PRESIDENT PAUL KRUGER

By the same author:

OLIVE SCHREINER—A Portrait (H. Keartland)
DE LA REY: LION OF THE WEST—A Biography (H. Keartland)
SWORD IN THE SAND: GIDEON SCHEEPERS (Tafelberg)
PRESIDENT STEYN—A Biography (Nasionale Boekhandel)
STORMBERG: A LOST OPPORTUNITY (Nasionale Boekhandel)
GENERAL LOUIS BOTHA—A Biography (Cassell)
THE COMMANDANT-GENERAL: PIET JOUBERT (Tafelberg)
SANDILE: THE FALL OF THE XHOSA NATION (Bulpin)
THE VOORTREKKERS (Cassell)

PRESIDENT PAUL KRUGER

A Biography

Johannes Meintjes

Cassell · London

CASSELL & COMPANY LTD

an imprint of
Cassell & Collier Macmillan Publishers Ltd
35 Red Lion Square, London WC1R 4SG
and at Sydney, Auckland, Toronto, Johannesburg

and an affiliate of The Macmillan Company Inc, New York

First published 1974

ISBN 0 304 29423 3

Printed by A. Wheaton & Company, Exeter
F874

TO MY MOTHER

also born on 10 October,
as a present for her eightieth birthday

He typified the Boer character both in its brighter and darker aspects and was no doubt the greatest man—both morally and intellectually—whom the Boer race has so far produced. In his iron will and tenacity, his 'never say die' attitude towards fate, his mystic faith in another world, he represented what is best in all of us.

GENERAL SMUTS to Emily Hobhouse on
Kruger's death in 1904

Preface

The great hearse, decorated by the artist Anton van Wouw, moved from the Suzanna Hall in Pretoria where the body had lain in State, and made for Church Square. Ahead walked Generals Louis Botha, De la Rey, De Wet and Burger, followed by dignitaries in rows of four. Thousands of people packed the route to the square where a decorated dais had been improvised at the church—which was in the process of demolition. There the first speeches were made since the Dutch ship, *Batavier VI*, had delivered the body at Cape Town. It had travelled slowly by train to the north, escorted by General Botha, stopping at all stations and sidings where silent crowds paid their homage.

The service at Church Square was conducted by the ministers of the three Dutch churches, and when the ceremony had ended the cortège moved along Church Street West, led by a mounted but unarmed commando under General Beyers. Followed by the generals and many Boer dignitaries, British militia and the Governor's representative in red jacket, the plumed hearse and horses, they passed the house with the white lions, and went on to the cemetery. There were so many wreaths that they were laden on mule wagons. Some twenty thousand people attended. As the coffin was lowered, all the bells of Pretoria began to peal and the guns of the British artillery boomed in the distance. It was the funeral of Stephanus Johannes Paulus Kruger, President of the one-time South African Republic, on 16 December 1904.

The Kruger story is a long one, lasting from 1825 to 1904, and, one can say, from 1904 until the present day. I have read about Kruger since childhood, have read more about his contemporaries than I can remember and have studied unpublished material covering a very wide field. My pursuit then was of other persons, but I knew that one day I would be involved with him, for he is the central figure of the period that has interested me most in South African history—1835–1935. The main problem was to keep the biography to a reasonable length, and above all to extract the man as a personality from a veritable bog of hostility and sentiment, prejudice and deification.

Paul Kruger was one of the most extraordinary men ever produced by South Africa, and the story of his life proves it. He was a professionally lonely man and a dreamer of dreams, a devoted husband and parent, a giant in the physical and mental sense, and in the end just a weary old man with an invincible faith in the will of God, waiting for what was to be revealed in His own good time. What Kruger was to become in the minds of men, of a nation, is beyond the scope of biography though it must inevitably be kept in mind. He was born about forty miles from where I live at Molteno and, having died in exile nearly eighty years later, he was buried by his own people with all the pomp, ceremony and evocation due to the greatest Boer in history. Two years later the Transvaal was given full Responsible Government, and the machinery was set in motion for the Union of South Africa, of which Louis Botha became the first Premier, with the home of Cecil Rhodes as his official residence at the Cape. Instead of fading into history, Kruger lived on as a vital force in South African politics and Afrikaner culture.

More nonsense has been written about him than anybody I know of. The reason for the distortion of the Kruger figure was firstly to justify an imperial policy and secondly to vindicate a war which should never have been. Further distortion came with the awakening of Afrikaner nationalism, swinging to the opposite extreme. I do not go into the rights and wrongs of the anti- and pro-Kruger campaigns at any lengths. I am primarily concerned with a personality and must accordingly see developments more from his viewpoint than from that of his detractors, but not with blind acceptance. Hundreds of writers have found that it is so easy to ridicule Kruger that they have become more concerned how to do it in a fresh rather than a just way, and in so doing have lost track of the human being.

The two guiding lights for the Kruger biographer are, of the older school J. F. van Oordt (he died in 1918), and of contemporaries, Prof. Dr D. W. Krüger. Their labours have been supplemented by scores of others who have dealt with every conceivable aspect of the life, times, thoughts and meaning of Paul Kruger. As his birth on 10 October 1825 is still commemorated annually, Kruger material has never ceased to flow and research continues on a subject which seems nigh inexhaustible when one might have thought that there remained little to add. All this however has little bearing on biography as an art, and I have made a considerable departure from my predecessors in structure and composition, in elimination and selection, in narrative, presentation and impartiality.

I acknowledge with gratitude the help given me by the State

Archives, the National Film Board, the Cultural and Kruger Museums of Pretoria, the Africana Museum and Library of Johannesburg, the Cape Archives and Central Reference Library of Cape Town, and the Regional Library of Grahamstown. Then there are the many private individuals, some no longer living, who have helped me in various ways, sometimes without even knowing it, to chart my course in retrieving living history while this was still possible, those who remembered and those who came after them with unclouded vision.

JOHANNES MEINTJES

Grootzeekoegat,
Molteno, 1974

Contents

Illustrations

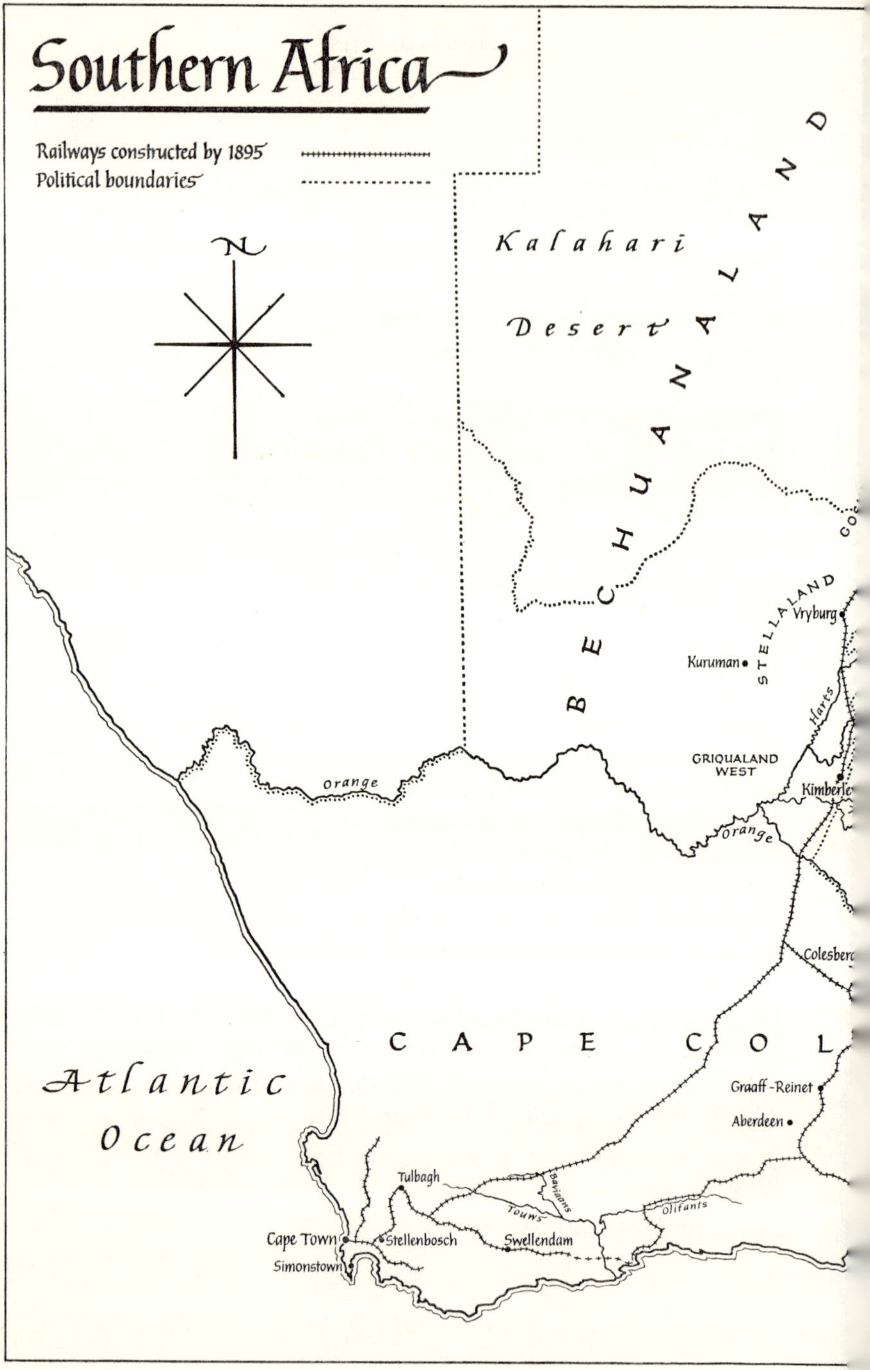
Southern Africa
Railways constructed by 1895
Political boundaries
N
Kalahari
Desert
BECHUANALAND
STELLALAND
Vryburg
Kuruman
Harts
GRIQUALAND WEST
Kimberle
Orange
Orange
Colesberg
CAPE COL
Atlantic
Ocean
Graaff-Reinet
Aberdeen
Tulbagh
Baviaans
Touws
Olifants
Cape Town
Stellenbosch
Swellendam
Simonstown

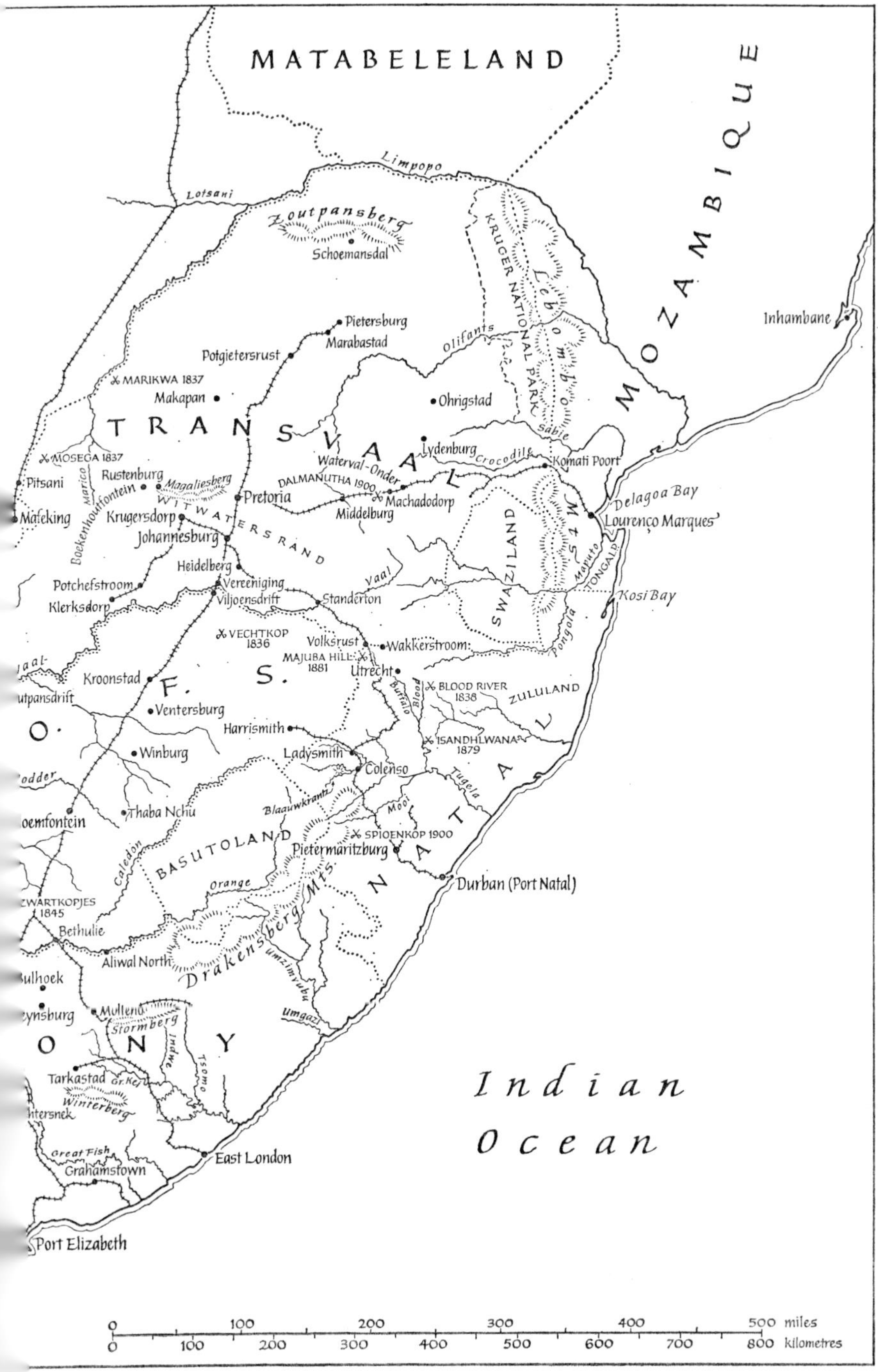
MATABELELAND
MOZAMBIQUE
Limpopo
Lotsani
Zoutpansberg
Schoemansdal
KRUGER NATIONAL PARK
Lebombo
Inhambane
Pietersburg
Marabastad
Potgietersrust
Olifants
MARIKWA 1837
Makapan
Ohrigstad
TRANSVAAL
Sabie
Lydenburg
Crocodile
Komati Poort
MOSEGA 1837
Waterval-Onder
Pitsani
Marico
Rustenburg
Magaliesberg
DALMANUTHA 1900
Machadodorp
Delagoa Bay
Boekenhoutfontein
Pretoria
Middelburg
Lourenço Marques
Mafeking
Krugersdorp
WITWATERSRAND
SWAZILAND
Johannesburg
Heidelberg
Maputo
TONGALD
Potchefstroom
Vereeniging
Vaal
Kosi Bay
Klerksdorp
Viljoensdrift
Standerton
VECHTKOP 1836
Volksrust
Wakkerstroom
Pongola
MAJUBA HILL 1881
Utrecht
Kroonstad
F. S.
BLOOD RIVER 1838
ZULULAND
Buffalo
Blood
Ventersburg
Harrismith
ISANDHLWANA 1879
Winburg
Ladysmith
Colenso
Tugela
Blaauwkrantz
Mooi
Thaba Nchu
SPIOENKOP 1900
BASUTOLAND
Pietermaritzburg
NATAL
Caledon
Orange
Durban (Port Natal)
ZWARTKOPJES 1845
Bethulie
Drakensberg Mts
Aliwal North
Umzimvubu
Umgazi
Molteno
Stormberg
Indwe
Tsomo
Tarkastad
Gr. Kei
Winterberg
Great Fish
Grahamstown
East London
Port Elizabeth
Indian Ocean
0 100 200 300 400 500 miles
0 100 200 300 400 500 600 700 800 kilometres

CHAPTER ONE

Young Paul

The funeral of President Paul Kruger heralded the resurrection of the Boer people as well as the birth of modern Afrikanerdom. More had been written on or about Kruger up to that time, 1904, than about any other person in South African history. And it continued on a major and minor scale up to the present day. He was also one of the most photographed men in the world, the one to feature in endless cartoons. As a personality he was more familiar to South Africa and the outside world than even Queen Victoria was. Such a man created many legends and total fabrications, but what is significant is that at his bier stood not only the peasant, the poor and defeated, but also the poet and intellectual. Paul Kruger was hardly a person any longer but a concept.

It is fitting that this giant of southern Africa should have been a child of the veld, born of and made by the soil of Africa. As a man of legend it is not surprising that there was even to be dispute about his exact date and place of birth. On South African soil the Krugers were soon to swell to a formidable clan, for the men fathered enormous broods of children, many of whom were boys, and marriage established kinship with scores of well-known families. The Krugers were, like the typical so-called Boers (Dutch/Afrikaans-speaking farmers), of mainly German, Dutch and French descent. They inherited national characteristics from those nations but were moulded by environment, hardship and isolation into what they became.

Paul Kruger's descent has been minutely examined.[1] In brief, the founder of his family came to the Cape as a soldier in the service of the Dutch East India Company in 1713.[2] He was Jacob Krüger (1690–1749) from Berlin who married Johanna Kemp of uncertain origin in 1718. In the same year he attained burgher rights—perhaps because of the loss of a hand—and established himself as a farmer to the north-west of Cape Town, in the so-called Sandveld. They had eight children. One son, Hendrik, married to Francina Cloete, had eighteen children, ten of whom were boys. Gerrit, born in 1750, showed traits for which his descendant was to become famous.

A most striking example features the Bushmen, the small nomadic race which caused so much trouble in the immediate interior. Theirs was a story of misunderstandings, violence and wanton extermination. Instead of being eradicated, Gerrit Kruger* maintained, the Bushmen should be taught the difference between livestock and game, and they were to be tamed. As the white man advanced, game became more scarce, so the Bushmen could be induced to drop their hunting activities by presenting them with small and large stock. This was a highly original idea, so it was to Gerrit Kruger's credit that he actually persuaded his neighbours in the ward behind the Sneeuberg to co-operate. They distributed 283 sheep among 118 Bushmen, some of whom became expert shepherds.[3] Other Krugers were to follow this example of sagacity, their only desire being to live in peace and to have law and order.

Gerrit or Gert Kruger married Suzanna Buys in 1769. The Buys family was among the first to penetrate the north-eastern Cape, and their descendants are still there. Gert Kruger's fourth son was Stephanus Johannes who married Sophia Margaretha Steenkamp in 1798. They started their married life at the parental farm Grootfontein until they branched out on their own. Their son Casper Jan Hendrik Kruger, born on 10 November 1801, was the father of Paul Kruger. It was to become fashionable to look upon these Krugers as backward peasants, whereas they were large landowners in an area stretching roughly from Graaff-Reinet to Colesberg and the future Steynsburg. By colonial standards one could even call them wealthy. They were prominent, influential men, leaders of expeditions and deputations, often original in outlook and very capable.

As the area in which they operated was mountainous and often sparse of vegetation, roamings went far and wide, even in search of water and good grazing. Trekboers were men of no fixed abode who roamed the interior as their moods and climatic conditions took them. Though landowners, the Krugers could be classed with the Trekboers, as they followed the example of all those on the outer fringes of the Colony in making sorties into what was still largely the unknown. Apart from an inherent restless spirit, drought was a major driving force, as well as locust plagues and buck migrations which destroyed grazing. Farming and roaming, or trekking, went together, but for the more established from a particular base.

At the age of seventeen Casper Kruger's roamings took him to the ward Brak River on the southern slopes of the Suurberg. This was a

* The umlaut, as in Krüger, was dropped by many families of German origin, only to be restored in more modern times.

farm called Bulhoek where Douw Gerbrand Steyn had been living since 1809, some miles from where the town of Steynsburg (named after these Steyns) was to be founded in 1872. The Cape history of the Steyn family dated back to 1668, and they were to play a major role in the history of Swellendam. The Steyns were affluent, politically minded and often aristocratic in their ways.[4] Douw Gerbrand Steyn bore the names of his Cape ancestor, and became a sheep farmer at Graaff-Reinet where he married Alida Barendina van der Walt in 1795 when he was eighteen. Such early marriages were common in isolated and sparsely populated regions. They had thirteen children, their daughter Elsie Francina being born on 6 May 1806 at the farm Gannavlakte near the future town of Aberdeen. Graaff-Reinet was then a vast district.

Elsie Steyn was a small child when her parents moved to Bulhoek, on the northern boundary of the Colony, where as a young girl she met the youth Casper Kruger when he visited them. Open house was held, any caller being your guest for as long as he wished to stay. These youngsters fell in love and planned to marry. In the way the outlying families knew one another from their roamings, the Steyns and Krugers were acquainted, and the union was given their blessing —in writing, as the children were minors. Elsie too had to put her consent in writing, and did so on 1 August 1820. She and Casper were married at the young town of Cradock by the Rev. Mr John Evans on 3 September 1820. Casper was barely nineteen, and Elsie fifteen. As was not unusual, several other couples were married at the same time, having first appeared in the Court of Matrimony, one of the brides being Elsie's elder sister Johanna.

Casper, Elsie, Johanna and her husband Casper Jan Hendrik Steenkamp (a relation of the Krugers) moved into the Steyn house at Bulhoek. Casper and Elsie's first child, a girl, was born there. Casper's father, Stephanus Kruger, who had again been roaming, settled down in the neighbouring ward of Renosterberg. There Casper and Elsie joined the Krugers for a while, and had their first son. Because of a frightful drought the Krugers left Renosterberg for Zoutpansdrift in the same ward. When another move was planned to beyond the Suurberg, Casper and Elsie decided to return to Bulhoek with their two small children, Sophia Margaretha Elizabeth and Douw Gerbrand. It was now 1825, and Elsie Kruger was again expecting a baby.

The child was born at Bulhoek on 10 October that year and given the names Stephanus Johannes Paulus Kruger. His first two names were those of his paternal grandfather; the Paulus was to remain rather a mystery, and yet the boy was always called Paul. The suggestion that Paul Kruger was actually born at Brak River on 1 October has been sufficiently disproved to be ignored.[5] He was baptized on 19 March 1826 at Cradock (distance usually caused late baptism), and his parents then followed in the tracks of his paternal grandparents.

Paul Kruger's immediate family was to remain comparatively small, for his mother died at the age of twenty-seven. The known facts of her life fill a short paragraph, even her burial place being unknown. The rest of the children, three boys and a girl, were baptized at Colesberg. If the Krugers lacked culture, the Steyns did not, and with the extreme limitations of schooling it was regrettable that Paul Kruger should have lost his mother at eight. In isolation the parents taught the children, the mother usually doing most, for she was the family scribe and kept the children occupied while the husband was away. The surviving fragment of Elsie's handwriting is neat and well-formed.[6] Books were scarce but every family had at least a Bible, and this was usually the first and sometimes the only book to which children ever had access. In the Old Testament these pastoral people found a parallel to their own lives.

Many eventually saw Paul Kruger as if he had stepped right out of the Old Testament, or at least belonged to any age except his own. He was however very much an early nineteenth-century South African of the interior, men who cannot possibly be judged in terms of culture and sophistication. They were largely self-taught, practical and skilful, bowing the knee to God alone, and finding in His Word and in their experience of life the solution to their problems. There were highly intelligent men among them, and to most, as in the case of Kruger's contemporary Piet Joubert, lack of formal education was to cause lifelong frustration and vexation. Kruger was to find solace in his own mental resources—and the most brilliant brains he could muster.

He shot up into a tall youth, big-boned and powerful. He was broad of shoulder, with large strong hands. Fully grown he is said to have been nearly six foot, but Bertha Goudvis told me that when she had coffee with President Kruger at Waterval Onder, just prior to his exile to Europe in 1900, she estimated his height at six foot two inches, even at that age. Much has been made of Kruger's ugliness. There are some faces which have nothing to do with beauty or ugliness. They are faces beyond time and place, faces which never blur, never remind you of anybody else and always involve a slight shock of recognition. Since the era of photography, five of the most famous faces in South African history have been General De La Rey, President Steyn, General De Wet, General Louis Botha and above all President Kruger. All five were to be involved with each other.

So the conventional picture is of a large, ungainly, ugly man. However, the young Paul Kruger certainly does not strike me as hideous in any way. He had a neat forehead, fine dark-brown eyes and a sensitive mouth, to judge by a photograph of 1855. Relations recalled the colour of his eyes and the way they seemed to have a glow in their depths. His hair was brown and very fine. Age was to bring its ravages, particularly an affliction of the eyes; but it is said that even well beyond middle age women were fascinated by Kruger's virility, even that they threw themselves at him—rather hopelessly, for he was no philanderer.[7] As for being ungainly, he could outrun anybody, was a superb jumper, swimmer, diver, shot and all-round horseman. He also had brains, far more than the anti-Boer world gave him credit for. Intellectuals like Leyds and Smuts could only marvel at them, and neither bore fools gladly. On the other hand there are those who will say that they were equally 'slim', meaning cunning.

Even by frontier standards young Paul's schooling was scanty indeed. He could have been taught to read and write before he lost his mother. What his father taught him, beyond religious instruction and manly pursuits, we do not know. A roving tutor called Tielman Roos took the education of the children in hand for a short period but it seems unlikely that Paul had more than three months' consecutive tuition from him. Paul's grandfather could also have been a help, as like him Paul was to use an odd little half-moon above the letter *u*. Then there was undoubted help from his step-mother, for Casper Kruger was to remarry, as was usual for all widows and widowers. His second wife was Heiletje Lavina Etresia du Plessis, and she was to bear him more children.

Although an English colony, the Cape of Good Hope had been founded and opened up by the Dutch. Their descendants by far outnumbered the English-speaking Colonists, and their daily language had undergone such modifications that it had virtually become another tongue, called Cape Dutch, the Taal (Language) and eventually Afrikaans. The Netherlands, France and Germany had long since become remote, to an extent which could only be gauged by the arrival of immigrants from those countries. The tie with the Dutch was stronger, for the Boer Bibles were all in High Dutch, and this was the language used for addressing the Almighty and on all formal occasions. Otherwise, Paul Kruger spoke Afrikaans like everybody else and reserved his Dutch for higher flights of speech. Had he not left the Colony at such a tender age, he would no doubt have mastered the English language. Of all Afrikaner statesmen he was the only one to use an interpreter all the time (Louis Botha only did so when he was nervous and fearful of misquotation). One does get the impression that Kruger's use of interpreters was more of a pose than a necessity. Great Trek leaders like Andries Pretorius and Piet Retief spoke English fluently. Paul Kruger did gain knowledge of the English language, somewhere, somehow and even inevitably, for he was heard to make the occasional remark and even to converse in English, particularly with lady visitors.[8]

If ever a man knew his Bible, that man was Paul Kruger. For the major part of his life he read in and from it every day. He also used it as others do a dictionary. Although he was to come to know the contents of the Bible by heart, he was always to find fresh interpretations, the answers to whatever bothered him at different times, the guiding lines he sought. He could also find a suitable quotation for almost anything. To him it *was* the word of God, and it was to be almost impossible for him to communicate satisfactorily with anyone not versed in it. Frontiersmen like the Krugers were very devout and reared their children in fear and trembling of the wrath of God. For Kruger there was also His love. The further civilization was left behind, the more reliance was put on the Word, on daily prayers and religious instruction. In his later life Kruger was to carry this to extremes, for indeed the Bible became the anchor of his turbulent career.

In the English version of Kruger's *Memoirs*, published while he was still alive, he is made to say: 'My parents were simple farmers, and I grew up at the farm like other farmers' lads, looking after the herds and lending a hand in the fields. With the exception that an old woman prophesied to my mother that her son Stephanus Johannes Paulus was destined for a superior position in life, I do not know that any one could have had the least notion that God would entrust me with a special mission.'[9] He could also have added: and would have provided me with a Handbook. That there was a special mission for him, Kruger was to realize or sense early in life. He built his career accordingly, and though everything that happened to him was seen in terms of the will of God, the key to the phenomenon of Kruger was his implicit belief that he was *called* by God.

Up to the age of nine, Paul's world was the old district of Colesberg (which embraced Steynsburg), a region of many climatic moods and bleak beauty, with sheer hills erupting from the veld to cast long mauve shadows, and with grassy plains and sudden far vistas. His childhood was spent mainly in the open veld, and it pleased his Biblical bent of mind to refer to himself and his father simply as shepherds, particularly in the company of the grand. From the spacious and romantic setting of Bulhoek with its dolerite-capped hills, he was taken to the farm Rietfontein on the Orange River, and then for some time along the Caledon River in the region called Transoranje, the Southern Free State. From his earliest days his was a strictly disciplined life, one of law and order, infused with the glow of a happy family life. He admired his father, dearly loved his mother—as he did his step-mother—and there was a strong bond of affection between him and his brothers and sisters. They were beset by many dangers, such as savages and wild beasts, and were at the mercy of the elements, but these things only strengthened the family tie, with each individual functioning like a cog in a machine.

Every day held its excitements, but there was to be no major change until 1836. Even before that time many people, mainly in the south-eastern parts of the Colony, had been considering the prospects of emigrating. Paul was too young to be concerned with the reasons for trekking, but he heard the general talk flowing in from Grahamstown, Graaff-Reinet, Colesberg and elsewhere. Up till that time his father had, unlike others, shown no animosity towards the Cape Colonial Government. Although the family and their relations strayed far beyond the boundaries, they always returned, paid taxes and gave an account of themselves. This applied to nearly all Trekboers, who must not be confused with Voortrekkers. The Krugers had apparently given little thought to emigration, and had no reason to do so.

Although much bitterness was aroused by the way in which the emancipation of the slaves was conducted (compensation being made almost impossible to obtain and certainly inadequate), this did not affect the Krugers as they had no slaves. Nor were they affected by the savage eastern border war of 1833–5, in which so many people were ruined when the tribesmen fell on them; the Krugers were far from the scene of pillage. As for resentment against the British administration, this did not apply as they were too far from the seats of authority to experience undue pressure. The Krugers were unmoved by political or economic motivations, and were quite happy where they were, along the Caledon, for instance, where there was beautiful grazing for Casper Kruger's 2,600 sheep. Without doubt, the notion that the Trek had been *ordered* by God had never occurred to them, nor did they feel that it was imperative to cast off the yoke of British oppression. As free men of the wide open spaces they knew no oppression, and they were not the sort of people to defy laws.

A kind of Kruger settlement had formed at the Caledon River. There were Casper and his family, his father, and his brothers Gert and Theuns with their families. With no water or grazing problems they remained there about a year. After being a shepherd, young Paul became a drover and herder of cattle as he grew older. Other families joined these Kruger encampments, and there they would possibly have remained but for the arrival of a tall, forceful man called Hendrik Potgieter. This was no Trekboer but a Voortrekker, or rather Emigrant Farmer as he styled himself, who had valid grievances against the Colony and was going to quit for ever. He also had political aspirations of no mean order, for he wanted to found a State and, what was more, to rule it.

Andries Hendrik Potgieter was born in the district of Graaff-Reinet in 1792 and was to become a farmer at the Tarka River, east of Cradock. From the Tarka to Colesberg he became a well-known personality and acquainted with the Krugers. He was over six feet tall, of powerful physique, and usually dressed in blue moleskin.[10] As a farmer he became affluent; he had his own slaves, 400 head of cattle and some 5,000 sheep. By the end of 1835 he had decided to play a role in the Great Trek. His reasons were not as clear-cut as those of other Trek leaders, but he had certainly had enough of the weak and wavering British policy on the eastern frontier, of Bushman and Bantu depredations and of the British in general. Of all the Trek leaders he was the only one to be overtly anti-British, his antipathy dating from the Slachtersnek execution of 1815,* the hanged men being personally known to him. Furthermore, he was the kind of man who preferred to move off rather than quarrel.

And so he gathered the flocks and herds of all those who wished to go with him, and headed north. On their trek the Potgieters located the Krugers. The Boers were born scouts and trackers, yet it is often amazing with what facility they located one another in the vastness of the interior. At the age of ten Paul Kruger beheld the man who

* The Slachtersnek episode was the result of an insurrection which followed the normal course of justice. The facts became much distorted, rebels becoming martyrs as a result of the manner of execution which began to symbolize British oppression of the Boer. See my *The Voortrekkers*, pp. 13–15.

was to bestride the South African landscape with a heavy tread. The boy was not one for hero-worship, not at any stage of his life, but apparently all the Krugers came under the spell of Potgieter, a man who was not only in accord with their rather narrow religious views but was also a born leader, commanding, practical and stubborn.

Nobody has tried to explain why the Krugers, who had no motivations for emigrating, threw in their lot so effortlessly with Potgieter. But it is not difficult to understand. Apart from his forceful personality, Potgieter not only knew what the Great Trek was all about (he was in touch with the pioneers Louis Tregardt and Johannes Jacobus Janse van Rensburg), but was ready to make a significant contribution towards it by founding an independent Boer State, preferably as far from the sea as possible, for, as he used to say, wherever you have the ocean, you have the English. Having become used to a nomadic existence, the Krugers felt that they had nothing to lose in following Potgieter for an orderly and godly life. If they also felt that Potgieter had been sent to them by God, as was felt about other leaders,[11] one need speculate no further.

In February 1836 Potgieter, the Krugers, Steyns, Liebenbergs, Bothas and other families with them made a raft crossing of the full Orange River at Winterhoekdrift, near the present Bethulie, just below the confluence of the Orange and Caledon Rivers. Nobody questioned the leadership of Hendrik Potgieter but he, in his middle forties, showed his mettle in having himself elected Commandant on independent soil, for he was not the sort of man to abide argument. Paul Kruger says that a meeting was held, 'resolutions were passed to which all the emigrants had to submit, and a sort of government instituted. But God's Word constituted the highest law and rule of conduct . . . The resolutions which came into general force contained, for example, the decree that it was unlawful to take away from the Natives, by force, land or any other of their property, and that no slavery would be permitted.'[12]

These decrees were depeated so many times that it becomes a source of wonder that British officials later managed to wrest from the Boers what was theirs by accusing them of land-robbery and slavery, the two things they held in abhorrence. That is why Paul Kruger makes special mention of it. We now see him at the age of ten walking beside the family wagons as a fleet of them, with thousands of animals, churned the veld to dust. Whips cracked like gun-shots, and the Potgieter Trek headed northwards to the unknown as men, women and children sang psalms to the glory of God.[13]

CHAPTER TWO

On Trek

Paul Kruger continued to have his religious instruction from his father. This took place after dinner which was at midday, and after supper when the children remained round a table or in a circle on the ground. Texts were repeated from memory and written down when this was possible, usually in the evenings. At various halts a hut was made of grass and reeds to serve as a school-room. The better educated among the Emigrants all took turns in giving instruction. When not studying, the children herded stock, collected firewood and joined in hunts. Indiscriminate shooting was not allowed, for ammunition was precious, and at night fires and the cracking of whips were found to be effective in chasing off lions.

Near the future Smithfield, Commandant Potgieter's trek was joined by a number of Colesberg farmers and by another great personality of the time, Sarel Cilliers, who was to win fame as the Prophet of the Great Trek. It seems probable that this combined Trek passed at a spot between the present-day Bloemfontein and Thaba Nchu and went on to the Vet River. At Thaba Nchu there was a mission station run by the Rev. Mr Archbell mainly for the benefit of the Basotho subjects of Chief Moroka. This spot became a convenient halting place or outspan in Great Trek history. The Potgieter Party dawdled for some time at the Vet River, as there was no urgency, and a lot of planning went into their various movements, such as splitting up into sections in order to ease grazing for all the animals they had with them.

A remarkable aspect of the vast stretch of country they travelled through was that it was almost devoid of human habitation. Remnants of broken and scattered tribes told the Trekkers of a frightful despot called Mzilikazi, a one-time Zulu general from Natal who had fled from his murderous king, called Shaka, and had founded a second warrior nation—the Matabele. These Matabele had been sacking the interior for some time, absorbing all those not destroyed on their paths of blood—tribes already decimated by the inroads of Shaka's regiments. Many fleeing tribesmen sought sanctuary in a mountainous region which was becoming known as Basutoland. Others, marvelling at the white men, their horses and rods of fire, emerged from hiding to seek protection. One of them was a chief called Makwana. He offered Potgieter the north-western Free State which had been the home of the Bataung tribe, wanting only a reserve for the remnants of his people, in exchange for some cattle and, particularly, protection against the Matabele.

Paul Kruger was still too young to participate in Potgieter's far-flung travels, for the Commandant was to lead exploring parties even beyond the Limpopo. Most families settled down in Makwana's territory, now ceded to them, to await the outcome of the expeditions. Though Potgieter had forebodings about the sea, he knew that his State would have to have a port, and so he sought one remote from the British sphere of influence, such as Delagoa Bay where the Portuguese had settled. Rumours reached King Mzilikazi (the Boers called him Silkaats) of a great influx of white people, and of particular note to him was the news that they had brought vast flocks and herds with them.

On 25 August 1836 the Matabele struck. The Trek groups had by that time fanned out right up to and even beyond the Vaal River. These were the victims of the sudden and ferocious attack in which the Liebenbergs perished. A stand was made, however, and the Matabele withdrew, taking much booty. They were of course to be back, and in this second and much larger onslaught the young Paul Kruger, now aged eleven, was to participate. This was the famous battle of Vechtkop of 16 October, in which six thousand Matabele stormed the laager of Hendrik Potgieter at a spot between the future Lindley and Heilbron. The laager consisted of some fifty wagons drawn into squares, the nearest thing to a fort the Trekkers could devise.[14]

Potgieter, aided by Cilliers, led the defence of the laager. Ever since his return from the north, just after the Liebenberg murders, Potgieter had been expecting another attack. There were only about forty adult men in the laager, and some twenty-five of them rode out to meet the Matabele who were under the command of one of their most celebrated generals, Mkhalipi. In the laager Paul Kruger and the rest of the children helped with the casting of bullets and with getting everything in readiness. This was young Paul's first experience of conflict with the blacks, and it was such an experience that he was to recall it in detail even in old age, giving a thrilling account to such receptive people as Olive Schreiner and her husband.[15]

The canopied wagons were chained together, the apertures filled in with the branches of thorn trees and firmly secured with leather thongs. There were two or three guns to every man, and basins with gunpowder and slugs stood about. These muzzle-loaders were cumbersome and had a powerful kick, but the men knew how to handle them expertly, even on horseback. It was becoming a Voortrekker tactic for a party to ride out to meet the enemy. When they did so on this occasion, the Matabele sank down behind their shields. Potgieter tried to parley with them, only to unleash a sudden rain of assegais and sticks. At a given signal his men fired and kept it up as they retired to the laager. Once inside, the single aperture was closed up. In the excitement some men rode clean past the aperture and thought it wisest to keep going.[16]

The Matabele at once surrounded the laager while their herdsmen rounded up the stock. Paul Kruger watched as they slaughtered cattle and ate them raw, then he turned his attention to Cilliers who had begun a religious service. This over, every man was at his post, with his wife and biggest children beside him, ready to load and pass on his guns. As the Matabele did nothing for some hours the suspense was great. At last came the onslaught, a shrieking multitude of black manhood in their war finery, raising a deafening din as they drummed on their shields. This violent action lasted about an hour, the Matabele doing everything possible to get to the Boers, jerking the wheels, slashing the canopies and throwing their spears aloft to drop inside the laager. Women stood ready with axes to chop off the hands of those who managed to scale the wagon-canopies. The whole laager was smoking with gunpowder.

All kinds of extraordinary things happened that day—no wonder it left such a lasting impression on Kruger—until the Matabele gave up and withdrew with a dreadful hissing. The Trekkers only lost two killed and fourteen wounded, while the Matabele dead lay in piles around the laager and all along their route of withdrawal. But their booty was enormous: 100 horses, 4,600 head of cattle and 50,000 sheep.[17] A patrol went in pursuit but only a few sheep were recaptured. The party was stranded without oxen, in want of meat and milk, and apprehensive about another attack. Three brave men, Hermanus Potgieter (the Commandant's brother) and two Coloureds (many non-whites had voluntarily joined in the emigration) offered to go to Thaba Nchu to seek help. Archbell and Moroka readily sent food and oxen. This coincided with the arrival of another important Trek leader, Gert Maritz.

The Krugers were to follow Maritz to Natal, where young Paul was to experience several shocks, mainly the murder of Piet Retief and his party by Shaka's successor Dingane, and the massacre of Blaauwkrantz which followed it. Potgieter, who had no interest in Natal as there was already a British settlement at the main port, meanwhile led an attack on Mzilikazi in his own stronghold and caused a rout. This was the first of several punitive expeditions. Later on, Paul Kruger took part in them, for his family decided to quit Natal and rejoin Potgieter. As a leader he was at first more to their liking than the dominating Andries Pretorius who was to become the Boer strongman of Natal after the deaths of Piet Retief, Piet Uys and Gert Maritz.

Vechtkop and his Natal experiences turned Paul Kruger into a man though he was only a boy in years. Already he had met the girl he wanted to marry, and at sixteen he would gain independence. As a soldier his training was soon to begin, and Potgieter, like a warrior prophet out of the Old Testament, was the man to mould him. Through cession, Potgieter had already obtained the north-eastern part of the Free State, with the town of Winburg as its capital, and he was going to obtain the Transvaal by conquest. As they saw it, Mzilikazi had tried to exterminate them without any provocation, so God would be on their side in giving him the punishment he deserved.

Through their extraordinary experiences and being the Biblical people they were, the Voortrekkers had developed a concept of themselves as a chosen people. Nothing swayed their faith, and even in the most hazardous situations they knew no fear. The happenings in Natal, culminating in the fantastic Battle of Blood River in which Andries Pretorius smashed the proud Zulu army without losing a man, as well as the British annexation of the Republic of Natalia which followed, were all seen in terms of God's will. Transoranje and the Transvaal together were becoming the Chosen Country for a Chosen People. Given their belief in being so singularly blessed, perhaps it is not surprising that so much squabbling and bickering took place among themselves. It was also in the nature of a man like Potgieter to be dictatorial and to arouse opposition. But he was a man to follow, and his dream of an independent Boer State, blessed by God, appealed strongly to men who were worn out by wandering, and yearned for peace, law and order.

Paul Kruger may never have given it a thought but he was very much like Potgieter, though perhaps fortunately for him this was later to be watered down by the influence of Pretorius. Although Kruger played little active part in the happenings in Natal, he had observed and heard enough henceforth to have an historical awareness of the Boers as a people. In Natal too he had found spiritual stimulation in his contact with the American missionary, Daniel Lindley, a man very much after the Boer heart, physically unafraid, manually expert, and a Christian in the truest sense of the word. Their paths were to cross again, for Lindley had a warm understanding of the Boers and was fascinated to watch the making of history. The name of Lindley, it was said, was ever after to sound glorious to the Boers.

Potgieter was very reluctant to go to Natal, but he went after all, because he wished to get a grasp of the situation and to obtain supplies such as gunpowder at Port Natal. He also led an expedition with Piet Uys against a Zulu force, an action in which Uys was slain and Potgieter's reputation considerably tarnished. He dismissed this with a shrug, believing himself in the right. It was also an excuse to leave Natal, a country he believed, more firmly than ever, to be accursed for them. So he quit, and welcomed back the Krugers in May 1838 when they settled at Liebenbergsvlei. As young Paul had implicit trust in his father, he shared his support for Potgieter whose 'Republic of Winburg' was becoming a reality.

At the beginning of 1839 it was an exciting adventure for Paul Kruger to accompany Potgieter on a punitive expedition against the Matabele, one of the series mentioned. Not all Boer livestock had yet been recaptured, nor had Mzilikazi's crimes been properly avenged. Potgieter left a wagon laager behind at Wonderfontein, near where he planned to found his new capital Potchefstroom across the Vaal, and set out with a mounted commando. The whole country through which they passed in the western Transvaal had been devastated. The odd destitute chief was to be found, such as Maghato in the Magaliesberg who was to become a lifelong friend of Kruger's. As Mzilikazi thought it wisest to withdraw from his old haunts in a western swing to beyond the Limpopo, the expedition came to nothing beyond letting the king understand that the Boers were ready for him.

'At last the wanderers had found a comparatively safe home,' Kruger remarked, reflecting on the great losses they had suffered in people and possessions. Potgieter formally annexed the territory evacuated by the Matabele, and with the territory ceded by Makwana now found himself lord of a large domain. Shortly before an expedition of 1840, he founded Potchefstroom, a town beautifully situated on the Mooi River. The Krugers settled at the foot of the Magaliesberg, an area henceforth associated with them, and young

Paul surveyed the possibilities of land wherever he went. The choice of two farms was soon to be his, one for grazing and one for cultivation.

Paul Kruger's legend was beginning. Of his physical strength and toughness there can be no doubt, but one marvels to hear that he began to shoot his first big game at the age of seven. As with all Boers, hunting was to be a passionate pursuit, not shooting for sport but for the pot and to clear specific areas of dangerous beasts. Hunting was so much part of his life that it was taken as a matter of course, but he did recall shooting his first lion at the age of fourteen in 1839. This was a lion that had been attacking their herds at the Rhenoster River, and six men, apart from Paul who did not count, set out to find the dangerous animal. For security they rode in two parties, a good distance apart.

Paul was with his father, a brother and an uncle, when the lion suddenly rushed at them. The horses were at once swung round to prevent them from bolting, and young Paul crouched at their hindquarters with his rifle, while his relatives dealt with their muzzle-loaders. The lion already seemed on top of them, crouching for a bound over Paul on to the horses. The boy got his shot in first, killing the beast outright as it came soaring over, nearly falling on top of him. It was at once established that the shot was true, and the men of the other party came riding up to them.

They all stood over the lion and marvelled at its size, particularly the teeth. As a man called Hugo crouched over the lion's head to measure the incisors, young Paul mischievously jumped on its stomach. The dead beast let out such a roar that Hugo fell flat on his back. This was an old trick, remaining breath being forced out, and all the men shook with laughter except for Hugo, who was ready to give Paul a thrashing. However, Hugo was pacified, and once over the shock laughed with the others.[18] Although he recalled being fourteen, there is a possibility that Paul might have been only eleven or twelve when this incident took place, seeing that as a member of the hunting party he did not 'count', as he says himself.

In the period 1839 to 1841 Potchefstroom formed the focal point of the Potgieter Party, and accordingly also that of the Krugers, the settlement being some seven miles to the north of the town that came into being. Originally it was called Vryburg, also Mooiriviersdorp, but as Potgieter's influence grew it was freely called after him as their *chef*.[19] This was the first town founded by whites to the north of the Vaal River. Families fanned out, the Krugers clinging to the region of the Magaliesberg, once a Mzilikazi stronghold, as it was wooded and well-watered. Casper and Gert Kruger were closely involved with Potgieter's activities. The country one can call his republic stretched from the Vet River in the Free State over a large region of the Transvaal. In 1840, before the coming of the English, this republic was briefly federated with that of Natalia where Andries Pretorius held sway, the central Government or Volksraad (council of the people) sitting at the Natal town of Pietermaritzburg, while Potgieter ruled over what was now vaguely called the Republic of Potchefstroom.

Paul Kruger's family farmed just to the north of the Magaliesberg at a place given the name of Zoutpansdrift. The farm granted him at sixteen was called Waterkloof (ravine of water), to the south of the town founded later with the name of Rustenburg. He was then fully grown, and again one gets a picture of a large clumsy youngster, 'a great shaggy bull',[20] but strength and overt virility went hand in hand with unusual agility, both physical and mental, shrewdness if not cunning, a lively sense of humour, tremendous vitality and a brain which cried out for development. The Great Trek, which had moulded him, was over, but not yet its history, and the lad was now able to enter the final phase with gusto—and a growing awareness of destiny.

CHAPTER THREE

The Young Farmer

Having been granted his burgher rights and farms, Paul Kruger wasted no time in getting married to the girl on whom he had set his heart. She was Maria du Plessis, daughter of the Voortrekker Casper du Plessis, whom Kruger had probably known since childhood. She was living south of the Vaal, presumably in the neighbourhood of Kroonstad, and was only fourteen when Kruger (who was seventeen) fetched her to be his wife in 1842. The Vaal River was in spate, quite impassable to anyone but Kruger. He drove his horses into the torrential waters at considerable risk, but as he was a powerful and expert swimmer, Kruger got safely across, much to the incredulity of the ferryman at that spot. On the return trip, to the relief of his bride, the river had subsided.[21]

They were married at Potchefstroom by the Landdrost (an official with wide magisterial powers), civil marriages being the accepted thing. At seventeen Kruger could no longer be considered a boy. A later associate, Carl Jeppe, was to wonder if Kruger had ever been young. But this applied to many Boers who reached prominence. Such a young couple were not only husband and wife but comrades, sharing everything—toil and hardship, gain and loss. And when her mate went on hunting expeditions, as all men did, it was not unusual for the wife to go along too. Voortrekker women were as much warriors as were their husbands, and often equally politically minded, giving of their bodies and minds to a point one would have thought beyond human endurance.

Life at Waterkloof started off in a primitive way: a shack to live in, rudimentary kraals (enclosures) for livestock, and cultivation on a small scale. What could not be acquired was made by hand, and hardly anything was ever thrown away. Very little is known about Maria Kruger, but she was clearly as capable as any of her sisters, and she was blessed with a husband who had already been noted for his regard and courtesy towards women. Even his most vicious detractors could find no criticism of him as a dutiful and loyal husband. Boer women were inclined to be critical, but in Kruger they could only admire the qualities of manliness and authority he displayed before he had even reached the age of twenty, and in Boer society there was no indulgence towards youth. Kruger appreciated intelligence in women, as well as modesty, and when interested showed attentiveness and courtesy astonishing to those who thought him devoid of all feeling.

Paul Kruger was about nineteen when he grew his first beard. It was considered unseemly to sprout whiskers at too early an age. The Voortrekker custom was to shave round the mouth and to wear beard like a fringe under the chin, a fashion also found elsewhere as in England and America. At times Kruger conformed to this custom, but he wore his beard at different lengths and on occasion grew a moustache which he shaved off when he tired of it. By the 1880s full beards had become the fashion, and perhaps because of it Kruger resumed the Voortrekker appearance. As his was still mainly an outdoor life, he was so used to wearing a hat that he disliked having his head exposed. In any case, a Boer never felt fully dressed unless he wore a hat. Kruger's deep voice was also of note, 'a real double-bass'[22] which could be startling, as well as authoritative and persuasive.

There are so many legends about Kruger the young man that it is no longer possible to sort fact from fiction. To judge by some revelations made in connexion with his later years, invention did take place. Hunting stories and various anecdotes were clearly introduced into the *Memoirs* to add to the interest of the narrative (which in some of the twelve translations was done in the first person throughout). The compilers Bredell and Grobler were more familiar with the world of books than was Kruger. The original Dutch text was edited and polished for the German edition (the first to appear) by the Rev. Dr A. Schowalter. From this was adapted the English version by A. Teixeira de Mattos for the British and American markets. The Afrikaans version follows the Dutch text (published shortly after the German) and can be supplemented endlessly by all the reminiscences and anecdotes that came afterwards.

But as far as possible fact must be sorted from fiction. Kruger was always to show a good deal of common sense and unusual powers of psychological insight at a time when psychology was still seen in terms of the vapours. A story not well known concerns Kruger and a young man who threatened to commit suicide. As he wanted to slash his throat with a razor, friends and relations kept the young man under constant observation. When it came to Kruger's turn, and the young Boer actually produced a razor, Kruger said he had something far more effective. He fetched a whip called a sjambok and gave the youth a sound thrashing, which apparently forthwith drove out the evil spirit in possession of him.[23]

Kruger was not the sort of man to boast of his days as a great hunter, at least not seriously. Like most Boers he did not hold his youth of much account. What mattered was the final product, not the formative years. Prodded, however, Kruger did admit that he had shot at least thirty to forty elephants and many other types of big game, killing five lions by himself, and countless others on expeditions. When he went out hunting he took a companion, often a black, and good horses with him.[24] On larger expeditions he allowed people in need of food to go with them by wagon so that they could have their share of the game. The meat, expertly cut, salted and dried, was called biltong, forming a delicious and nourishing stock of food which could last for months.

It was on a hunting expedition in the north-western Transvaal that Kruger lost his left thumb, one of the most famous stories concerning him. There are many versions, but it boils down to his hunting a rhinoceros, which he wounded, when his gun exploded and blew off the top of his thumb. He had to flee for his life from the maddened rhino until the creature collapsed. At camp his wife tried to staunch the profuse bleeding of his hand with turpentine. In spite of all kinds of treatment gangrene set in, and they all knew what that meant. By pretending that his hand belonged to somebody else, Kruger amputated what was left of his thumb with his jack-knife, a very painful operation, as he said in a matter-of-fact way.

He then pushed his hand into the warm stomach of a freshly killed goat. When it came to the turn of the second goat, the awful swelling began to go down, and he knew his hand was saved. Kruger ascribed this old Boer remedy's success to the large number of herbs eaten by the goats. The wound took over six months to heal, but he was out hunting again before it had done so.[25] Kruger was self-conscious about his mutilated hand, even in old age, and was inclined to edge it away from cameras. In Europe, when a dentist was not available, Kruger once dug out a painful molar with his knife, the impression being given that he was quite impervious to physical pain. From that it was but a short step, as his enemies deduced, to being totally insensitive to the feelings of others.

The stories of Paul Kruger streaking ahead of ferocious wild beasts are legion. One of the most amusing was told by him to a caller who persisted in questioning him about his hunting days. 'One day,' Kruger began wearily, and then suddenly becoming interested in his own story, 'I wounded an elephant cow with particularly fine teeth in dense bushveld. Too late I saw that she had a calf and was at her most ill-tempered. There wasn't time to reload, so I took to my heels with the screaming elephant after me. Because of the density of the bush I hared along an elephant path. Suddenly, there in front of me, was a lion. I could not turn back, nor sideways, so could only hope to give the lion a fright. Just then the elephant started trumpeting and the lion bounded off. But as I was going at full speed, I passed the lion, the elephant crashing after us. The lion passed me, but once more I got ahead, and so it went on—the best race I've ever had. But all this time the elephant was gaining on us—' Just then Kruger was urgently summoned to the Volksraad, and the open-mouthed man was left in dreadful suspense, for he was never to hear the end of the story.[26]

Paul Kruger's sense of humour was boundless, and he enjoyed practical jokes and leg-pulling. This was usually done with a grave countenance, but a twinkle of his dark eyes or a mischievous expression around the corner of his mouth would give him away. In youth he never tired of playing pranks. When he helped to build the first church at Rustenburg, the laying of the ridge-pole beam moved him to climb to its highest point, there to stand on his head. Kruger's energy became proverbial. Not for him the ordinary mounting of a horse, but an expert vault into the saddle. And when he wished to be on the other side of a team of oxen, he used the whipstick for a pole-vault over the team. Swimming, diving, running, jumping—thus we see the young man in endless exploits. He was also given to friendly but painful slaps, embraces and pinches which were frightening to the timid.

Kruger's self-assurance at times verged on exhibitionism, but in the lives of great men this is not unusual. Cowardliness and ungodliness were the two things he most despised, intelligence and practical ability what he most admired. He possessed qualities of leadership and could recognize it in others, had a balanced view of things and rarely really lost his temper. Though his father was an important man under Potgieter, and other relations were influential, Paul Kruger's rapid climb in life was on his own merit. In youth he had a kind of joyousness which was infectious and a lightheartedness which people found difficult to reconcile with the solemn man he was to become. Always, however, there was to be humour, though some of it was at the expense of others.

Paul Kruger's first major excursion after his marriage was another

Potgieter expedition. Dramatic things had been happening in Natal, for as Potgieter had feared and had indeed prophesied the British annexed the territory in 1843. There was resistance under Pretorius, but it was not a united stand and Potgieter, as it appeared to some, abandoned them to their fate. He disassociated the Winburg-Potchefstroom Republic from the Natal Volksraad which continued to function at Pietermaritzburg, the Voortrekker town named in honour of Piet Retief and Gert Maritz. Potgieter was involved in a new constitution of thirty-three articles, known afterwards as the Potgieter Constitution, and renewed negotiations with the Portuguese about Delagoa Bay as a harbour.[27]

Paul Kruger became a deputy veldcornet (field-cornet) in 1842, a singular honour at seventeen, but he considered this of little importance in comparison with becoming a full veldcornet ten years later. Even so it meant something to be part of the expedition of 1845 as a deputy 'to colonize the conquered territory'. Every member of the expedition was promised a farm in the north-eastern Transvaal. Potgieter had led a commission, of which Kruger's father was an important member, to Delagoa Bay the year before to negotiate, apart from harbour facilities, a mutual frontier. The Lebombo Mountains were decided upon as the dividing line between Boer and Portuguese territories. As the necessity was felt to have a town nearer to Lourenço Marques than Potchefstroom, Kruger was present when Potgieter founded the town of Andries-Ohrigstad, named after himself and the Dutch trader Ohrig who had been tantalizing the Voortrekkers with marvellous prospects for years.

After a period of comparative peace, the Emigrant Farmers were again in a state of flux, for after the British annexation of Natal they came streaming back to the Free State and Transvaal. The Winburg-Pochefstroom people were fanning out, and were mainly loyal to Potgieter, which the ex-Natalians were not. A period of strife began which became only more marked with the arrival of Pretorius. It was the wish of many to see a reconciliation between these two forceful men. Although Paul Kruger's relatives, particularly his father and uncle, were much involved with the political intrigues which came about, he preferred to stay out of them, and also to leave Ohrigstad because of fever, cattle-sickness 'and other evils'. To Paul Kruger the Magaliesberg was home, and when he was back again he extended his farming activities by acquiring additional farms by barter.

Early in 1846 tragedy struck just as Paul Kruger was finding his feet. His wife and the baby she had recently had both died that

January. It would appear that this was a result of malaria contracted at Ohrigstad, and not death in childbirth.[28] Personal attachments among the Voortrekkers were very close, as one would expect from people who shared so much. But the Bible taught them resignation to the will of God, and after a lapse of time a new mate was sought. Kruger's choice fell on a cousin of his late wife, Gezina Susanna Frederika Wilhelmina du Plessis. He had met her as a small plump child at the Caledon River, for her family had formed part of the Potgieter Trek. She was called Gezina and also Sanna du Plessis, and was born on 6 May 1831, the daughter of Jan Adriaan du Plessis, a farmer from the Tarka-Colesberg region. Paul Kruger married her in 1847.

This was to be a perfect match, lasting fifty-four years. They were to have sixteen children, nine boys and seven girls, some of whom died young. Their first child, Casper Jan Hendrik, was born on 22 December 1847. Gezina Kruger was a small rotund woman, gentle, very feminine, friendly and hospitable. She shared her husband's devoutness and capabilities, and was to become a haven of peace as Kruger's career became more and more turbulent. Gezina was not in the least put out by her overpowering consort, and perfectly content to have him as he was and to remain quietly in the background. Even as First Lady of her land over a long period, Gezina never obtruded herself and was actually very rarely seen. But she was very much there, a quiet, gracious and kindly woman who clearly loved her husband with selfless devotion. In their house in Pretoria I have always been more aware of her than of him, while he dominates Church Square nearby, and by no means solely on account of his monument standing there now.

As a Calvinist, Paul Kruger belonged to a rigid branch of the Dutch Reformed Church called the Gereformeerde Kerk, members of which were called 'Doppers', not unlike Quakers. The Doppers have always been outnumbered by members of the mother Dutch Reformed Church, and perhaps for that reason were clannish and critical of their more 'worldly' countrymen. They frowned on ostentation of any kind, on frivolities like dancing and general light behaviour, but narrowness varied with the individual. Even in early Trek days one could recognize Doppers by their mode of dress and even by their distinctive basin-cut hair. Because of their clannishness they were inclined to form settlements in particular areas, as at Rustenburg, for long Kruger's stamping-ground. He was to remain unswervingly loyal to his church, but as will be shown Kruger was not as narrow-minded as he has been given out to be, and indeed as a young man religion did not weigh as heavily with him as it was to do later on.[29]

At the outset of his farming career his main concern was to find reliable workmen. Potgieter's campaigns against the Matabele had inevitably liberated various tribes and had also saved some from total annihilation. Although these people were willing to work, they had much to learn, and it was another matter to get them to work well. Thieving and unreliability seemed to be part of their nature. Also, no longer living in terror, these once starving peoples began to prosper in the reserves Potgieter created for them. With prosperity came an assurance and arrogance which were to complicate white and black relations. Kruger played many pranks on these illiterate savages, without ever being really malicious, and the comicality of some pranks tickled him ever afterwards, not that Boer humour was seen in an indulgent light by the prejudiced.

Because of the political squabbling caused by the returning Emigrants from Natal, Potgieter felt the need to have faith in him reaffirmed. The result was that he was re-elected Chief Commandant in May 1845. At Ohrigstad two parties came about, that of Potgieter and the so-called Volksraad Party under J. J. Burger from Natal. Burger was an ardent republican and dead set against Potgieter's dictatorial ways, not that Potgieter paid much attention to him. Potgieter had his friend Gert Kruger appointed Commandant of Potchefstroom, and resumed his customary negotiations with Native tribes and the Portuguese as if Burger did not exist. Rivalry and a clash of personalities produced two governments in 1846 which headed for an inevitable collision a year later.

The farm granted to Paul Kruger in the fever belt where Andries-Ohrigstad was founded had the name of Swartkop at the Steelpoort River. On his quitting the region, the Volksraad confiscated this farm, something which gave Kruger little concern as he had lost all interest in living there and was concentrating on his salubrious Waterkloof. Ohrigstad (the full name was rarely used) was clearly doomed, many people already moving to a healthier region where they founded a town called Lydenburg in commemoration of all their sufferings. Far from the scene, Kruger and many of his relations remained uninvolved in the furious dispute which arose between the Potgieter and Volksraad Parties. The Krugers, no lovers of disputes, would probably have remained passive but for the arrival of Andries Pretorius (1798–1853), the hero of Blood River, who was looked upon by many as their true and God-given leader.

The year 1848 heralded a whole series of excitements, for a new Cape Governor, Sir Harry Smith, felt that the Colony could not afford the loss of such a large number of people, to some extent the cream of the Colony, and that the solution lay in proclaiming the Queen's Sovereignty to the north of the Orange River. As his plan apparently went no farther than the Vaal River, Potgieter felt no particular alarm, while Pretorius who had many supporters in Transoranje could not remain aloof. As the Pretorius Trek prepared to quit Natal for good, Sir Harry Smith came tearing over the Drakensberg to try and induce them to stay, for Natal too could not afford to lose them.

Sir Harry confided to Pretorius that he was planning to annex the territory beyond the Orange, and was nonplussed when Commandant-General Pretorius told him not to do anything of the kind, as the larger number of the Emigrants would not have it, particularly those in the northern parts. Sir Harry then came to an agreement with Pretorius not to do anything until the people were sounded on the matter. Pretorius was only too ready to do so, but hardly had he left camp when Sir Harry issued his proclamation of annexation, no doubt because he, like his predecessors, looked upon the Emigrants as British subjects no matter where they went, and also because he had made up his mind, annexation being one of his joys in life. In the uproar that followed, Sir Harry blamed Pretorius for stirring up rebellion. This being the case, Pretorius felt he had no option but to lead the rebels at their invitation.

The upshot was the dreary Battle of Boomplaats of August 1848 in which the Boers put up a poor show and Sir Harry Smith had the astonishing experience of having his 'children' firing at his person.[30] Commandant-General Andries Pretorius was a superb military leader, in the same class as Sir Harry, at least, as he had proved at Blood River, when his men were united. In the southern Free State there were many Boers who were not Voortrekkers and were still loyal to the British Government, as indeed the Krugers had been. Some genuine Voortrekkers, worn out by squabbling, welcomed the British plan. But by far the greater number of them cherished the republican ideal, wished to have nothing to do with British rule, and were even beginning to show the fervour of Boer nationalism. Although the Krugers wished to avoid strife, Casper and Gert were drawn into the Pretorius commando and most reluctantly into battle.[31] Not so Paul, who watched the exasperated return of his father and uncle. South of the Vaal, Sir Harry now created his Orange River Sovereignty, put a price on the head of Pretorius, and tried to woo Potgieter, of all men.

Andries Pretorius, though not a Dopper, also had a farm at the Magaliesberg, between the confluence of the Crocodile and Magalies Rivers, which he called Grootplaats. His brothers Piet and Bart were near by, and a warm friendship with the Kruger clan was established. As Andries Pretorius was physically one of the most impressive men of his time (some say he was nearly seven feet tall), and a living legend after he had broken the old-time power of the Zulus, Paul Kruger was fascinated by him. I have said earlier that Kruger was not a man for hero-worship, but in Pretorius he found much to admire, although he too had his detractors. It was the scope of his mind which interested Kruger, and he was to be a frequent caller at Grootplaats where a gracious home was built by two imported British artisans.[32]

Pretorius was not the rough pioneering type, but a man of breeding and means. His stand against the British annexation of Natal, futile as it turned out to be through lack of co-operation, was already part of history, and as a maker of history he was by no means done. Apart from Kruger's admiration for the man, there was also a bond of sympathy between them, for Pretorius liked Kruger and was perhaps the first person to recognize that behind his rough exterior was a most singular person with an intellect all the more remarkable for being almost entirely self-developed. Devoutness too was a bond between them. It was entirely unostentatious and devoid of sanctimoniousness. They shared, one can say, a nobility of soul, and it is surprising that the influence of Pretorius on Kruger has gone almost unexamined. To the elderly Kruger, Pretorius would have been 'worldly', for he enjoyed entertainments, music, balls and banquets, but for the youthful Kruger this was a very admirable man.

It was the aim of Pretorius to unite the various Boer districts that had come about. He still held the rank of Commandant-General of his Natal days, but Potgieter claimed that of Chief Commandant. The Volksraad could see the only solution as having a Commandant-General for every district. At the mass meetings of 1849 when it was decided to have one central Volksraad (literally Council of the People), Potgieter did not attend. He was also absent when he was appointed Commandant-General for the Zoutpansberg region, along with Pretorius for Magaliesberg and Mooi River, W. F. Joubert for Lydenburg, and J. A. Enslin for Marico. These appointment gave the impression of four separate republics but were in fact the beginning of a movement to unite them. Paul Kruger was veldcornet to General Pretorius.

Kruger's political awareness can be dated from 1850, and it was in no small measure given him by Pretorius. Like his mentor he wanted law and order and submission to authority, as well as British recognition of their independence. Although Pretorius had fought the British in Natal and the Free State, he was not anti-British. Neither was Kruger, for as yet he had no particular reason to be so. But for the unity of the State, recognition of independence was essential as long as the Cape Government held that they were still British subjects. The Great Trek had of necessity had a military structure as an organization, but now supreme authority had to be vested in a properly constituted Volksraad. In Kruger's opinion the four commandant-generals were unnecessary, two of them definitely redundant, for Enslin was too ill to be politically active and Joubert threw his weight behind Pretorius. As Potgieter remained aloof in the north, Kruger too stood by Pretorius. The general swing to him was becoming marked.

In the Sovereignty too there was unrest. Most of the Boer inhabitants resented British rule, no matter how prudently administered by the Resident, Major Henry Warden. Moreover, he had become involved in a disastrous war with the Basotho under King Moshesh (also known as Moshoeshoe and Mosjesjwe). The Winburg Emigrants appealed to Pretorius to take over the Government imposed on them, and Moshesh too sent an envoy to Pretorius to ask him to restore law and order in the Sovereignty. This was in 1851, and Pretorius, still outlawed, began a diplomatic correspondence with Warden and conferred with his council of war, or Krygsraad, of which Paul Kruger was now a full member. Warden informed Sir Harry Smith that unless a compromise was reached with Andries Pretorius, now the most powerful man in the interior, and also an honest and sincere one, the Orange River Sovereignty would be wrecked.[33]

Sir Harry, fast losing favour with his Home Government because of his theatrical treatment of Natives and reckless annexations of huge tracts of country, had no option but to recognize Pretorius and send two commissioners to the Sovereignty to investigate the situation and make recommendations. The two men were Major W. S. Hogge and C. Mostyn Owen. They turned up at Major Warden's military post, Bloemfontein, on 27 November 1851. For a meeting with General Pretorius a spot on the Sand River, the farm of P. A. Venter, was selected. The main endeavour of Hogge and Owen was to nullify any further threat from the north, and this could only be done by the formal acknowledgement of the independence of the Emigrants beyond the Vaal. This was exactly what Pretorius wanted, but Potgieter feared that should it become an issue everything could be lost.

In January 1852 Pretorius and his party set off for the Sand River. Paul Kruger was one of them, as well as his uncle Gert Kruger. His father had also been deputized but was too ill to go. At twenty-six Paul Kruger was present at the signing of the historic Sand River Convention on 17 January, the crowning achievement of General Andries Pretorius. According to this document the British Government guaranteed in the fullest manner that the Emigrant Farmers beyond the Vaal would have the right to manage their own affairs 'and to govern themselves according to their own laws without any interference on the part of the British Government, and that no encroachment shall be made by the said Government on the territory . . .'

There was general jubilation, and it was but a matter of time for Pretorius and Potgieter to be reconciled. Their joint aim was the founding of a united South African Republic. Both also wished to work for the withdrawal of the Sovereignty, Transoranje to become the Republic of the Orange Free State. The union of these two republics would no longer be an impossible dream. With the death of Potgieter at the end of 1852 followed by that of Pretorius six months later, one can see the Great Trek period ended. Not its effects, however, for the Pretorius and Potgieter parties remained active, and independence merely escalated a war of personalities.

Paul Kruger came through this period as a Pretorius man. It was in his nature to be loyal, but not blindly so, and Potgieter's hold on him as a youth had long since been replaced by that of Pretorius, whom he had been privileged to know far more intimately. Both were great men, and just how strong their personalities were was henceforth to be revealed to him in the activities of their successors, activities which prompted Kruger to a definite line of action which was to reveal him as the true heir of both men.

Kruger never lost his interest in farming but it was to be much curtailed. In 1852 we see him reaching his prime, straight as a ramrod, his bulk and the broadness of his shoulders making him appear less tall than he was. He was compared to a rock, an eagle, a lion, and many other things and creatures when viewed in retrospect. What he was actually like then is only seen in outline and can be quickly sketched. He had a habit of contracting his eyebrows and narrowing his eyes, but when excited his eyes opened wide. Already he was a heavy smoker, and there was always a Bible next to his favourite chair. The corners of his mouth were tightening, his lower lip slightly pendulous from all that pipe-smoking.[34] When deep in thought his face became quite expressionless. He dressed simply, still wearing old-fashioned flap-trousers, and was particularly partial to meat and milk.

CHAPTER FOUR

The Young Warrior

It was not yet permitted to become a veldcornet before the age of twenty-five. But for this regulation Paul Kruger might have been pushed into a military career sooner than he was, for Native unrest was becoming a serious problem. No longer menaced and starving as in the past, tribes re-established themselves, and became bold and aggressive. Open to a multitude of new influences, they flaunted authority and became more and more prone to attack whites and one another. On the whole Kruger got on well with the blacks. They admired his size and physical strength, his horsemanship and abilities as a hunter. In races he often outran the fleetest of them, and they marvelled at his ability to mimic the cry of birds.[35] On his trips Kruger invariably had Native companions, and with many of them he had warm and enduring friendships. Traitors and criminals, however, could expect little mercy from Kruger.

One of the disturbers of the peace was Chief Setshele of the Bakwena tribe of Bechuanaland, who was aged about forty-two in 1852. The Matabele had driven this tribe into the Kalahari Desert. Their scattered remains only got back to their ancestral haunts after Potgieter's successful onslaughts on the Matabele military towns of Mosega and Egabeni in 1837. They submitted willingly to the protection of Potgieter's Potchefstroom Government and caused no trouble. Early in 1846 Dr David Livingstone began his labours among the Bakwena, Setshele being his first convert. The tribe had begun to flourish and regained self-assurance. The Commandant of Marico reported to the Volksraad in 1850 that the Bakwena had gained possession of considerable quantities of arms and ammunition, and were clearly planning an attack on the Boers. Livingstone appeared to be implicated, for he looked upon the Boers as predators.[36]

The matter came to a head when a Kgatla chief, Moselele, fled to Setshele for protection after stealing livestock from the Boers. Kruger believed he had committed several murders. Setshele was told to hand Moselele over, but he refused to do so, it being an ancient Bantu custom to give asylum to those who sought it. Setshele went further in being deliberately provocative by calling on other tribes for a general rising. So a commando was raised under Commandant Pieter

Ernest Scholtz, with Paul Kruger promoted to Deputy Commandant, to deal with the matter. One member of the commando was a short powerful man, Petrus Jacobus Joubert, always called Piet, aged twenty-one, whose life was to be closely linked with that of Paul Kruger for the rest of his days. Piet Joubert, like some of the other men, had his wife with him, and she was ever after to accompany him on all his campaigns, something Kruger's Gezina never did.

The commando arrived at Kolobeng on Saturday, 28 August 1852. Again Setshele was asked to surrender Moselele, but he sent a message to say that they could try and get him, that he would not fight on a Sunday, and that he was in need of coffee and sugar. Scholtz replied that he had no coffee and sugar to give away, but Setshele was welcome to pepper on the Monday, a reply which delighted Kruger. On the Monday he was well in front when the battle began, firing a four-pounder loaded with coarse shot. Setshele's town lay on a mountain, and as the Boers began to take it their gunner Louw du Plessis hit a large rock. The ball rebounded and hit Kruger on the head, knocking him unconscious. A comrade bound his head, while his Hottentot servant held the Natives at bay with his master's gun. When Kruger revived, he saw Natives creeping up behind rocks and boulders and at once ran to warn and lead those in the most dangerous positions. As he did so, Kruger was swiped by a bullet across the chest which ripped his jacket without wounding him. Both escapes seemed miraculous.

When the Bakwena were routed, Scholtz sent some of his men to investigate Livingstone's house which was near by, the doctor being away. 'Here,' said Kruger, 'Pretorius' (this was the great Andries, only nominally in command, for he was suffering from dropsy and near the end), 'found a complete workshop for repairing guns, and a quantity of materials of war which Livingstone was storing for Secheli [*sic*].' As this was a contravention of the Sand River Convention—no arms or ammunition to be supplied to Natives—Scholtz confiscated the 'arsenal'. That is all Kruger has to say about the campaign, switching over to Livingstone's subsequent slanders of the Boers. But some very contentious things did take place, such as the sacking of Livingstone's house, the destruction of his medical equipment and library, the books being torn to shreds.[37] Then there were all those prisoners, men, women and children, taken by the Boers.

According to Van Oordt the action itself was brisk and lasted some six hours, only four Boers being killed and five wounded.[38] According to Livingstone, who was at Kuruman, thirty-five Boers and sixty of the Bakwena were killed. Setshele said that twenty-eight Boers fell, and that the reasons for their attack on him were first his refusal to be 'in their kingdom' and second because he was said to allow Englishmen and Griquas* to pass through his territory to the north.[39] Of Moselele there is no mention. Nearly all Livingstone's facts, gathered at Kuruman, are muddled, for he says there were 600 Boers, when in fact there were 300; that they were accompanied by 700 Natives and Coloureds, when there were about half that number; that the Boers carried off women and children to make slaves of them, 'savage Boers, many of them half drunk . . . shooting down women and children without the least provocation . . .'[40] Setshele in his turn accused Kruger of being drunk when he never touched liquor.

In their Cape Colonial days the Boers had become used to the campaign of various missionaries against them, their readiness always to take the side of the black against the white, no matter what the evidence. Injustice, misrepresentation and heinous slander of the Boer had encouraged the Great Trek. Now the Setshele affair opened the eyes of Paul Kruger to this sort of thing, and also to the difficulties still to beset them, for Livingstone's distortion of fact spread throughout England. His slanders were also taken up by two local missionaries—Rogers Edwards and Walter Inglis—and to a lesser extent by Robert Moffat, Livingstone's father-in-law. The Boers hotly denied all the allegations made against them, and when Edwards and Inglis persisted, Scholtz had them arrested and brought to trial at Rustenburg on a charge of libel against the State. They were found guilty and ordered to leave the country within a fortnight.[41]

At Waterkloof, Gezina Kruger thanked the Lord that her husband had gone through the campaign unscathed. Perhaps God had a special mission for him, she felt, seeing that he had been twice saved from what looked to be certain death. All round, Kruger had made a strong impression, and instead of reverting back to Veldcornet, he was promoted to the rank (soon to be dropped) of Lieutenant, between a veldcornet and a commandant. With this rank he was sent to the western border where, as a result of the Basotho risings in the Free State, tribes were becoming restive—particularly the Barolong of Chief Montshiwa, who were partial to Boer cattle. Other than that, friction was inevitable as the Convention had not seen to a clear definition of the western border. Montshiwa was called to account

* Griquas were persons of mixed blood who even proudly called themselves 'Bastards'.

and, as he refused to surrender the stolen cattle, a commando was sent against him in December 1852.[42]

Andries Pretorius was again only nominally in command, and for the last time. Although he went along, he had almost nothing to do with the campaign, not that there was much of it anyway. The commando set out for the region between Schoonspruit and Marico, on the Harts River. In a snowfall Montshiwa had raided a large number of Boer cattle, murdering one of the owners. The chief had fled to Setlagoli in Bechuanaland, so the commando set off in pursuit. Because of a huge swarm of locusts, the dust raised by the horses went unobserved until they were close to Setlagoli. Kruger was sent to the chief to demand that Montshiwa should come out and explain his behaviour. But he was no longer there, so Kruger went off in pursuit, only to land in an ambush. He and his companions promptly charged their attackers and dispersed them.

Back with the main commando, Kruger's horse was so done in that he proposed to lead an attack on foot. Commandant Schutte, standing in for Pretorius, refused this and gave Kruger his groom's horse. In a patrol of forty men, Kruger led an attack on 500 Natives and put them to flight. The Boer cattle were there all right, and Kruger took custody of their drovers in order to take them back to their town that same evening. As night began to fall before they got there, Kruger explained to his captives that he and his men had not come to fight but only to recover their property. So, fearing another ambush, he released them. The next day a patrol found Montshiwa's great place Mahikeng (Mafeking) deserted, so the commando went home, Pretorius having long talks on religious matters with Kruger as they trotted along.

Kruger had been in close contact with Natives since childhood. He knew many dialects and spoke some fluently. As some Natives also picked up Afrikaans with apparent ease, there was no lack of communication. In time people were to say that no man knew the Transvaal Natives better than Paul Kruger. 'Native politics in a Republic such as ours,' he was to state, 'where so many Kaffir tribes live among us and all around us, offer very exceptional difficulties. The chief principle that must always be borne in mind is that savages must be kept within bounds, and always ruled with justice and morality . . . Every Kaffir tribe within our boundaries must be taught to respect the authority of our Government, and, in order that the laws, by which these tribes also benefit, may be equitably administered, they must bear their share of the public burden . . . I cherish the hope that some time, under God's blessing, it will come to this, that order, industry and the fear of God will make the Kaffir also a happy and contented subject of the South African Republic.'[43]

General Andries Pretorius died on 23 July 1853 at the age of nearly fifty-five. Towards the end he pleaded for unity and love amongst his people, dictated letters in which he urged people to fight party strife, to curb wild ambitions and to love their Church. He dissuaded Mpande, King of the Zulus who had fought with him against the former King Dingane, from an attack on the white inhabitants of Natal. He received envoys from Mzilikazi and Moshesh, as well as chiefs and indunas from various tribes who knelt beside him and kissed his hands.[44] Loyalty, trust, kindness, justice and love must prevail among all, no matter their race or colour. Feeling the closeness of death, Pretorius sent for Kruger, but the messengers did not reach him in time, and Kruger was left wondering what Pretorius had wanted to discuss with him in his last moments.

'And you, my brother, who are to succeed me,' Pretorius had written in his farewell message to his Krygsraad, 'lead God's people in humility and manliness, in all justice and honesty. Know that the Lord will look upon you also from Heaven. Ask Him His blessing and His aid, and He will uplift you. Do nothing for your own increment, but in everything aim at the glory of God and the well-being of land and people.'[45] These words could have been directed at Paul Kruger. Pretorius had not named a successor as Commandant-General, such a person having to be elected. But it was taken for granted that his successor was his son Marthinus Wessel Pretorius, now aged thirty-four, living near the parental home of Grootplaats at Kalkspruit.

Andries Pretorius had undoubtedly recognized qualities in Paul Kruger which he knew his own son lacked. It is also likely that he knew that, when the time was right, Kruger was to play an important role in the history of the Republic. But for the time being, as Pretorius had no doubt expected, his son Marthinus would do. The young men had known each other for years and had come to manhood under his guiding hand. The man who should perhaps have been his successor was Gert Kruger, but it was decided to follow the example of Potgieter who was succeeded by his son Piet as Commandant-General of the Lydenburg and Zoutpansberg districts.

Paul Kruger's next campaign was in August 1854[46] against Chiefs Mapela (his real name was Mankopane, but he was usually given the name of his grandfather, a Ndebele chief of the Langa tribe) and Makapan (Mokopane) in the Waterberg region. This featured a horror story which was told all over South Africa. Herman Potgieter, a brother of the late General Potgieter, being well known as an elephant hunter and splendid shot, had been invited by Chief Mapela to come and see an exceptionally large herd of elephants in his country. It was also to be an opportunity for Herman Potgieter to check his cattle which were in Mapela's care, he having the use of the milk of the cows, an arrangement which had been made at Mapela's request. Potgieter, never giving foul play a thought, set out with his son Andries, his coloured groom and some friends to visit Mapela. Black conspiracies were usually quickly exposed, but this time nobody had any notion that Mapela and Makapan had come to an arrangement to kill all the whites in their territories, perhaps because there was no such arrangement.

There are various versions of what happened, but as Paul Kruger's informant was Potgieter's groom and he had the proof of his own eyes, there is no reason to question what he tells. At Mapela's kraal the party was given a friendly reception, and as usual it was decided to leave the wagons there while they went after the elephants. About to go, Mapela's warriors suddenly fell on them, killed Andries Potgieter and the other men, while they held on to Herman Potgieter whom they dragged to the top of a hill. With wild yells they skinned this great powerful man alive, and merciful death only came when they dragged out his entrails. The groom, whose life was spared, later showed Kruger where Potgieter had met his ghastly end. It has been said that a karos, a kind of coverlet, was made of his skin.

While this was taking place, Chief Makapan, whom everybody had thought to be friendly, attacked a party of women and children travelling from Zoutpansberg to Pretoria, and butchered all of them. Legend has it that they were cut up and boiled, their hands roasted on spits, for the inroads of Mzilikazi had driven some tribes to cannibalism. The two murders appear to have been mixed up by a chronicler like Van Oordt,[47] but it seems certain that all the murdered were mutilated in the most horrible fashion, before or after they died. A plausible explanation for Mapela's execution of Potgieter is that an argument broke out shortly after their arrival at the kraal, one of Mapela's sons being particularly insulting. Potgieter, a man with an explosive temper, shot him dead in front of everybody.

Whatever the true details were, the fact remains that a certain number of people had been murdered and that the culprits had to be brought to book. The Boer principle had been to allot certain districts to certain tribes proportionate to their size, on condition that they spurned the white man's arms and lived in peace. They were allowed missionaries, free grants of land for churches and private purposes, and were to be encouraged to attain civilized ways. Barbarism in any form was not to be tolerated, certainly not by those who had survived the horrors of Blaauwkrantz in Natal. Veldcornets began to commandeer men in their various districts.

For this campaign Paul Kruger attained the full status of Commandant under Commandant-General Marthinus Wessel Pretorius. They set out with 200 men from Pretoria (not a town yet but a *kerkplaats* or farm where church was held), while 100 men under Commandant-General Piet Potgieter set out from the Zoutpansberg. Before the commandos united, there was an attack on Potgieter's laager, these Natives being easily repulsed. When the two commandos came together the men numbered 550. Scouts reported that the tribesmen had taken to the mountains and were hiding in caverns. This meant a siege, the first of many. The so-called Caves of Makapan, a future archaeologists' paradise, consisted of some huge caverns and formed natural fortresses.

Paul Kruger was in command of the Rustenburgers. Sympathizers brought arms and ammunition from the Free State, and Van Oordt mentions a number of Englishmen joining the commando. On 25 October an attempt was made to charge one of the largest caves, but this proved hazardous because of hidden snipers who had learnt to handle the white man's arms with skill. Sieges are wearisome things, and this was no exception, reliance having to be put on lack of water and food to force capitulation. Paul Kruger managed to slip into one cave and exhort those inside to surrender. He succeeded in getting about 180 women and children out, but Piet Potgieter was furious that he should risk his life like that and ordered him away from the caves. In one engagement Potgieter, standing close to a rocky wall giving orders, was mortally hit by a sniper. Large of body like his father and uncle, he crashed down into an entrenchment in front of the cave. At once, under heavy fire but given cover by his comrades, Kruger scaled the barricade and retrieved the body, having to exert all his strength to do so. He could well imagine what would otherwise have happened to his General's body.

The campaign came to an end with the surrender of several captains who were promptly court-martialled and shot; but both Makapan and Mapela escaped. It was estimated that 3,000 of the enemy had already perished, mainly of starvation, and as an epidemic of horse-sickness was causing alarm, the men were ready to go home.

Kruger had already left the scene, a captive having offered to show him a cave where stacks of ivory had been secreted. It was an unsuccessful ruse to ambush him and his companions. On this trip Kruger came upon a number of bloodstained garments, which could only have belonged to the murdered women and children, as well as the remains of portions of human bodies roasted on the spit.

After campaigns like these it was always a problem what to do with the captive women and children, for they could not just be left to their fate. So they were usually taken home, booked in with various families, clothed and fed. Their welfare was under strict legal supervision, and when they were able to fend for themselves, they were allowed to go if they wanted. That this system gave the impression of slavery is not surprising, and all protests of humanitarian motives availed nothing in the outside world. Because of heavy casualties among the enemy, there were always large numbers of orphans, and the most sensible thing seemed to be to look after them and give them training. There was no question of enslavement in the Boer mind, and it is true that many of these 'apprentices' felt the same and became so devoted to their adoptive families that they refused to leave them. Gezina Kruger had such a maid whose marriage she eventually arranged, and she gave her a dowry.[48]

The siege of the Caves of Makapan having ended, M. W. Pretorius sent Kruger to the town of Chief Maraba where it was believed a large number of Makapan's cattle was kept. Kruger was ordered to attack should there be any resistance. But there was none. The Marabas said that they had no part in Makapan's crimes and were quite willing to hand over his cattle, a thousand head, so Kruger took them and returned to his commando. Mapela had got off the most lightly, but he and his subjects had fled so far away that pursuit was ruled out. The men contented themselves with retrieving wagons and goods which had belonged to their murdered people found on a hill near Mapela's town. They then went home, feeling uneasy that savages like Mapela and Makapan should still be on the loose.

The Boers in the Orange River Sovereignty were resentful that those beyond the Vaal had gained a formal grant of independence, while no such prospect was immediately held out to them. Soon enough, however, they were soothed by rumours that the Sovereignty was to be abandoned, apparently if it could be done without loss of dignity. Sir Harry Smith's rather startling role in South African history was abruptly ended by his recall, and his successor Sir George

Cathcart was more in tune with the Home Government in believing that the Sovereignty should never have been proclaimed. There were already Native and financial problems enough without looking for more. The Basotho war brought matters to a head, particularly after Major Warden's humiliating defeat at Viervoet. British authority, it was clear, could only be exerted by maintaining a large military force at great expense. Cathcart himself came near to disaster in his campaign against the Basotho at the end of 1852.

A hope of dignified withdrawal was seen when King Moshesh began to sue for peace, the only remaining snag being that quite a large number of the Emigrants wished the British to stay. In April 1853 a special commissioner, Sir George Russell Clerk, was sent to act on recommendations already made by Hogg and Owen. International affairs were tense and there was a world-wide economic slump. Clerk was in Bloemfontein by August and the conferences began which were to lead up to the Convention of Bloemfontein of 23 February 1854 which ended the Orange River Sovereignty and heralded the Republic of the Orange Free State. The first Volksraad assembled in March, a Constitution was ratified in April, and in May the first President was elected. He was the crippled Josias Philippus Hoffman who wished to lose no time in befriending Moshesh.

Across the Vaal, M. W. Pretorius watched these rapid developments in the Orange Free State with mixed feelings, for he wished to see one Boer Republic and felt that at least the territory ceded to Potgieter in the Great Trek days rightfully belonged to the Transvaal. But for the time being any kind of union was ruled out by civil strife, in both republics, made all the more unpleasant as the Church could not remain uninvolved. A draft Constitution or Grondwet for the Transvaal was only formulated in September 1855, Kruger being a member of a commission of eight, and was only adopted in January 1858 because of the resistance of the districts of Zoutpansberg and Lydenburg.

One would have expected the Voortrekker town of Winburg to be the capital of the Orange Free State, but it was Warden's military post Bloemfontein which rapidly turned into a sprawling town, with a considerable British element. In the Transvaal the capital remained Potchefstroom, while Pretoria became the seat of government. Pretoria, as has been mentioned, began as a church farm in 1854, the central point where a minister (not yet easily found) held services. A year later it became Pretoria-Philadelphia, though known only as Pretoria in memory of the late General Andries Pretorius. The land was bought and laid out by his son Marthinus. He had a house built for himself on Church Square in 1856 but never lived in it.[49]

Paul Kruger remained resident at Waterkloof, west of Rustenburg, and was to live there until 1873. He moved to his other farms periodically, such as Boekenhoutfontein which he acquired in 1862, but for the time being was quite content with his base. Like many farmers, Kruger was to have a house in Pretoria for occasional use, a *tuishuis*, but he only lived permanently in Pretoria as from 1881, and yet this town was to become permanently and even emotionally linked with him. The Commandant belongs to the days of Waterkloof from where he participated in the creation of the South African Republic.

The slain Piet Potgieter was succeeded by Commandant-General Stephanus Schoeman, an influential man who strengthened his position in the north by marrying Piet Potgieter's widow. Allied to the stubborn, dictatorial and uncompromising Potgieters and their adherents, he was now their leader and virtually President of Lydenburg-Zoutpansberg. M. W. Pretorius felt the need to strengthen his position in the south, particularly after Gert Kruger, his senior and a far more experienced man, had retired to his farm after being passed over as Commandant-General. Pretorius could rely on the loyalty of Commandant Paul Kruger, and he was to have much help from a learned Hollander who had come to the Transvaal with high hopes of stimulating Dutch immigration, Jacobus Stuart (1803–78). In his opinion the various commandant-generals merely caused dissension. What was needed was one Head of State.

Stuart was right, for in the early fifties a chaotic element marked the territory beyond the Vaal. Up to the Limpopo there were only six towns by 1855: Potchefstroom (1838), Schoemansdal (1848—originally Zoutpansbergdorp), Lydenburg (1849), Rustenburg (1851), Piet Potgietersrust (1854) and Pretoria (1855). Settlements like Ohrigstad were abandoned, while most of the others were very far apart. There was a great need for teachers and ministers of the Church. The Volksraad did not meet regularly and had little power as there was no proper Executive Council. Financially the situation could not have been worse. The country was thus run by the commandant-generals, their commandants and veldcornets, as well as a few landdrosts, which meant that there was no central authority.[50]

Apart from personal clashes, a dispute arose among the various church councils whether to be part of the Cape Synod or not. This dispute was fanned by the Rev. Mr Dirk van der Hoff on his arrival from Holland, for he wanted an independent church. The result was a serious rift between north and south, contributing to the establishment of the Republics of Lydenburg and Utrecht.* It was the unenviable task of M. W. Pretorius to unite all these dissenting groups before he could fulfil his dream of federation or unification with the Orange Free State. The first step was the draft Constitution of 1855, though Lydenburg and Zoutpansberg dissociated themselves from it, wanting a federation similar to the United States of America.

Pretorius was not discouraged and held mass meetings at Rustenburg, Potchefstroom and Pretoria, achieving a kind of people's commission or Volks-Commissie of twenty-four members for an acceptable Constitution. Paul Kruger was one of the members, attending the session of 16 December 1856 at Potchefstroom. The significance of 16 December lay in that it commemorated the Battle of Blood River, but as a day of thanksgiving it still had to be proclaimed. General Schoeman promptly created his own Volksraad and called upon the support of Zoutpansberg and Lydenburg. Something nobody could have believed possible became clear in 1856—the prospect of civil war.

The Potchefstroom Constitution made provision for the election of a president, a command-general and an executive council. The People's Committee formed by the Commission unanimously elected M. W. Pretorius President. When it came to electing the Commandant-General everybody looked at Paul Kruger, but he at once made it clear that he was not available for office and proposed General Schoeman, considering this a diplomatic move to bring about unity. Schoeman flatly refused to accept the office under Pretorius and, according to Van Oordt, behaved like a madman.[51] H. S. Lombard and M. A. Goetz were appointed to the Executive, with J. H. Visagie as State Secretary.

On 6 January 1857 Marthinus Wessel Pretorius was sworn in as the first State President of the South African Republic. The Transvaal flag, the Vierkleur (four colours) was hoisted for the first time. The ceremony aroused only hilarity and ridicule in the north, but Pretorius may well have thought it the dawning of a new age. To a considerable extent his helpmate was Jacobus Stuart, probably the most highly educated man in the Transvaal at that time, author of an important book with a title that can be translated as 'The Dutch Afrikaners and their Republic in South Africa', which was published in 1854, a year

* Utrecht formed the south-eastern corner of the Transvaal and united with Lydenburg in May 1858. From 1902 the district of Utrecht fell in Natal.

before he helped with the first draft Constitution. Stuart is perhaps best remembered as the man who paved the way for a reconciliation between Hendrik Potgieter and Andries Pretorius in 1852.

The position of M. W. Pretorius in 1857 as President was odd in that he was President of only a part of the Transvaal, the Schoeman-Potgieter party refusing to recognize him. Although M. W. Pretorius was not as tall as his father, he was of powerful build, with brilliant blue eyes. Born in the district of Graaff-Reinet on 17 September 1819, he was nineteen when he accompanied his parents on the Great Trek. He took part in the smashing of Dingane and in fighting the British at Port Natal (Durban). On quitting the country beyond the Drakensberg in 1848, it was he who led the Pretorius Trek, his father being away on a diplomatic mission in the Eastern Cape. They were living at the Magaliesberg when plans were made to oust the British from the Orange Free State. After Boomplaats, M. W. Pretorius was one of the delegates who helped to arrange a meeting between Major Warden and his outlawed father, a man of such powerful personality that it was only after his death that Marthinus was able to come into his own.

He had regular features and a rather stern countenance, adorned in later life with a sweeping moustache. An impetuous and irritable man, M. W. Pretorius suffered in comparison with his father, particularly from the day of his elevation when it suddenly dawned on his people that he was a far cry from the great Andries. Even his most loyal supporters became sharply critical. Paul Kruger was one of them, not that this made him in the least disloyal. It was the general opinion that President Pretorius should have given immediate attention to domestic matters, such as ending the dispute with Zoutpansberg-Lydenburg and working for smooth administration. Instead he looked south, holding unification with the Orange Free State of primary concern. It amazed people that he should look upon the Free State as an inheritance from his father, when everybody knew that the Potgieters had the prior claim.

The man who had become their leader by 1857, Stephanus Schoeman, was a remarkable character. He was born in Cape Colony on 15 March 1810 and had played a significant role during the Great Trek. Schoeman was one of the first to settle beyond the Vaal and as a staunch Potgieter man only gained in influence. On the deaths of Hendrik and Piet Potgieter, Schoeman (who had also married into the Potgieter family) was unhesitatingly proclaimed leader of the north. He was perfectly justified in considering himself a national leader and had more qualifications for the job, including seniority, than M. W. Pretorius. The way Pretorius carried on struck Schoeman as presumptuous. He did not approve of the Potchefstroom Constitution, and the action of the Pretorius supporters convinced Schoeman that they would do anything to oust him from his leadership.

Only five weeks after being sworn in as President, M. W. Pretorius, accompanied by Goetz, went to Bloemfontein, apparently expecting an enthusiastic reception. It was just the opposite, for his federal plans were known, and the Free Staters were not impressed either by his grand manners, or by the way he appeared to cash in on the reputation of his father. The President of the Free State at this time was Jacobus Nicolaas Boshof, successor to Hoffman in 1855. The Volksraad was in session, their independence day was being celebrated and their own flag and coat of arms approved by the King of the Netherlands were being inaugurated. Pretorius declined to attend the festivities and added insult to injury by sending a message to Moshesh to meet him at Bloemfontein. Pretorius was confronted by outraged members of the Volksraad who received such a haughty reception that he, their self-appointed saviour, was told to be out of Bloemfontein within twenty-four hours.[52]

The Republic of Lydenburg reacted with full scorn. But M. W. Pretorius was only getting into stride. He left a member of his Executive, H. S. Lombard, behind as Acting President in the Free State and formally dismissed Stephanus Schoeman as Commandant-General, the office he had refused. Pretorius then issued a proclamation which verged on a declaration of war on Lydenburg. On 7 March 1857 the Transvaal Volksraad elected J. F. Dreyer Commandant-General. As it had become known that the Free State Government had begun to take steps against the supporters of Pretorius among them, General Dreyer was ordered to warn the Free State that if these steps were not discontinued forthwith, a commando would be sent against them. The Free State rejected the ultimatum with indignation, so President Pretorius ordered General Dreyer to call up the burghers.

Paul Kruger was away on business when these excitements took place, and he was surprised to receive a message to return at once. When he heard the reason, he was utterly dismayed. Kruger located Pretorius, Dreyer and the commando at the Vaal River. President Boshof at the head of 700 men was already at Kroonstad. The Transvaal commando consisted only of 300, and Kruger spoke out freely about the folly of the whole enterprise. Then he heard that

Boshof had called on Shoeman and his Lydenburgers for military assistance. This was a grave matter, for what could simply have been an armed protest could now turn into a bloodbath, and of brothers at that. Kruger did some quick thinking.

Though he deplored the rashness of Pretorius in having caused such a situation to arise, Kruger felt he had to stand by him. They were to act at once before Schoeman came, and a march on the Free State was promptly called. The commando crossed the Vaal River and headed for Kroonstad. When President Boshof observed the approaching Transvaalers, he sent an officer with a proposal of peace. He found the men playing games, and though relieved to find that the spirit was not really warlike, the Free State officer was peeved that his side should be held to lightly. Pretorius asked Kruger to meet Boshof, and this the Commandant readily did under a white flag. Kruger told Boshof of his disapproval of the whole business, adding: 'But you are quite as guilty as your adversary. Why do you take up arms, instead of impeaching Pretorius before the Volksraad? He would certainly have been punished.'[53]

There was a strong, big man present, Koos Venter, who began to rail against Pretorius, saying that he would like to wring his neck. Kruger stood up for his President and offered to fight Venter, the result to decide the matter. But Venter had no desire to fight Kruger, for he knew that they had equal rights in standing up for their presidents. So it was decided to nominate a commission of twelve men from each side for a conference at the Vaal River, the Transvaal commando to encamp beyond it. As a member of this commission, Kruger showed his loyalty in defending Pretorius in spite of his disapproval. A compromise was reached by which Pretorius relinquished whatever claims he felt he had on the Free State, claims Kruger had held as 'unjust' from the start.

One of the terms of the agreement was that offenders of the Free State and the Transvaal should be punished by their respective countries. So two Free Staters who had sided with Pretorius were promptly charged with high treason and sentenced to hang. Pretorius was not going to have this and sent Kruger to tackle Boshof once more. To punish, Kruger told him at Bloemfontein, was his right, but to punish means not merely to chastise, but to warn and to correct by means of chastisement. Boshof demurred, so Kruger produced his Bible, as he was to do so many times, and showed the President where it said that there is a distinction between punishing and chastising and that to kill a man is to chastise without punishing him. The Free

Staters relented, commuted the sentences to fines, and Kruger even succeeded in having these reduced. Who then was the strong man of the Transvaal, the Free Staters had to wonder: Pretorius, Schoeman or Kruger?

Many people were to ask themselves whether this 'civil war' would ever actually have led to bloodshed, for armed protest was to become part of the Boer way of life, a demonstration of force without a shot being fired while negotiations took place.[54] They had gone through so much together, and their number was so small, that it was inconceivable that they would start killing one another. Paul Kruger was no pacifist like his future generals Joubert and De la Rey, but the shedding of blood was abhorrent to him. In any sort of conflict, including tribal risings, he always preferred negotiations to actual combat; but if it came to a fight he would be in the front rank, the 'bravest of the brave' as he was so often called. But he enjoyed mental combat more, invariably having the last word in finding confirmation of his views in the Bible, and his countrymen had no argument with Holy Writ. Natives posed rather different problems.

Paul Kruger's service for land and people can be dated from 2 June 1857 with the signing of the treaty between the Transvaal and Orange Free State. His name had already become a familiar one in the interior, and the stories about his skills, strength and fearlessness had begun. Nobody questioned his abilities as a warrior, but now it was noted that he also remained loyal even in opposition, that he had singular powers of persuasion and argument, and that he had the ability to lead men and command their respect. In all kinds of tricky situations and emergencies, as in the case of President Pretorius, reliance was put on Paul Kruger to find a solution. Whether one liked him or not, there was comfort in having him near by.

CHAPTER FIVE

The Young Mediator

In persuading M. W. Pretorius to withdraw the claims he felt he had on their State, the Orange Free Staters gained much satisfaction. And having the friendship of Stephanus Schoeman, they hoped to talk this recalcitrant general into a more accommodating attitude towards his fellow-Transvaalers. It was significant to the Free Staters that their country formed the geographical heart of a developing South Africa, ideally situated for mediation, a role that they were indeed to assume to a greater extent and over a longer period than Paul Kruger could have imagined.

He was deeply concerned about the Lydenburgers who still appeared keen to fight it out. They were a much more formidable band of men than the rather placid Free Staters. Kruger now proposed negotiation for the creation of a commission of arbitration to sit at Rustenburg. He went to Lydenburg and conferred with Schoeman who was more ready to talk to him than to Pretorius. Kruger persuaded him to agree to the commission he had in mind, on condition that two members of their Executive Council, H. T. Bührmann and C. Potgieter, joined in the discussions.

The session was held in January 1858, and attended by a large number of armed men from both sides. Kruger saw to it that there were no ugly incidents. The fact that the session was held at Rustenburg shows how much he had to do with it, for Rustenburg looked upon him as their man. Schoeman was prepared to be reasonable on condition that an entirely new Constitution was drafted, so a commission was at once appointed to this end. Most of the articles of 1856 were retained, but the changes Schoeman wanted were made and the new Grondwet approved. The Zoutpansberg region accordingly became part of the Republic, Pretorius was sworn in all over again as President, and Schoeman became the first and sole Commandant-General[55] of an almost united Republic.* Paul Kruger's role in the proceedings marked him as a future statesman.

It April the same year it was again necessary to take up arms against Chief Mapela. The attack on him some four years previously had not subdued him, and a fresh series of plunders and murders

* Lydenburg and Utrecht joined in 1860.

showed that he was emboldened by a plentiful supply of arms and ammunition obtained from hunters, traders and irresponsible persons. Commandant-General Schoeman called up a commando and promoted Paul Kruger to Assistant General. Spies informed Mapela of their coming, so he and his people entrenched themselves in an almost impregnable position on the summit of a high mountain called Magagamatala, with sheer walls of rock on all sides, some sixty-five miles to the north-west of Piet Potgietersrust.

Kruger called for volunteers to storm the position, and a hundred came forward to be taken to the foot of the mountain that night. The men were told to take off their shoes for a noiseless ascent of a steep gorge, the only way of access to the top. Kruger went ahead with a patrol and was about half-way up when a sentry discovered them. He fired at Kruger, but the gun stuck, so Kruger shot him. Firing now came from all sides, Kruger's gun-bearer falling, so he hurried back, ordered the men to don their shoes and to storm the gorge. In a great rush Kruger led them to the top where they took up positions and waited for daybreak. The tribesmen had fallen back, but as soon as they could see the first group of Boers, they charged. A brisk engagement followed in which, Kruger said, 'our fire mowed down the blacks in rows, and they rushed away in wild flight'.[56] The fugitives threw themselves from the heights and fell to death. Again Mapela escaped.

The Orange Free State Government, impressed by the dash shown by the Transvaalers in mountainous terrain, asked Pretorius, Schoeman and Kruger what could be done to establish better relations with their wily neighbour, Moshesh, and his raiding Basotho. This was a nation fashioned out of the members of tribes who had survived the inroads of the Zulu tyrant Shaka and had found safety in a mountainous corner of the eastern part of Transoranje. Basutoland (Lesotho) had also fallen under British jurisdiction during the Sovereignty. Moshesh had his capital on a mountain fastness called Thaba Bosigo which proved impregnable. The raids his subjects made on Boer cattle invited constant punitive expeditions, a war in fact, which seemed to go on for years, causing great loss and much hardship. Moshesh is usually described as wily and treacherous, but was certainly a highly intelligent man with gifts of diplomacy guided by his French missionaries.

Kruger, accompanied by President Pretorius and some fifty men, responded to the appeal made by the Free State, for a settlement of the Basotho problem was in the interest of both Republics. They made for Osspruit on the upper Sand River in June 1858 where they joined a Free State commando. That same night the Basotho raided the cattle they had with them. Kruger sent Veldcornet Boldenstein with the Transvaalers to get them back, and in this they succeeded. From Winburg they went on to Bloemfontein where the Government gave Kruger General J. J. Pick, Marthinus Schoeman and J. A. Cronjé as escort. They set off for Thaba Bosigo. From the foot of the mountain Kruger sent a message to say who he was, that he had come in peace and wanted to talk about peace. Not caring to wait, Kruger climbed the mountain and reached the town just as Moshesh was coming forth to meet him. With the king was Chief Maghato, Kruger's old friend from the Magaliesberg region, on a visit to the Basotho king.

Maghato introduced them, saying: 'This is Paul Kruger.' Moshesh, a tall thin man, beamed with pleasure, saying that he had heard so much about Paul Kruger that he had expected a much older man. He took Kruger by the arm and led him to his European-style house and sat them down to refreshments. In the discussion that followed Kruger pointed out that the king was cutting his own throat by allowing the war to drag on, for it meant that all the high roads to his territory were blocked and that all trade ceased. From their conversation, as given by Kruger,[57] one can see his easy manner with his black countrymen, the humour and fondness for argument, for which the Natives were also noted, as well as mutual respect and courtesy. Moshesh was clearly impressed by Kruger's campaign against Mapela. It did not matter that two of his daughters were married to that chief, for he did not approve of the atrocities committed by him.

Kruger spent some time with Moshesh and succeeded in having a peace treaty, then thought satisfactory, drafted. Moshesh promised to call in his warriors the moment it was ratified by the Free State Government. Kruger says this treaty drafted by himself and Moshesh brought an end to the first Basotho war. (The second began in 1865.) One searches in vain for more information of this visit by Kruger to Moshesh, and his part in the treaty.[58] But Kruger was certainly at Thaba Bosigo in 1858, and apparently talked so much sense that the king pressed him to prolong his stay and gave him a fine saddle-horse as a gift, the Basotho being in the process of becoming a nation of horsemen. Kruger would have liked to stay but received an urgent message from President Pretorius to return at once.

The reason was that a chief on the Harts River, Gasebone, had raided cattle, murdered some of the owners and abducted two women.

Kruger spent fifty hours on horseback in three days, passed only a day at Waterkloof and then rode for Elandsheuvel (Klerksdorp) where the punitive expedition was waiting for him. The commando was poorly equipped with ammunition and provisions but it was hoped to acquire slaughter-cattle on the way. A message was sent to the Free State to ask for assistance, and in order to conserve ammunition game was driven into the bends of the Vaal River and clubbed. On reaching Gasebone's place the 200 men were joined by Commandant Piet Venter with another 100, white and coloured, from the Orange Free State. It was found that Gasebone had fled to Chief Mahura, his nephew, up the Harts River Gorge.

As Assistant Commandant-General (an appointment made on 28 June 1858), Paul Kruger called on Mahura to surrender the two women, Gasebone and the stolen cattle. Only the women were released, so the commando moved up to Mahura's great place, both chiefs coming on the attack. As usual Kruger had hoped to avoid bloodshed; but this was now out of the question, and there were two engagements in which many of the enemy fell. Gasebone fled in the direction of what was to become British Bechuanaland, but was found in brushwood on 13 August by a Boer patrol and shot. His head was sent to Mahura as proof of his death, no novelty this in frontier war.[59] Mahura pleaded for forgiveness through his missionary, saying truthfully that he had had nothing to do with Gasebone's raids. Kruger pardoned him and appointed him Chief of Gasebone's Batlapin. His spoils, 2,800 head of cattle, 4,000 sheep and goats, 165 horses and 23 wagons (giving some idea of the extent of these Native raids on the Boers) were returned.

Kruger was relieved to be back at Waterkloof and to have some rest. He was both physically and mentally exhausted, for he was going through a kind of spiritual crisis, a *geloofstryd* as the Boers called it. It was only at the age of thirty-two to thirty-three that Paul Kruger was what he considered adult, and it came about with intense soul-searching in establishing his relationship with his personal Saviour. In the mountains at Waterkloof he did battle with God, like Jacob, and for three days went without water or food, to the concern of his family and friends. It was a kind of conversion from which he emerged as if he had walked through fire, purged and cast into shape. From statements made at various times one can guess at some of the things that bothered him: pride, arrogance, aggressiveness, insubordination, intolerance, self-aggrandizement. From now on he could know self-respect only in prostration before God, action only by the guidance of God. Never again was his faith to be shaken, a faith which struck some of his contemporaries as being of childlike simplicity.

Carl Jeppe, who knew Kruger well, says: 'To what height his marvellous intellect, coupled as it was with indomitable will power, would have risen, if it had been properly disciplined—it is difficult to imagine.' Jeppe refers to Kruger's 'strength of purpose, his diplomatic abilities, his rough but most effective eloquence', his powerful sermons, his amazing knowledge of Scripture, his abilities as a lawyer, his humour, his self-possession, nerve and stoicism.[60] He was certainly to need all these qualities in the storm which were now to start rocking the Transvaal. One can also take it that it was his personal pact with God which gave him the courage and wisdom to save the Boer people from themselves.

A fresh church dispute began in November 1858 with the arrival from the Netherlands of the Transvaal's first Dopper dominee or minister, Dirk Postma (1818–90). The origin of the name 'Dopper' is obscure, but Kruger himself believed that it derived from the Dutch word for a candle-snuffer, the snuffing process being self-explanatory. The Dopper Church adhered strictly to the decrees of the Synod of Dordrecht of 1618–19. For example, only psalms—no hymns—were to be sung at services. The State Church was Dutch Reformed, and it was only with the coming of Postma that the Christelijk-Gereformeerde Kerk seceded and established itself at Rustenburg in 1859, Kruger being one of the first to join and thereafter a life-long member. As only members of the State Church, according to the Constitution, were to function in public affairs, the Doppers for the time being found themselves in the rather odd position of not being fully qualified burghers.

The two Dutch Reformed ministers already in the Transvaal—P. A. C. van Heyningen at Lydenburg and D. van der Hoff at Potchefstroom—regarded Postma with hostility. However, a meeting was held in April 1859 to iron out their differences. As a result Postma was recognized, and the procedure at his services left to his congregation. By that time Kruger and his fellow-Doppers had already separated from the Mother Church, stood aloof from the Cape Synod and refused to have Dutch Reformed ministers officiating in their midst. Frictions among such an intensely religious people, thinly scattered over a vast land, took on singular proportions, and one must also bear in mind that membership of the Cape Synod was seen as an extension of the British sphere of influence. My ancestors, for example—the Rev. Mr Meent Borcherds of Stellenbosch and the

Rev. Mr P. B. Borcherds of Riversdale—though retaining cultural ties with the Netherlands, staunchly supported the Cape Colonial Government, and so did their colleagues, nearly all of whom had frowned on the Great Trek.

President Pretorius went to Zululand in 1859 for border and harbour discussions for King Mpande. In his absence H. S. Lombard was Acting President. People were becoming rather used to intrigue, but even so it caused something of a sensation when Jan Kock, well known as a hothead and hell-raiser in early Trek days, issued a proclamation that July in the name of Commandant-General Schoeman. In it, claim was again made on the old Potgieter territory between the Vaal and Vet Rivers. As this was a contravention of the treaty with the Orange Free State, the Acting State Attorney, Hermann Jeppe, published a protest in the Government newspaper of which he was the editor—the *Staats-Courant*, printed at Potchefstroom. Schoeman at once issued a counter-protest. There was considerable speculation as to how far Schoeman, Kock and Pretorius were implicated (Kock was related to Pretorius by marriage), and whether their troubles were to start all over again.

President Boshof resigned just then, and Jacobus Venter was recommended as the next President of the Orange Free State. The desire for union with the Transvaal had been steadily growing, mainly because of Basotho trouble which seemed endless, so the so-called Union Party sent in a requisition for President Pretorius to stand in the Free State election. Nothing could have suited his schemes better, so Pretorius accepted with alacrity. And he was indeed, past differences having been forgotten, elected by an overwhelming majority as President of the Orange Free State. His success was partly ascribed to the fact that King Moshesh had great regard for the Pretorius family.

But how could M. W. Pretorius be President of the Transvaal and the Free State at the same time? His own Constitution made it illegal. The Transvaal Volksraad, not being against this surprise development, sought a way out of the deadlock by granting Pretorius six months' leave, no doubt hoping that he could achieve a union of the two States in this period. On his departure for Bloemfontein, Johannes Grobler became Acting President of the Transvaal. Pretorius should have known that he was putting himself in a spot, but he was blinded by ambition and so keen to live up to the glorious name of his father that he ignored the cross-currents among his people.

On 8 February 1860 Marthinus Wessel Pretorius was sworn in as

President of the Free State. The very next day a deputation was sent to Pretoria to negotiate union. Paul Kruger knew that the British Government frowned on such a union. Two years previously they had made it clear that any kind of amalgamation would be contrary to the Conventions of Sand River and Bloemfontein.[61] Kruger knew there would be trouble. And he could not approve of a dual office, no matter how lofty the ideal, when it was illegal. Many people agreed with Kruger, and so at a full session of the Transvaal Government the Orange Free State deputation was given a cold reception. M. W. Pretorius was more or less told that if he wished to be President of the Free State he had to stay out of Transvaal affairs.

This was not only a blow to his vanity but to his plans. The Transvaal Volksraad went even further. Their State Secretary who had accompanied Pretorius to Bloemfontein was dismissed and replaced by J. H. Struben. As far as the Transvaal was concerned Pretorius was officially on leave, and only on his return would he be given a hearing. Should he meanwhile be confined to the Free State Volksraad that was his own concern. All prospects of union faded as the weeks passed. When Pretorius's leave was due to expire on 2 August 1860, the Free State felt that he could not be spared, though willing to give him three months' leave in their turn.

Paul Kruger watched this tussle with close attention, for there were indications of serious developments, and he knew that he would be involved. It was to be one of the unhappiest periods of his life, and he was also in desperate financial straits. He had seven children by this time, who were still too small to help with the farming; and although he was lord of a large domain (after military campaigns he was usually rewarded with a gift of land) this was almost meaningless for lack of money or the means to earn it. His farming activities were constantly curtailed by demands made on his time, such as the expeditions against warlike tribes which took him from home for months on end.

Commandant-General Schoeman was furious that Johannes Grobler should be Acting President in the absence of Pretorius, as he felt that the office should have been his. He was not wrong, as his office made him second only to the President, but on the other hand his reputation as a difficult man and his unpopularity in some quarters had made it advisable to get a more innocuous person. It should have been clear that this was no way out, for Schoeman as a Potgieter man was not going to stand aside for anybody. If he should be Acting President, he would be, and he forthwith began to hold angry meetings, again arousing the Zoutpansberg-Lydenburg-Utrecht region where it was still an effort to take President Pretorius seriously.

On the return of Pretorius to the Transvaal, the Volksraad met on 10 September with Cornelius Potgieter, Landdrost of Lydenburg, as 'its leading spirit'.[62] The illegality of holding a dual office was again brought up, and Pretorius was told to make up his mind whose president he wished to be. After a heated argument Pretorius, angry, hurt and exasperated, resigned as President of the Transvaal, for he felt that he could not abandon the Orange Free State at this stage, not having just won her trust. Apparently it was not expected that Pretorius would sacrifice the Transvaal for the Free State, for there was an outcry among his supporters, and even Stephanus Schoeman was clearly taken aback, for he needed Pretorius to further his own ambitions.

A mass meeting was held at Potchefstroom on 8 and 9 October. Resolutions were passed by those present that so far as they were concerned M. W. Pretorius was still their President, but with the difference that Stephanus Schoeman was to be Acting President while Pretorius was given a year's leave of absence. As there was no longer confidence in the Volksraad (hardly surprising, as Schoeman was determined to get his way), it was held to have ceased to exist, and it was proposed that a new council be elected on the return of Pretorius. As Acting President, Schoeman naturally had the enthusiastic support of the old Potgieter party, but not of an unbending constitutionalist like Paul Kruger. He had no axe to grind with Schoeman, although he could see this man as the source of untold woe, but stood by Grobler as their legal Acting President.

Kruger had by this time moved to his farm Boekenhoutfontein but had not yet built his substantial homestead. He was being referred to as the Lion of Rustenburg, a designation which became like an order of merit among the Boers. When he heard that Pretorius, who was on a brief visit from the Free State, was planning a meeting similar to the one held at Potchefstroom at Rustenburg on 13 October, Kruger attended it in the company of his faithful friend and staunch ally, William Robinson. Both rose in protest against the Potchefstroom proposals. Although Kruger had long been of the Pretorius party, he refused to support what he considered an illegal course, no matter if relations between the families of Kruger and Pretorius should henceforth be strained. He proposed a special court to consider the proposals, but this was turned down.

Determined to assume the reins of Government, Schoeman left for

Pretoria and called for a meeting of the very Volksraad he considered abolished on 14 January 1861. Furthermore, he went to the Government Office and demanded the State papers. Acting President Grobler refused in indignation and appealed to Kruger for advice. Kruger said that there had to be another general meeting, for they were heading for an impasse. Schoeman and his supporters acknowledged this, agreed to the meeting, but then Schoeman appointed Johannes Steyn Commandant-General before it was held, something which in any case he had no legal right to do. Kruger set off for Pretoria to attend the meeting, only to be halted at Daspoort by armed burghers with an order from Schoeman to stay where he was. Kruger told them what to do with themselves and with the order, resumed his journey to Pretoria and went straight to Schoeman's house. It was bristling with armed men, while Kruger and his companions bore no arms. A Krygsraad was in session, with the newly-appointed Steyn in the chair.

Kruger stalked in, and on finding Schoeman reproached him for trying to stop him from attending a meeting to which they had both agreed. Steyn told Kruger to give up with good grace and accept the new state of affairs. Kruger ignored Steyn and took Schoeman to task for allowing his men to be armed. Kruger would consequently have nothing to do with the meeting. As he turned to leave, some of Steyn's officers tried to seize him but were at once stopped by others. Kruger strode out unmolested and made for his encampment. Schoeman then had a gun loaded with shrapnel pointed at the Kruger party. One of them was the Potchefstroom newspaperman, Hermann Jeppe, who was wanted by Schoeman for the printing and quick distribution of proclamations. Kruger refused to hand Jeppe over, but Jeppe was so alarmed at the threatening attitude of Steyn's men that he skipped from behind Kruger and rushed over to the other side.

Kruger began to inspan, and as a party of Schoeman's men passed, shouted: 'Once I've crossed the Magaliesberg, you must look upon me as an enemy!' The wagons began to move and were halted by an outburst of shouting. Pretorius had just arrived in Pretoria, and there he was with a number of Schoeman's followers. They begged Kruger to stay, for after a long period of antagonism Pretorius and Schoeman had buried the hatchet and wished to stand together for the good of both republics. This alliance was not as strange as it appeared. Pretorius needed the support of Schoeman in getting the union he wanted, and Schoeman needed Pretorius in order to legalize his position. Sooner than cause civil strife, Kruger was told, the men would cast away their arms. If that was the case, Kruger told them, they were to submit to their legal Volksraad in deciding who was in the right and who in the wrong. This was agreed to, so Kruger told his drivers to outspan.

The Volksraad met, and Schoeman was found guilty of breaking the law. He was dismissed as Commandant-General and replaced by Theunis Snyman. The new Acting President was to be Willem C. Janse van Rensburg, with J. H. Visagie as State Secretary. Schoeman, who had obviously relied on firm support from Pretorius, burst from the court room in a fury. In the Potgieter tradition he was not going to take orders from anyone. He ignored the plans for the election of a new State President, the ballot papers having to be in by 14 October 1862. The men recommended by the Volksraad were Paul Kruger and Cornelius Potgieter, but Schoeman was not prepared to stand aside for either. If Pretorius was finally to be ruled out of the Transvaal, Schoeman looked upon himself as the obvious new State President. Kruger had gone home after the Volksraad session and was hunting along the Crocodile River when he received a message to say that new troubles had broken out and that his presence was urgently needed in Pretoria.

What strikes one about Kruger in this phase is his steadfastness. Nothing seemed either to shock or surprise him. Legal procedure was the only thing that mattered to him, not the personal ambitions of men like Pretorius or Schoeman, or even his own. Legality, he was convinced, would triumph. His reply to Pretoria was that it was all very well to summon him there, but in fact his church membership gave him no political standing. President Van Rensburg at once had a resolution passed conferring equal rights to members of *all* Evangelical churches. One can see Kruger smiling with satisfaction, and of course he left for Pretoria straight away. He was clearly set on a course from which nobody and nothing would deflect him.

Pretoria appeared to be divided into two hostile camps, the one under Van Rensburg, the other under Schoeman. Kruger went to see Schoeman and again proposed a meeting to come to an amicable solution. What was wanted, he said, was a mass meeting of all the burghers of the Republic and their decision *had* to be final. The Schoeman Party agreed, as usual, until they had second thoughts. Kruger went home to get his Rustenburgers together. Like him, they stood by Van Rensburg and Snyman, and knowing the Schoeman-Potgieters they thought it advisable to adopt the usual precautions when going on commando. They were not surprised to hear that when at a large meeting in Pretoria it was resolved that a separate court should settle each separate question, Schoeman had objected and had begun to call up his supporters.

Acting President Van Rensburg and Commandant-General Snyman summoned a Krygsraad and stationed pickets at points around Pretoria in order to prevent Schoeman's messages from getting out. But his messengers simply rode these men down. Snyman ordered that should it happen again, the picket should fire at the horses. When it did happen again, a horse fell and a messenger was wounded in the arm. 'Thus,' said Kruger, 'was the first shot fired that started the Civil War.'[63] It was actually more a period of strife than of war, for fortunately little blood was spilt, but it was extremely distasteful and an episode in their history which the Boer people have tried to forget. This 'civil war' was perhaps inevitable, the seeds having been sown during the course of the Great Trek, and the man who was to emerge from it all with full honour was Paul Kruger.

On the evening of the day on which Schoeman's messenger was wounded, Snyman issued orders for the arrest of Schoeman. But somehow he and his men managed to escape and rode hard for Potchefstroom where they hurriedly assembled a commando. Snyman dealt with Schoeman adherents still in his midst, got his men together and set out for Potchefstroom accompanied by President Van Rensburg and Commandant Kruger. The real leader of the commando of some six hundred men was Kruger. When they reached Potchefstroom, Van Rensburg sent a message to Schoeman in which he proposed a joint commission to settle their differences. To this proposal Schoeman again agreed, obviously playing for time, having Jan Kock and other cronies on his side of the commission, while Kruger led the Government side.

The delegates met halfway between the two camps. Jan Kock's first words to Kruger were: 'So you want to make your church the State church!' This was the first Kruger heard of the surprising rumour that he was out to make the Church of the Doppers that of the State. It was quite contrary to what he had in mind, for nearly all the men with him, including the President and all the officers, were Dutch Reformed. Moreover, it was the principle of the Dopper creed that Christ and no other was Head of the Church. Nevertheless, the false rumour gained many adherents for Schoeman, even far from the scene, and one wonders if he started it. But it could also have been Kock who had had many years of experience in spreading intrigue.

As the commission failed to reach agreement, Snyman sent Kruger with a number of men to bombard Potchefstroom from the south.

This was not to be a real bombardment, but part of the show of force which belonged to an armed protest. Schoeman replied with his one gun and rifle-fire. The duel went on all day—a sad waste of ammunition, Kruger must have thought—but he did succeed in putting Schoeman's gun out of action. On the following night of 9 October, Schoeman planned a surprise attack and led his commando from the town, but the sharp-eyed and nimble-minded Kruger knew his every movement and led a fierce resistance in the hills. Though it was quite an engagement by master shots, one wonders how serious it could have been, as only three of Kruger's men were wounded, while Schoeman lost one man and had fifteen wounded, including himself. Schoeman's commando was routed and fled into the Orange Free State. With them went President Pretorius who had turned up on leave in the hope of restoring order.

Paul Kruger took possession of Potchefstroom on his birthday, and Schoeman was formally banished from the South African Republic. But such a man was not easily got rid of, nor subdued. Across the Vaal he rallied his supporters and, when Kruger led a march on the Klip River, leaving Potchefstroom unguarded, Schoeman slipped back and reoccupied the town with a larger force than he had had before. Kruger hurried back, contemplating laying a siege, but was met by President Pretorius who saw mediation as the only way to find a solution. The rival parties accepted the proposal, and their representatives met midway between the camps on 24 and 25 November. Kruger was accepted as spokesman for the Government Party, while Pretorius was ready to argue for Schoeman.

It was Kruger's proposal that a new election be held for both President and Commandant-General, but that for the time being the existing Executive Council was to remain in office. Men who had committed crimes during the upheaval were to come before a special court, presided over by an outsider like the Chief Justice of Natal, Walter Harding, or the Free State advocate, H. A. L. Hamelberg. It was perhaps not expected that both gentlemen would decline to preside. All sentences of banishment, confiscation and fines were to be suspended until 12 January 1863 when the special court would go into session. Arms were to be laid down and the men to go home. Argument went on for hours, but this time agreement was reached. Kruger packed up to go home, believing the 'war' to have ended.

From what is known about Stephanus Schoeman by now, it is only to be expected that he would not allow any court to sit in judgement on him. Characteristically he entrenched himself with an armed force in Pretoria, ready to oppose any decisions of the court, the members of which he looked upon as his enemies. Kruger had no option but to leave for Pretoria with the men he could raise at short notice. He pitched camp just outside the town and sent out appeals for men to join him so that law and order could be enforced. Such was his influence now that they came in large numbers. Accompanied by two men, and unarmed, Kruger entered Pretoria with the announcement that he wished to have no bloodshed but was compelled to see that justice took its course. He was not hindered, Schoeman adherents too being weary of all the squabbling. Kruger placed a strong guard on the court house, ready for the session to start on 20 January.

A violent thunderstorm broke the day before, so torrential that it afforded Schoeman the opportunity to break out of Pretoria with some of his most ardent supporters. Heading for the Free State, they took two guns with them and, still hopeful, the State flag. The court met as arranged, and consisted of three Landdrosts and a jury of twelve for each case. Shoeman and some others were found guilty of rebellion against the State and were banished, their property confiscated. Apart from the leaders, the rest were handled leniently. The session of the special court having ended, the election of the new leaders of the State would follow.

From the small number of votes it was clear that the troubles were not over. The result of the election was announced at the session of the Volksraad of 20 May 1863. The President was to be Van Rensburg, and the Commandant-General, as one would expect, Paul Kruger. They were both unhappy about the small number of votes cast and proposed a fresh election. The outcome of this was rather better. On 12 October, 1,206 was announced for Van Rensburg, 1,065 for Pretorius, and a decided majority for Kruger. Twelve days later C. W. Janse van Rensburg was sworn in as State President of the South African Republic, one of the lesser-known figures in Transvaal history. His opponents refused to recognize him as President, holding that the voting papers had been tampered with. Kruger's majority was so decided and his abilities so well-proven that his election aroused no opposition, though he too had his enemies. M. W. Pretorius was back in their midst, having resigned as President of the Orange Free State the previous June, and he was not sitting still.

The new Commandant-General was thirty-eight and still in the prime of manhood. His officers were now to discover his reserves of energy and relentless drive. Paul Kruger's face had become somewhat strained, and there was an indication of future bagginess under the eyes, eyes which were dark and glowing. The strong nose was broadening, and he was still fully bearded. Kruger looked and dressed like a farmer, even officially, for full-dress uniforms lay in the future. He had gone through deep water, physically, spiritually, financially and politically, but he had taken everything in his stride. Perhaps he also knew that far more difficult times were to come, for it is said that he had indisputable psychic gifts. He could, as it were, see beyond the horizon, even being able to tell hunters where they would find game, and what kind. It was too much, and he asked God to take the gift away from him.* But did He?

* In unpublished Memoirs his future State Secretary, F. W. Reitz, made reference to this. Reitz was very fond of anecdotes, and these are widely scattered, but he was a literary man, and not averse to invention.

CHAPTER SIX

The Commandant-General

A revolt now came from the Marico in the western Transvaal. It was as unexpected as it was sudden, led by Commandant Jan Viljoen. It was his contention that Paul Kruger, now being second only to the President, was pushing through his plan to make the State Church that of the Doppers. Why this unfounded rumour should again have been current is difficult to understand, unless one looks in the direction of M. W. Pretorius,[64] for all this had happened before—the exploitation of religious differences for political advantage by Schoeman, Kock and now Viljoen, all of the Pretorius Party.

In Jan Viljoen (his first names were Johannes Willem), 1812–93, another interesting character is introduced, short and explosive, a renowned hunter, friend of Moffat, Livingstone and Mzilikazi. He took part in the Battle of Boomplaats and was punished by having his property confiscated. He moved to the Transvaal and settled near the future Zeerust on a farm called Ver Genoeg (Far Enough)—which it was. Viljoen campaigned with Kruger in the war against Setshele in 1852 and must have met him many times in the following ten years. Being a staunch supporter of the Dutch Reformed Church in that period of his life, he disapproved of Kruger as a Dopper, and as a friend of Schoeman and Pretorius he was prepared to take up arms on their behalf.[65] After Kruger's elevation, all three were forced to the acknowledgement that this 'backveld Boer Dopper' could thwart all their ambitions.

Commandant Jan Viljoen led an armed force into Potchefstroom on 10 December 1863. He dismissed officials, appointed others and proclaimed himself leader of what was styled the Army of the People, *Volksleger*. Commandant-General Kruger was just at this time on his way to the Free State in order to settle a dispute over the exact boundary between the two States in the western part. Viljoen's surprise move was reported to Kruger, Viljoen's objective apparently being to take him captive. Kruger raised 150 men to put down the rebellion, far too few to deal with Viljoen's superior numbers. In defiance of Viljoen, Kruger's force was called the Army of the State, *Staatsleger*. As things began to move, a section of Kruger's force under Veldcornet Sarel Eloff was cut off and forced to surrender, though Eloff managed to escape.

This is the first mention of the name Eloff in connexion with Kruger, a name to become very familiar in his life as three of his daughters married Eloffs. Kruger offered mediation, even a fresh election for a president, but Viljoen was unbending, his main purpose being to neutralize Kruger. As more of Kruger's men were captured and he could see no way clear of effecting anything, Kruger slipped over the Vaal and took Eloff with him, sending a message to Viljoen to say that he had decided to quit the Transvaal for ever. Stephanus Schoeman at once rushed to Potchefstroom with high hopes, but Viljoen refused to hand over the command to him. Schoeman's eclipse had come in this fresh war of personalities. His wife saw it clearly, and she handed over the State flag which she had had in her keeping all this time.

Kruger gave out that he could no longer bear all the disputes in the Transvaal, 'bought' a farm in the Free State and sent a message to his family that they must prepare to leave in order to join him. It is doubtful if many members of the Volksleger believed all this, for on 23 December they left Potchefstroom for Pretoria. President Van Rensburg and the Staatsleger were encamped at the Crocodile River and sent Kruger messages about what was taking place, the Government having evacuated Pretoria for Rustenburg. Kruger thus had no problems in returning to the Transvaal, where he found that Viljoen's masterful conduct had swung most of the burghers to Van Rensburg. Kruger and Eloff raised a large force with rapidity and led these men to the Crocodile River, while Viljoen issued proclamations warning men against joining Kruger, proclamations which only encouraged them to do so.

On 5 January 1864 the two opposing forces met at the Crocodile in a fight which, though it barely lasted an hour, was momentous. Any hopes of mediation Kruger might still have had were dashed when his friend Hans Enslin was hit and fell dead in his arms. Blind with rage, Kruger led an attack which was so violent that one could hardly see for smoke. And suddenly it was all over. Casualties were far less than one would have expected, perhaps because of the strategic positions taken by Kruger. He lost only two men, while Viljoen had five killed and thirty wounded. As the Volksleger took flight, Kruger stopped the shooting and sternly forbade pursuit. Both armies then went into laager.

In the remarkable way he managed to flit about, M. W. Pretorius turned up at Viljoen's laager on the morning of the 6th and sent a message to Kruger's encampment to express regret at what had happened and an offer of mediation. Pretorius should have done so before the blood of brothers was spilt, but perhaps he had not expected that it would come to this, and the Volksleger were after all his supporters. Kruger agreed to a conference which began on the 8th and lasted for six days. It was his contention that the elected Government should be held legal by the Volksraad until a new presidential election could be held and that points of argument should be referred to a court of arbitration. On the 15th these points were ironed out by Kruger and Pretorius as the spokesmen for both sides, and the men disbanded, feeling foolish and ashamed over this unnecessary chapter in their history. Yet, it had significance as it betokened the emergence of Paul Kruger as their greatest son.[66] Not only had he remained completely consistent, but was also fully aware of the importance of the Pretorius image and influence among his people.

In the presidential election that followed soon afterwards, Marthinus Wessel Pretorius was once again elected, gaining 1,519 votes as against Van Rensburg's 1,118. Kruger insisted that he too should be put to the test and was gratified when he gained more than two-thirds of the votes as Commandant-General. Pretorius was sworn in at Pretoria on 10 May, and as a general amnesty had been proclaimed, peace and the rule of law mercifully prevailed.

The civil strife in the Transvaal, however, had made a bad impression all round: on President Brand of the Orange Free State (who had advised against a court of arbitration), on Cape Colony, on Natal, and not least on the Natives. The Transvaal found herself with an empty treasury, salaries were in arrears and taxes appeared irrecoverable. Pretorius had a most unenviable task in putting everything right, but it was he, more than anybody else, who had been the cause of most of the strife. Fortunately for him, he had an unbending constitutionalist as his pillar of strength, no matter that a chill permeated their once warm friendship. It must have been hard for Pretorius to have to take Kruger's criticism and disapproval all that time, and to find it right; but Kruger showed what sort of man he was by having a salute fired at the swearing-in of President Pretorius.[67]

Towards the end of 1864 Kruger accompanied Pretorius to the district of Utrecht. This was originally Zulu territory at the foot of the Drakensberg which had been ceded by King Mpande to a group of Boers in 1854. The eastern border (like the western) was, however, so ill-defined that there was a constant influx of Zulus. Mpande being old and ailing, his son Cetywayo had become the strong man of Zululand. He was no friend of the Boers and indifferent to the fact that his father had once fought on their side for the overthrow of Dingane. Nevertheless, Cetywayo sent envoys to meet Pretorius and Kruger at Utrecht, and a boundary was properly defined and beaconed. The President and Commandant-General then went home, only to hear some months later that Cetywayo had had the beacons pulled down.

This caused another of the endless Zulu scares. A Zulu threat was never taken lightly by those who had experienced the horrors in Natal, and the stories of what was perpetrated in the Trekker days were passed on from generation to generation. As the signs pointed to a Zulu invasion, the Boers in the south-eastern districts went into laager, and Kruger raised a large commando and moved it to Wakkerstroom. Cetywayo had second thoughts, for he too knew the traditional stories, particularly the Battle of Blood River which had made a lasting impression on the Zulu mind, and sent messages that he had no hostile intentions.

At Wakkerstroom, Kruger again met a powerful stocky man farming at the farm Rustfontein in that district. This was Veldcornet Piet Joubert who had received orders to commandeer men in the Zulu scare. Kruger had met Joubert on various occasions, the last time being at the Crocodile River when Pretorius came to offer mediation between the armies of People and State. Joubert was a friend of Jan Viljoen and accordingly a member of the Volksleger—in opposition to Kruger, an opposition which was to be maintained. Although Piet Joubert (1831–1900) had recently become a member of the Volksraad representing Wakkerstroom, and had already shown a forceful personality and exceptional organizing abilities, Kruger could have had no idea that this emotional man, whose voice rose to sudden squeaks, would play such a major role in his life. Although both men were capable of warm friendship, this was not to happen between them, and Kruger was to find that no matter what he said or did he only put Joubert's back up.

In the Orange Free State a second shattering war with the Basotho had broken out. If the Zulu menace was great, that of the Basotho was equally so, if not greater, for it invariably triggered off tribal unrest to the west. President Brand called up his burghers to deal with Moshesh. The Cape Governor, Sir Philip Wodehouse, issued a proclamation in which he demanded strict neutrality from British subjects. President Pretorius said that his burghers were of course free to go to the assistance of the Free Staters. Many would have liked to have gone, but because of the political turmoil in the past three years and the current Zulu threat, all they desired was to get back to their neglected farms and do some hard work. Just then the members of a Transvaal party under Pieter Pretorius, an uncle of the President, were returning over the Drakensberg from a trading mission to Natal when they were brutally murdered by the Basotho. This was on 27 June, when Kruger was at Wakkerstroom during his negotiations with Cetywayo, and thus prevented from taking immediate punitive action.

By August the Zulu army had begun to disband. Pretorius was now able to send a message to Moshesh to demand the murderers and compensation for the goods seized. Moshesh ignored the message, so Pretorius proclaimed martial law and sent Kruger with nearly a thousand men against the Basotho. Pretorius went with them, impressed by Kruger's stern disciplinary measures. It was September, and the enemy was first tackled at Witzieshoek where a rout took place, huts were burned down and livestock taken. But at the end of the month the Basotho (Kruger says three thousand, aided by four thousand Zulus)[68] made a nocturnal attack under cover of rain and mist, and landed right in their midst, killing five Boers and wounding ten others before they were driven off. Kruger's secretary, having been drunk the previous evening and consequently tied to a wagon wheel, slept right through the fight.

The Transvaalers joined forces with the Free Staters and launched a vigorous attack on Malapo, one of Moshesh's most important captains, who promptly set fire to his own town and fled. But a large number of livestock was captured, and Malapo's district was annexed. This was on Kruger's birthday—invariably something eventful seemed to happen on his birthdays. A successful action against the Basotho followed on the 25th, more livestock being seized. The hopes that farms would be granted them in the annexed territory invigorated the Boer fighters, and they were furious when President Brand informed Commandant Fick, in command of the Free Staters, that the Transvaalers would *not* be given land in the conquered region. The Transvaalers forthwith withdrew from the campaign and, to quote Kruger in words which were to become over-familiar (they were used by General De Wet after the fall of Bloemfontein), 'the burghers of the South African Republic refused to fight any longer and went home'.

Many of the enemy had been killed and vast numbers of livestock taken. Kruger pleaded, wheedled and threatened, but it was to no avail, and the Free Staters watched in disgust as the Transvaal commando headed north on 30 October. It is even said that Kruger wept with rage and vexation, for he knew that the attitude of the Free State would be that, having sated themselves with booty, the Transvaalers had left their brethren to their fate. The gradual disenchantment with Paul Kruger in the Orange Free State began in October 1865. He knew that his men were weary of strife and war and were longing to get home, but even so it was alarming to a general to see his men simply go off. President Johannes Henricus Brand (1823–88), in office since February 1864, one of the most honoured and beloved of Orange Free State presidents, was never again to look with a benign eye on Paul Kruger. Their temperaments and background were, in any case, worlds apart.

Kruger returned to Rustenburg in a black mood. He was also dispirited by diseases among his livestock and by financial problems. For a couple of months he gave undivided attention to farming, then in February 1866 he had to go to Potchefstroom for a session of the Executive Council, of which he as Commandant-General was a member. On his way back, at the farm Schoonkloof, near home, he impatiently charged a ditch, capsized his cart and broke a leg. On one leg and with the help of his small Native companion, Kruger lifted the cart back on its wheels and sat in frightful pain as his four mules jogged on for an hour and a half. This accident put Kruger out of action for nine months—torture for such an active man—and his left leg was ever after to be slightly shorter than his right.

Incapacitated Kruger might have been, but not mute. Some of his early letters have survived, but as Commander-General he now had a secretary, P. Nijhoff, who handled the correspondence to which he put his laboured signature: S. J. P. Kruger. All kinds of interesting things were happening, such as a scheme for Scottish immigration organized by Alexander McCorkindale (he managed to bring out only fifty, as well as an enormous amount of gunpowder). Then there were the various schemes to remedy the Republic's chaotic financial situation, the growing Native unrest in the Zoutpansberg region, and wholesale gun-running on the western border—arms and ammunition being supplied to tribes like the Bangwaketse, Bakwena and Bamangwato by hunter-traders. Powerless to do anything himself, Kruger insisted on an acting commandant-general and proposed men he thought suitable.

He was particularly concerned about the lawlessness prevalent in the Zoutpansberg among both blacks and whites. Theal even goes so far as to say that these whites 'were the most lawless of their colour in all South Africa'.[69] Many of those on the frontier had no connexion whatever with the descendants of the Voortrekkers, but consisted of a motley collection of adventurers, traders and hunters of all nationalities, mostly after ivory and gold. The decent families kept to themselves and expressed alarm at the conduct of these 'robbers', the dangerous feuds among tribes, the arms acquired from illicit traders and the general disorderliness, even debauchery, seen at Schoemansdal, the most distant outpost of the white man.

At the Volksraad and Executive session before his accident, Kruger had been asked to restore law and order in the Zoutpansberg. Now on crutches, he proposed that T. P. Pretorius should take his place. However, T. P. Pretorius declined, so the President decided to lead a commando himself. M. W. Pretorius commandeered twelve hundred men, of whom only five hundred turned up, the attitude being that the Zoutpansbergers were themselves responsible for the lawlessness in their midst. Pretorius achieved almost nothing, but as an inter-tribal war had broken out, black and white relations temporarily not being the issue, he disbanded his unwilling men. By the beginning of 1867 the warring tribes had settled their differences and swung their attention back to the whites, resuming their customary depredations. Although Kruger had not yet fully recovered, he offered to lead a new commando—even if he had to be carried on a stretcher.

Two thousand men were commandeered, and again only 500 responded, no matter that Kruger himself would be in command. Because of a shocking lack of ammunition (McCorkindale's still lay at Durban) and the lack of funds to buy it, Kruger wondered how he was to effect anything, but men from the troubled region assured him that there were lots of powder and lead to be found in the Zoutpansberg. Because of climatic conditions, a commando only operated in winter in that region, so Kruger set off in June 1867. While he attacked Native robbers, a court of three landdrosts were to punish white criminals of the Zoutpansberg district at Schoemansdal.

Kruger's strong sense of duty and his faith in humanity (yes, he still had it) were to have some rude shocks on this campaign. His commando was too small to deal with armed Natives in their mountain fastnesses, and moreover his men were insubordinate. This may have been partly due to his new rule that captured stock were not to be distributed among them but sold for the benefit of the commando as a whole. His disciplinary measures were resented, and his religious fervour was thought excessive on active service. Furthermore, the powder and lead were not there and none was forthcoming from Pretoria. Disease was rife among cattle and horses. In only two attacks on black robbers he exhausted nearly all the ammunition. Order appeared impossible to maintain. For example, two men who appeared before the special court at Schoemansdal on a charge of theft from a chief, were sentenced to a fine and ordered to return the cattle. But an unruly mob promptly released them and broke up the court room.

At Schoemansdal, Kruger was outraged by this lawlessness and alarmed by reports of a general Native attack on the town. If he could not exert control and lacked the means to defend Schoemansdal, the only solution appeared to be evacuation. But he hesitated to take such a step, knowing how serious it would be. On the other hand, from a military point of view the town was badly situated, and the town's water supply came from heights infested by the enemy. He took a snap decision and ordered the inhabitants out. Hardly had they done so, when Chief Katlakter fell on Schoemansdal and set it alight, totally destroying the town and its surroundings, while Kruger with his commando and the inhabitants were some six miles to the south. The sacking of Schoemansdal caused an outcry, Kruger being blamed for it, and the town's Dutch Reformed minister, N. J. van Warmelo, was to hold it against him all his life.[70]

Although the evacuation was not Kruger's decision alone but that of a council of war, the subject was to be raised several times in the Volksraad, as it was thought a disaster and a disgrace to have abandoned a once flourishing town to barbarian hordes.[71] All that survived of Schoemansdal were the doors and windows of the church which the indignant Rev. Mr Van Warmelo had had the foresight to take with him. Although President Pretorius was to consider the loss of the major part of the Zoutpansberg region the greatest disaster since the founding of the Republic, Kruger was formally exonerated, the evacuation being ascribed to factors beyond his personal control, as indeed they were.

Kruger moved the evacuees to a place called Marabastad. As he crossed Makapanspoort, he received complaints about the raids of a chief they called Machem who lived with his people in a refuge of caves, ravines and earth-holes. Kruger sent him a summons; the chief came but his subjects refused to do so. Kruger ordered a siege, captured women and children taking water and food to the rebels, and landed up in a brisk fight in which he was under fire. Kruger routed the enemy, placed a guard at Makapanspoort and distributed captives among members of the commando as apprentices. Machem was allotted a new residential area.

Kruger returned to Pretoria where he faced a storm of criticism. The Schoemansdal affair was bad enough, but the distribution of captives was thought highly irregular, as these were not people left destitute on a field of battle. He was censured for it by the Volksraad on 9 September. Chief Machem showed willingness to co-operate and to live in peace in future, so the captives were sent back to him. Kruger was puzzled by the to-do, for the apprentice system was generally accepted and had actually been started by the British in Cape Colony. But times were changing and, as he was to find many times, he was not always in step with them, or the mere fact that *he* followed a certain example proved it wrong.

Early in 1868 President Pretorius announced that he wanted a commando of a thousand men to assemble by 20 February to deal with the Zoutpansberg. Should they not come, the district would be abandoned. Only 260 turned up. 'When the law rules again,' Kruger wrote to Pretorius at the time, 'then I hope with the aid of the Lord again to ensure the safety of our land, as it appears to me thus far that those who tirelessly help to hold our land are suppressed and held to mockery, while those who wish to live without the law and heed no laws go scot-free.' As always it was his firm intention to restore law and order, to ensure the safety of the State and to crush their enemies.[72] But it was a mystery how he was to achieve that with a mere handful of men.

And yet it was done, in a manner, Kruger believed, devised by God. Chief Mapela (Mankopane) had risen once again after a period of professing to be loyal. Kruger asked Pretorius to proclaim martial law. Every male capable of bearing arms was to be called up. When nothing happened, Kruger tackled the Volksraad so forcefully that more paper money was issued, some ammunition obtained and a commando of 900 men raised. On 13 June, Kruger attacked Mapela's mountain and conquered most of it, killing some 300 of the rebels, while two of his men were slain and eleven wounded. The campaign was abruptly ended by the outbreak of an intertribal war, involving some of the most powerful clans. And what the Boers could not achieve was done by a sudden and massive onslaught on the Zoutpansberg by a Swazi impi (regiment) that October. The blacks having spent their rage on one another, peace was sought all round.

In his customary manner Kruger had interviews with all the chiefs and talked to them in fatherly fashion. That they held him in esteem, more so than his own men did, was clear. In restoring order Kruger had the support of his old enemy, Stephanus Schoeman, for the people who still looked upon him as their leader were now able to trickle back to the farms. A general truce was in sway by December 1869, but marred by an outbreak of malaria so violent that the small town of Piet Potgietersrust had to be temporarily abandoned for Marabastad which was turned into the seat of the Landdrost of Zoutpansberg, Van Nispen. Schoeman regained some favour by becoming diplomatic agent for the Government.

From 1864 until 1869 Paul Kruger was constantly on the go and was subject to a great deal of vexation and frustration. By October 1869 his normally robust constitution began to break down. One by one, too, members of his family were prostrate with malaria, the uncomplaining Gezina also being decidedly unwell. But there was to be no respite for General Kruger. All along there had been talk of minerals, gold in particular, and as from 1867 of diamonds. The Boers had not given much thought to minerals, for they were a pastoral people and knew little or nothing about them. Rich discoveries, however, betokened good things to come, as well as new problems—as if they did not have enough. Even the most simple-minded could see that mineral wealth could bring both prosperity and new threats to their hard-won land.

Boundaries were still in need of clarification : between the South African Republic and the Zulus, in regions between the two republics, particularly to the west and south-west. In 1870 Kruger was a member of a commission sent to Mpande to come to a final agreement about the disputed stretch of land in the Utrecht district. He noted that the Zulus were strongly opposed to white occupation of this land and advised Pretorius to halt his plans for cutting it up into farms. The matter was allowed to slide for the time being. Kruger was also a member, with Piet Joubert, of a commission to finalize the exact boundary between the Orange Free State and the Transvaal. The issue was submitted to the arbitration of the Lieutenant-Governor of Natal, Robert William Keate, at Harrismith, for if the Free Staters had their way the Transvaal would lose most of the district of Wakkerstroom. Keate decided in favour of the Transvaal, much to Joubert's relief.

The diamond discoveries in Griqualand West posed far more serious problems. Part of the territory, according to Pretorius, fell within the district of Bloemhof and was accordingly part of the South African Republic. Various chiefs felt differently, as had their white advisers who were flocking to the diamondiferous areas. Kruger was a member of a commission appointed to deal with the western and south-western border towards the end of 1870, and he says that he had a very friendly reception from the English miners gathered there. He was not much involved in this complicated business of diamonds on both sides of the Vaal River, for he disapproved of Pretorius's idea of another court of arbitration. 'The Republic,' he said, 'did not need and should never accept arbitration regarding her own possessions.'[73] He also felt that it would be a mistake to call in Keate once more to arbitrate, for a rapidly expanding English settlement was forming there, and the British Government was unlikely to abandon them and their interests.[74]

But Keate was called in all the same and acted in the way Kruger had predicted. He was a member of a commission which lodged a protest with the Volksraad. They felt that Pretorius had acted without their sanction and had totally bungled argument, allowing an unnecessary dispute about their own possessions. In the uproar that followed at the prospect of losing both territory and wealth, President Pretorius had no option but to resign. He admitted sadly that he was not competent to deal with the intrigues that had arisen, intrigues that even foxed a much cleverer man like President Brand out of Kimberley which, before the discovery of diamonds, had been undisputed Orange Free State territory.

Marthinus Wessel Pretorius began to fade from the Transvaal scene as from 20 November 1871, but not entirely though, for he was to live until 1901. He had resigned before, as at the end of 1867, but had been persuaded to withdraw his resignation. No doubt he hoped that this would happen again, but it was not to be. Kruger consoled himself that their protest had at least saved the village of Christiana for the Transvaal, but it was the Barolong and Batlapin who had won the day in the contested region. The resignation of Pretorius having been accepted, a member of the Executive Council, Daniel Jacobus Erasmus, was appointed Acting President.

The forthcoming election for a new president aroused much interest. Commandant-General Kruger was asked to stand, but he declined, knowing that feelings were divided about him, that the Transvaal needed a man of education and subtle diplomacy. He was in any case not yet ready for such an elevation, and he knew that many people felt a positive aversion towards him. The rumour persisted that his aim was a Dopper Republic; and many were still critical of his role in the civil war, even more so after what had taken place in the Zoutpansberg. People felt that they had had enough of both Pretorius and Kruger, and some even felt that Kruger should resign as Commandant-General, not that there was any justification for such a step.

Paul Kruger was now forty-six and again in excellent health, even fighting-fit, as he showed in his campaign for William Robinson as presidential candidate. This presidency was preferably to be for two years only, during which time the republics could possibly find union under President J. H. Brand. The general feeling was indeed for someone from outside the Transvaal, and Brand, steadily gaining renown for his sagacity and all kinds of sterling qualities, would be the ideal person. Perhaps he would have been, but he was not interested. Brand drew attention to the Rev. Mr Thomas François Burgers of Hanover in the Cape. This in his opinion was the best man available, no matter that Burgers was a controversial figure. He had landed in a dispute with the Cape Synod because of his unorthodox views and had successfully fought a move to oust him from his pastorate. There were various reasons why Burgers was anathema to the Doppers, among them the fact that he did not believe in the personality of the Devil. On the other hand, Burgers was so learned, so handsome, such an eloquent preacher and generally so charming that he seemed the only man after Brand declined to stand. Burgers would also counteract the influence of the Doppers. His success was assured, and he gained 2,964 votes as against 388 for Robinson.

On 1 July 1872 Thomas François Burgers (1834–81) was sworn in as State President of the South African Republic. Paul Kruger was present, and the oath of office having been taken, rose majestically and addressed Burgers: 'Your Honour, I have done my best to prevent your election, principally because of your religious views, which appear to me to be mistaken. But, as you have now been elected by the majority, I submit as a good republican to this vote of the people, trusting that you are a more earnest believer than I thought, in which case I will congratulate you with all my heart.' Burgers turned his hazel eyes on the burly bulk of Kruger. 'Those,' he said gently, 'who voted against me on the grounds of conscience are as dear to me as those who voted for me.'[75]

The elegant and gracious Burgers was born in the district of Graaff-Reinet, and was nine years younger than Kruger. Burgers graduated at the University of Utrecht in the Netherlands in 1858, the year in which he married a brainy Scottish lady, Mary Bryson. On his return to South Africa his liberal views soon evoked criticism, but he showed that he was quite prepared to stand by them. Kruger was to acknowledge that he was a man of keen intelligence and of very great gifts, but of too advanced ideas for the Transvaal of his day—a man, it was generally remarked, who had hitched his wagon to a star. And yet his eyes, likened to those of a prophet, instilled confidence in those without religious prejudice.

Although Paul Kruger was capable of considerable religious tolerance—as I will show later—he felt no confidence in Burgers. The régime of this President was to reveal various flaws in Kruger's character. Did he, for example, resent the fact that not more pressure was put on him to stand for President, or that Burgers showed him up as an uncouth backveld Boer of no education? Was he thwarted in his ambitions and humiliated, wounded in his patriotism and religious convictions? Whatever his motivations were, the fact remains that Kruger sincerely believed that Burgers could bring no good to the Transvaal, and as it turned out Kruger was more far-seeing than the majority of his countrymen. Religious scruples aside, a dreamer like Burgers was not the sort of man to rule a rough, backward, unstable and bankrupt State.

Kruger was still Commandant-General and accordingly member of the Executive Council. But the election of Burgers caused him to lose interest in the job. He had begun to establish himself more permanently at Boekenhoutfontein, particularly after he and some helpers put up a substantial homestead, reminiscent of the Karoo style, which still exists.[76] Kruger was again feeling run down, and his wife and children were all suffering from malaria. He began to absent himself from the Executive sessions in 1872, Gezina being so ill that he did not wish to leave her side. All this was true, but it also appears that Kruger had lost interest in public affairs and that he in no way wished to be associated with the various steps of the Burgers administration, particularly a new education law which Kruger thought obnoxious because it made no proper provision for the religious instruction of children.

The waves of animosity emanating from Boekenhoutfontein made it clear to President Burgers that he had to get rid of his Commandant-General, and as soon as possible if he wanted the young Cape advocate, James Buchanan, in the Executive. In May 1873 Burgers must have given a sigh of relief when Kruger asked for an honourable discharge. Hints had clearly been passed on to Kruger to do so, and he was pleased to take them up. His resignation having been accepted with the usual regrets and expressions of gratitude for services rendered, it was proposed that the Postmaster-General, Fred Jeppe, should present Kruger with a sword of honour as a memento. A week later Burgers, to ensure that Kruger would not be back, had the office of commandant-general abolished in peacetime—one of his series of blunders.

CHAPTER SEVEN

Paul Kruger and President Burgers

The forebodings Kruger had at the outset of the Burgers administration at first appeared to be unfounded. As there were no properly trained officials, one of the first things Burgers did was to import them from the Netherlands, looking for the best men he could find. Importing Netherlands officials was a policy Kruger himself was to adopt, in his case mainly to keep the Transvaal Dutch. Kruger could only be grateful to Burgers for his example and for the men he was to inherit from him. Behind all the schemes of Burgers was his dream of a united South Africa under its own flag. The British High Commissioner at Cape Town, Sir Henry Barkly, a disciple of the Colonial Minister, Lord Carnarvon, who had succeeded in the federation of Canada, said to Burgers shortly after his inauguration: 'Well, Your Honour, I shall be most happy to assist you in bringing about your idea of a United South Africa.' But he was determined that it should come about under the British flag.[77]

The discoveries of mineral riches in South Africa one after the other (such as the goldfields of Lydenburg in 1873) began to draw worldwide attention and it was freely prophesied that they would bring about the end of the continued independence of the Transvaal. The British take-over of Griqualand West on the flimsiest of pretexts caused both republics deep concern and gave many a national awareness they had not had before. Burgers was gradually to find himself threatened as much from outside as from within. His downfall was being waited for by the various churches and also by the British, both the external element and the steadily increasing number within his own borders. There were also men in the Government, like the new State Secretary N. R. J. Swart, who were working against Burgers.

At the start however one would have thought that a new era had dawned. Burgers began to put finances in order, to plan telegraphic communications and a major undertaking—a railway line to Delagoa Bay. Foreigners, whom the Boers called 'uitlanders' (those from other lands), were streaming into the country in high hopes of good fortune, as at the goldfields of Lydenburg. Newspapers were founded, and for the first time attention was given to a planned educational system.

Burgers were determined to fight the Keate decision on the western border, and there were so many things he wanted: Dutch immigration, loans, allies, a new flag, a new coat of arms, a port, ships, development of national resources, a stable economy. . . . Hardly had he begun to tackle Barkly on the issue of the diamond fields, when the gold of Lydenburg became the subject of the day and aroused fears in Burgers that Barkly would 'jump' these fields as well.[78]

The dreams, hopes and fears of President Burgers were known to Paul Kruger, some more easily dismissible than others. He became vitally concerned when the new education law stipulated that religious instruction would no longer be given within school hours, but after hours. The whole Dopper community rose in uproar. Kruger declared that Burgers was the enemy of Christianity. Once convinced of this, Burgers could as well have been a butterfly circling a rock. Van Oordt was to comment that Burgers could revolutionize the Government but never the character of the people, for he did not understand it.[79] Of Kruger, Burgers certainly had no understanding whatever at this stage, and little patience with him, though both were to have kinder thoughts in later life.

As a 'Godless' person was now their Head of State (he was even called the anti-Christ), many—and mainly of the Dopper community—felt that their country would no longer know the blessing of the Lord and that it was better to trek. A new pass law, giving greater freedom of movement to Natives, would in any case soon make the country uninhabitable. There seemed no option but to cross the desert in the west for Damaraland or Ovamboland where, it was reported, there was good ranching country. People from the Marico, Rustenburg and Waterberg came to see Kruger, and pitched their camps at the Crocodile River. Would he, like Moses, lead them through the desert? Kruger was touched but undecided. Some members of his family, including his step-mother (who was now married to Piet Venter after the death of Kruger's father), were determined to go.

The result was the tragic Dorstlandtrek or Thirstland Trek in which many perished. Among them was Kruger's step-mother who, after a life of trial and hardship, found her last resting-place in an unknown grave in the wilderness. The movement for this trek began in 1873, but although some people started leaving in 1874, it was only really attempted in the following year. Piet Joubert of Wakkerstroom who was becoming more and more influential was also asked to take a lead. But, like Kruger, he declined, for opposition to Burgers was becoming so strong that it appeared unlikely that he would stand a chance in the next election. Furthermore, Kruger felt that such an exodus of members of his 'true church' would greatly weaken it. He would in any case have preferred to fight it out rather than run away. There was also a general belief that Burgers had not long to live. In March 1874 he was thought to be already at death's door.

By September, Burgers had sufficiently recovered to assemble the Volksraad, with Piet Joubert as president. In contrast to Kruger's hostility to Burgers, and perhaps also because of it, Joubert was friendly (though disapproving) towards him, for he greatly admired intelligent and learned men. Burgers invariably caused a flurry, such as by giving representation to two members of the new mining population, and then by handing out sovereigns struck from Transvaal gold bearing his effigy. Such a *Burgerspond* is today almost beyond price, only 1,000 being minted. Kruger was disgusted by such self-glorification, but when the time came a whole range of coins was to bear his profile, in copper, silver and gold, not to mention endless medallions struck by the nations of the world or to commemorate special occasions. The Transvaal's first stamps were designed by Fred Jeppe who had them printed in Germany and put into circulation from 1870.

Once Burgers got talking he had great powers of persuasion. He was positively inspired when it came to the railway line to Delagoa Bay, no matter the astronomical cost and the difficulty of the terrain. He himself, he proposed, would go to Europe to raise £300,000 to build it. In any case, his health necessitated a trip to Europe. It would also be an opportunity to gain full publicity for the Transvaal. Now a few surprise moves followed. Burgers wished to entrust his office to a triumvirate in his absence, but the Raad decided on Piet Joubert as Acting State President. This sudden elevation left the ambitious Joubert quite dizzy with delight—but not for long. Before 1874 was out Paul Kruger was again member of the Executive Council, after being an outsider for some eighteen months.

The reason for Kruger's surprise reinclusion, much against the will of Burgers and his mouthpiece *De Volksstem*, was because the contentious Education Law had been satisfactorily amended, and because the opposition party in the Volksraad had insisted on a reshuffling of the Executive by replacing Fred Jeppe with Paul Kruger. As a Government paper, *De Volksstem* was founded at the invitation of Burgers by the Cape journalist, Johannes François Celliers, and was to play an important role in Transvaal politics, countering papers like the *Gold Fields Mercury* and *Transvaal Advocate*. On the departure of Burgers on 17 February 1875, Joubert took his place, careful not to commit himself to anything in particular. When the new flag was pulled down in Pretoria by an old patriot called Hans Steyn, Joubert recognized it as symbolic of the mounting feeling against Burgers, and had to wonder how to counteract it.

As Kruger was again a member of the Government and the changes for religious instruction in schools had been made, he dropped some of his hostility towards Burgers. A smell of disaster was in the air, and Kruger was not a vindictive man. He was also true to form in his loyalty to the State, and when the majority of the Volksraad acted on public opinion and restored the old flag and coat of arms, he stood by the majority, for to him the voice of the people was the voice of the State, and of God. Kruger was perturbed by reports of speeches made in various parts of South Africa, such as Natal, that the British sphere of influence should be extended over the Transvaal. Joubert showed Kruger letters from Burgers in which he commented on his meetings with Lord Kimberley, Lord Carnarvon and others while in London, intimating the same sort of thing. Internally, a flare-up with Chief Sekhukhune seemed imminent and was bound to be exploited by the foreign element of the Lydenburg region.

Kruger was to reflect on President Burgers at various stages for the rest of his days, and particularly when he had to face very similar difficulties. His political awareness, given him by Andries Pretorius, was licked into shape by Thomas François Burgers. The President's exaggerated liberal views could be used in many advantageous ways. The Bible could also be used as a decisive factor in argument on a goggle-eyed people indoctrinated over the past thirty years to believe themselves the Chosen. Whatever went right, and whatever went wrong, could conveniently be ascribed to the will of God.

One can resolve much soul-searching in seeing things in terms of the will of God: one's own blunders, own misfortunes, the cruelties of nature, droughts, diseases, death—and if a man should be broken in the process it was also the will of God. Burgers understood this way of reasoning, a reasoning which gave absolution to those who plotted his downfall, for were they not, after all, the instruments of God? Kruger was far too clever a man not to make full use of the powers and latitudes God gave him, the only difference between him and an unscrupulous person being that he believed, utterly believed, that he, as a child of God, was right. In this concept lies a great deal of what is usually relegated to the 'enigma' of Paul Kruger, and it was the dilemma of Burgers (who was never at any time irreligious) and the gamble of Kruger to find the balance between the will of God and political expediency.

The Bapedi tribe of Chief Sekwate had first been involved in war with the Boers in 1846 when they were defeated. In 1852 they again gave trouble and were taken to account. Four years later they were given a reserve in the then Republic of Lydenburg. On the death of Sekwate (or Sekwati) in 1861, his son Sekhukhune I took over the leadership of the tribe. Perhaps he would have remained at peace, had it not been for the gold discoveries. Arms and ammunition were easily obtained, no matter that it was a contravention of the Sand River Convention, and the mining population made no secret of their desire for British annexation. Lord Carnarvon, who had set his heart on the federation of all South Africa under the Union Jack, saw his chance should the Boers again attack the Bapedi.

While Burgers was away, Chief Sekhukhune became rampant, committing murders, and plundering with impunity. Complaints and appeals poured into Acting President Joubert's office. Burgers had warned Joubert not to become involved in a Native war in the year of his absence, so Joubert was at a loss as to how to punish the Bapedi. Burgers himself did not know what to advise him to do, for he was well aware that with Sir Henry Barkly's connivings to the west and those of Theophilus Shepstone, Natal Native Administrator, estranging Boer and Zulu to the east, a Sekhukhune war could spark off a conflagration. The Bapedi had by this time become so outrageous that the farmers were forced to go into laager.[80] The Pilgrims Rest diggers, just to the north-east of Lydenburg, spread the word that the Government failed to protect them (actually they were instigating the Bapedi) and the Lydenburg farmers threatened to take up arms on their own account. Joubert and his Volksraad sent warnings to Sekhukhune and resolved, the moment Burgers was back, to send a military expedition against him.

President Burgers, on his return after a most memorable European sojourn, knew that he had to act at once. The British looked upon the Bapedi as an independent tribe, whereas they were subjects of the Republic. Burgers called on Paul Kruger to lead the expedition. Much to the bafflement of Burgers, Kruger declined. The President did not want this war, for it would halt his railway programme, retard a loan from Holland, and because he sensed a growing conspiracy against the independence of the Transvaal. He turned to Piet Joubert who had also shown exceptional abilities in Native wars of the past, but Joubert too declined. Burgers again approached Kruger, and a third time, but Kruger refused to go. If the President had seen fit to abolish the office of commandant-general, he was not to be reinstated as the President's whims took him. Kruger proposed that Burgers should lead the expedition himself, taking such veterans as M. W. Pretorius and Nicolaas Smit with him. Pretorius was perhaps no great shakes as a soldier, but Nicolaas Smit was a general born.

Various reasons for Kruger's refusal can be considered. The way the office of commandant-general was abolished could only be interpreted as an insult to him personally. Secondly, any military campaign organized by Burgers, Kruger believed, would not have the blessing of God, no matter who accompanied him, and certainly not if Burgers went along. 'I cannot lead the commando if you come,' Kruger is made to say in his *Memoirs*; 'for, with your merry evenings in laager and your Sunday dances, the enemy will even shoot me behind the wall; for God's blessing will not rest on your expedition.'[81] Piet Grobler and Manie Bredell, compilers of the *Memoirs*, skip over this issue as if it were of little importance and make Kruger refer to himself as if he was still Commandant-General. Another reason may be that both Kruger and Joubert considered a Native war politically unwise at that stage. Also, Burgers, having no military experience, was bound to interfere should he accompany the commando.

The President called up 2,500 burghers and some 3,000 non-whites. He also appealed to the Swazis for help, they having been allies of long standing. Van Oordt comments that Kruger would perhaps have gone had Burgers stayed home and had he entrusted the entire military operation to him.[82] According to Burgers's biographer, S. P. Engelbrecht, it was the *Executive* which forced him to go in person, and that he went most reluctantly after Kruger, Joubert and other stalwarts had 'flatly refused' (to quote Burgers) to go. So Burgers went, wearing a top hat and taking his Sash of State with him, on a campaign which soon turned out to be a fiasco. As Kruger was a member of the Executive, one may even deduce that he wished to see Burgers stew in his own juice. His enemies certainly made use of his absence to the extent that the President was made to feel 'betrayed and deserted'.

At Lydenburg there was a kind of insurrection going on. Captain Conrad von Schlickmann, a volunteer from Kimberley who raised the Lydenburg Volunteers for Burgers, wrote to the President on 15 August: 'I think that the Government officials and English residents of the district are trying to induce the population to ask for the interference of the English Government and in the state of intimidation or panic in fact, which is existing here, I am afraid that without your immediate appearance there is a good chance of their success.'[83] At the same time Sir Henry Barkly telegraphed to the Colonial Office that the Bapedi were pursuing the Boers up to Pretoria. This was quite untrue. The Boers were not routed, but had disbanded, and Sekhukhune was to be put down by the volunteers for whose maintenance Burgers levied a special tax.

This tax coming on top of that already levied for the railway scheme was too much. Kruger for one considered the special tax illegal, as it was imposed without the consent of the Volksraad in order to cover a loan of £20,000 from the Cape Commercial Bank. Even when the Volksraad did approve, Kruger considered the special tax unnecessary to finance handsome young Von Schlickmann and his volunteers.[84] Though Kruger had become more cordial to Burgers, he did not hesitate to take the President to task for whatever aroused his disapproval, and as from the time of the Sekhukhune War starting in May 1876 everything seemed to go wrong for this haunted man. Kruger was also much too ready to believe all kinds of slanders against him.

Propaganda against an independent Transvaal throughout South Africa and also in England was reaching alarming proportions. The South African Republic, it was said, was too weak for self-rule, and the Native tribes within and along her borders suffered constant aggression and suppression from the inhabitants. The *Gold Fields Mercury* published at Pilgrims Rest described President Burgers as 'utterly selfish, cruel and even cold blooded'.[85] Most of the Transvaal towns were becoming predominantly British as immigration and trade increased, and even ministers of religion such as J. P. Jooste and F. Lion Cachet advocated annexation. Lord Carnarvon, so far from the scene and usually given incorrect information, first sent the historian J. A. Froude to study the possibilities of confederation, and when he proved unsatisfactory sent Colonel George Pomeroy Colley who reported favourably. His views were supported by Theophilus Shepstone who conferred with Carnarvon on a visit to London.

The machinery for annexation, which was vital for Carnarvon's plans, was gradually set in motion. General hostility towards Burgers had created a curious apathy about their future among the Boers. They were farming people in any case and were indifferent to the excitement reigning in some towns. The death of Burgers had not occurred, but his term of office was ending. Many people went to Kruger and urged him to stand in the next election. At first he declined, but as there was such general dissatisfaction, Kruger allowed himself to be persuaded. Imminent annexation by Great Britain was common talk, but then there were so many other wild rumours and fabrications current—even that the Boers were the aggressors and not Sekhukhune. An actual cancellation of the Sand River Convention on whatever pretext appeared too fantastic, and too contrary to British honour, to contemplate.

When it became clear to Kruger that he stood more than just a good chance of becoming the next President, he went to see Burgers. 'I promise,' Kruger told him, 'to bring over the majority of the burghers to your side, if you will promise me to take strong measures against annexation and to defend our independence. If this is your intention, you must make it plain.'[86] Kruger was quite sincere, for he did not favour the candidature of the Chief Justice of the Orange Free State, Francis William Reitz. Kruger did not feel that he himself could possibly shine in a diplomatic war and he felt that a man with polish and brains should fare all right if he stood behind him. Kruger still had a lot to learn about Frank Reitz. 'You know,' Kruger wrote to Piet Joubert, 'that I opposed the President on his election. You also know why, his liberalism, my fear for the fall of Christianity, and particularly when the School Law took the children from the Church, but as that has now been rectified, the cloud has lifted.'

The other thing that meant a lot to Kruger was their continued independence, and as Burgers had given him his word that he would fight for it, Kruger was prepared to stand by him. 'Burgers is a Liberal and a Freemason, so is Reitz. Mr Burgers wants our independence; I am not so sure of Mr Reitz. Mr Burgers wanted to fly; his wings were clipped; now he will have to crawl with us. The wings of Mr Reitz are unclipped . . .'[87] As it turned out, Mr Reitz, a Cape Colonial born in 1844, had begun to identify himself far too much with the Orange Free State to give serious consideration to the Transvaal. And Kruger, though he had vowed to give Burgers his full support, knew that if he stood in the next election he would win it.[88]

The person who began to loom larger than life on the Transvaal scene was Sir Theophilus Shepstone (1817–93), son of an 1820 British settler, one of South Africa's most distinguished Bantu administrators, and recently knighted. In his opinion the Conventions of Sand River and Bloemfontein should never have been concluded, and he believed that a closer connexion of all South Africa with the British Crown would be to the benefit of both white and black. Lord Carnarvon's schemes were wholeheartedly supported by Shepstone, and Carnarvon could think of no one more able to pull off the annexation of the Transvaal, should the larger part of the population or the Volksraad wish it. The Sekhukhune War offered an ideal pretext, but it was already over by the time Shepstone could act.

This did not in the least deter him. Shepstone wrote to President Burgers on 20 December 1876 that it was his intention to visit Pretoria in order to 'make special inquiry into the origin, nature and circumstances of the disturbances, and of the several questions the existence of which is a source of so much danger, with a view to the securing, if possible, the adjustment of existing disputes and difficulties, a settlement of the questions out of which they have arisen, and the adoption of such measures as may appear less calculated to prevent their recurrence in future . . .'[89] Burgers could understand Shepstone's concern over the Native Question, his labours in this field being well known, but he could not know of Shepstone's dreams of a greater Natal, of federation with the Transvaal, of finding a pretext for annexation to please Carnarvon. Least of all was it expected that Shepstone would at this stage of his life embark on an unfamiliar and perilous political course.

Paul Kruger knew of Sir Theophilus Shepstone's departure from Pietermaritzburg on 27 December, accompanied by various gentlemen and twenty-five members of the Mounted Police of Natal. He also knew of Shepstone's arrogant and curiously ambiguous letter to Burgers. But of the man himself he could not have known much, though he had undoubtedly heard the name. Burgers was clearly rattled by the impending visit, sensing that Shepstone had something up his sleeve. It was suspicious that a representative of H.M. Government should find it necessary to come to Pretoria to confer on the Transvaal's internal affairs, now that gold was found and the country filling up with English. Everybody knew the story of the diamond fields.

As the Shepstone party approached Pretoria, Burgers proposed to Kruger that they should both withdraw from the forthcoming election and give their support to a new man. Such a step would unite the Kruger and Burgers parties and accordingly upset Shepstone's 'design', whatever it was. Kruger refused to withdraw, saying that Burgers could if he so wished. Burgers was certainly not going to give the Kruger party a clear field, not with the existing lack of unity in the Transvaal. Another civil war would give the British a humanitarian excuse to intervene in the interests of both white and black. Burgers invited the Executive to his house, Kruger among them, to discuss a formal reception for Shepstone as Queen Victoria's special commissioner.

He was thus given full honours, even the presidential carriage, and the pro-British element jubilantly welcomed him. Of impressive appearance, benign and impassive, a hint of a smile lurking in his shrewd eyes, Sir Theophilus began to wine, dine and generally befriend the people of Pretoria. On old and young, Briton and Boer, gifts of all kinds were showered. The only two people who really knew what he was up to were Lord Carnarvon who had given him his 'commission' and Sir Bartle Frere, now Governor of the Cape and due at Cape Town towards the end of March 1877.[90] In Shepstone's initial talks with the Transvaal Government there was no mention of annexation but hints of a kind of federation to safeguard British possessions in South Africa. If Carnarvon had grievances against the Republic, both Burgers and Kruger felt these should be dealt with before anything else was tackled. They proposed a commission of inquiry of two members from each side. Shepstone was not enthusiastic but could not very well refuse such an inquiry, so he appointed M. Osborn and J. Henderson, while the Government nominated Paul Kruger and Dr E. J. P. Jorissen.

They met on the last three days of January 1877. Dr Jorissen was one of the scholarly gentlemen imported by President Burgers from Holland. Although trained as a theologian, Eduard Johan Pieter Jorissen (1829–1912), switched to law in order to become Burgers's State Attorney in 1876. It struck Jorissen in 1877, according to his memoirs, that the Transvaalers as yet had no concept of a Fatherland. As king of his domain, a Transvaaler's chief concerns were his friends, his clique or church when forced to take a stand in the political field. It was Shepstone, Jorissen observed, who was to shake the Boers as a people into an awareness of being burghers of a specific land.[91] Burgers had originally intended Jorissen for an educational appointment, but as there was nothing suitable he took the plunge into law. He was a rather grim, critical and humourless man, and yet to become noted for his epigrams.

The cultured Jorissen and the unpolished Kruger made a curious combination, one which was to be repeated several times. Jorissen, liberal in outlook, a disciple of J. S. Mill and a Freemason, was far more in tune with Burgers (whom he revered) than Kruger; but it must be borne in mind that Kruger was not incapable of close friendship with such a man. They had no trouble in revealing the alleged British grievances—such as that against slavery—to be mythical. At a ball given by Shepstone, Jorissen remarked to an English colonel: 'We are dancing on the grave of the Republic, but then we all believe in a glorious resurrection.'[92] He, apparently, had a clearer grasp of Shepstone's design than anybody else, perhaps because he was not really perturbed either way.

The inquiry not having got him anywhere, Shepstone became impatient, and as the weeks passed was at a loss to explain his continued presence in Pretoria. On calling on Burgers one day, the President candidly asked him why he was still there. Shepstone was equally candid, even astonishingly so, Burgers thought, for he replied that he had come to annex the country. It took three months, involving Burgers in high drama, a drama which takes up the major part of his biography by Engelbrecht. Kruger was in the wings, watching in stupefaction as Burgers played into the hands of Shepstone. Burgers was eventually to write a heated vindication in which he related the sequence of events but left unexplained such curious matters as the lassitude of his people. Apart from a party of Boers turning up to find out what Shepstone's business in Pretoria was, the Transvaal simply seemed to slide under British rule—because, as Afrikaner historians hesitate to concede, she either wanted it or could not be bothered.

Kruger made strong protests against federation under existing conditions, while Burgers grabbed rather wildly at Constitutional reform. One session of the Volksraad followed the other. At one of these Kruger was appointed to the new post of Vice-President at a salary of £300 per annum, much to the disgust of Piet Joubert who had automatically expected the office. Both he and Kruger had interviews with Shepstone at his residence, and there was fiery talk which needed no interpreter, for Shepstone spoke fluent Afrikaans. In the circumstances the presidential election, which Kruger knew he would win, was postponed. This suited Shepstone admirably, for he knew that Kruger was a much harder nut to crack than Burgers. Only many years later did Kruger realize the nightmare Burgers went through, for he was to experience much the same sort of thing himself, but in a far more involved and calculated way.

A large measure of Shepstone's success can be ascribed to the Volksraad which *opposed* all the reforms proposed by Burgers (constitutional, financial and military) and then by *passing* them, only caused increasing bewilderment and division. Shepstone was bent on annexation, even if he had to invent pretexts. Even if fraud (as the Opposition in England saw it) was to be committed, a start had to be made in taking the Transvaal. It was imperative for a united

British South Africa. Whenever Shepstone found obstacles, he spoke of an imminent Zulu invasion, something which scared nobody.[93] The potential mineral riches of the Transvaal and a possible rail link with Delagoa Bay would in time make the country too strong for incorporation with the other colonies and would seriously undermine British paramountcy in South Africa.

'We fear the inherent weakness of the State,' Shepstone said. The only way it could save itself was to come under Her Majesty. Manfred Nathan wondered why, if the State were so inherently weak, Carnarvon and Shepstone 'were not content to wait until the structure fell to pieces of its own accord'.[94] But Shepstone could wait no longer, and on 12 April 1877 the ceremony of annexation took place, the proclamation being read in a trembling voice by Melmoth Osborn, Shepstone's private secretary. His hands were shaking so much that his assistant, the future novelist Rider Haggard, had to hold the papers. President Burgers made formal protest, saying that it was not in his power to take up the sword against mighty England. And it was at once decided to send a deputation, Kruger and Jorissen, to London to plead their cause.

A man who certainly had an awareness of Fatherland was Paul Kruger. The concept of independence was henceforth to obsess him. Although he had strongly opposed President Burgers, he could not watch his going unmoved—he was a man who had done everything in his power, even sacrificing his private means, to save the State. In the end Burgers was powerless against the forces working his downfall, with the people divided (many of them even thinking that Shepstone would not make a bad President) and with so many slanders—such as the claim that he simply *gave* the country to the English—current. And how much active support did he really have from Kruger and Joubert? Burgers often had to wonder about this in the lonely years ahead.

Whether Kruger had qualms of conscience we do not know. He wanted Burgers out, and now he was. By going to London and talking things over, it would appear that he felt confident that Shepstone's annexation would be annulled, for surely the solemn Sand River Convention was irrevocable. As Kruger planned his first trip to Europe he had much to reflect on. There were the wiles of British diplomacy; the future of his country; relations between Boer, Briton and Bantu; his allegiance to the Union Jack now fluttering in Pretoria; and his continued role in governmental administration. What may have come to him as a revelation, as one notes in his speeches in the Volksraad and in talks with Burgers and Shepstone in the early months of 1877, was that he had reserves of power which appeared divinely inspired.

Kruger's physical strength as a young man had already become legendary. What he now felt was a similar kind of strength which came from the mind and the spirit—not that he had lost his physical prowess, given him by God to move mountains. As Burgers was out of the scene, and Joubert was sitting on his farm, it was Kruger's task to make the future of the Transvaal his life. Backveld Boer he might be, but if it was the will of God that he should be used to regain Transvaal's independence and as a leader for his people, he was ready. He was also ready to do away with men like Burgers and their ilk in one mighty swipe, for what he felt was right and just and blessed by God for the Transvaal was—Paul Kruger.

CHAPTER EIGHT

The Two Deputations to London

Paul Kruger was about to have his first sight of the ocean. As a boy in Natal he had not visited the port which was becoming known as Durban, and his movements up to the age of fifty-one had been restricted to the interior. At this stage he wore a beard at a length never to be seen again in photographs of him, as well as a full moustache which looks strange to those familiar with his shaven upper lip. His hair parted on the left was neatly slicked down and was already turning grey. His dress was baggy and usually black in public, the short-cut jacket and black hat in the Dopper fashion giving him a rather quaint appearance.[95] The great shoulders, once capable of lifting a laden wagon, showed a slight sag. The eyes had a fixed and determined look about them, quiet and observant. To his whole person clung the odour of Magaliesberg tobacco, a weed so potent that younger men blanched when he offered them his pouch.

It was at Kruger's request that he was accompanied by Dr Jorissen, who had a wide knowledge of classical and modern European languages. As secretary they had the cultured Willem Eduard Bok (1846–1904), another of Burgers's importations, a skilful scribe and versed in modern languages. To these two Hollanders their Boer companion was a constant source of wonder, for to them, as to many others, Kruger was a living anachronism belonging to the seventeenth century. President Burgers having resigned, Kruger was still Vice-President and looked upon himself as the lawful leader of his people. As Sir Theophilus Shepstone had shown astuteness in making as few changes as possible, Kruger and Jorissen were still members of the Executive Council.

The trio set off in May 1877, almost immediately after the Annexation. They travelled by coach to Bloemfontein where Kruger conferred with the Free State Government, then on to Kimberley and with cart and horses to Worcester where Kruger boarded a train for the first time in his life.[96] They had hardly left Pretoria when Shepstone tried to scotch their mission by informing Lord Carnarvon that both Kruger and Jorissen had given him the assurance that, should their mission fail, they would quietly submit to the new Government. 'I declare this statement to be absolutely untrue,' Kruger was to remark.[97] And he soon proved it to be so, though it is not unlikely that Jorissen, whose involvement with the Transvaal had only been of about a year's duration, had said something of the kind.

On reaching Cape Town they had a meeting with Sir Bartle Frere who carefully avoided contentious matters, beyond saying that Lord Carnarvon would surely give them a hearing, but that any possibility of having the Annexation revoked was to be put from their minds. Present at the interview was a goggle-eyed Major Owen Lanyon, Administrator of Griqualand West, who made notes as Jorissen translated what Kruger had to say. One of Kruger's statements was that should independence be restored, a federation would be possible as far as the Natives were concerned. Frere sent his report on the interview to London, as determined as Shepstone to see the deputation fail in their mission before they even got there.

The Annexation was still too recent to have sunk in, even in the Transvaal, so the Afrikaner Cape Colonials were not in evidence, perhaps even thinking it a good thing that British law and order would curb the turbulence of the Transvaal. Kruger was never unaware of scenic beauty, and if there were few Afrikaners to see, there was all the glory of the Cape Peninsula to behold. Here his South African ancestor, the young German Jacob Krüger, had landed in 1713, more than a century and a half before.

In the harbour lay their ship, the *Dunrobin Castle*, and on board Kruger met a burly young man from the Orange Free State, aged nineteen, on his way to Europe to study law. He was Marthinus Theunis Steyn, and Kruger knew that if they sorted things out they would no doubt establish kinship. But he felt little in common with this jolly, fun-loving young man and barely spoke to him on the whole voyage.[98]

It lasted some twenty-six days to Plymouth, and to Kruger it meant a whole new world of experience. Many people were to be surprised how quickly Boers who had never even seen the ocean were to appear at home on it, as if they automatically reverted back to the days of their ancestors.[99] Kruger was no exception, and he became a familiar figure on deck, under clouds of smoke, as he pensively watched the ocean. Did anyone realize how courageous this step of his was? At home, his wife and one of the children were ill, and this was of deep concern to a man utterly devoted to his family. He lacked the funds for an undertaking of this sort. One can only guess at his knowledge of the English language. But perhaps his most serious concern was who in fact he was representing, apart from a now non-existent

Government. And what were the true feelings of the Transvaalers?[100]

When not immersed in his own thoughts, Kruger listened to Jorissen and Bok as they discussed, on one particular bright starlit night, the heavenly bodies and their movements. When it penetrated what they were saying in their cultured Dutch voices, Kruger told them to shut up, for if he had to believe them, he could as well cast his Bible overboard. To Kruger the world was flat, and anything that touched his faith was not to be tolerated.[101] Kruger's stern gaze would wander to the ebullient Theunis Steyn, always hanging round the Fraser family from Philippolis. The young man seemed in affluent circumstances, and Kruger could only think bitterly of the miserable thousand pounds on which he and his companions were to execute their mission when twice that amount had been promised.

From Plymouth they travelled by train to London and the Albemarle Hotel. What was the Transvaal in comparison with this hive of human activity? And who was he, Paul Kruger, in a city like London where every street was redolent of history? But he was not ruffled. Kruger was never easily ruffled by anything. But he certainly marvelled, as much at people and buildings as at the incredible greenness of the countryside. It was the beginning of July 1877, and it was warm and humid. As President Burgers had done on his visit, the trio turned to one known to be sympathetic and influential, the shipowner Donald Currie, a man of the same age as Kruger. For business and political reasons Currie was much interested in matters South African.

It was he who showed them the sights and arranged a meeting with the Secretary of State at the Colonial Office. Kruger, Jorissen and Bok were received with courtesy, no matter what Jorissen was to say in his memoirs, and there was a kind of old-world dignity in every encounter. Formal protest was made against the Annexation. It had taken place, said Kruger, against the will of the people and went contrary to the Sand River Convention. He was not overawed by Henry Howard Molyneux Herbert, 4th Earl of Carnarvon (1831–90), and nearly trapped him into agreeing to a plebiscite, had not Jorissen, who was more ready to submit to the Annexation than he gave out, gone off on tangents. Then too there were the misleading reports from Shepstone and Frere, as well as a communication from the Rev. Mr J. P. Jooste to the Press that Paul Kruger was not a representative of the broad will of the people but only of the small Dopper community.

It infuriated Kruger to be described the leader of a 'handful of irreconcilables' by a minister of Potchefstroom, and he rose to remarkable heights of oratory, surprising to his colleagues who had no grasp of his scope of mind, and to Carnarvon who did not expect this from a backveld peasant whose every word had to be translated. As far as Carnarvon knew—and this was confirmed by reports from South Africa—the Annexation was considered a boon. He was prepared to spend £100,000 on the development of the Transvaal, on roads, railways and telegraphic communication. Import duties on goods from Natal would be waived should there be federation with that colony. Everything was for the best. Kruger, although still unsure of his facts, had an intuitive feeling that opinions against the Annexation had begun to stir and again proposed a plebiscite. But this was dismissed as being too much trouble, too expensive and obviously unnecessary.

So nothing came of the Deputation. Even the Liberal Opposition, barring Leonard Courtney who sympathized with the Boers, showed scant interest, and Jorissen felt that aid from Irish parliamentarians would not further their cause. By 28 August their mission was over. The courtesy shown all round was impressive, and it is usually said that Queen Victoria gave them an audience. After so many—mostly humorous—anecdotes and even scenes in films, it almost comes as a shock to find that Kruger never did meet Victoria. This disclosure was first made by Prof. D. W. Krüger in 1961, refuting Dr Manfred Nathan's statement: 'They were taken to Windsor, and presented to Queen Victoria'. A person of interest whom Kruger did meet was the distinguished politician William Ewart Gladstone, also through Currie, aboard one of his steamships on the Thames to Gravesend.[102]

Before returning home, the trio wished to visit Europe, particularly the Netherlands and Germany. Much had been made of President Burgers on *his* tour, various orders being bestowed on him, but Kruger was to find little interest on the Continent in what had subsequently happened in the Transvaal. So he busied himself with people of all walks of life from his own church, arguing on such points as the Boer antipathy towards missionaries and the equality of the races. On the whole Kruger made a strong impression because of his unpretentiousness, even simplicity, his staggering knowledge of Scripture and for being a dedicated brother in Christ.[103]

Back in London, Kruger turned fifty-two, and the same day his daughter Elsie, married to Frikkie Eloff, gave birth to a daughter six thousand miles away.[104] Thoughts must have been much with his family that day. An invitation to Lord Carnarvon's country seat, Highclere, was accepted, but the luncheon in splendid surroundings and the host's geniality failed to impress him. Jorissen noted Kruger's grumpiness and that he only seemed to cheer up when he scanned the magnificent countryside, the stables and splendid horses. Kruger was naturally depressed by the failure of their mission, but he was also exhausted and longing to get home. He did so just before Christmas after the longest period he had ever spent away. In the peace of the Magaliesberg it must have seemed difficult to credit that all *that* existed in the outside world.

Hardly home three days, Kruger was drawn into what he had expected—a general movement to regain independence. When President Burgers had quitted office, he had urged everybody to remain quiet and undemonstrative until the return of the Deputation. Kruger had asked them the same on his departure. While he was away, one frequently heard men say: 'Wait until Paul Kruger gets back.' And now that he was back sixty men rode up to escort him to Rustenburg to address a meeting, and on 5 January 1878 over a thousand men waited eagerly to hear his report, a cavalcade taking him from Meintjeskraal to the centre of Pretoria. What Kruger had felt intuitively in London had come about—even grim Dr Jorissen, State Attorney under the British régime, was struck by it—a national awakening.

It was literally that, like a man stirring from the torpor of sleep into sudden awareness. Shepstone too felt it. His military precautions show that he was nervous of the meeting held at Kruger's request on Church Square. He told his audience all that had happened, saying provocatively that as Carnarvon clearly had no intention of revoking the Annexation there was nothing more to be done about it. A famous old Boer warrior, Henning Pretorius, rose to the bait: 'Rather than submit to the English,' he said, 'I will give my blood for my country.' It was reminiscent of the Voortrekker women in Natal who threatened to cross the Drakensberg barefoot rather than remain under British rule. There was a murmur of approval; the old Boer spirit was revived.

The Paul Kruger story now becomes one of endless meetings, resolutions, counter-resolutions and demonstrations, an interesting denouement of revolt. However, the confines of biography permit only a brief résumé, the focus remaining on Kruger's development as a personality. As a Calvinist he believed in submission to legal authority, always bearing in mind that the will of the people was the will of God. As God had chosen him, and this he believed by now, to lead the people back to independence, his intention was to do so along peaceful lines. For this reason he informed Shepstone of his every move. So much has been made of Kruger's 'hatred of the English' that it may come as a surprise if I say that he had never been anti-British and that even the Annexation had not made him so. True, his mission to Carnarvon had failed, but he still believed that once the British realized that they had made a serious mistake, they would rectify matters. What he felt later is another story.

As Shepstone was away in Zululand towards the end of January, Kruger wrote to the Government Secretary, M. Osborn, to say that he had found great dissatisfaction among the people on his return from England. In order to maintain peace the only solution was a petition to Lord Carnarvon in order to prove to him how many were either for or against the Annexation. 'Should the majority favour the annexation, I will be ready, as I have said, to remain under the government of the Queen of England and to obey her, and I believe I may be fortunate enough to persuade my countrymen accordingly.' By now he knew perfectly well that the majority opposed the Annexation. 'Although not a few of my countrymen are in a state of great excitement, and would not have hesitated to regain their freedom with bloodshed, I am glad to say that it appears to me that I can persuade them to take this measure in a calm way and to work for their independence in a peaceful manner.'[105]

On his return to Pretoria, Shepstone warned Kruger against any move which could cause unrest, the Annexation being irrevocable. A plebiscite, he knew, would reveal the Annexation for what it was, what the changeable British politician, Joseph Chamberlain, called 'an act of force, fraud and folly', or one of sheer brigandage, as the South African judge, Sir John Kotzé, implied. On Shepstone's triumphal tour through the Transvaal a while before, reports of which had been sent to Carnarvon, his rapturous reception came largely from the Uitlander element. Kruger soon established this and went on quietly with his work; he appeared at meetings where he dealt firmly with hot-heads, and he arranged the holding of his plebiscite through the ex-Republic. This revealed 6,591 against the Annexation and 587 in favour of it. The next step was to send a new deputation to London with the outcome.

Shepstone did everything he could to halt proceedings but Kruger stuck to a strictly legal course. For once he also had support from Piet Joubert who had been sitting on his farm at Wakkerstroom nursing all kinds of grievances. He too had found a new kind of national awareness, and all this time his influence was growing steadily to the extent that he was becoming as much representative of the east as Kruger was of the west. In the election for the Second

Deputation, Joubert even gained thirty-six votes as against Kruger's twenty-nine. Jorissen was not considered, his performance during the First Deputation and his speeches on his return having put him in a bad light. But Bok was still in favour as an intelligent and competent secretary, interpreter and adviser.

Another overseas adventure held little appeal for Kruger, but he more or less forced himself to go out of a sense of duty. This time at least there were to be more funds, but he knew well enough that there was strong criticism of his going. Although Kruger had not taken the oath of allegiance, he was still in the Executive. That he should draw a salary out of the usurper's pocket some found unforgivable, while Joubert, who had refused to have anything to do with the new régime, enjoyed increasing popularity. The reason why Kruger did not step down was because he believed the régime to be merely temporary, because he wanted to be at the helm of things, and because he needed the money. Joubert was in a different position, for he was not a member of the Government at the time of the Annexation. He was also a born businessman and, though his fortunes were to fluctuate, on the road to becoming very wealthy.

Kruger, Joubert, Mrs Hendrina Joubert,[106] her daughter and grandchild, and Eduard Bok arrived at Cape Town on 1 June 1878. An interview with Sir Bartle Frere had been arranged for the next day. Sir Bartle was courteous, but not encouraging as he thought their mission futile and that the outcome of the plebiscite would be ignored. He was genuinely puzzled why the Boers wished to reject all the blessings brought by the new administration. 'Under the English flag,' he said, 'you will have everything you may desire. But the flag will have to go on waving over the land.' Joubert was quick to retort: 'Over the land perhaps, but over the people—*never*.'[107]

The one thing about Joubert which Kruger never had reason to doubt was his patriotism. Although he knew that Joubert did not like him, Kruger could not help holding Joubert in some affection, perhaps because he found him ridiculous at times. That Kruger himself cut rather an odd figure in the eyes of some, like Frere, did not occur to the Lion of Rustenburg. Everybody who knew Joubert was familiar with his difficult temperament which swung from open-handed generosity to white-hot fury. He was always scheming and conniving, his voice rising to startling squeaks, his eyes never looking directly into one's own. But it was impossible not to like him. When he chose he could be most agreeable and amusing, and always he was intelligent and, when not thwarted, generous. He and Kruger had very much the same sort of background as children of the Great Trek, but Joubert was far more polished, had acquired considerable legal knowledge and had made himself familiar with the English language. He even had literary aspirations, and as an orator, once one got used to his voice, he was exceptional and full of surprises.[108]

The *Conway Castle* reached England safely and the party were in London on 29 June, booked in at the Albemarle Hotel. In their mail was a letter from Shepstone in reply to one from them of 11 May. They had delivered it personally, along with a copy of the petition they were taking to H.M. Government, but Shepstone first wished to study the contents before making comment. Kruger and Joubert had warned that chaos (*verwoesting*) was imminent should H.M.'s authority not be withdrawn from the Transvaal. 'No two people in the Transvaal,' Shepstone concluded his letter, 'have contributed more to make general chaos, which you wish to avert, possible than the two of you . . .' At least, Van Oordt was to comment, Shepstone made it plain that he recognized the influence of Kruger and Joubert beyond the Vaal.[109]

In another communication Kruger found that as he was agitating against the Government he had been dismissed from the Executive Council. This certainly ended an anomaly, and one can only wonder, apart from the reasons already given, why Kruger had ever allowed himself to be taken over by a Government he did not recognize. Various English writers, J. P. FitzPatrick among them, have praised Joubert for turning down his salary and showing greater consistency than Kruger, but as I have already pointed out he was no longer a member of the Government and drew no salary. Kruger had even asked and been granted a rise in salary. From the correspondence as published by E. B. Iwan-Müller one gathers that an additional reason for Kruger remaining in the Government was the persuasiveness of the Administrator, Shepstone, who had even kept him on after the First Deputation. But as Kruger now had more power to his elbow, his agitation was seen as manifestly inconsistent with an official position.

The Earl of Carnarvon had meanwhile been succeeded by Sir Michael Hicks Beach (1837–1916), later Lord St Aldwyn, commonly referred to as 'Black Michael'. This was a very different man from the courteous 'Twitters', and Kruger and Joubert soon found that Hicks Beach could be incredibly rude and appeared to be in a perpetual rage.[110] Kruger was not in the least put out by what he heard beforehand, but poor Joubert spent a sleepless night and trembled like a leaf before their first interview. (Rather hysterically he wrote all this down.) It was a cold reception, Sir Michael listening crossly as Bok read out a long declaration, carefully and even brilliantly prepared, in which the illegality of the Annexation was examined and the true will of the people presented.

When Bok had finished, Hicks Beach declined to comment, saying that he would write. In wonderment he murmured: 'Have you ever heard of an instance where the British Lion has ever given up anything on which he had set his paw?' Kruger at once retorted: 'Yes. The Orange Free State.' Sir Michael clearly knew little or had forgotten all about that. Apparently those were the only words said by Kruger, and the quaking Joubert did not after all have to say anything at all. From now on there was to be correspondence as the weeks dragged by in a heatwave. Hicks Beach, imbued with the imperialism of Disraeli, briefed by Shepstone and Carnarvon, as well as by others who held that the Boers were weak, cowardly anti-English savages,[111] never gave the Deputation much thought; but he was eventually forced to put in writing that the Annexation would not be revoked. He maintained that the Deputation represented only a small section of their people, that Shepstone's popularity was immense and that the signatures against his administration had clearly been obtained through pressure.

Further argument was pointless. The Turkish Question was the topic of the day, and only a few men like Leonard Courtney showed the slightest interest in the remote Transvaal. One sympathizer gave Kruger a gold ring engraved with the words: 'Take courage, your cause is just and must triumph in the end.' He wore this ring for the rest of his days and was to have reason to look at the words many times. From London the trio and the others in their party went on to the Netherlands, France and Germany.

What struck Kruger was that there was considerably more interest in the Transvaal on the Continent than he had found previously. There too it had taken time to grasp that Britain had simply pocketed the Transvaal, but once it had been grasped there was sympathy for the Boers and some indignation. It was autumn in Paris where a great International Exhibition was being held. There Kruger saw his first balloon. It was reminiscent of the young Kruger that he readily took part in an ascent and drifted over Paris. On their descent the aeronaut presented him with a medal 'to remind me of my journey through the air'.[112]

The Deputation had much more publicity than the previous one, and it can be taken that this was arranged by Joubert, with his astute business mind. Their lengthy reply to Hicks Beach was published in the British Press as an open letter; they showed all their papers to the Dutch ambassador in London; they had an interview with the Minister of External Affairs at The Hague; and their various moves aroused general interest. According to Mrs Joubert they went through the whole of the Netherlands, and they were particularly struck by all that water and all those who lived by it and on it.[113] Back in London, Kruger and Joubert sent Hicks Beach their final message. Unless the Annexation was revoked, voluntary federation would be out of the question. Only by restoring independence to the Transvaal would co-operation with the rest of South Africa for the good of the whole be possible.

On 24 October the party embarked for home. The trio's next step, it was decided, would be to tackle Sir Bartle Frere at Cape Town. He had shown courtesy to both deputations, and had not exactly been unsympathetic. After their useless and disagreeable mission, they hoped they could perhaps prevail on Sir Bartle to do something for them. Joubert felt the failure of their mission more keenly than Kruger, for it affected his personal pride. Naturally he had hoped to succeed where Kruger had failed, and so had many who had wished him to go. Joubert totally lacked Kruger's capacity for resignation, and was inclined to brood and fret.

On reaching Cape Town they found that Sir Bartle Frere had gone to Natal. Apparently British and Zulu relations were about to go up in flames. But they were determined to see Frere and went back on board to sail for Durban. On 28 November, Kruger and Joubert were in Pietermaritzburg where they asked Sir Bartle Frere to grant them an interview.

CHAPTER NINE

The Fight For Independence

If the Zulus had had high hopes when Sir Theophilus Shepstone was appointed Administrator of the Transvaal, they soon came to look upon him as a double-dealer. After first giving Cetywayo support in his claims on the disputed stretch of land in the Utrecht district, to which reference has been made (see pages 60–1), Shepstone changed his mind after his assumption of office and upheld the Boer claim. A warrior nation like the Zulus was not going to tolerate this and prepared for war. The explosive situation had demanded the presence of Sir Bartle Frere, and he was quite pleased to hear of the arrival of Kruger and Joubert, men familiar with Native wars—not that the British had, usually for ulterior motives, approved of their measures.[114] Of course he would see them, but at the same time he wished them to meet his Commander-in-Chief, Lord Chelmsford.

Kruger knew that the Zulu danger was far too serious for him to get an attentive hearing on the subject which had brought him there. So he talked amiably to Lord Chelmsford (until recently bearing the name of Frederic Augustus Thesiger) and gave him military advice. Chelmsford clearly underrated the fighting abilities of the Zulus and could make a blunder in leading an attack in open veld against the superbly organized Zulu regiments. The soldiers were to form laagers as the Boers had done in the days of the Great Trek and still did in the open, and there was to be advance scouting all the time. Sir Bartle Frere knew that Kruger was talking sense and asked him if he would accompany one of the columns. But Kruger shook his head. He was prepared to take only 500 men to mop up Zululand, but he was not going to do so unless he was assured of the restoration of their independence.

In further talks with Chelmsford, who had only just brought to an end the 9th Border War in the Eastern Cape, Kruger impressed on him the necessity of going into laager at every halt in a Zulu campaign. Perhaps Kruger had been told of the remark Chelmsford made at a ball in Pietermaritzburg, that the campaign was bound to turn out a mere promenade. Kruger could only smile, as he did later on receiving a letter from Shepstone asking him to raise a Boer commando to assist in putting down the Zulus. Kruger replied that the bitterness caused by the Annexation made Boer military aid to the British out of the question. General Chelmsford did not take Kruger's warnings seriously, so the result was the Battle of Isandhlwana of 22 January 1879 in which 858 British soldiers and 471 camp-followers were surprised and butchered by the Zulus, one of the most ghastly happenings in South African military history.

On reaching home, Kruger found the aggressive spirit among his people even stronger than after his first mission. Dr Jorissen as State Attorney, or rather Attorney-General in the British administration, had also been dismissed by Shepstone, on the recommendation of Chief Justice J. G. Kotzé who held that Jorissen was not suitably qualified for the office. This step no longer endeared these two gentlemen to him. Further, Kruger heard that J. F. Celliers, editor of *De Volksstem*, was at loggerheads with the Government, and that there had been a feeble expedition against Sekhukhune in his absence. Kruger and Joubert were expected to report on their mission, so a mass meeting was arranged at Wonderfontein in the district of Potchefstroom for 10 January. Further interesting news was that Shepstone was leaving for England at the end of the month. Even Uitlanders had begun to agitate against him, and his financial problems appeared insurmountable.

Sir Bartle Frere heard of the planned Wonderfontein meeting and had an open letter published, addressed to Kruger and Joubert, in which he confirmed that in no circumstances would British rule be withdrawn from the Transvaal. But, he added, all the pledges made by Britain would be redeemed. Sir Bartle Frere's aspirations for a united South Africa under the British flag made no allowance for Boer republics but demanded the settling of the Native Question. To stop the Wonderfontein meeting, however, was beyond his powers, and a crowd estimated at between two and three thousand people turned up to hear what Kruger and Joubert had to say. This meeting marked the beginning of the struggle for independence which moved rapidly to a climax.[115]

In his speech at Wonderfontein Kruger expressed his satisfaction at finding such a united front among the people. Only through unity, regularity and obedience would they succeed. When Hendrik Schoeman, a son of the controversial General Stephanus Schoeman, rose and said: 'Who wishes to subject himself to Her Majesty's authority?' there was a roar: 'We would sooner die!' But Kruger was not interested in bloodshed. There was in any case a serious shortage of arms and ammunition. Their next step should be to get Sir Bartle

The Young Paul Kruger, 1864

'On Trek' by W. H. Coetzer

Gezina du Plessis, Paul Kruger's Second Wife

Father and Son:
Andries Pretorius

Marthinus Wessel Pretorius

President Thomas François
Burgers

The Commandant-General:
Petrus Jacobus Joubert

Stephanus Schoeman

The Third Deputation, 1883. Standing, left to right: G. J. Beelaerts van Blokland; General N. J. Smit; Ewald Esselen. Sitting: President Kruger and S. J. du Toit

A Contemporary Dutch Cartoon of the Jameson Raid

Three British Administrators:
Sir Bartle Frere

Sir Theophilus Shepstone

Sir Hercules Robinson

President and Mrs Kruger

Frere to the Transvaal in order to show him the true state of affairs and to let him hear the voice of the people. This was agreed upon, and Piet Joubert was chosen to take the invitation to Frere who was still in Natal.

Sir Henry Bartle Edward Frere (1815–84) was appointed Governor to the Cape in 1876, also being High Commissioner for all British South Africa. He was hand-picked by Lord Carnarvon for his dual office, with the understanding that he would be the first Governor-General should confederation be successfully achieved. Kruger and Joubert had no idea to what extent he was committed and how difficult his plan of procedure had been made by Shepstone's annexation. It had cost him the support of prominent Afrikaner leaders of the Western Cape, had aroused the suspicion of the Orange Free State and was now stirring the Transvaalers to revolt.

Joubert found that panic prevailed in Natal after Isandhlwana. Frere was in no mood to receive him, nor to hear that the Transvaal was determined to be independent. Frere could only repeat that the Annexation was irrevocable. But as High Commissioner he was willing to grant self-government and a free Constitution. Joubert said all this was very well but the *people* wanted to be *free*. 'I would have thought,' Frere replied, 'that you and Mr Kruger would have explained to your countrymen that you will be as independent as you wish, or ever have been—your own Government, as well as given protection for your possessions, even as in Cape Colony. Should you reject my offer out of ignorance, this will be your responsibility, and should the Transvaal people soon find themselves on the edge of an abyss, reflect on my warnings . . .'[116] The invitation to the Transvaal, however, Sir Bartle was prepared to accept.

Joubert reported back to the people's committee or *Volks Comitó* which had been formed, consisting of thirty-two members. They decided to have another meeting, at Kleinfontein, thirty-six miles from Pretoria, on 18 March. Notice of this meeting was sent to Frere and to the new Administrator of the Transvaal, Colonel William Owen Lanyon (1842–87; knighted 1880). Nobody had expected that Shepstone's visit to England would also mean his exit, but so it was, and the choice of his successor was generally considered 'unfortunate'. It was more than that. Lanyon was Acting Administrator that March, his appointment soon to be confirmed. He was a swarthy little man, resembling a caricature of the Administrators of his day. But he was not as incompetent as he has been made out to be, though he was certainly totally out of touch with the Boer people and consequently prone to absurdities which Shepstone would never have committed. He was also tactless and imperious, and from the day of his assumption of office, 3 March 1879, he was held in mounting contempt. Lanyon could not even follow Dutch, and he despised the Boers.

As 18 March came, the Transvaalers streamed to Kleinfontein to form the largest gathering in their history. The men alone numbered up to five thousand, and most of them were armed. To add to the martial aspect, the wagons brought by families were drawn into a traditional laager. The spot had deliberately been chose near Heidelberg on the main road to Pretoria, Sir Bartle Frere's route from Natal. Many familiar faces were seen again, old Voortrekkers, famous warriors, ex-President M. W. Pretorius, even Dr Jorissen who had swung his allegiance back to the Boers. Although Frere left Pietermaritzburg on the 15th, there was no sign of him and the people began to wonder if he was dawdling deliberately in the hope that the great assembly would disperse.

It would have been only human if Frere had bitter thoughts about Kruger for not raising a commando to help against the Zulus. On the other hand, Frere had established that the Zulus had been deliberately incited against the Boers by the British in the past, and had Chelmsford but followed Kruger's explicit instructions Isandhlwana would never have happened. The massacre caused a sensation in England, and but for Queen Victoria's personal intervention Frere might have been dismissed.[117] While the Boers were waiting for him, Owen Lanyon asked members of the Volks-Comité to meet him in Pretoria. They went, Kruger being the main spokesman. He was reluctant to go over all the old arguments about the Annexation and forthright in saying that Lanyon had no understanding of the independence movement. As yet it was peaceful, but Kruger could give no assurance that it would remain so. This threat either went over Lanyon's head or he preferred to ignore it.

He appealed to the Kleinfontein gathering to disperse as such a large assembly of armed men was causing disquiet. This was true as far as the pro-British element was concerned, so the Boer leaders gave their assurance that they were there voluntarily, had no hostile intention and were waiting for Sir Bartle Frere. In their three weeks of waiting (Frere blundered in this respect) the burghers had their first real opportunity to have full discussions of the independence movement, to weigh the pros and cons of war against England, to assess armament, strategic positions and to plan a military campaign. For amusement there were military exercises which also proved to be instructive. Instead of making them lose patience and disperse, Frere gave the Boers the opportunity to plan a revolt in some detail.[118]

At last, on 9 April, His Excellency turned up at Heidelberg; he was bright-eyed but serious of countenance, and sported a drooping moustache. Colonel Lanyon came to meet him, and Frere was clearly rattled to find all those Boers still there. He tried to excuse himself but was held to his word and conducted to the laager on horseback by members of the Volks-Comité. Frere, Lanyon and various officials passed through two dense rows of Boers, who stood in complete silence with unsmiling faces, to a conference tent. There it was decided to have formal talks two days later, 12 April, at the farm called Erasmuskraal on the Hennops River, some six miles to the south-west of Pretoria. Frere then departed, unnerved by his cold reception.

Paul Kruger was not only the soul but the architect of the struggle for independence. Frere had long before acknowledged him as a man of considerable ability and shrewdness, and it is doubtful if he still found Kruger's appearance 'clownish'. It was indeed formidable, as observed that day at the Hennops River when Kruger, in his black Sunday-best, took the older man to task, his forceful words translated by the Rev. Mr G. W. Stegmann whom Frere had brought with him from Cape Town as interpreter. Perhaps astutely (as various politicians were to do through the years), Frere had the meeting opened with prayer by Stegmann. On the other hand, the High Commissioner was sincerely devout.[119]

In Frere's own words the meeting was notable for 'tall talk', from himself particularly. His accusations that they were not representative of the people and that many had been forced to be present were eloquently refuted by Kruger. He went on to say that the Annexation had brought dishonour to the British Crown and led up to a proposal that a new petition be sent to H.M. Government. Frere naturally did not want the Annexation repealed, but he could hardly refuse to pass on such a petition, with a covering letter. In this case there was no mistaking what Kruger meant when he repeated that he was doubtful how much longer he could restrain the people. The stern eyes of the forceful Mr Kruger must have lingered in Frere's mind, for he was much more friendly when they met again, perhaps also reassured that Kruger would not allow His Excellency to be held hostage, something he had dreaded all along.

There were two Sir Bartle Freres, Kruger was to discover, the one who talked to him and the one who talked to Downing Street. In time there were to be even more of them. Also, what Frere gave with the one hand he removed with the other. Certainly a charming old man, of the same school as Twitters Carnarvon, but quite unreliable. Jorissen, who was becoming adept at this sort of thing, drew up the new petition. Frere submitted his covering letter to the leaders of the Volks-Comité who found it satisfactory. The burghers then went home to await the outcome, only to find that there appeared to be none as the months went by. Elsewhere there were developments: the British army smashed the Zulus at Ulundi on 4 July 1879 and took Cetywayo prisoner. Sir Bartle Frere's authority in the Transvaal was withdrawn and restricted to Cape Colony. The Governor and High Commissioner of the Transvaal and Natal was now Sir Garnet Joseph Wolseley (1833–1913), a soldier of distinction.

Having subjugated Zululand, General Wolseley set off for Pretoria. Near Wakkerstroom he was met by Piet Joubert who did not hesitate to have a record of their conversation published.[120] The gist of what Sir Garnet said was that the Transvaal would for ever form an integral part of British South Africa, but a new Constitution would provide a measure of self-government. This then was the outcome of their memorial, and it was repeated by proclamation in Pretoria towards the end of September 1879. Joubert had warned Wolseley that the Boers would not co-operate, but he simply ignored this and even offered Kruger a seat in the new Executive Council he formed just after his induction. Kruger refused the offer, apparently with startling rudeness.

Having proclaimed the new Constitution, Wolseley prepared for the final subjugation of Chief Sekhukhune, without Boer help. This was an odd irony, that after all that had been said about the Boers in this respect, it was to be the British who were to subjugate the Native tribes of South Africa. Wolseley seized Sekhukhune's mountain fastness on 28 November with a few regiments and eight thousand Swazis, a forceful action in which five hundred Swazis perished and about a thousand Pedi were slain. Sekhukhune was captured and incarcerated in Pretoria. Kruger and his countrymen were not in the least impressed.

The Volks-Comité of which Kruger was the undisputed leader continued its work for independence. Deputations were sent to the Orange Free State and Cape Colony. President Brand did not want to be involved, though his Volksraad felt differently. And in the Cape there was growing sympathy with the Transvaal among its large Afrikaner population, now that the resentment against the Annexation was being understood. A Cape leader of stature was emerging in the person of J. H. Hofmeyr who must have guessed that sooner or later he would have dealing with Paul Kruger.

At fifty-four he still felt ready for anything, and he looked forward to a mass meeting planned for 10 December, again at Wonderfontein. Sir Garnet Wolseley, involved with the smashing of Sekhukhune, was annoyed when he heard of the projected meeting and issued a proclamation from Fort Weeber on 16 November in which he uttered warnings and threats. As he was storming the Pedi fastness, the Boers were already streaming to Wonderfontein, this time six thousand of them. The tent of Paul Kruger formed a central point as armed men came riding up from all directions, their leaders proudly bearing the Vierkleur, the flag of their fathers.

In his first speech (he always addressed the burghers as 'friends and brothers') Kruger said that if there should be any persons present against their will they were to leave at once. Nobody left, and proceedings were delayed for the arrival of M. W. Pretorius who had fallen ill. When he turned up, it was down to business and this time it became clear that the time for speech-making was past. The spark of patriotism had turned into a flame. 'The steps you wish to take,' Kruger said severely, 'are a matter of life and death. You know that England is a mighty power, while our forces are small and insignificant in comparison with what she can bring into the field . . .' Past history gave him deep concern over any vestige of lack of unity. 'Consider carefully before you shout "Yes! Yes! We want to fight!"' Piet Joubert was in complete agreement with Kruger on this point and spoke in similar vein.

On 15 December an important *Volks-Besluit* (Decision of the People) was taken unanimously to have their independence along peaceful lines and to restore their own legal Government. Sir Garnet Wolseley and his Administrator, Colonel Lanyon, were informed accordingly by M. W. Pretorius, chairman of the committee, and Eduard Bok, secretary. They were promptly clapped into gaol on a charge of high treason. This was a major blunder, for Pretorius was a national figure, and they were quickly released after Jorissen cabled the news to W. E. Gladstone who had since become leader of the Opposition in England. It was the beginning of 1880 and war very nearly broke out then and there. Wolseley hastily offered Pretorius a seat in the Executive, which it must have gratified him to refuse.

Paul Kruger did not want a war. It was against his principles as long as their objective could be reached along a legal course. But he had done all that could be reasonably expected from him, such as keeping the authorities informed of their every move, without any success whatever. As always, he held that the Government was put there by God, but in this case the Government to which he owed his loyalty was that of the South African Republic and not the usurper. Although the Republic was not recognized by the British, it existed more firmly than ever in the minds of his people, and to fight for it was the duty of every Boer. On the other hand, a solution could lie in the outcome of a fierce electoral campaign in England. The leader of the Liberal Party, W. E. Gladstone, seemed almost certain to bring down the Beaconsfield ministry.

Gladstone had on several occasions spoken of the injustice of the Annexation. Should he win, independence could be painlessly restored as a prelude for a wider scheme of things. A scheme for South African confederation had already been worked out by Sir Michael Hicks Beach and submitted to the Cape Parliament. There was much to recommend in the scheme, but should it be passed independence would no longer even be a talking-point. An independent Transvaal could voluntarily enter a confederation, a totally different matter to being annexed and coerced into it through the violation of a solemn Convention. The Volks-Comité had already laid its viewpoint before the Free State and Cape Colony, even Natal where sympathy was found in Alfred Aylward, editor of the *Natal Witness.*

The Transvaalers had made up their minds not to be simply absorbed without protest, and as British subjects at that. As the confederation scheme was to be raised in the Cape Parliament, Kruger and Joubert were at once deputized to go to Cape Town and fight it through the M.P.s sympathetic to their cause. Actually, by this time sympathy for them was widespread throughout South Africa, and also in England. As the two men prepared to leave in March 1880, they heard that Gladstone had defeated Lord Beaconsfield (Benjamin Disraeli) at the polls. So Gladstone was in office when Kruger and Joubert left Potchefstroom on 10 April, travelling via Beaufort-West to the seat of Afrikanerdom, Paarl, where they had a rousing reception.

These Afrikaner Colonials were mostly loyal to the Queen, but the Annexation struck them as a crime and they wished to see it revoked for the honour of England. Although Joubert was not so well known, Kruger was already a man of legend, and they aroused much interest at Paarl and on their journey to Cape Town where they took rooms at Haylett's boarding house. They were joined by Dr Jorissen who travelled down independently; they were given an encouraging reception at the Commercial Exchange, and also on a visit to the town of Malmesbury. Kruger had become stern but could still be amusing. The sort of self-government they had been offered in their annexed country, he said, was like putting your head in a noose and being hung up, free to kick your legs about as much as you pleased.[121]

To their satisfaction the confederation plan fell through. It was not popular in South Africa, the Gladstone ministry opposed the further incorporation of territories and the strong protests of the Transvaal, supported by Afrikaner Colonials, could not be ignored. This signalled the end of Sir Bartle Frere's career at the Cape. He asked for a private interview with Kruger and Joubert. Kruger asked his emissary which Sir Bartle Frere wished to see them, as by this time he knew four of them. 'The first came to us at Kleinfontein and assured us that he had not come with the sword, but as a messenger of peace. But, later on, I read in an English Blue Book that, on the same day, a Sir Bartle Frere, the second, therefore, had written to the British Government: "If only I had had enough guns and men, I would have dispersed the rebels." '

Kruger continued: 'I made the acquaintance of the third Sir Bartle Frere through his answer to our petition for the repeal of the Annexation: he then said that he had informed the British Government that he had met some five thousand of the best Boers at Kleinfontein and that he recommended their petition to the Government's earnest consideration. Afterwards I saw in the English Blue Book that, on the same day, a Sir Bartle Frere, obviously the fourth, had informed the British Government that he had met only a handful of rebels. Now these four cannot possibly be one and the same man; if, therefore, you can tell me which of the four Sir Bartles wishes to see us, we will think about it.'[122]

Apart from J. H. Hofmeyr, Kruger and Joubert also had the support of such powerful Cape politicians as J. X. Merriman and Saul Solomon. Kruger and Joubert were in the public gallery when Sir John Gordon Sprigg, Cape Premier since 1878, thought it wisest to withdraw the confederation proposal. The embittered Frere held Kruger and Joubert entirely responsible for the withdrawal, and they certainly had a hand in it, for they wrote to Leonard Courtney that they had done their duty and had used all lawful influence to wreck the proposal for a conference and the confederation scheme itself.[123] They also wrote to Gladstone to appeal to him to see that right would prevail, to revoke the Annexation and to honour the Sand River

Convention 'so that peace can prevail between the representatives of Her Majesty the Queen of England and the Boer Emigrants, the founders of the South African Republic'.[124]

Kruger and Joubert were not blind to the benefits of confederation, as they also told Sir Gordon Sprigg and the Attorney-General, Sir Thomas Upington, but this could only be contemplated once the Transvaal was free. To Kruger the Transvaal came first in everything and they were first to get their own house in order, a programme which included a port and a railway, before he was prepared to contemplate a tightening of links. Joubert was not so obsessed but he had a secret dream of one Boer Republic, with the Transvaal and Orange Free State as nucleus. How far he hoped it would stretch one can only speculate.

It was wet and misty in Cape Town, so it was agreeable to them to be back in the dry and bracing air of the Transvaal in June. They reported on their mission to the Volks-Comité gathered at a farm near Heidelberg. There it was decided, though further meetings seemed pointless, to have another gathering of the people on 8 January 1881 some forty miles from Pretoria at a farm called Paardekraal, a name to become historic in Boer annals. A fuller report and general discussion was needed, as well as time to negotiate with the British Premier who had condemned the Annexation in his Midlothian speeches.

Kruger was shocked by Gladstone's reply. It was written on 8 June and in his hands about a month later, a rather short letter in the circumstances. But Gladstone took the circumstances into consideration, saying that 'those applying to the Transvaal as well as the rest of South Africa, and to the necessity of preventing a renewal of disorders which might lead to disastrous consequences, not only to the Transvaal but the rest of South Africa, his Government did not feel free to advise the Queen to withdraw her Sovereignty.' Without prejudice to the rest of the population, the white inhabitants were to enjoy the fullest liberty to manage their own affairs, a liberty which could be easily and promptly obtained in a South African Confederation.

So there were also two Gladstones. Kruger still had to learn how often different tunes were sung when an Opposition came to power. What more could they do to gain independence along peaceful lines? There was nothing, so they had to arm. Unostentatiously, rifles and ammunition were acquired over a wide area, in the Free State also, and no suspicion was aroused. Sir Garnet Wolseley did not for a moment consider that the Boers would go to war with England. His administration evoked much criticism and dissatisfaction, particularly in Natal, and he was no doubt relieved to be able to continue his career elsewhere. His successor was General Sir George Pomeroy Colley (1835–81) as from March 1880. Wolseley so underrated the Boers that he withdrew large numbers of troops on quitting the Transvaal. Nothing suited the Boers better. All they needed now was a spark to start a conflagration, and when such a spark is needed almost anything can provide it.

The British Government had been very lenient about taxation, for they knew that the population of the Transvaal was largely impoverished and they did not wish to arouse hostility. Many burghers in any case refused to pay as a matter of principle, and those that did, did so under protest. Now, as everything appeared to be so quiet, Sir Owen Lanyon began to tighten measures to raise taxes. The landdrosts of the various districts were informed accordingly and were to issue summonses to those in arrears. Of these there were many in the district of Potchefstroom, duly summoned by Landdrost Goetz. One man who was not going to stand any nonsense was Pieter Arnoldus Cronjé, a controversial personality farming in the district. Paul Kruger had known Piet Cronjé for years, and Van Oordt who knew them both personally suggests that Kruger had a hand in what now took place.[125]

On 7 October, Cronjé, accompanied by some 130 men, handed in a written statement to the Landdrost in Potchefstroom which said that they were prepared to pay taxes to their own legal Government but not to a usurper, and that if they should be forced to pay, receipts should be made out to say that payment was done in protest and that the money should be held in trust. Goetz forwarded the letter (it was very rude indeed) to Lanyon who instructed him to deal with the defaulters forthwith. One of the first was a man called Piet Bezuidenhout who, having paid what he thought was due from him, was assessed for more. Refusing to comply, his wagon was seized and put up to auction on 11 November. Piet Cronjé was on the scene, put a stop to the auction and removed the wagon. He informed Kruger of what he had done, while Landdrost Goetz appealed to Lanyon.

The Administrator, blinking in his owlish way, served summonses on Bezuidenhout, Cronjé and others. Had he known more South African history, such as the connexion of the name of Bezuidenhout with Slachtersnek and Boer martyrology, he would have hesitated. Perhaps it was just as well for the Boer cause that he did not, for Paul Kruger now cast his scruples aside, summoned Piet Joubert from Wakkerstroom and declared: 'I can no longer restrain the people, and the English Government is entirely responsible for the present state of things.' The Volks-Comité was hastily summoned to the farm Kaalfontein near Potchefstroom on 1 December. Troops were being poured into the town, so the Government Secretary, George Hudson, hastened to the meeting to plead restraint. 'You know perfectly well that the people were planning to gather at Paardekraal on 8 January,' Kruger told him. 'Why could you not wait until then? Why must you incite the people now with enforced taxation? You are to blame for everything; I can do no more; see what you can make of it; I wash my hands of it.'[126]

The patience of Paul Kruger could be remarkable. He talked to Hudson for no less than three hours. He had talked and talked all over the place in South Africa, England and Europe. Nobody heeded him, so now the will of the people, which was the will of God, would prevail. He, like Joubert, did not particularly like Piet Cronjé but found him useful, and the needed spark had been set off. Instead of having the great meeting on 8 January it was decided to have it at once, on 8 December. Even at such short notice some five thousand burghers turned up at the farm Paardekraal. It was a scene of tremendous excitement, even impressing small children deeply, and every stone heaped on a pile to commemorate the meeting had a particular significance.[127] A monument was to bestride these stones, dominating a new town called Krugersdorp.

The Paardekraal meeting grew to some ten thousand people, just about the largest ever held by whites in South Africa up to 1880. It was also perhaps the most united crowd assembled up to that time, and for long afterwards. 'I stand here before you,' Kruger boomed, his bulk holding all eyes, 'called by the People. In the voice of the People I have heard the voice of God, the King of Nations, and I obey!' What he obeyed was the resolution taken nearly a year before, to restore their own Government, to summon their Volksraad as Vice-President, to be in fact the will of the People. This was a tremendous responsibility and not an easy one to assume for a law-abiding man. Kruger turned to the only person he felt could help and strengthen him, not Joubert or Pretorius, but Jorissen who, charged with the import of the historic occasion, had become infused with a kind of divine fire of justice. Even the pacifist Piet Joubert was so transported that he accepted the office of commandant-general, something he could have had no intention of doing and which certainly he would never have believed would be his for the rest of his life.

The leadership of the people was now vested in a Triumvirate of Paul Kruger, M. W. Pretorius and Piet Joubert. The *real* Triumvirate, D. W. Krüger pertinently points out, was Kruger, Jorissen and Bok.[128] M. W. Pretorius had become purely ornamental in Transvaal affairs, while Joubert, though popular, did not easily co-operate with anybody, least of all with Kruger for whom he had an aversion and against whom he never stopped scheming. Kruger knew his feelings and did not hold them against him, but at the same time he was not going to give such a man his confidence. Dr Jorissen was again State Attorney and Bok State Secretary. They issued a proclamation which was sent to Sir Gordon Sprigg, Sir Owen Lanyon and Sir George Colley—a proclamation which could only be interpreted as a declaration of war against Great Britain.

Paul Kruger now emerges in full stature, rocklike, unbendable, with full faith in God and British justice. He was not only determined to triumph but convinced that he would, once a united Transvaal showed the world their true feelings in all earnestness.

CHAPTER TEN

The First Boer War

The proclamation of independence contained thirty-eight clauses. It was essential to have it printed at once and widely distributed, for the document would give full explanation of the reasons for their step, their hopes and aspirations, and could possibly forestall bloodshed. The only sympathetic printer appeared to be Johannes Philippus Borrius of Potchefstroom, a protégé of Hermann Jeppe in 1860, and by 1877 editor and owner of his own pro-Boer paper *De Transvaal.* Commandant Piet Cronjé was entrusted with the proclamation and ordered to take it to Borrius with an escort of four hundred men, for it was known that an effort would be made to prevent the printing. Though threatened by a charge of high treason and in spite of some two hundred Royal Scots sent there to deal with tax defaulters, Borrius, his staff having deserted him, had the printed proclamation ready on 16 December 1880.

On the same day the Boers converged on the town of Heidelberg, Kruger having decided that this would be their best choice of a capital, and took it—the men being described as 'inflated toads' and 'mortal cowards' by Sir Owen Lanyon.[129] It had become fashionable during the British administration to look upon the Boers as 'cowards', so it gave satisfaction to Cronjé's men at Potchefstroom to taunt the Fusiliers with shouts of 'Why don't you fight, you damned cowards!' At Heidelberg, Kruger acted with dignity; he gave the Acting Landdrost written notice, demanded the keys of his office and had the Vierkleur hoisted at sunset. A laager of about two thousand men had formed, but everything remained orderly and there was no molesting of residents. News of the taking of the town was sent to Lanyon by the Landdrost who felt that he saved face by not surrendering the front-door key, though he left it conveniently in the lock.

The Triumvirate passed a copy of their declaration of independence on to Lanyon with a covering letter written the previous day in which he was addressed in the name of the People of the South African Republic. 'We declare most solemnly,' they said, 'that we have no desire to shed blood and do not wish to resort to arms. It is up to you whether we are forced to take up arms in self-defence. If, God forbid, this should happen, we will do so with the most profound respect for

Her Majesty the Queen of England and for her Flag. Should it come to this, we will defend ourselves with an awareness that we are fighting for the honour of Her Majesty, as it will be a fight for the sanctity of the treaties made by her and which have been abused by her officials.' It was an ultimatum, but one in which full co-operation with the British Government was promised in the hope that the keys of the Government Offices would be surrendered without bloodshed in the same way as the Boers had given them up in 1877.[130]

Sir Owen Lanyon, who knew what had been going on since the Paardekraal meeting, and who had taken his first steps in forbidding armed meetings within a mile of any town, was not really perturbed, for he refused to believe that a spirit of unity could possibly prevail among the Boers. This was also what he wrote to Sir George Pomeroy Colley, but Lanyon showed some caution in sending a detachment of the 94th Regiment to Pretoria straight away. The Heidelberg documents were delivered to him by H. J. Schoeman on 17 December. By then the first shot had already been fired at Potchefstroom—on the Boers, fracturing the arm of Commandant Robbertse. This was where the war began. As Heidelberg and Potchefstroom were in Boer hands, Lanyon issued a threatening proclamation on the 18th, as if proclamations could still achieve anything. The only person who had the jitters was Piet Joubert who felt that they should not be at Heidelberg at all but at Paardekraal.[131]

But he was to pull himself together and, as I have shown in my biography of him, as Commandant-General his was to be the starring role of the war, though the military honours go to General Nicolaas Smit. Kruger, though he had far more military sense and experience than Joubert, played the diplomatic role, assisted by Jorissen and Bok. Kruger's active military career was over; the politician, diplomat and statesman now set to work in earnest—and with surprising assurance for a man who had still so much to learn. This was one aspect of Kruger which was to fascinate many people—his superb self-confidence. It sprang of course from his conviction that he was guided by God. It will be recalled that in his younger days he was much less sanguine.

The British were at a disadvantage from the start. Their military strength had been much weakened by withdrawals, and they had almost no comprehension of the fighting abilities of the Boer. They also failed to understand his earnestness and were bewildered that anybody could possibly wish *not* to be a British subject. Garrisons, before it had really dawned what had happened, were smartly laid siege to at Potchefstroom, Pretoria, Standerton, Lydenburg and Marabastad by 2,800 Boers. The rest of them mobilized to deal with the British reinforcements expected from Natal. Their obvious route of influx was Laingsnek (also known as Langenek), the main pass across the Drakensberg. Once General Joubert grasped the military situation, he secured an excellent position and showed the gift for organization which was to bring him renown.

Heidelberg had hardly been occupied when a report was received of a detachment of British troops moving from Lydenburg to Pretoria. Commandants Frans Joubert and Nicolaas Smit were instructed to take 160 men in order to turn this detachment of the 94th Regiment back to Lydenburg. The small commando met the British near Bronkhorstspruit under their commanding officer, Colonel Anstruther. The Boers ordered him to turn back, but scornfully he refused, and the result was a lightning action in which nearly 100 of his men were killed and 114 wounded.[132] The rest surrendered. This sensational event happened on 20 December, some thirty-six miles from Pretoria. Another detachment making their way from Wakkerstroom to Pretoria promptly fell back on Standerton and entrenched themselves. The action at Bronkhorstspruit was described as a 'massacre' of redcoats, and from 'cowards' the Boers graduated to 'barbarians'.

On the contrary, they had done what they could to avoid a conflict, and when this had failed showed wounded and prisoners the greatest consideration, as was acknowledged by the dying Philip Anstruther. The Boers were appalled by the bloodshed caused in twenty minutes, particularly when they discovered that most of the redcoats had had their rifles wrongly sighted. But the spoils were great and the laden wagons of their convoy (there were 30,000 rounds of ammunition) were sent off to Heidelberg where Paul Kruger 'bowed down in the dust before Almighty God in inexpressible gratitude', to use his own words,[133] for such a victory with a loss of only two men. He and Joubert knew that the British could not let this go unavenged.

While Cronjé held Potchefstroom, the garrison besieged in a make-shift fort, General Joubert moved nearly two thousand men to the Drakensberg to take possession of the passes and particularly the key position at Laingsnek. He knew that General Sir Pomeroy Colley was preparing to lead his troops into the Transvaal. The Boers had long since developed a superb scouting system, their mobility was thought amazing, and it was to their advantage that most of them knew every inch of the country and that their needs were few. As a result of Joubert's clever dispositions, Colley was forced to lead the expected assault on Laingsnek, to be repulsed, losing 7 officers and 76 non-commissioned officers and men killed, and 111 wounded. Joubert lost 24 men in the shelling (Van Oordt gives 14 in killed, 30 wounded).[134] Colley, who knew Joubert and had even dined with him at his house in Pretoria, made a humiliating retreat back to his base. It was 28 January 1881, and Colley waited for reinforcements from Pietermaritzburg.

Although one military success followed the other, Kruger, no matter that he believed in the blessing of God because their case was righteous, was realistic enough to reject the possibility that independence could be regained by force of arms. Once England began to pour troops into her colonies and led a determined assault on the Transvaal all would be at an end. Hostilities had become inevitable, causing the Lanyon administration to collapse, and having taken their stand they were now ready for negotiation. In a tent at Heidelberg, Kruger, Jorissen and Bok put their heads together for a political victory, while General Joubert and his commandants controlled the military situation and remained on the defensive.

Kruger's capacity for work was becoming legendary also. One can only wonder if he had a moment's rest during the war, for having assumed the reins of government, he was involved with a multitude of tasks, domestic and military; he conducted a huge correspondence, made personal appearances, controlled restless tribes, dealt with crime, treason, armament, postal delivery, and so on. He visited commandos at Potchefstroom, in the Drakensberg, at Standerton and Rustenburg, making rousing speeches in which he exhorted the burghers. The Boer cause had begun to draw international attention, as well as sympathy, in the Netherlands, Belgium, Germany and even in England where the Liberal Government had begun to do some soul-searching. Natal was rather indifferent, but in Cape Colony agitation had begun for a special commissioner to investigate the revolt. Though President Brand tried to remain neutral, the Orange Free State was, as one would expect, largely sympathetic and also of material and physical assistance.

Colley's reverse at Laingsnek was followed by another at Schuinshoogte, near Ingogo, where General Smit, who had set out to intercept a wagon supply train from Pietermaritzburg, clashed with two British detachments on 8 February. This was one of the most heated and prolonged actions of the war, on terrain sodden by downpours, lasting till nightfall. Colley's losses were seventy-six killed and sixty-seven so badly wounded that they had to be left on the battlefield. Smit had eight men killed and six wounded. The frightful weather ruled out pursuit, which the Boers thought unChristian anyway, and a thoroughly shaken Colley regained his base at Mount Prospect unmolested. In General Nicolaas Smit he had met more than his match, a modest but great soldier.

Alarm was beginning to spread throughout South Africa that the Transvaal war would spread into a clash between the two white races all over, a possible conflagration should the Native tribes decide to rise. In the Transvaal, Kruger kept a close watch on tribal affairs, particularly to the west, for in no way did he want Natives involved in a white man's quarrel. It must be remembered that nearly all the menfolk were away on commando and their farms were left in the charge of their wives and daughters. Gezina Kruger was of course in this position, and she was alarmed to receive a report that Chief Maghato's tribesmen, living in the region between Boekenhoutfontein and Rustenburg, were about to attack them.

Women and children from neighbouring farms fled in panic to the large homestead at Boekenhoutfontein. There were forty of them altogether. An advance party of Natives came yelling round the house, breaking windows, sticking their hands through to pull down curtains. The women stood guard at the windows and doors with whatever weapons they could handle. The situation was all the more harrowing as one of the neighbouring children had arrived ill and was clearly dying. Gezina organized everything and everybody, and it was like an act of God when a tremendous storm broke and brought the river down in such spate that it was impassable for a week, giving Kruger the opportunity to rush to the scene.[135]

It was mainly thanks to him that apart from this one disturbance the Natives remained quiet as the war moved to its climax. Deeply concerned was President Brand, for if the Free State were to remain uninvolved, hostilities had to cease at once. Many were convinced that the one man who could *make* them cease was Johannes Henricus (Sir John) Brand. Brand's Volksraad received a letter signed by Kruger which asked, 'Is there nobody to protect us, nobody, not a single British statesman, not even to mention a foreign power, to come to our aid? Whether we win, whether we die: freedom will rise in Africa like the sun from the morning clouds, inasmuch freedom rose in the United States of North America. Then it will be from the Zambesi to Simons Bay: Africa for the Africander.'[136]

The word 'Africander' or Afrikaner must not be taken literally here. It had come to mean all those to whom Africa was home, Dutch and

English. This is merely an excerpt from a lengthy communication, the concluding words of which were to cause repercussions for years. From it was deduced, when this was convenient, that the Afrikaners were hatching a conspiracy to grab most of South Africa for a vast Boer Republic. Ironic, when the South African-born wives of British mining magnates, like Lady Florence Phillips, spoke of themselves as Africanders. Furthermore, the slogan was undoubtedly not that of Paul Kruger, but that of Dr Jorissen. Only Jorissen could have dreamt up something like 'Africa for the Africander'.

In England, Leonard Courtney worked ceaselessly for the retrocession of the Transvaal. He had been the principal member of a committee which had opposed the Annexation and remained in close touch with the Boer leaders. His opinions were shared in Portugal and France. Internationally the name of Paul Kruger was becoming known, and rather romantically at that in some quarters. For President Brand it had no enchantment. Though still wary of becoming involved, he knew he had to do something and got into contact with General Colley, the British Minister of Colonies, Lord Kimberley, and the new Cape Governor and High Commissioner, Sir Hercules Robinson. Free Staters had begun to stream into the Transvaal to help their kinsmen, and Brand's Volksraad had become increasingly restive. A sign of the wind was when Lord Kimberley instructed Colley to ask Brand to persuade the Transvaalers to lay down their arms. Should they comply, H.M. Government (Gladstone knew that Kruger still had faith in him) would do everything possible to find a way out of the impasse.

Brand sent a messenger at top speed to Heidelberg to see Kruger. But he had just left for the Drakensberg to deal personally with Colley, having written impassionedly to him that they sought no strife with the Imperial Government, that he had no objection to a Royal Commission to examine the situation, and that the Boers would vacate their virtually impregnable positions should the British troops be withdrawn. This letter, sent on 12 February, only received a reply on the 21st. Colley had been in telegraphic communication with Lord Kimberley and was awaiting more detailed instructions as Kruger's proposals were seen in a favourable light. Colley now wrote to him that should the Boers lay down their arms, commissioners would be sent to arrange a settlement. 'I must add that,' he said, 'when this proposal is accepted within forty-eight hours of receipt of this letter, I have the authorization to cease hostilities from our side.'[137]

Colley's delay in sending his reply nearly wrecked everything,

Kruger having left for Rustenburg to deal with restive tribesmen. General Joubert informed Colley of Kruger's absence and that the letter had been sent on to him by express. As Joubert read the letter before he sent it off, he assumed that hostilities had already ceased. He relaxed discipline and waited for Kruger's return. It was a time of torrential rain, but with his usual vigour Kruger covered the great distance to Rustenburg and back to Heidelberg in record time. On receipt of Colley's letter on the 28th, Kruger accepted his proposal with alacrity, oblivious that Colley had been lying dead on Mount Majuba since the previous day.

The Battle of Majuba of 27 February 1881 was the last and also the most sensational of the war. Colley was expecting reinforcements under his second-in-command, Sir Henry Evelyn Wood, and knew that this outstanding soldier would almost certainly replace him. Not having yet heard from Kruger, and as Wood was still on his way, Colley saw his opportunity to have another attempt to prove the superiority of British arms and also to save his reputation. The Boer positions were dominated by a mountain they called Spitskop, better known as Amajuba or Majuba, the Zulu hill of doves. On the night of the 26th Colley led his troops towards the summit. At dawn the next morning the first person to spot the redcoats there was Mrs Piet Joubert, a woman whose eyes never missed anything, and her husband immediately ordered an assault on the Kop.

As Colley yet had no guns on the summit, what followed was a rout in which 90 British soldiers lost their lives, 133 were wounded and 57 captured, while their small band of attackers lost only one man. Among the dead lay General Sir George Pomeroy Colley, facing his foe. Apparently he had had a premonition of personal disaster, but it was more than that, for few things were to rankle more in the British army than the shame of Majuba. Even if Colley had been suffering from temporary insanity, Majuba simply could not go unavenged, for in the anti-British world the news of the Boer triumph was received with amazed delight, even a thrill of wonder, and the humiliation of the British armed forces in South Africa was complete. The Boers were now acknowledged to be born soldiers of outstanding ability. But in this case too there was no gloating, the victory being seen as given them by God, but there was no denying that the way the survivors fled from the heights of Majuba was simply scandalous.

Paul Kruger was filled with dread that this victory would nullify all his work. Both he and Joubert spoke sharply to their men. 'It is the God of our fathers,' Kruger told them at Laingsnek, 'to whom we have been praying and pleading for four years for salvation who has helped us.'[138] General Piet Joubert, though Majuba made his name world-famous, never claimed credit for it, and was no doubt amused by the many portrayals of him on horseback, pointing to the mountain, even rendered on porcelain ware.[139] Kruger went further in pretending that Majuba had not happened, and he continued his negotiations, fortunate in that Gladstone was not a vengeful man. Colley had after all brought disaster on himself, and this at a time when the Boers had believed the war to be over. Joubert sent eloquent condolences to Lady Colley, while Kruger conveyed his personal sorrow over Colley's end to President Brand. Kruger was much concerned with honour, irrespective of race, and the word occurs frequently in his correspondence.

Joubert was often to annoy and exasperate Kruger but their only monumental row happened at this time. Brand was in touch with Sir Evelyn Wood (1838–1919) who had automatically succeeded Colley as Commander-in-Chief. Wood had moved up with a considerable force, so a meeting between him and Joubert was arranged for Sunday, 6 March, half-way between their respective camps. The main purpose of the meeting was to decide on an armistice. It went well, for Wood, a veteran of Xhosa and Zulu wars, was a shrewd as well as charming man. Joubert was always susceptible to charm and particularly when it was combined with intelligence. He also took a strong liking to those who clearly liked him. To Kruger it appeared as if Joubert was clay in Wood's hands, for the terms of truce concluded as from the afternoon of 6 to 14 March made no reference to independence in any form and could give Wood the opportunity to bring up even more troops from Durban. Happily Joubert wrote to Kruger, including a copy of the agreement, addressing his colleague as *UHoogedele* (Your Honour or Excellency), for Kruger was still Vice-President and generally referred to as 'the President'.

He received Joubert's communication on the evening of the 9th at Heidelberg. Joubert, still in session with Wood, referred to a grave lack of food supplies and restiveness among his men, and had clearly gained hope from the draft armistice. Any armistice, in Kruger's opinion, in the circumstances and unconditional about their gravest concerns, would be sheer folly. Should the British take advantage of it to treble their force, which could be done now, the Boers would be swept from the Drakensberg in one swoop and everything would be lost. A very annoyed Kruger, J. P. Maré, M. W. Pretorius and Dr Jorissen hurried off to Laingsnek in pouring rain. Joubert, realizing that they would have difficulty in getting there on time, trustfully asked Wood for a peaceful continuation of their talks.

Kruger reached the Boer camp on the 14th and received a warm reception from his waiting men who seemed to have dropped all discipline and caution. Kruger snapped Joubert out of his holiday mood by telling him what a fool he was. Both he and Smit seemed to fade as Kruger became the most dominating person there. The cold, wetness and lack of food were as depressing as was the thought that everything might now depend solely on the goodwill of the British Government. Kruger had come to know a type of soldier like Sir Evelyn Wood, steel underlying all that charm, and Kruger would not have been in the least surprised had Wood made a sudden move to avenge Majuba, something he was in fact contemplating. Had Kruger been in his position he would have done the same, making full use of the four days gained by Joubert's armistice.

A cloud would have lifted from Kruger's mind had he known the contents of the telegraphic communication which had already taken place between Sir Evelyn Wood and the Colonial Minister. The main proposals were amnesty for all the Boer leaders so that they could empower persons for negotiation, the appointment of a Royal Commission to investigate the military situation and retrocession with self-government under British suzerainty, a British Resident to be posted in Pretoria and British control of the Transvaal's foreign affairs. On 16 March at ten in the morning representatives of the opposing parties met in a blue-lined marquee midway between Laingsnek and Prospect Hill.[140]

Paul Kruger was accompanied by his co-members of the Triumvirate, Pretorius and Joubert, and the members of their Executive: Jorissen, Chris Joubert and Jacob Maré. (Bok does not appear to have been much on the scene lately.) Sir Evelyn had with him Colonel Redvers Buller, his chief-of-staff, and Majors Fraser and Clarke. Interesting was the observation of Buller, who knew his South Africa and was to play a major role in it, that 'any peace now agreed to, will not be a lasting one'. He clearly felt that the British wished to retain too much control over the Transvaal. Discussions lasted for eight hours, Sir Evelyn mainly directing himself to Joubert whom he found much more agreeable than Kruger. But in the presence of the formidable Mr Kruger, Joubert seemed to wilt.

Even before the conference began, Kruger could draw satisfaction from the knowledge that they were no longer looked upon as rebels but the representatives of a legitimate war party. That was at least something Joubert's armistice had achieved. Now Kruger made everybody blink, even those who thought they knew him well. To the British, Paul Kruger was a man of mystery and legend, in coarse contrast to the handsome uniforms, the well-tended moustaches and beards, but once his deep bass took over, appearance was forgotten in a man of such passion and superior intelligence. Kruger also showed an unexpected grasp of the situation—that all they could hope for was qualified independence. But he showed his determination to have these qualifications annulled or modified. Argument began about the Royal Commission.

The men proposed to form it were Sir Hercules Robinson, Sir Evelyn Wood and Sir John Henry de Villiers, Chief Justice of the Cape, with President Brand as an impartial adviser. Kruger and his party felt this commission too one-sided and wanted one representative to be their own. Secondly there was the question of 'suzerainty' and what it meant. A tricky question was the procedure of British withdrawal from the Transvaal. Sir Evelyn Wood, a military historian of the future, enjoyed the conference when he realized that it was not to be a walk-over, not with Kruger, Jorissen and Joubert around. Sir Evelyn was at his most charming, amiable and amusing (Kruger too warmed to him) as the whole thing became like a game of chess between himself and Kruger. It was Kruger who outwitted him in turning an armistice into a declaration of peace, but concessions were a different matter.

No snap decisions were to be taken. The weather remained inclement, rain coming down and mist at times enshrouding everything and everybody. The English side was in contact with Lord Kimberley, while the Boers awaited the arrival of President Brand. When the parties gathered again it was in a small cottage at the foot of Majuba, still remembered as O'Neil's Cottage. They came in driving rain, and it was so cold that newspaper reporters huddled over a fire in the tiny kitchen. Horses were dying of exposure. General Joubert was there on his own as Commander-in-Chief of the Boers, and Kruger and Joubert were glum when he reported back that the concessions wanted had been turned down by the Colonial Secretary. But they could still play for time, until midnight of 21 March. Kruger felt that they simply had to have representation on the Royal Commission, and Joubert agreed with him that it would be unwise to vacate Laingsnek before the British garrisons left the country.

Kruger was besieged by men who were quite willing to resume the war. One of them was General Smit who held meetings in his tent. An improvement in the weather soothed tempers but the resolve to continue the war, because of the unsatisfactory conditions, only strengthened. The Free Staters who had joined them, such as C. J. de Villiers, said they were quite ready to raise a commando to attack the British in their rear from the north. Dr Jorissen drew up his so-called 'Third Proclamation' in which he made a rousing call on the people. It was such an explosive document that it was perhaps fortunate, all things being considered, that it was decided *not* to have it published.[141] President Brand, delayed by the weather and after having nearly drowned in a flooded river, turned up on the 20th and darted from one camp to the other. His main and seemingly impossible objective was to make the Boers withdraw without written guarantee, and it was he who protested against the publication of Jorissen's latest proclamation as it could draw the whole of Afrikanerdom into the conflict.

Various persons have now and then been given the title of 'the first South African', the embodiment of the two white races in a specific country. Brand is one of them, though his later acceptance of a British title rather clouds the issue.[142] One thing is certain, though, that it was Brand who enabled the opposing parties to come to an agreement. Lawyers always fascinated Kruger and their powers of argument could elate him. Thus it was thanks to Brand that Kruger, though they were apparently never on good terms,[143] unbent. At the important conference of the 21st at R. C. O'Neil's cottage, he waived representation on the Royal Commission as well as the simultaneous withdrawal of the opposing forces on which he had previously insisted. Thanks also to Brand, Wood was in a more accommodating mood than he had been previously. The outcome was that a preliminary treaty could be agreed upon with the men now acknowledged to be the lawful representatives of the Transvaal people.

Kruger caused a flurry when he insisted on having the terms in writing, for Wood held that the minutes would do. A properly signed document would be to Kruger in itself a peace treaty and binding for the Royal Commission. 'I cannot understand,' Kruger said through his secretary and interpreter Karel Rood, 'how an honest man can first agree to something, and then refuse to put his name to paper in confirmation of that promise.'[144] Only then was the document drawn up, signed by Sir Evelyn Wood and the Triumvirate. Suzerainty would be maintained but the Transvaal was to have full self-government as regards internal affairs. Within six months the Republic was to be restored. The Royal Commission was to deal with Native districts and their protection, as well as compensation to either side for acts not justified by the necessities of war.

Although this was only a preliminary treaty, the seven thousand Boers at Laingsnek appeared content and began to prepare to disperse, longing for their farms and families. 'Not one of the Boer leaders,' J. F. van Oordt remarked in 1896, 'was as steadfast as Paul Kruger; only when he saw that he *had* to concede partly, did he do so, and to him personally the mild attitude of the Free State President was by no means agreeable. Indeed, after so many years one may assert, that had matters been left wholly in the hands of Paul Kruger and Dr Jorissen, better conditions would have been obtained from Sir Evelyn Wood or a decision would have been taken to resume the war.'[145] To Prof. D. W. Krüger in 1961 this *signed* preliminary treaty was a crowning achievement of Kruger's statesmanship.[146]

Ratification of the treaty (the contentious aspects will be dealt with as they arose) was received on 23 March, and Sir Evelyn Wood was a privileged spectator the next day when he attended a full Boer military parade on the battlefield before dispersal, for this was something which had rarely if ever been seen by a British commanding officer. Four thousand men took part, carrying their rifles in their right hands, an amazing spectacle of pastoral men who were born soldiers. Evelyn Wood and Piet Joubert shook hands, the Triumvirate spoke in turn, and then Joubert gave the dismissal. Within a matter of hours all the Boers were gone, seeming to vanish into the veld. Kruger, though exhausted by those strenuous weeks and yearning for his family, was not so fortunate as to vanish with them, for as Vice-President it was his duty to assemble the Volksraad at Heidelberg.

'With a feeling of gratitude to the God of our fathers,' he said with visible emotion on 15 April, 'who has been near us in battle and danger, it is to me an unspeakable privilege to lay before you the Treaty . . .' He then went on to make one of his 'most notable utterances', in the opinion of Dr Manfred Nathan,[147] one which many writers from both sides have preferred to ignore: 'I consider it my duty plainly to declare before you and the whole world, that our respect for Her Majesty the Queen of England, for the Government of Her Majesty, and for the English Nation, has never been greater than at this time, when we are enabled in this treaty to show you a proof of England's noble and magnanimous love for right and justice . . .' He went on to avow his faith in the Royal Commission and expressed his desire for a peaceful and obedient people, with a progressive government. From his side too Kruger was responsible for the coining of a new word, 'Majubanimity', soon a term of scorn among the British.

'It is better to receive half an egg than an empty shell,' was the opinion of General Joubert. For a further six months the Union Jack was still to wave over over the beloved land. This could be endured, but the Royal Commission had to be watched. Kruger knew that the removal of an inch of land would unleash a fresh storm. It is unlikely that he knew of Queen Victoria's displeasure over the outcome, but he must have realized that Gladstone showed remarkable strength of character in granting the Transvaalers their heartfelt wish in the face of a storm of disapproval and when British military prestige in South Africa had been reduced to what it was. Anxiously Kruger awaited 30 April 1881—the first meeting of the Royal Commission at Newcastle in Natal.

Others also watched in painful suspense for different reasons. Already on 11 April, S. J. Meintjes had written from his farm Arcadia (which was to become one of Pretoria's best-known suburbs) to his son Dr S. J. Meintjes, in English :

> We have been in Camp besieged for 103 days when Peace was proclaimed, the further terms are not known to us. It is to be settled by a Commission. There are so many rumours afloat that one does not know what to write or say. Some say the Country is to be given up or at least annexation rescinded, others that we will agree to a free Constitution under British rule, others that the Country will go back and the Republican Government again established, then that a piece will be cut off from the 30th degree from S. to N. with the Republic but a small piece, hemmed in all round, the Boers swear they will then have a second fight, and we will see, God knows what the upshot will be.
>
> One thing is certain, the English have had a most shameful licking three times running—and that England's prestige is not worth a straw, and if she gives up the country as it is said she will, then I for one will never believe in anything she says.
>
> For her Ambassador said as long as the sun is in Heaven the Country will never be given back, which now appears bombast and a direct lie—what is to become of the loyals—I am just ruined all over again, and the picture I hung up to myself, to sell Arcadia and go back to you has become a soap bubble . . . I am of opinion that peace won't last. Why not have given the people the promises made at the Annexation [autonomy] and all would have been well,

> but instead of that they have been tampered with and an Autocratic Rule established. If England wants to make the Transvaal one of the finest and most prosperous countries, she must maintain her rule here under an elected Volksraad by the people, by withdrawing her rule the Banks will close and the whole of the Country plunged into downright dire misery which I am afraid my countrymen[148] cannot see, they have been grossly misled by their leader . . .[149]

Sir Theophilus Shepstone was still upset a decade later. 'The Boers did not really want to fight,' he wrote to Rider Haggard, 'and we are always pusillanimous enough before we make up our minds to begin, so we did not want to fight either, but it appears that the Home Government did want to undo the annexation. Nothing could have been done more easily, or have looked more gracious to those concerned. Why not have plainly told me their wish and authorized me to carry it out? We should have parted with embraces and the best of mutual good feeling; as it is, we have earned the contempt as well as the hatred of the Boers, and very much puzzled the native races . . .'[150] For Shepstone the retrocession was the final humiliation.

To newspapermen Kruger expressed his dismay over the British attitude towards Majuba. 'People say we think we conquered the English . . .' He paused, blowing out a cloud of smoke, then continued in his forcible way, voluble and prone to gesture: 'We think that the English did not know what were the wishes of our people when they took the country away from us. Then we said, we will show them that we do love our country. We knew that England was much stronger, but we said, sooner than have our country taken away from us unjustly, we will fight until we die. Then the English people saw that they were in the wrong, and they gave us back our country.'[151] Many years later Paul Kruger was moved to remark that the only England he cared to remember was that of William Ewart Gladstone.

CHAPTER ELEVEN

Retrocession

The only South African on the Royal Commission was Sir Henry (later Lord) De Villiers (1842–1914) who always strove for total impartiality towards Boer and Briton. At Newcastle he, Sir Hercules Robinson (later Lord Rosmead) and General Sir Evelyn Wood began their sessions by dealing with the people who claimed that they had suffered losses through Boer depredations. The beginnings of their work only indirectly touched Paul Kruger, and there was comfort for him in the restraining influence of De Villiers and the commission's adviser, President Brand, on Sir Evelyn Wood who was keen to claim a large part of the eastern Transvaal. In the wetness of the Drakensberg, Kruger had contracted a cold and was later confined to bed with pneumonia as the members of the commission resumed sessions at Pretoria which were to lead up to the signing of the Convention of Pretoria, in the drafting of which Sir Henry de Villiers played the leading role.

As the Liberal Party felt concern for the lot of the Natives, they felt more at ease having a permanent Resident or Agent at Pretoria to whom appeals could be made. Suzerainty, a nomenclature to be dragged up with monotonous frequency in the future, meant in the main control over the Transvaal's external affairs. Kruger did not like the new fashion of referring to his country as the Transvaal State, for to him the name South African Republic held a particular significance.[152] But he had to bide his time for the changes he wished to see made. The session of the commission at Pretoria lasted some three months, all their decisions being referred to Downing Street for approval. The more Kruger reflected on their work, the more obnoxious he began to find the idea that they had regained their freedom subject to British Suzerainty. The British were welcome to their Resident at Pretoria, surely no more than a kind of glorified ambassador, but to be hamstrung in their relations with foreign powers was a serious matter.

The performance of Sir Evelyn Wood in the prelude to the signing of the Convention (it still had to be ratified) showed that he felt he had a score to settle with the Boers, while Sir Hercules Robinson hardly opened his mouth. On 3 August 1881, and about time too it was felt, the document containing thirty-three articles was signed by the members of the Royal Commission, General Joubert and M. W. Pretorius. Kruger was still confined to bed but determined to attend the official retrocession. Many agreed with the *Volksstem* that the new Convention had apparently been drafted 'for the benefit of the Kaffirs', one of the articles being that Chief Sekhukhune, overpowered and incarcerated by the British, had to be released. There were other things too that tickled the Boer sense of humour, but they felt insulted when Sir Hercules, in an address to an assembly of Native chiefs and their escorts, said that slavery in any form whatever would not be tolerated. As the British military band then struck up with *Ten Little Nigger Boys*, the High Commissioner's speech rather lost impact.[153]

Although far from well, Kruger prepared for the official retrocession on Monday, 8 August. An armed mounted escort set out to meet the Vice-President and Eduard Bok, his State Secretary. People had been pouring into Pretoria for days, outspanning their wagons on the squares and other open places, law and order being maintained by Assistant Commandant-General Hendrik Schoeman and the men under his command. But there were no wild scenes, the hoisting of the Vierkleur after four years was far too solemn an occasion for demonstrations. The British element in Pretoria mistook this solemnity for lack of enthusiasm; they were still beyond grasping what this segment of Africa meant to these people.

The main function was on the stoep of the Treasury Building, and Kruger, in his address to the crowd, spoke with surprising brevity. They were not there for self-aggrandizement, he said, but in humble gratitude to God for His blessing. Kruger apologized for feeling too unwell to say more, so Pretorius spoke and the flag was raised. Speeches by Bok and Joubert followed, and there was a service of thanksgiving in the afternoon. The British garrison was tactfully confined to camp, and there were also no incidents from that quarter, except from an unidentified man found in the evening trying to sever the cord which held the Vierkleur aloft. This was in a way symbolic of the Transvaal in the second half of 1881. Whatever jubilation was felt was not generally shared. As has been shown, from the economic viewpoint some leading Afrikaners even saw the retrocession as a disaster. But the date was significant—as was pointed out by the Rev. Mr H. S. Bosman—it being the 38th anniversary of the Voortrekker abandonment of Natal.[154]

It has been made clear by now that Kruger was never vindictive.

And from him and a man like Joubert flowed a large measure of the cordiality towards the British and 'disloyal' Afrikaners who were to remain in their midst. There was no interference with their property and there was no victimization. Even men who had borne arms against the Boers were to become members of the Volksraad, R. K. Loveday, F. Watkins, E. P. A. Meintjes and C. Jeppe, men who were to play a significant but little-advertised role in the life of Kruger. It was due to this peaceful reconciliation, Carl Jeppe was to point out, that so many old opponents 'threw in their lot without doubt or hesitation, and almost to a man, with the Republic' on the outbreak of the Second Boer War.[155] But we are dealing with the First, the war which changed the entire course of South African history and makes a fresh look at Paul Kruger imperative.

'Be faithful but trust nobody,' he was to say henceforth. Van Oordt endorses it, adding that also from now on the retention of their independence was to be the all-consuming passion of Kruger's life.[156] Nobody can write on him without studying Van Oordt's *Paul Kruger en de Opkomst van de Zuid-Afrikaansche Republiek*, a tome running to 904 pages (not indexed; not translated into English), and on the various occasions I have gone through it, I have often wondered if Kruger ever read it, while I am sure that General Joubert did. Johan Frederik van Oordt (1856–1918) also wrote voluminously under the pseudonym D'Arbez and in English as James King Hill in younger days. His study of Kruger (considered his masterpiece though remote from the art of biography) has particular value in that Van Oordt repeatedly interviewed the President in the course of writing it and had access to many State documents up to 1897. Van Oordt's extraordinarily long pointed ears must have caused Kruger intense amusement ('D'Arbez' was derived from zebra), and it was well known that this frail, industrious little man was an alcoholic.

The next step in Paul Kruger's career, as he knew to be inevitable, would be his election as State President. Although he loved farming, public duties had become so overwhelming that he could no longer have Boekenhoutfontein as his headquarters. He was nearly fifty-six and looked it, though he showed little loss of energy. All that travelling to and from Pretoria took up too much time. So the farming was handed over to his son Piet, and Kruger and Gezina made their final move to the town that August. The Kruger house still in existence on the western part of Church Street (by then already turning into one of the longest streets in the country) is within easy walking distance of Church Square.[157] Apart from the large trees which lined the stoep, and minor alterations, the Kruger home is still much as it was built for him.

Here Gezina Kruger was to live for the rest of her days, never complaining and always doing something. She was becoming more and more stout, her face round like a bun in which her eyes gleamed like currants. At the back of the house she kept her own cows. Fresh vegetables, meat and oranges came from Boekenhoutfontein, either sent or collected, for their ties with the farm were to remain. Mrs Kruger rarely went out, only perhaps to attend the Dopper church opposite her home. In 1896 the old church was replaced by the one which still exists, the church where Kruger often used to preach.[158] Gezina Kruger was so rarely seen that many people who lived in Pretoria for years never clapped eyes on her. But he was seen everywhere.

It was about this time that Kruger shaved off his moustache and most of his beard, leaving a kind of fringe around his chin. Bagginess under the eyes was growing, but the eyes were still fine, the gaze penetrating. The mouth revealed was resolute, the droop to the lower lip more pronounced. In appearance he was again reminiscent of the Voortrekkers of yore, and this might have been deliberate, for the shaven mouth was unusual at that time. (Lord Kimberley also shaved his upper lip but not his chin.) More than ever the face of Kruger was not easily forgotten, and the gleam of humour in the eyes the most favourably remembered. The days of carriages and coaches to his office were still to come, so many watched the large man striding along Church Street with the gait of a farmer.

His days followed a fairly set ritual when he was home. Grace was always said before and after meals, women not wearing bonnets being required to place their serviettes over their heads. Gezina was never seen without a bonnet. Kruger rapped on the table, surveyed everybody there, and said : 'Let us pray.' This he did in High Dutch, and at length. For luncheon a typical menu was stewed meat, baked sweet potatoes, potatoes done with the meat, samp (a form of maize) and stewed peaches with raisins. For dessert there were preserved peaches with custard, followed by coffee. Always beside Kruger was a bowl of bread in milk.[159] His partiality for milk has been remarked upon—all his life he was never to feel comfortable until he had had his bowl of bread and milk, even in exile, a habit he probably acquired from the Native herdboys with whom he grew up. Kruger was partial to milk food of all kinds, particularly flakes or *snysels.*

Although their house, built by James Clark, was not as grand in any way as some of the stately homes, like Melrose House, to rise in Pretoria, it was comfortable and had room enough, not being a cottage or bungalow as some describe it. To Gezina it was perfectly adequate. A granddaughter described her as quiet, sympathetic and loving, and recalled how hard she had worked in the Boekenhoutfontein days when Kruger was often away for such long spells and she had to keep her eye on all the farming activities, including sugar and coffee plantations, the making of candles and soap. Morally she was just as strong as her husband, of whom she had an instinctive understanding; she always understood problems, and never left anyone in the lurch—even if they had brought disaster upon themselves—and could only be loved for her generosity and total unselfishness.[160]

It was usual for the entire family to retire very early and to rise at dawn. After early morning coffee, Kruger moved out to the stoep where callers were already assembling. Gezina sent out trays laden with coffee and rusks, often to some forty men at that early hour. This session over, family prayers would follow, psalms being sung to the music of an organ played by one of the children. The whole house was permeated with the aroma of coffee and things baking as Gezina bustled about. Under her bonnet trimmed with lace and ribbon she wore her hair parted in the middle and in a bun. To church she wore satin and lace, and black low-heeled shoes, taking a seat beside her husband on special chairs which always stood ready for them. But even to cross the street was to become too much for her because of increasing corpulence. A woman was engaged to help her with dressing and baths, and in her own little parlour she received, her hands always busy doing something. Gezina's needlework was considered exquisite, and it might be from her that some children and various grandchildren inherited decided artistic gifts.*

The bustle of valets, maids, secretaries, grooms, coachmen, postilions, guards and so on was still to come, but made no difference to the Krugers. In the house Gezina was only seen when fully dressed, and then there would be the baking of cake, bread and rusks, the making of sausage and biltong, jams, dried fruit and all the usual products of farmers' wives everywhere during the different seasons. Once Kruger had a steady salary, his wife was paid a monthly allowance, and from this she was always ready to help the needy. She also dealt with the formidable Paul on behalf of others. She was not in the least scared by him, and he clearly hated to deny her anything, even when it was to help an undeserving child or grandchild.

* One of them was the sculptor Fanie Eloff.

It has been observed that the Paul Kruger of 1881 was not the same man as he had been in 1877.[161] He had become self-confident, the earlier feelings of unworthiness and incompetence having left him. Kruger certainly needed his new assurance, for the immediate consequence of the retrocession was an economic slump, and as Carl Jeppe observed, Pretoria was not a happy place. 'The banks, established during the interregnum, initiated a policy of scuttle and run; they called in all outstandings, and ruthlessly enforced their claims. This was followed by the withdrawal of much other capital invested there. The value of property depreciated to an alarming extent. The large sums spent by the British garrison and the well-paid officials no longer found their way into the till of the shopkeeper. The Transvaal Government was soon on the verge of bankruptcy . . .'[162]

Kruger's first concerns were finance, education and Native affairs. For four years hardly any attention had been given to education. And it was true that finances were just about as bad as in the time of Burgers. As extraordinary circumstances demand extraordinary measures, to quote Kruger, the Triumvirate somehow hit upon the idea of granting monopolies. This was done in good faith in order to make some quick money by men who were not economists and only with the best of motives. One wishes that someone could have given them better advice. At a meeting of a newly elected Volksraad on 21 September 1881, Kruger referred to a commission to see to the needs of the widows and orphans of some fifty men slain in the war, as well as of the dependants of the wounded. He then went on to a revision of the taxation system, the problem of the national debt and the granting of monopolies in order to boost industry. He felt the need to create a State Artillery, and they had to have a superintendent of education, a properly qualified man, imbued with Christian principles.

This personage had already been found, and introduces the Rev. Mr S. J. du Toit (1847–1911) of Cape Colony to Transvaal history. He was indeed a capable man and of great energy (almost too much so) whom Kruger had met back in 1873 when Du Toit had visited Rustenburg as a student of divinity. The slender young man with his glowing dark eyes and lively personality had impressed Kruger, perhaps also because of his hostility towards President Burgers. Notice was taken later of Du Toit's passionate pro-Republican stand when he edited the first Afrikaans newspaper, *Die Patriot*, at his hometown Paarl in the Western Cape. Du Toit was an innovator in many spheres, the founder of an important political movement called the Afrikaner Bond, a Bible translator, a leader of the first movement for the recognition of Afrikaans as a language in its own right, and he also made a name for himself as a prolific and versatile author. When Kruger invited him to become their superintendent of education, Stephanus Jacobus du Toit (whose political aspirations were not yet known) accepted joyfully.

At the Volksraad session the next day, the Convention of Pretoria came up for discussion in a heated way, for several members could not reconcile themselves with it. 'You may choose,' Kruger said quietly, 'either to approve the Convention or to return to Laingsnek.'[163] He naturally agreed that some of the terms were unsatisfactory, but in his opinion the Triumvirate had signed out of love for the Fatherland and in concern for the welfare of South Africa as a whole. Argument before ratification was to continue until 25 October, and even then considerable resentment remained, for Gladstone did not see his way clear to modify suzerainty in such a way that it meant not to control but merely to keep an eye on foreign affairs. Nor did he feel free to curtail the powers of the Resident by making him merely a representative of the Queen. There also appeared to be no question of paying compensation for a take-over of Swaziland, which the Boers looked upon as part of their domain, and the territory retained by the British to the west. Many burghers were keen to resume the war, and Sir Evelyn Wood in Natal would have welcomed it.

Monopolies, concession, education, a State Artillery, telegraphic communication and the passionate dream of a railway to Delagoa Bay—such matters took up the rest of 1881. Concern also remained about Native unrest to the north and the west. It was Kruger's proposal that 16 December should, as the Voortrekkers had vowed at the time of the Battle of Blood River in 1838, be made a national day of thanksgiving—at Paardekraal. The first festival on a national scale was arranged from the 13th to the 16th, and large crowds came, gathering around the pile of stones heaped there prior to the war. The well-known monument over an increased pile of stones was erected eight years later, Kruger speaking there every five years, like a prophet, with countless allusions to God, the Lord and the Bible, all their woes and joys being seen in terms of God's punishment or blessing.[164] Even Kruger stalwarts had to admit that these speeches could become most wearisome.

The most active person in the Triumvirate in the first half of 1882 was General Piet Joubert, for it was his task to deal with various rebellious chiefs in the south-western regions. Rumour had it that the members of the Triumvirate were not on the best of terms, and the general feeling was that the time was right for a new State President. One of the names put forward was that of the Cape politician, Jan Hendrik (Onze Jan) Hofmeyr as he had resigned from the ministry of Sir Thomas Scanlan. The Cape Afrikaners had no intention of losing Hofmeyr, and the Transvaal did not really want him. Both Kruger and Joubert, after seeing much of Hofmeyr while in Cape Town in 1880, had had their confidence in him shaken when he failed to take a more positive stand in their independence agitation. But Hofmeyr was a great man, and his young kinsman with the same name must have speculated a good deal when he wrote his biography what would have been the course of South African history had Onze Jan become President of the Transvaal. Hofmeyr found it necessary to publish a denial of his candidature in the *Volksstem*.[165]

Politically Hofmeyr's destiny was tied up with Cape Colony, and particularly the Afrikaner Bond. This society, formed in 1876, developed from the Farmers' Defence Association, aimed at a South Africa united in the interests of its own people, with its own flag, defensively and protectively Dutch. Du Toit's hostility towards the British connexion was not felt by Hofmeyr, his successor as leader, who was more interested in influencing than capturing government.[166] The Afrikaner Bond tried hard to spread its wings throughout South Africa but, despite General Joubert's support, it never particularly took root in the Transvaal, perhaps because Kruger found its interests too wide-flung at a time when he was totally obsessed with whatever pertained to his South African Republic.

Joubert had begun an endless bombardment of the Volksraad with letters, and one of 4 July was particularly notable.[167] As federation with the Free State, he said, now appeared to be out of the question, and as a continued existence of a Triumvirate could create dissension, he felt that what was needed was a return to the old Constitution and the election of one Head of State. There was already talk of a Kruger Party and a Joubert Party, with some people eagerly awaiting a new outbreak of discord which could wreck everything. Personally, said Joubert, he did not want the office of State President for himself, but he was ready to give full support to the candidature of S. J. P. Kruger who was already their Vice-President. Joubert's writing is often so involved that it has to be rephrased, but this was more or less what he said. And about his sincerity on this occasion, I have dealt in my Life of him.* The idea of writing such a letter at that time almost certainly came from Dr Jorissen.

* See my biography, *The Commandant-General*, p. 27.

On the day Joubert's letter was read and discussed, Kruger was absent, but he was there the next day when the minutes were read and the letter repeated. When he rose to comment, Kruger said that his main concern was that it should not appear as if there was discord among the Triumvirate. He was sure that General Joubert had not meant to imply this. As to the desirability for a State President, Kruger was in full accord. So was the Volksraad, and a unanimous decision for an election was taken. The campaign began on 15 January 1883 and was concluded on 15 February. As Kruger was to have Joubert's support, Kruger was ready to give him his.

As Vice-President, Kruger had begun to calculate every word he uttered for his local audience and now for an international one. Should he be elected, he declared, 'God's Word should be my rule of conduct in politics and the foundation upon which the State must be established. The promotion of agriculture; the opening up of fresh sources of the country and their exploitation through the creation of new industries; railway extension towards the east; restrictions on immigration—' He paused, with a smile. 'I apprehend the least danger from an invasion from Holland . . .' But there had to be some restriction—or control, he could have added—for this was to be much on his mind 'in order to prevent the Boer nationality from being stifled'. He wanted 'a friendly attitude towards England and a closer alliance of the South African States; the maintenance of the authority of the Government towards the Natives and the friendly treatment of obedient Native races in their appointed districts; the furtherance of all efforts which would bring the life of the people under the influence of the Gospel, *and above all*, the advancement of instruction for the young . . .'[168]

Kruger's replies to requisitions were amplifications of the various aims he had for his 'Theocracy' which made some people think of the one that had once held sway in Israel.[169] Oddly enough, he showed a greater awareness of the Native Question than his successor, General Louis Botha, was to do, but then Botha's primary concern was inevitably the reconciliation of the two white races after a devastating war. Kruger wished to follow General Hendrik Potgieter's aim of seeing the various tribes in their own reserves, and believed that through orderliness, industry and piety the Native could become a happy and contented subject of the Republic. 'The one,' Kruger said, 'who found a suitable solution for the Native problem would be the greatest benefactor of South Africa.'[170] As the rebellious Chief Mapoch was just then the topic of the day, the subject was very much on Kruger's mind, and he knew well enough to what degree incitement of Natives within and along the borders was due to elements hostile to the Republic.

The election was curious in that the opposing candidates handed in requisitions and voted for each other. Joubert was always to overrate his own popularity, but he undeniably had a strong following and from among the best brains in the country. Joubert was realistic and enlightened, and in time he was to be referred to as progressive, his followers inevitably becoming 'Progressives'. Though some outstanding men were among them, the hard core of the Transvaal never forsook Kruger. The War of Independence had brought Joubert far more fame than Kruger, and accordingly general esteem in the Transvaal, but when the election results came, there were 3,431 votes for Kruger, 1,171 for Joubert. The Lion of Rustenburg was not surprised, and with quiet dignity prepared to don the green Sash of State, emblazoned with the Transvaal coat of arms, over his left shoulder.

Once he had made up his mind, Paul Kruger was not easily swayed. Christianity was to be the fundament of his State. I have already referred to his religious tolerance, something he has not often been credited with. His was a Christian State, but all were welcome to it, and he never lost patience with anyone on religious grounds, believing that they all worshipped the same God in their various ways. Among his closest friends were Jews and Roman Catholics, even the Free Thinkers of the era. He was very much like an orthodox Jew himself, and this may in part explain the fascination he had for men like Alois Nellmapius and Samuel Marks. The motto of the Orange Free State was Freedom and Immigration; Kruger too wanted immigration, but a steady and selected influx. The foreign *invasion* which had already begun posed problems of fairness for all if the voice of the people was to remain the voice of the State. The authority of the people rested on justice and independence—and his obsession with the concept of independence was, as some thought, to work like a madness in his brain.[171]

'What impressed me most,' Dr J. W. Leyds, successor to Jorissen, was to remark, 'was his dignity.' Now Leyds was a most polished and dignified man, learned and sophisticated, who was to work with Kruger from day to day for nearly fifteen years. The picture Leyds gives of the Boers and particularly of Kruger is very different from the grotesque portrayals that were to become so commonplace. 'It was typical of the Boers in those days,' Leyds told Kees van Koek, they were very well-mannered. Nobody would for example dream of entering anybody's house with his pipe in his mouth . . . Paul Kruger's name and fame he made himself . . . It is sometimes said that he was illiterate. This is of course nonsense . . . He was certainly not learned, but he had a thorough knowledge of many things. It was customary for him to sit with his eyes closed, listening to bills and memoranda as they were read to him, and years later he could still recall the smallest detail and alteration, for his memory was amazing . . .

Then too he was not narrow-minded. His inclination was to be liberal, an enlightened man, in politics as well as in matters relating to religion.

Leyds explained that he had refused to have his own children baptized, and Kruger never held it against him. When circumstances necessitated it, Kruger even condoned work on Sunday—large of him as a Dopper. 'He could be as refined as a woman in small attentions. Although he and his pipe were inseparable, he never smoked when I was with him, for he knew that it affected my throat. Although a devoted family man, he would not allow any of his sons to enter the civil service. His honesty was like the Bible. Once he got up in the middle of the night to come to my house to tell me that he had done me an injustice. He refused to use any information he had against his enemies dating from the years of friendship, and he was utterly loyal to his officials. In his own office he would blast them, but in the Volksraad he stood by them to the man.'

Leyds went on to speak of Kruger's never-ending concern about the disunity among his people. 'But he was clever enough not to go too fast. He always made sure first that his people followed him, and he never over-shot his target . . .' Leyds spoke of Kruger's large-heartedness, and recalled the time when he returned from Europe and the bulky personage awaited him on the Pretoria railway station, a signal honour indeed. Kruger took Leyds to his home in his carriage, taking both his hands in his as they drove along. 'Doctor,' he said, 'I miss you so much, and while you were away I prayed for you every day. You know, your blood is warm, and so is mine, and when we touch the sparks fly . . .' Leyds could only wonder who could not love such a man.[172]

But what Leyds, and later General Smuts, saw was one side of the picture. A study of Kruger the man moves between extremes, from saint to snuffy mendacious savage. Onze Jan Hofmeyr showed the balanced view in honouring him primarily for 'the love he ever displayed for his land, his people, his language, for his national and ecclesiastical institutions' and could only admire Kruger for 'his unbending will-power, his unlimited courage, his unshaken faith, his deep religious feeling, his faithfulness unto death . . .'[173] E. B. Iwan-Müller gave what he thought an objective assessment:

> Nothing could be more grotesque than the soubriquet, bestowed on him by his admirers, of 'the South African Bismarck' . . . In the lower spheres of diplomacy Mr Kruger was a master. He was quick in detecting the false moves made by his opponents, and an adept in turning them to his own advantage; but of the large combinations he was hopelessly incapable. To secure a brilliant and conspicuous success today he was ready to squander the prospects of the future, if, indeed, he had the power of forecasting them. He was what I believe soldiers would call a brilliant tactician, but a hopeless strategist.[174]

CHAPTER TWELVE

First Presidency

On 9 May 1883, Paul Kruger ascended a platform in front of the orginal Government Building on Church Square in Pretoria. Apart from the Vierkleur, there were the flags of England, the Netherlands and the United States of America. There were two guards of honour of infantry and cavalry. Members of the Volksraad and other dignitaries took their seats, while the Rev. Mr Bosman glanced at his notes for the induction prayer. A large crowd thronged the sombre square which was now brightened up with flashes of colour and there was a general feeling of festivity. Everybody fell silent as the ceremony began, horses snorting and stamping. As he delivered his inaugural speech, Kruger spoke slowly and clearly.[175] The odd observer, perhaps because High Dutch was an effort to one who normally spoke Afrikaans, thought he had a speech defect. The conclusion of his speech was greeted by a gunfire salute. Other speeches, including one by the British Resident Rutherfoord, followed.

Kruger's public image was first groomed by Dr Jorissen, later by Dr Leyds—his dress, the trappings of his entourage, even his style, if one may call it that. For the rest he remained a simple man, determined to be easily accessible to all whose intentions were honourable. The Jorissen–Bok–Leyds combination (Dutch protocol, I believe, being among the strictest known) could not in any way interfere with his easy manner towards people. He was a Transvaaler and belonged to the Transvaal; that was one reason why he maintained his political ascendancy, despite mounting criticism and waning popularity—no mean feat, Prof. J. S. Marais decided, when these adverse tides were only to be expected in the life of a political figure, and among such rugged individualists.[176]

Marais was ready to see Kruger as a typical Boer 'but no ordinary specimen of the type'. Everybody has to acknowledge that. One can challenge the idea whether his republic was really a theocracy, and whether the Bible played the role it did or was merely a useful instrument of statecraft. Like all major politicians, Kruger was a superb actor, but even men of genius can have a curious simplicity if not childishness, and there is no reason to think that he did not believe implicitly that God had marked him for His own. Those who could not believe such a concept possible in a man of the nineteenth century called him a sixteenth-century zealot.

As Kruger assumed office the two topics of the day were new gold discoveries near present Barberton and the murder of Chief Sekhukhune by his half-brother Mampuru. The richness of the new gold discoveries caused a fresh influx of foreigners and a new community of diggers. 'This gold is still going to soak our country in blood,' General Joubert prophesied many times. When Kruger expressed his concern to him over the ever-increasing foreign population, Joubert said he could as well try to push back the ocean as stop it. Sekhukhune who had been set free the previous year had clearly been sincere in professing that he would henceforth be loyal to the Republic. But then on 18 August 1882, he, his son and thirteen followers were butchered. Mampuru tried to escape arrest by fleeing to the neighbouring tribe of Njabel (also known as Mapoch) who refused to give him up.

This was the usual code of honour, but such murders could not go unpunished, so General Joubert called up the burghers. For a change they came readily, some three thousand of them. At his reinstatement as Commandant-General, Joubert had protested once again that he was not suited for the office. At the same time it was flattering to him to hold such an important position, and also, after the shock of the outcome of the election, to be unanimously elected Vice-President. The Njabel or Mapoch campaign was again one of siege in cavernous terrain. President Kruger visited the commando in December and was impressed by Joubert's clever dispositions. Their relationship was friendly for a change, and Kruger readily agreed that their artillery left much to be desired and promised to order guns from the Free State and Cape Colony.

Not only was Njabel harbouring Sekhukhune's murderer, but he also refused to pay his taxes in such an insolent manner that he had to be brought to book promptly as an example to other tribes. Sir Garnet Wolseley had resorted to dynamite on his campaign, so Joubert followed his example in blowing up caves, something which was most repugnant to such a humane man. It was also essential to prove to the world that the Transvaal was strong enough to deal with insurrections within her borders. Nevertheless, this turned out to be the longest campaign of its kind in Transvaal history, fresh commandos having to be commandeered at intervals, as it lasted until July 1883 when Njabel and Mampuru surrendered. They were tried by Chief Justice J. G. Kotzé and sentenced to death, a sentence H.M. Government hoped to see commuted.

From the eastern Transvaal attention swung to the west where disputes between various chiefs dated back to the days of Hendrik Potgieter. It had since become the scene of considerable missionary activity and formed the base of many fortune-seekers and big game hunters, ivory still being in great demand. These chiefs called on the whites in their midst for assistance and offered them land as a reward. Many went, also Boers from the Transvaal and the Orange Free State, and such were the grants of land that they were to form two small fledgling republics given the names of Stellaland and Goshen. Such a development naturally brought no solution to the border disputes already in existence. As from 1881 these became serious, for the spotlight was thrown on the South African Republic's foreign relations.

Sooner or later this was bound to happen because of the clauses of the Pretoria Convention which Kruger had attacked and which had generally aroused criticism and resentment. As turbulence increased on the western border, the Volksraad decided to make an attempt to have some the clauses of the Convention revised. A deputation would be sent to London 'to endeavour to have the Convention of 1881 replaced by one more in harmony with the people', to quote Kruger.[177] It appears that he had surmised that there would be such a deputation, and he himself would be a member. The solution of the western border dispute, so unsatisfactorily handled by the Royal Commission, was also vital for the future of the region called Bechuanaland.

State Attorney Jorissen had been unwell for some time, so he was given leave to go to Europe for medical treatment and, while in London, to pave the way for the new deputation. Though Jorissen's mission was unofficial and at his own expense, he was given a courteous reception in London, Lord Derby listening attentively and sympathetically to what he had to say. The Secretary of State for Colonies agreed that the status given to the Transvaal State according to the Convention of Pretoria could hardly be considered satisfactory. As far as he was concerned, formal suzerainty for one thing could be waived. Also in London was Sir Hercules Robinson, and he supported Jorissen in his plea for a complete revision of the western border and a reduction of the national debt. Jorissen did good work. He had every reason to expect to be a member of the new deputation. Then like a bolt from the blue, while still in London, he received notice from the Transvaal of his dismissal as State Attorney. The new régime did not consider him suitably qualified for the office. To Jorissen, who knew nothing of the Rev. Mr Du Toit's plotting in conjunction with Justice Kotzé, the news was shattering.[178]

Why did Paul Kruger allow this to pass? He referred to the proceeding as discourteous and in the highest sense unjust, and also that he protested in vain. But surely he could have put up a stronger resistance? Van Oordt put the blame for Jorissen's brutal dismissal squarely on the Superintendent of Education, Du Toit, and made no reference to J. G. Kotzé who, as will be remembered, had first agitated against Jorissen in the days of Shepstone.[179] I have said earlier that Kruger was no hero-worshipper, but there is no denying that some men at various stages seemed virtually to mesmerize him. Du Toit had become one of them, not that Kruger yet grasped the extent of his political aspirations, his ambitions and dreams of glory.

In Du Toit's mouthpiece, *Die Patriot*, still being published at the Cape, there were fulminations against Jorissen which were largely libellous and considered disgusting (*walgelijk*). How much Kruger knew of all this one does not know. He could not go through all the newspapers himself, and only the information considered of interest to him was read by his secretaries. That Du Toit had gained a curious hold on him cannot be disputed, and the dismissal of Jorissen made it possible for Du Toit to become a member of the Deputation. General Nicolaas Smit, also a member, had become equally fascinated by Du Toit. As General Joubert was once again to be Acting State President in their absence, a job which elated him, he was indifferent to plots and intrigues which posed no threat to his position.

The Deputation prepared to leave for Cape Town via Kimberley on 18 August 1883. Kruger first put in an official appearance at Rustenburg, his main purpose being to beacon off a reserve for Chief Maghato in consultation with a new British Resident, George Hudson. There were flags, escorts, salutes, arches, processions, speeches, an official luncheon—a foretaste of what Kruger was henceforth to experience as Head of State. His second official function was to attend the opening of the Transvaal's first factory at Erasmusspruit, run by a friend and also one of the first concessionaires, Alois Hugo Nellmapius. This was a distillery, to be taken over by the firm of Lewis & Marks. A cold picnic luncheon was served with champagne and beer, and milk for the President.

It was an elegant function, for apart from the members of the Deputation (Kruger, Smit, Du Toit and the secretary Jan Eloff) various prominent persons, like General Joubert and Justice Kotzé, had been invited with their ladies. In his speech Kotzé declared that it was an honour to serve under a man of so much character as President Kruger. The 'liberal' side to Kruger was illustrated when he said that though he himself disliked liquor, he could not see its production as a sin, only its abuse. 'Drink is a gift from God,' Kruger continued, 'given to man for moderate consumption, and in that there is no sin.' On commando he had not forbidden the use of brandy, but drunkenness he had never tolerated. He could well understand that a drink after a hard day's work could be both refreshing and invigorating.[180] After the singing of Psalm 134, the members of the Deputation said their goodbyes and left by passenger coach. At all their stops they were fêted in a most heartwarming way.

There was a banquet at Kimberley, at Victoria West a railway saloon was put at their disposal by the Governor of the Cape, and receptions were held all the way to the Mother City. It was noted that Kruger was wearing a new suit and of better cut than usual, his beard was trimmed and his black boots shone. Only for the most formal occasions did he don his Presidential Sash (a costume, with some modifications, which was to be revived when a united South Africa became a Republic). Top hats, cigars and pipes, beards and frock-coats, swirling skirts, flowers, speeches, food and wine featured in their trip through the breathtaking Boland to Cape Town, where they were given a reception worthy of royalty and were put up at Government House.

The newspapers gave detailed descriptions of this progress, and on looking at the speeches one notes that the journalists were impressed by Kruger's references to them all as *sons of South Africa*, his belief in the necessity of unity between the colonies and states, their interdependence, need of co-operation and the welfare of South Africa as a whole. To underline it Kruger spoke of a direct railway line from Cape Town to Delagoa Bay as his ideal. Was this a new Kruger? I do not think so. Years before it had given him no effort of the imagination to see the Transvaal as part of a confederation, something the Annexation had ruled out, and to think of his country now as an integral part of South Africa was only common sense. But what Kruger had perhaps not revealed to the Cape Colonials before was his historical awareness, not only of what had gone before but what he was in fact trying to make.[181]

It appears significant that they sailed from Cape Town on the *Rosslyn Castle* on the President's 58th birthday.[182] In the party was an addition, the Rev. Mr D. P. Faure, a Free Protestant minister of Cape Town who had ben recommended as interpreter to Lord Derby by Sir Hercules Robinson. It is likely that Kruger did not at first approve of Faure, not so much because of his rather liberal religious views but on the grounds of what he had written on the Transvaal in the past. Feeling towards Faure was to become more cordial, and in his memoirs Faure gives a picture of Kruger sitting placidly on deck with his pipe and a bag of Transvaal tobacco at his side, studying the English language by reading a Bible printed in English and Dutch in double columns.[183] As diversion Kruger and Smit told hunting anecdotes, often hilariously, for the one tried to outdo the other in fantasy.

The voyage to Plymouth lasted nineteen days, and on disembarking there were a number of Afrikaner students from Edinburgh University to bid them welcome. Kruger was to find this a very different visit from his previous ones, for he was not on a begging mission; the world knew who he was, and he was President of a potentially wealthy Republic. But he could hardly expect the British to take him to their hearts. Queen Victoria shared the general disgust over the outcome of the war. She held that withdrawals always led to hasty improvised returns at enormous cost. 'To make peace immediately after a defeat like Majuba,' she declared, 'before honour had been retrieved, was especially short-sighted. I fear future difficulties are being laid up there. Above all, I loathe the idea of handing over African natives to the Boers, a most merciless and cruel neighbour, and in fact oppressor.'[184]

The new Lord Mayor of London simply ignored the Deputation, but the 15th Earl of Derby (E. H. S. Stanley) 1826–93, who had become Secretary of State for Colonies towards the end of the previous year, was courtesy itself. A real menace was the Rev. Mr John Mackenzie (1835–99) from Bechuanaland who was also in London and had set his heart on the extension of the British sphere of influence over the region. He was to fight any revision of the western border in the Transvaal's favour tooth and nail. Derby was indifferent, saying that as far as he was concerned Jorissen could have both the abandonment of the suzerainty and of the Convention. 'I think we should wash our hands of the Transvaal altogether.'[185] Sir Hercules Robinson, still in London, was ready to give advice and counsel restraint.

Kruger was not always on his best behaviour in the series of meetings at the Colonial Office and once, on his own admission, nearly knocked Sir Hercules down in front of Lord Derby when he thought himself insulted.[186] Sir Hercules apologized, and Kruger calmed down. They were to become good friends, the only High Commissioner with whom Kruger was to exchange private and confidential letters. Perhaps Kruger's irascibility can be ascribed to impatience after so many years of argument, to his sensitivity to anything that touched the Transvaal, and because he had had quite enough of fooling about with empty talk. The disgust felt at the retrocession grieved him. He was tired and irritable, and he was so depressed by the English winter weather that he preferred to remain in his hotel when the younger men went out sightseeing.

They were staying at the Albemarle which had become a kind of Boer–Afrikaner rendezvous. On arrival the Deputation was startled to find Dr Jorissen still installed there, and on the same floor. His dismissal needed some explaining, and Jorissen was determined to justify himself. Being snubbed, he used an intermediary until Kruger relented and had it out with him. This was not satisfactory, and Jorissen could only conclude that Du Toit, who had done his utmost to prevent his session with Kruger, was his arch-enemy and had a 'fatal' influence on the President.[187] Instead of returning to the Netherlands, Jorissen packed his bags for South Africa, determined to make his presence felt in Pretoria. His feelings of outrage were justified, for it was he who had put Derby in such an accommodating mood. On the other hand, Du Toit and Kotzé were not wrong in considering Jorissen unsuited to the office of State Attorney, though they also had political motivations.

The Convention of London was signed on Majuba Day, 27 February 1884. Except for the vexed western boundary line, now complicated by the German take-over of South West Africa, as well as John Mackenzie's hysterical outpourings in the Press, Faure considered the achievement of the Deputation as 'completely successful'.[188] The Transvaal State would again have its original name of South African Republic, the national debt had been reduced and suzerainty dropped painlessly. At for the western frontier where there was the traders' route to the north, Kruger naturally wished to draw full benefit from it for the Republic. One can hardly see this logical desire in terms of territorial expansion, not when various European powers annexed huge tracts of Africa as their whims took them. Kruger wanted the boundary as defined at Sand River in 1852 restored, but by this time the whole South African scene had changed so much that the possibility was becoming daily more remote.[189]

As their formal objective had been realized, though not fully, Kruger and his friends embarked on a triumphal progress (*zegetocht*) which left an indelible impression on them all. Lord Derby gave them a banquet, at Edinburgh they were given a rousing reception by the many

South Africans studying there, and at Birmingham Kruger was shown all the stages in the manufacture of a modern rifle. One of those who called on them was Sir Bartle Frere who left his card, Kruger being out, and who repeatedly tried to arrange a meeting. But Kruger did not want to see him, not knowing which Sir Bartle he would meet this time. Kruger was pleased, however, to meet again W. E. Gladstone who to his mind personified the concepts of justice and fair play ascribed to the British people. Hostility and disapproval were only to be expected, but there were numerous other interesting meetings and new friendships. They had a new secretary in the handsome young Boer Ewald Esselen, found in London, who had switched from medicine to law.

It was in a pleasant frame of mind that Kruger and his companions left for Rotterdam. Their reception in Europe was beyond all expectations. Throughout March one banquet followed the other, the stand of a handful of Boers against the British Empire having caused a sensation on the Continent. They were dined by the Prince of Orange and enthusiastically entertained by various festival committees as blood-relations in the Netherlands. '*Leve President Paul Kruger*!' was the roar in Amsterdam. Back in The Hague they were granted an audience with King William III and Queen Emma, Kruger wearing the Sash. Their Majesties, though stiffly formal, were clearly fascinated by these men, and particularly the rugged President Kruger. So too, but in a warmer manner, was the King of Spain when the party passed through Madrid on their way to Lisbon for a discussion of Delagoa Bay railway matters. There were fêtes all the way, and Kruger's glass of milk when it came to toasts became the accepted thing. Their main base was Amsterdam where Kruger felt so much at home that he made some speeches in Afrikaans, as also in Belgium where Flemish (not such a far cry from Afrikaans) was spoken.

It was a novel experience to be given an ovation by up to a hundred thousand people, but Kruger took it in his stride. His impassivity was misleading, for his eyes hardly ever missed anything. Notable too was the reception given them in France where the exploits of General Joubert had aroused much interest, and now there was Du Toit, also of French descent. Kruger was keen to negotiate a trade treaty with France. Back in Holland there were consultations with bankers for a Transvaal National Bank, and the foundations were laid for the Netherlands South African Railway Company, primarily to build the Delagoa Bay line. They also put out feelers for a new State Attorney. Various unsuccessful approaches ended when legal professors suggested one of their most brilliant students who had just completed his studies —Dr Willem Johannes Leyds.

He was only twenty-four, tall, fair and handsome, on the brink of his career, and he was by no means moved to transports of delight by the rather astonishing offer made him. His uncertainty is shown in that he was prepared to accept the office only provisionally for three years, and there was to be no lightning dismissal as in the case of Dr Jorissen. The only reason why Leyds accepted even provisionally was because of the impression Kruger made on him. A salary of £1,000 per annum and the opportunity of a perhaps unique experience were also not to be dismissed, as he explained to his fiancée who was opposed to the whole idea. That Kruger put such faith in young men was quite contrary to Boer tradition. It shows that brains meant more to him than years, and between him and Leyds there was to be such a peculiar chemistry that in time to come people were to say that the real Kruger was Leyds. And yet Leyds was a man of the world, fluent in Dutch, English, French and German, a polished diplomat, one of the best in his profession, and also a Free Thinker. 'Think what you like,' Kruger growled, 'as long as you do your duty faithfully and honestly . . .'

Kruger also met the King of Portugal, the Belgian royal family, the President of France and in Germany Kaiser Wilhelm and Bismarck on whom he made a great impression. Bismarck was ever after to have a soft spot for Kruger and paid high tribute to him. They were perhaps similar in many ways, even physically, except for Bismarck's small voice which surprised people in coming from such a large man. Then there were all their other learned and aristocratic hosts, with diversions such as a visit to the Opéra in Paris (*Sappho*) and the Plaza de Toros in Madrid where Kruger found the bullfight revolting.[190] In Portugal Kruger's first decoration was bestowed on him by the King, the Order of the Great Cross of the Immaculate Conception. In the fields of finance and diplomatic relations satisfactory arrangements were made and, having appointed Jonkheer G. J. T. Beelaerts van Blokland, the jurist who had accompanied them everywhere, Envoy Extraordinary and Plenipotentiary of the Republic at various Courts (he had declined the office of State Attorney), the Deputation sailed from Southampton and reached Cape Town on 11 July 1884.

'The independence of the land,' Kruger said in the Volksraad on the 28th, after a rousing progress to Pretoria, 'has in the first place been regained; the Suzerainty no longer exists, and the Republic has been admitted to the row of Nations . . .'[191] He had been away for nine months, had dined and wined with kings and the most learned of Europe, had gone through all the motions of a Head of State and been exposed to the cream of European culture. Roaring crowds, bands and speeches, flags and flowers, military parades (as in Germany), all the glitter and colour, palaces and churches, elegance and glamour—had it touched him at all? It did not appear so, and the glint of almost sardonic humour in his eyes was still there. His legend now embraced a whole new collection of anecdotes, humorous and mostly invented: that on presentation to Queen Victoria he had refused to bow, as he only bowed to God, and that at dinner he had poured his coffee into his saucer to cool it, and Her Majesty had followed suit.[192] Dining with Wilhelm I he had drained his finger-bowl, the Kaiser having no option but to do so as well. And so it went on, even total fabrications part of the price paid for fame.

A number of English writers tell a story that while in London the Deputation ran short of funds and were unable to pay their hotel bill. They appealed to a friend of theirs on the Stock Exchange, Baron Grant, who came to their assistance on condition that Kruger would publish an assurance that British settlers would be welcomed in the Transvaal and be given rights and protection. The Baron was particularly interested in the gold concessions of Lydenburg, and Kruger readily complied.[193] From this the naïve deduction was later made that the Uitlanders were there at Kruger's own invitation and were entitled to the rights he had promised in 1884. Dutch and Afrikaner biographers make no mention of this 'invitation', but it is found repeatedly in the mass of Rhodes literature.

Kruger had once again been impressed by the men which the Netherlands produced in the fields of theology, law and general education. Furthermore, the bulk of his people regarded the Netherlands as their mother-country, so it was the obvious place to find officials with the qualities so badly needed in the Republic. True, they could also be found in Cape Colony, and to a lesser extent in the Orange Free State. But these persons had all come strongly under the British sphere of influence, and instinctively Kruger felt that the mother-country supplied the better answer. This might also have been the influence of S. J. du Toit who believed that such a source could only strengthen Dutch Afrikanerdom. It has been suggested, by Van Oordt among others, that after their intimate months together, Du Toit's hold on Kruger was stronger than ever.[194] On the other hand, Kruger was merely following a policy begun by President Burgers, who had since died at Richmond on 9 December 1881.

Kruger's partiality for Hollanders was to come in for much criticism, by the British because it weakened their influence and by his own people because they found these Hollanders insufferable. They certainly gave themselves airs and looked down on everything pertaining to the Boer, even his tongue. Mrs Leyds went so far as to say that enlightened Cape Afrikaners were so ashamed to speak Afrikaans that they switched to English when talking to her.[195] It would be more correct to say that she, a snob if there ever was one, was so embarrassed by the Taal that she preferred speaking to Afrikaners in English. Kruger did not like the Hollander airs either, but he believed that the importation of officials from the Netherlands could only strengthen the Boer identity.

Many Cape Afrikaners were already semi-Englishmen, and with the tremendous influx of Uitlanders into the Transvaal—not that they were all British—all of them could turn 'English' without much effort. Men from the Netherlands would be less susceptible, apart from being better trained, and could, as some indeed did, bolster the Boer identity by giving him an awareness of his own cultural heritage. The idea of 'to each his own' which was to play such a significant role in South African politics and race relations began with Kruger.[196] But the rift between Afrikaner and Hollander was already there and only increased as the concept of Afrikanerdom grew. Kruger knew this also, so he did not dismiss Cape Afrikaners altogether, not if they were nationalists like Du Toit, and in time was even to prefer them to the 'detested' Hollanders.

During his presidencies Kruger was often to reflect on the tragic President Burgers. M. W. Pretorius, having been pensioned off, was still around but aroused little interest beyond being an ex-President and the son of Andries Pretorius. When Kruger gave his attention to immigration, education and the Delagoa Bay railway line, it was Burgers of whom he thought. 'Burgers dearly loved his land and people,' Kruger was heard to say, 'but was far ahead of his time.' As the years passed and his troubles grew, Kruger's sympathy for Burgers deepened, and he paid warm tribute to him at his reinterment which took place in Pretoria in 1895.[197] Even by 1884 nobody was permitted to speak of Burgers in Kruger's presence in a disparaging way, and it is not surprising if he had qualms of conscience, for he had had much to do with the downfall of the man who 'strove to erect a structure of marble, with no material in hand but clay, and no builders'.[198]

Since 1882 Kruger had looked with increasing alarm at the turbulence along his western border. 'Don't part with an inch of territory to the Transvaal,' an impassioned young man called Cecil John Rhodes had wired to Cape Town when the Transvaal–Bechuanaland border dispute again broke out. And back in the House he made his pronouncement: 'I look upon this Bechuanaland territory as the Suez Canal of the trade of this country, the key of its road to the interior . . .'[199] The outcome was that the Transvaal boundary was not relaxed and that a British Protectorate was proclaimed over the Bechuanas at the time of the signing of the Convention of London. The fate of Stellaland and Goshen was in the balance, and particularly when John MacKenzie was superseded by Rhodes as Special Commissioner.

Cecil John Rhodes had come to South Africa as a youngster to be cured of a tubercular tendency, ending up a multi-millionaire, Premier of Cape Colony and founder of a country. He was Kruger's junior by twenty-eight years, and was to develop into a large, clumsy-looking man, with striking eyes. Brilliant, simple in his tastes, grandiose in his visions, warm-hearted and yet totally unscrupulous, it is no wonder that there have been so many biographical studies of him and that they are still being written. This was a man who felt himself akin to the Emperor Hadrian, and as an organizer of British South Africa he probably was. Rhodes was to Oswald Spengler the first man of a new age, the first precursor of a Western type of Caesar, falling before maps into a kind of poetic trance.[200] His maps were of Africa and he wished to see them all in the red then used for the British Empire. All Kruger's aspirations for the independence of the Transvaal knew no more dangerous man.

The scramble for Africa was in full swing in 1884. Rhodes, having achieved his Bechuanaland Protectorate, wished to see the end to Stellaland and Goshen which fell inside it and which the Transvaal appeared likely to incorporate. While he was concentrating on his 'Suez Canal', the Germans proclaimed their Protectorate over South West, something which gave Kruger no particular concern. The Germans had always been kind to him, had given assurances of support, and he was after all of German descent himself. In August General Joubert was sent on an inspection of the western border, a meeting with Rhodes also being arranged. The General was in one of his grumpy phases. He had not approved of the Deputation to London, perhaps thinking it undignified. The latest Convention did not satisfy him, and he had snorted over the Deputation's glittering European tour—such a waste of money. Above all it was galling to be again second fiddle to Paul Kruger.[201]

On the other hand, he was able to act more freely. Joubert was always an exemplary Acting President, cautious not to put a foot wrong and very careful with expenditure. With Kruger back, he could be more venturesome and spoke freely to his cronies about the golden opportunities for expansion to the east and the west. Goshen and Stellaland should be snapped up, he felt, before they were incorporated into Bechuanaland. And to the east the same should be done to a new republic being envisaged there. This was land granted by Dinuzulu, the son of Cetywayo, to the Boers who had helped him to come to power. Joubert had already been invited to become President of this new republic, but while Kruger was away he did not feel entitled to any step beyond putting down a Native dispute in the Zoutpansberg. In future, he told the chiefs, they were to bring their grievances to the Government and not take the law into their own hands.

The Krugers moved into their new, and from now on their permanant, house in Church Street as Joubert was preparing to leave for the frontier. They gave a dinner on 14 August to celebrate the occasion. This is the house already referred to, one of South Africa's best-known museums. Joubert was off at the end of the month and began his tour of some weeks. He met Rhodes and saw him several times, at the 'capital' of Goshen called Rooigrond, at Lichtenburg and at a spot called Vrijwilligersrust on 25 September. Rhodes was equally keen to restore order between the 'volunteers' of the two 'republics' and the four chiefs involved, a confusing situation of split loyalties and personal aspirations.

Rhodes came to terms with Stellaland, but the Goshenites were defiant and up in arms against Chief Montshiwa who appealed to Joubert to be taken under the protection of the South African Republic. Rhodes naturally wanted Bechuanaland for England and he was not having any little republics blocking his canal to the north, one he saw reaching as far as Cairo. He tried to make his plans for the annexation of Bechuanaland more palatable by keeping the Imperial factor out of it, and warned against a second Majuba, the annexation having to come from Cape Colony. When Goshenite filibusters attacked Montshiwa at Mafeking, they were told that they were making war on the British Government.[202]

While Rhodes and Joubert were negotiating with each other and with everybody involved (claims and counter-claims of land, those wishing to be British subjects, Transvaal subjects or independent republicans), there came a surprise move from Pretoria, the outcome of a 'tremendous intrigue'.[203] On 16 September, Joubert received a Government despatch to say that he had to return to Pretoria immediately for his formal swearing-in as Commandant-General (he had recently been re-elected). To replace him as Special Commissioner at the border was the Rev. Mr S. J. du Toit who was already on his way. Two days later Kruger published a proclamation in which he, 'in the interest of humanity', took Chiefs Montshiwa and Moshete, at their request, under the provisional protection of his Government in order to put an end to bloodshed on the western border. With this proclamation Montshiwa's letter to Joubert in which protection was asked was published.

Joubert nearly had a seizure at the folly of this step which made an utter fool of him in his delicate negotiations with Rhodes. Joubert at once sent in his resignation as Commandant-General. He knew that Du Toit had been plotting against him for some time, in the same way as he had got Jorissen out of the way, and this whole new intrigue smelt of Du Toit—since when had Kruger ever referred to the interests of humanity? It was soon perfectly obvious. Eyes aglow and bursting with expansionist and political zeal, Du Toit turned up at Rooigrond where he made a fiery speech on 3 October, and then with a 'theatrical gesture' [204] hoisted the Vierkleur and renamed the place Heliopolis. Kruger had not realized that Du Toit would go as far as that and, shaking off his mesmerism, ordered the immediate striking of the flag. Its implications were so serious that he telegraphed rather frantically to Lord Derby on three successive days that the whole thing was just provisional and subject to Her Majesty's approval. A stunned silence was his only reply, while people streamed to meetings in Cape Colony.

On 8 October, Sir Hercules Robinson, outraged that Kruger's telegrams had gone over his head to Derby, called upon Kruger in the name of H.M. Government to disavow his proclamation as it was a violation of the Convention of 1884. Eight days later Kruger did so, saying that as his provisional proclamation had achieved its object in restoring peace to the border, the way was now open for the Governments concerned to come to a friendly arrangement for a durable peace. This was not enough for Robinson, for he put pressure on Derby to send a military expedition under Sir Charles Warren to Bechuanaland in order to expel freebooters, deal with robbers and to tidy up the border. Here then came the involvement of the Imperial factor which Rhodes had perhaps really tried to avoid. Warren

(1840–1927) at the head of four thousand regular troops and volunteers, as well as a Native corps, and accompanied by the detested John MacKenzie, set out for Bechuanaland in December.

There were some stormy scenes in Pretoria, for Joubert had also resigned as Vice-President and Superintendent of Native Affairs. He took care at first not to give any explicit explanation for his step, as he sensed tricks and traps everywhere. Du Toit had naturally been recalled, and Kruger had to bear full responsibility for what he had done. When Joubert felt more assured, he described Kruger's original proclamation as 'untimely and irresponsible'. The abrupt way in which he, Piet Joubert, had been replaced by an upstart like Du Toit was particularly infuriating, but Joubert calmed down when he realised that it was Du Toit who had lost patience and wanted the glory of territorial gains for himself. Joubert was equally ambitious in this connexion, though not as openly, but it was Kruger who could now be called a land-grabber by Rhodes, his friends and admirers. The myth of Kruger's territorial ambitions takes up an astonishing amount of space in Rhodes literature, particularly when there is no proof that he wanted anything beyond the restoration of the original western border and an outlet to the sea.

On 24 January 1885, Kruger met General Warren, ahead of his 'expedition', Cecil Rhodes and John MacKenzie at Fourteen Streams for a conference lasting two days on the border issue. This was the first time that Rhodes and Kruger met. They were all rather constrained, Rhodes towards the self-opinionated Warren as a representative of the Imperial factor, and Kruger towards MacKenzie as an enemy of the Boer people. Warren in his turn was disgusted by Rhodes's shabby appearance (he cared little for dress) and blunt manner, and Rhodes knew that MacKenzie should not have been present. Kruger, who had his new young State Attorney, Dr Leyds, in his party, apparently commented on Rhodes: 'That young man will cause me trouble if he does not leave politics alone and turn to something else. Well, the race-horse is swifter than the ox, but the ox can draw the greater loads. We shall see . . .'[205] On the British element Leyds made the odd impression of being a pleasant but a rather feeble Hollander.

Kruger told Warren that there was no necessity for a military expedition—four thousand men to drive out fifty, or even a hundred undesirables. He was worried by this large force which naturally excited his burghers, and he told his commandants to keep them quiet. Kruger dismissed the 'flag incident' as having taken place without his consent. All he wanted was law and order, and Warren was not to be provoked. 'Let there be no more talk of "Shoot the Englishman",' he told his men, 'or of "damned Englishmen". . . Let the burghers of the Transvaal and Land of Goshen guard their tongues as well as their actions, otherwise they'll pay dearly for their words . . .'[206] Transvaalers were to stay in the Transvaal, and wrongdoers among them could expect no mercy from him. If the Boers in Bechuanaland had had hopes that Kruger would stand by them and their claims, they now knew that he would not.[207]

At the conference itself, Rhodes was so conciliatory that he almost appeared pro-Boer. This was mainly because of Warren, and later on this general's antics made many question the balance of his mind. Rhodes said that the British themselves shared in the blame for the troubles on the border. He made some snide references to Joubert, having heard that there was not much love lost between the two Boer leaders. Kruger remained impassive, too much so in Leyds's opinion, for he made no objection when Rhodes proposed to send police over the border into the Transvaal after stock thieves. Kruger also agreed that the defining of the border should be left to two border commissioners. As Sir Charles Warren was still determined to have his expedition through Bechuanaland, Kruger showed some irritation in saying that it was both unnecessary and foolish. He then took his leave to proceed to Pretoria. A messenger was sent off to the Goshenites, who had hoped to become part of the Republic, to order them to get out if they knew what was good for them. Within a month there was hardly a white left in the region.

Bristling with self-importance, Warren proclaimed martial law and marched off, descending on an empty Land of Goshen. He caused trouble for Chief Khama, and proposed that only settlers of pure British blood were to enter Bechuanaland. Warren so alarmed and offended everybody, and the cost of his so-called 'expedition' was so enormous, that he was recalled.[208] It was a relief to Rhodes to have the blockage caused by Stellaland and Goshen removed. A link-up between the Transvaal and Germany across the Kalahari Desert had been forestalled (were there any such plans?). The southern part of Bechuanaland was now a Crown Colony, the northern part a British Protectorate. The scene was set for Rhodes's subsequent career, for Kruger showed scant interest in further developments to the west and even less north of the Limpopo—so much for his dreams of a Boer empire.[209]

Kruger's role in the western border issue came up for discussion in the Volksraad session of May. An uncomfortably familiar face was back in the ranks—Dr Jorissen, elected member for Pretoria some two months previously. He had many grievances to settle, first with Du Toit (fast losing favour and confidence through antagonizing Leyds), then with Kruger. When the President submitted his report, Jorissen was at once on the attack, causing Kruger to reply in mounting anger. Further argument was pointless. There was peace at last on the western border, and though Kruger had gained nothing, he had also lost little, except dignity and some of his political reputation—soon regained. Even Joubert relented and allowed himself to stand for Commandant-General once more. He was elected by an overwhelming majority and sworn in on 8 June. He was, however, no longer Vice-President, and this was to rankle, but at his swearing-in, Joubert and Kruger were on quite affable terms, having apparently ironed out their differences in private.

It was again a time of depression. The worst times the Transvaal had known economically were 1868, 1876 and 1885. Every time it was to appear as if they were really God's chosen, for when things appeared at their worst, the earth suddenly revealed riches—diamonds which, even if the British grabbed them, created markets; the first gold discoveries; and now, when things were so bad and within a matter of months, the greatest repository of gold in the world—not that the full extent was yet known. The gold discovered along the Witwatersrand in 1886 put the spotlight of the world on Paul Kruger.

CHAPTER THIRTEEN

Kruger and the Witwatersrand

Gold discoveries in the Transvaal date from 1852, but previous finds were nothing compared with the reef confirmed to be there in 1886. Kruger was directly informed of it in July of that year, and an affidavit was handed in by an Australian, George Harrison, to an official of the Department of Mines, in which he stated simply that he thought it a payable goldfield.[210] The news was out at once and prospectors streamed to the scene, outcrops being found over a distance of thirty miles. Kruger was petitioned to have the goldfields proclaimed, and this was done according to the Gold Law recently drafted by young Leyds. A site for a town was selected and given the name of Johannesburg, presumably after the veldcornet of the area, Johannes Petrus Meyer. On the other hand the name Johannes (John) was as common then as it is today.

Johannesburg rapidly became a city, the largest in southern Africa. It has been rebuilt several times in the course of its history, and there still is no end to it. Paul Kruger kept a close watch on this town, erupting as it were on the bare veld, over a period of some thirteen years and was to visit it on a number of occasions, visits more memorable to some than to others. To leave Pretoria for Johannesburg was like going to another country, and yet one could get there within six hours on horseback. Natal and Cape Colony naturally wished to establish trade links with the new goldfields by rail, but Kruger first wished to see his Delagoa line established, as he feared for the independent trade of the Republic. From now on the story of gold is the story of South Africa, something Kruger had to accept as inevitable, and it still applies to the present day.

Kruger also knew that these riches put the fate of the South African Republic once again in the balance, and his concern for their independence only became more fanatical as strangers poured through the gates. Within a matter of months, import duties alone jumped from £7,000 the previous year to £48,000. The revenue of 1886 of £196,000 escalated to nearly four million ten years later. Everything was changing and nothing could ever be the same again. This was impressed upon Kruger on his first visit to Johannesburg in the middle of February 1887. The digger population gave him a hearty welcome. But they were aliens seeking their fortunes, and they had grievances about property rights, the cost of stand licences and import duties, the lack of postal facilities, the need for a municipality and a licensing court. Even at that early stage they were ready to tell him how to run his country. Yet, Kruger was prepared to say 'Welcome in our midst' and to deal with grievances, but there were also laws, and laws had to be obeyed.

As Great Britain was steadily strengthening her position in South Africa, President Kruger was watched closely in case he should add an inch to his country, no matter that the 'scramble' for, if not 'rape' of, Africa was still the order of the day. Swaziland, once a Boer Protectorate, was to remain independent according to the Convention of London. The so-called 'New Republic' to the east, of which Joubert had declined the presidency and now run by Lucas Meyer, a large charming man, was seeking incorporation with the S.A.R. and not Natal. This aroused outside concern, but was incorporated all the same in 1887 at the request of the farmers who had been given the land by Dinuzulu. Rhodes, at this time still involved with diamonds and rather slow to turn to gold, kept his eyes beyond the Limpopo to which his 'Suez Canal' led. The south-eastern Transvaal was of little note in comparison.

The businessman Nellmapius had again been in the news. In the past he had rendered valuable service in the Sekhukhune and Njabel campaigns in the supply of dynamite, and he had became one of the President's intimate friends, something which was useful to him in gaining various concessions. The intricacies of his business entanglements now led up to a charge of embezzlement. Nellmapius was found guilty and sentenced. Kruger, believing like many others that he was innocent, was instrumental in his release, thus interfering with the judiciary and acting unconstitutionally, which, commented Manfred Nathan, 'though he may have acted in entire good faith, was completely indefensible'.[211] This was where Kruger's reputation as an autocrat began.

In the course of 1887 a new presidential election was announced, as Kruger's term of office was to end the following year. His opponent, almost inevitably, was again to be General Joubert. This gave Kruger no concern as he dealt with the changing scene. In order to settle differences among the diggers and to enable negotiation between them and the Government, a Mining Committee was formed, as Kruger wanted friendly settlements and did not wish to be 'compelled to have recourse to force'.[212] He wondered if he should not show more consideration for the feeling of the ever-swelling Uitlander population, but nobody was again to accuse the Transvaal of 'inherent weakness', and happenings at Kimberley were a warning of what could happen in Johannesburg—a British take-over. Also in 1887 the first conference was held to establish a closer alliance with the Orange Free State.

'I insisted,' says Kruger, 'that the Orange Free State should not permit a railway to be built through her territory which would connect the South African Republic with any of the British colonies in South Africa. I was opposed to a closer connexion . . . so long as the independence of the Transvaal was not guaranteed by the possession of a railway of her own, and I feared that the construction of the only possible self-supporting railway, for which the Government had made itself liable, would be delayed, or the railway rendered unproductive, if other lines were started in the meantime . . .' [213] He also wanted an offensive and defensive alliance with the Free State. This desire caused indignation in Cape Colony. President Brand remained evasive, not wishing to commit himself. He personally felt much closer ties with Cape Colony than the Transvaal.

The *Volksstem*, concerned over the enormous changes taking place in the South African Republic, felt that Kruger and Joubert should combine forces in support of a new man to run the country in which the foreign element would apparently soon exceed the original population. But Kruger and Joubert, though they acknowledged that they belonged to the Voortrekker era and had their limitations, felt that they could deal with the changed scene. They had reached a stage of full challenge to their ambitions and political acumen. It was also to their material advantage to hold on to the offices they held. Kruger, like Rhodes, was not interested in money for its own sake but what he could do with it. Joubert's fortunes had begun to climb as he snatched at new opportunities, and he was on the road to great wealth which would be a help in ousting Kruger as President.

People had begun to refer to Kruger familiarly as 'Oom Paul'. A form of address in Afrikaans to men usually about twenty years older than oneself is 'oom' or uncle. It is felt to be less formal than *meneer* (mister or sir) but courteous, and its usage is still general. In talking of Kruger the new population referred to Oom Paul, either in affection or disparagement. Nobody had to wonder who was meant, and it became so usual that one heard it throughout South Africa and eventually abroad, as in Germany. 'I seem to be uncle to the world,' Kruger once remarked. Actually, except for members of his own family, nobody dared to call him Oom Paul to his face. He was always addressed as President or Your Honour, and the misguided were told gruffly that they were not related.

The influx into the Transvaal was becoming more and more alarming, from the colonies, Great Britain, Australia, the United States, Germany, the Netherlands—what was to become of the 'old population', Kruger wondered with ever-increasing concern. But he continued to welcome them. 'It rejoices me to see,' he said, 'that they are working together with the inhabitants of this State; that they follow the dictates of law and order; that they subject themselves to the laws . . .' In his view the newcomers fell into three classes: those who wished to settle permanently and to be naturalized; those who wished to make their fortunes and then leave; and those who wished to stay without surrendering their nationality. Anyway, they were welcome, 'but I place you under the care of the old burghers,' he added hopefully.

John Xavier Merriman (1841–1926) left Cape Colony to venture into the Transvaal early in 1887. Gold production was only to start in May, but Johannesburg was spreading rapidly, the most curious place he had ever seen, with 'seedy individuals talking glibly of thousands of pounds, in a little shanty that would not be considered a decent place for a stable'. Pretoria struck the Cape politician as a 'sort of tumble-down untidy Dutch village'. Merriman noted the water flowing in the furrows and the large Dutch church (demolished 1904–5) in the centre of the main square. There were many shops and hotels but a singular lack of bustle in the streets. True, the imposing buildings of Pretoria still had to be built, but according to many it was a lovely town even then, almost smothered in roses.

Merriman called on President Kruger and found him 'fatter' than he had last seen him when he had called on him at Kalk Bay in 1880, 'but otherwise is the same dirty-looking stolid fellow'. J. X. Merriman was known for his cynicism and barbed wit and also for being unnervingly candid. Kruger did not receive him very cordially, and this was hardly surprising after the way the Cape politicians had treated him. They talked of the customs. 'Kruger is very sore at his treatment by the Colony and at the rudeness of Upington,' Merriman wrote home, referring to Kruger's advances on railway and customs. 'Over and over again he made use of the homely simile that the Transvaal was like a puppy that used to be blind but now had its eyes open.' Merriman noted, however, that Kruger was sincere in his desire for a commercial union, though he feared that the English Government could suddenly withdraw from any agreement made.

After Kruger, Merriman called on General Joubert at his new and what he considered rather pretentious house in Visagie Street. Joubert was much more vivacious and easier in manner than Kruger, cleverer too, perhaps, but Kruger was the more interesting man, for he belonged to a by-gone day. As it was Joubert's birthday, there were streams of callers, and Merriman noted with interest that the General spoke of Kruger slightingly several times as he poured the drinks.[214] When not writing to his wife, Merriman showed more restraint, as to J. G. Fraser some weeks later. The Transvaal, he said, was beautiful, fertile, and he was struck by the magnitude of the gold discoveries, the order and content that seemed to prevail, 'and the evidently honest intention in the mind of the rulers of the country to do their best to meet the odd circumstances of the body politic.'

And then follows these remarkable observations, taking into account that it was February 1887:

> Unless some gross mismanagement takes place, the Transvaal is bound to become a populous, highly prosperous republic in which the Dutch South African and British South African races will fuse into some new compound. My reason for thinking that the Government will remain a republic is that in no quarter did I hear the slightest wish for any return of the British Government, even from the most loyal Englishman; everyone is perfectly content with the republic, if it expands with the times and respects the rights of everyone. I think I saw also evidences of a sincere desire for fusion among the more intelligent of the so-called Afrikaners. Such a republic will be the leading state in South Africa. It will set the policy for the rest. Confederation becomes not only possible but from every point of view desirable. The idea of a British Empire in South Africa is at an end, and that of the United States of South Africa, under the friendly protection and possibly in some undefined connexion with Great Britain, takes its place.[215]

Kruger's next visit to Johannesburg was on 24 September 1887 and again he was enthusiastically received. The growth of the town and its population within a matter of months also staggered him. Kruger felt like a foreigner in his own country, and this apparently affected his temper, for at a banquet (tickets were four pounds each) that evening, he arrived late, showed irritability, and left before the toast list had ended. He had made the acquaintance of mining men before, at Lydenburg and Barberton, but these rowdy crowds of all nationalities, some shrieking 'God Save the Queen' to his face, gave him a tightening of the heart. But they were to be welcomed, to be treated equally. And yet, should they have the franchise within five years and demand representation in the Volksraad, what would happen to his country?

In this connexion Kruger spoke freely. He also repeated that he was aware of the importance of rail links for the Rand but that the Delagoa line had to be finished first. Strain was added to the Johannesburg banquet by demonstrations in the street outside, and elsewhere, against the appointment of the notorious Adriaan de la Rey as commissioner of police for the goldfields. This was a huge man whose motto was that blood must flow and who had been a holy terror in Stellaland. Even so, Rhodes had won his friendship and even became godfather to his grandchild. But this De la Rey (a cousin of the famous general) was even a reputed murderer, and J. X. Merriman, again in the Transvaal at the time, thought the appointment 'monstrous'.[216] One hears no more of it. Grievances and demonstrations there were, but on the whole Johannesburg was friendly and courteous towards President Kruger in its formative years.

The election of January 1888 caused little excitement, for its outcome was a foregone conclusion. To General Joubert, however, whose hopes had soared again, it was shattering—834 votes for him and 4,483 for Kruger. But never again was he to have such a licking. The results proved that faith in Kruger was stronger than ever, and he was determined to be worthy of that faith in the changed circumstances of his land. Kruger was sworn-in in May and addressed the Volksraad on the 7th, surprising his audience in hardly referring to the goldfields and the changes he obviously had in mind. One interesting point was his references to the appointment of a consul to Matabeleland at the request of Mzilikazi's successor, Lobengula.[217]

An important change was to be the elevation of Leyds to State Secretary, replacing Bok who was to have the new post of secretary and minute-keeper to the Executive Council. As Leyds was not yet thirty, he had to wait a while as this was the minimum age for the office. The Transvaal was getting into his blood, and though the Boer people often got on his nerves, Leyds felt that they had an historical right of existence. There was also his deepening friendship with 'the old man'—after they had nearly parted their ways as a result of Kruger's interference with the judiciary in order to help his friend Nellmapius. Nobody could question the absolute integrity of Leyds. His relationship with Kruger had entered a new dimension since the night the President came to him to ask his forgiveness. Many were beginning to believe that Kruger was now being mesmerized by Leyds as he used to be by Du Toit. In the eyes of some there was an unholy alliance between the brilliant beardless young man and the grumpy old warrior. It is not generally known that each was offered and declined a British knighthood.

Piet Joubert's active opposition to Kruger was intensified because he was again passed over as Vice-President. On the resignation of Chris Joubert, the Volksraad almost unanimously elected General Nicolaas Smit, an honour he richly deserved. Smit's friendship with Kruger remained unclouded, and they had many a laugh together, still enjoying incredible hunting stories. Joubert also could not help being fond of Smit, a man so capable and yet so totally unpretentious. Joubert once asked Smit why he did not oppose Kruger when he deserved it. 'Old friend, it is like this,' Smit said. 'I *do* stand up against him, I know he is wrong and I tell him so; but first he argues with me, and if that is no good he gets into a rage and jumps round the room roaring at me like a wild beast . . . and if I do not give in then he fetches out the Bible and . . . he even quotes that to help him out. And if all that fails he takes my hand and cries like a child and begs and prays me to give in. Say, old friend, who can resist a man like that?' Joubert, in his turn, aroused much amusement by making impersonations of Kruger, his mannerisms, buffalo rushes around a room, and bellowings. Meetings of the Executive were apparently no picnic.[218]

But the whole of 1888 was eventful. There was the 'Grobler Affair', P. D. J. C. Grobler, appointed consul to Matabeleland, having been murdered in territory in dispute between Lobengula and Khama, Chief of the Bamangwato. As Grobler had been to Bulawayo and had presented Lobengula with the treaty, drafted by Kruger, by which the King placed his country under the protection of the South African Republic, and which was fully approved, the murder caused no small sensation. 'There is no doubt whatever,' Kruger remarked, 'that this murder was due to Cecil Rhodes and his clique.'[219] Rhodes's designs on the interior had become common knowledge, and the fact that Khama now paid Grobler's widow a yearly pension of £200 caused much comment. It is a long and involved story, told in full in Gustav Preller's *Lobengula* which, though written in English, could not find a British publisher and was brought out decades later by an Afrikaans firm.

Dr Schowalter gives an anecdote of Rhodes calling on Kruger in Pretoria on his way from Cape Town to Beira. 'We must work together,' Rhodes said. 'I know the Republic wants a seaport; you must have Delagoa Bay.' Kruger was amazed. 'How can we work together there? The harbour belongs to the Portuguese, and they won't hand it over.' Rhodes smiled. 'Then we must simply take it.' Kruger was horrified. 'I can't take away other people's property. If the Portuguese won't sell the harbour, I wouldn't take it even if you gave it me; for ill-gotten goods are accursed.'[220] It is possible that Kruger did tell this story to Schowalter. If he had he could also have explained why he had taken so long to do anything about Lobengula who had persistently asked him for a treaty, not that Rhodes enthusiasts agree on this. The reason was simple. Kruger was not the territorial expansionist he was so clamorously made out to be, and he was looking east, not north. He only woke up when he realized that the north was about to be cut off. The character of Grobler, the waywardness of Lobengula and the innocence of Rhodes are not matters for argument here, but of importance is Kruger's distrust of Rhodes which began to influence his attitude towards the Witwatersrand.

In July 1888 Sir John Brand died of a heart-attack after a long reign. He was succeeded as President of the Orange Free State by the country's Chief Justice, Francis William Reitz, a charming, clever and amusing man. In the republican sense Frank Reitz was looked upon as more dedicated than Brand, proud to be an Afrikaner and keen to see Afrikaner ties strengthened. That Brand was a great man nobody could deny, but somehow he and Kruger never hit it off. Reitz's attitude towards Kruger was entirely different. Reitz was nearly twenty years younger than the Transvaal President and was to outlive almost all his contemporaries, for he only died in 1934. Of interest is that he had seven sons and one daughter by his first wife, and six sons and one daughter by his second. His sister Frances was married to the Cape politician, W. P. Schreiner, in 1884. The name of one of the sons, Deneys Reitz, lives on as a writer. The whole family was very gifted and had a lively sense of humour. They were all fascinated by President Kruger, and Reitz was to have intimate contact with him at different levels for the rest of his days. Their first conference as Heads of State was fixed for Potchefstroom in March 1889.

Kruger endured criticism from many quarters, for his apparent reluctance to join a customs union, for his 'Hollander Policy' (a concession had just been granted to the Netherlands Syndicate for a tramway from the Boksburg coalfields to Johannesburg), for not making sufficient reductions on import duties destined for the Rand, and for certain salary increases, his own being stepped up from £3,000 to £8,000 per annum. There was also personal criticism of Kruger for apparently believing himself to be divinely inspired, for ascending the pulpit of the Dopper church opposite his house and preaching to the people once a month, for believing that the sun went round the earth, and so on. The grossness of his personal behaviour was continually exaggerated (spitting was quite common in an era of pipe-smoking, as were elegant spittoons which it is said he invariably missed). In descriptions of his table-manners, dress and general eccentricities, it was to become fashionable with the alien elements (and others not alien at all) to make the President as grotesque as possible.

But it is true that he seemed to get more and more averse to opposition of any kind as he grew older, and he flew into some monumental rages. People were not always sure in how far these storms were genuine or feigned, but when it came to criticism of something like his plans for coastal connexion, his fury could not be doubted. As 1888 neared its end, Kruger gave much thought to another bay, that of Kosi, a paradise of nature, to be reached by an alternative route through Swaziland. Negotiations with this aim in view were to go for months, and it was Kruger's obsession with eastern coastal connexion which enabled Rhodes to talk Lobengula into granting a mining concession, which led to the formation of a British South Africa Company and an inevitable Matabeleland take-over under Royal Charter.

The President visited Johannesburg in December 1888. This was his most formal visit thus far, for he had an escort of artillery and was received to the strains of the Transvaal national anthem. There were addresses of welcome from all sectors, American and German included, and there was a display of fireworks. The warmth of the reception put him in a good mood, and he showed keen interest in mining operations on his inspection of the Robinson Mine. Of course there were the usual requests for the redress of grievances, for a municipality and more officials, but the mood was friendly and Kruger was willing to co-operate. He repeated that he made no distinction between those who wished to settle and those who were there only temporarily, and laid the foundation stone of a building for the Y.M.C.A. When Kruger laid a foundation stone it is said that he carried out his duty in no perfunctory manner. He spent time in testing the exact position of the stone with spirit levels, for he was, after all, a practical man believing in co-ordination between head, hands and usage.[221] In a flurry of flags, bands and trotting horses, the President took his departure.

His conference with President Reitz early in 1889 was highly satisfactory to both parties. A treaty of peace and amity—an important defensive alliance—was made between the two republics, and import duties, with few exceptions, were waived. Both sides saw the desirability of a federal union, and agreement was reached on railway matters, the one State to consult the other on any extensions until such time as the Delagoa Bay line was completed. The Free Staters were delighted to have easy access to the Johannesburg market, and Kruger at last had at least one sworn ally.[222] A sour note was usually introduced by General Joubert who, on a visit to Natal, declared that he would give his full support for a line from that Colony to Johannesburg, but Kruger could handle him and actually showed amazing tact in his dealings with this tricky opponent.

'I never ceased thinking,' Kruger remarked, 'how I could meet the wishes of the new population for representation, without injuring the Republic or prejudicing the interests of the older burghers.'[223] Too much was wanted too soon in Johannesburg, like municipal status, but they could have the increased number of judicial officers desired at once. Representation in the Government posed many problems, but Kruger was well aware that the Uitlanders had to be given a voice. He thought he had hit on a solution when he dreamt up something rather amazing—a Second Volksraad, 'my own idea,' he said, 'for which I alone made myself responsible.' To this body matters relating to the interests of the Johannesburgers would be relegated, gold laws, telegraphic connexions, and so on. Many of even Kruger's own supporters took a dim view of this Second Volksraad, as it was almost meaningless, and some even thought it one of his biggest mistakes.

On 6 May he had a proud moment—laying the foundation stone of the new Government Building or Raadzaal to the west of Church Square, the largest and most opulent building to be erected in the Transvaal up to that time, symbolic of new-found wealth. 'Who would have believed,' Kruger said slowly and clearly, having been asked to speak thus, 'five years ago that such a building was possible?' Now the position and dignity of the State demanded such an edifice. But, and always one notes Kruger's historical awareness: the old building of 1864 on the same site was not to be forgotten, not after all the well and woe they had gone through there. In the same way the hardships of the past were to be remembered, and the new bounty to be seen solely as thanks to God's mercy.

This building, designed in the Italian Renaissance style by the Government architect, Sytze Wierda, provided Kruger with two offices to the left of the main entrance. When finally completed in 1891, the building cost £155,000, with an internal telephone system and electric light. (Kruger's private residence was also fitted with electric light, and had a telephone.) The central tower of the Government Building was topped by a female figure, either a Minerva or an allegorical figure representing Freedom or Liberty, nobody seems to be sure, and the story goes that it was at Kruger's special request that the bare-headed lady was equipped with a helmet, as it was not seemly for a woman to stand up in public with her head uncovered. Kruger took a lively interest in every stage of this 'costly pile', and it has remained intimately associated with him.[224]

Johannesburg did not watch the changing face of Pretoria with any enchantment, for during most of 1890 there was to be a slump, a kind of hangover which followed on the gold intoxication of the previous years. Fortunes were not, after all, to be made overnight, and deep-level mining posed technical problems remote from old-fashioned digging days. Kruger had to wonder how rich the Reef really was, whether it would last, if the earth would really give up her riches so readily. Among his other concerns one again proved his loyalty towards a friend. This involved Bok whom Kruger was determined to have as Secretary and Minute Keeper to the Executive, with a seat in it, at £1,000 per annum, something strongly opposed by those who had had enough of Bok. Leyds had meanwhile reached the age qualification for Secretary of State, an office superior to that of State Attorney which was non-political.

Education remained of great concern to Kruger. He mooted the rather startling idea of a University of Pretoria. His Government, once their surprise was overcome, gave the idea enthusiastic support, only to find opposition from Amsterdam where the Free University had no intention of losing their Afrikaner students. The Second Volksraad came up for close scrutiny, a draft act having been published. The new legislative body, as well as an alteration of franchise requirements, had heated discussion in the May session, some feeling that too much was granted, others too little. But, as Kruger insisted in an impassioned speech, he could see no other way to safeguard the independence of the State and the authority of the people. Representation of some kind there had to be, but easy voting rights would be their undoing and had to be tightened up. This debate moved from 1889 into 1890.

In March of the new year, Kruger was on his way to Blignautspont to confer with the High Commissioner of South Africa and Governor of Cape Colony, Sir Henry Brougham Loch, who had succeeded Sir

Hercules Robinson in December 1889. The coming of Loch coincided with Cecil Rhodes's elevation to the Cape Premiership. From Pretoria Kruger first went to Johannesburg on the 4th in order to meet various deputations. With Leyds beside him in his carriage, artillerists trotting alongside, they entered Orange Grove on the northern outskirts of the town. They were met by a member of the Volksraad and were followed by some sixty vehicles to the Wanderers terrain. There some ten thousand people had gathered, a restless crowd, bursting into British patriotic songs previous to the arrival of the presidential cavalcade. But there were rousing cheers as Kruger heaved his bulk from his carriage and mounted a rostrum. The usual welcoming addresses were read out to him, and, apart from a certain restiveness, there was nothing ominous to be noted. Kruger said that he would meet the various deputations and bodies that evening.

He was driven off[225] to the house of his host, Captain Carl von Brandis, the man who had been the Witwatersrand's first Mine Commissioner and was now Special Landdrost of Johannesburg. A crowd had gathered both inside and outside the whitewashed Von Brandis dwelling. Kruger sensed that there was something wrong, and knew it when he heard that some hotheads had pulled down the Vierkleur at the Landdrost's office and had torn it to shreds. But he was not alarmed, and nobody accosted him in an insulting way, though there was some frank talk. To a man who told him that he treated the new population with contempt, Kruger replied: 'I have no contempt for the new population, only for people like yourself.' The man flung himself from the room and outside a riot began which Van Brandis tried his best to control until police reinforcements came up.

Kruger could no longer ignore the restlessness in the town and was puzzled by the excitement prevailing. After all, it was not in his power to concede to all their wishes on the spot. The railway, he told his audience, would be constructed as speedily as possible from Delagoa Bay via Pretoria to Johannesburg, and he was beginning to see his way clear for a rail link between the Rand and Bloemfontein. When he expressed his displeasure with the riotous element, he was assured that the respectable people of Johannesburg had no part in it. The Chamber of Mines offered an apology, which was accepted. Kruger knew that many suspicious characters had come on the scene, but was sincere in believing that the bulk of the population of the Witwatersrand was law-abiding, looked for no political quarrels and merely wished to seek their fortunes.

But the occurrences during his visit to Johannesburg in March 1890 were more ominous than he realized. The 'old population' were outraged that a riotous mob should gather anywhere near the President and that the National Flag should be insulted. As Kruger prepared to leave for his meeting with Loch, he told those who rallied around him not to fuss, as the incidents came only from a small riotous element and could be ignored. The news, however, spread far and wide, and this was the point where the rift between the Transvaalers and the Uitlanders began. Paul Kruger was a national symbol, and any insult to him was an insult to the Boer people. His contemplated alterations, restrictions and innovations began to make sense to both those who thought him too liberal and to those who thought him too restrictive.

Hardly had Kruger left Johannesburg, when a mass meeting was held on the town's market square. Eloquent speeches for various reforms were made. Van Oordt describes it as 'a sudden volcanic eruption'.[226] But it was not as bad as all that, being symptomatic of a period of economic unsettlement. Silly rumours, such as that burghers from Standerton were about to attack Johannesburg, were deliberately spread by agitators. The President sent a message to his Government to ignore it, and they did so, waiting for his return from Blignautspont.

Sir Henry Loch met Kruger as arranged at the border between the Republic and Cape Colony. His Excellency was much intrigued by the rumours flying about the country. 'What is all this I hear about a *riot*?' he wanted to know. 'Sir Henry,' Kruger explained, 'you see, those people remind me of a baboon I once had, which was so fond of me that he would not let anyone touch me. But one day we were sitting round the fire, and unfortunately the beast's tail got caught in the fire. He now flew at me furiously, thinking that I was the cause of the accident. The Johannesburgers are just like that. They have burnt their fingers in speculations and now they want to revenge themselves on Paul Kruger . . .'[227]

CHAPTER FOURTEEN

Intrigue

With Sir Henry Loch (1827–1900), Kruger encountered Cecil John Rhodes and William Philip Schreiner. The main purpose of the conference was to discuss matters relating to Swaziland, railways and customs. Loch had already gained 'the entire confidence' of Rhodes, according to Sir Lewis Michell. Rhodes was at the head of the De Beers Mines, was playing a role of growing importance in the development of the Transvaal's goldmining industry, was the 'guiding spirit' of the Chartered Company, and he was Prime Minister of the Cape.[228] Loch had in fact within a matter of months become a Rhodes disciple, and as talks began, it was soon clear that Loch and Rhodes were obsessed with the north, while Kruger was primarily interested in Swaziland.

Rhodes had spread so many wild stories about Kruger's territorial ambitions that he had perhaps come to believe them, in the same way that Sir Henry and most of Rhodes's biographers did. Rhodes and Loch expressed their concern to Kruger about a rumoured Boer emigration to Mashonaland. He tried to bring the subject back to Swaziland, a territory, except for the east, bounded on every side by the Republic. Everybody knew that the Swazis had been Boer allies of long standing against insurgent northern tribes, had enjoyed Boer protection and had granted them concessions. But in this case also, it would appear that Kruger was more interested in a way through Swaziland to the sea than the actual incorporation of the country.

Sir Hercules Robinson had acknowledged his desire for a port to be perfectly understandable. Sir Francis de Winton, sent by the British Government to investigate the scene, had reported in favour of the Transvaal's claims. But according to the Conventions of 1881 and 1884 the independence of the Swazis was assured. Loch and Rhodes were now willing to come to an arrangement. Should Kruger agree to enter a South African commercial union and to abandon all aspirations of northern expansion, he could have his way to the sea through Swaziland.

Kruger was not opposed to a customs union, nor to a railway between Durban and Johannesburg, but then he had first to be sure of a port of his own, particularly when he could clearly see such an 'arrangement' steering towards South African confederation under British predominance. He could not possibly gamble with their independence, not when he had high hopes of a major port like Delagoa Bay and had reason to have doubts about inferior Kosi Bay on the Swazi route. No decisions were reached, and negotiations were to resume later that year.[229]

Kruger was back in Pretoria on 19 March 1890. He now had greater clarity about Rhodes's designs on the north and knew the man to be in deadly earnest. The rumour of a Boer trek to Mashonaland, organized by Louis Bowler, was true, so Kruger tried to ease tension by forbidding it. But, as he knew, once a Boer had made up his mind to trek it was no easy matter to stop him. Only now did he realize what a sensation had been caused by the riot in Johannesburg and the insult to the Vierkleur. Kruger insisted that there was no reason to get excited and that he did not hold the Rand in contempt because of the behaviour of some drunken louts. But even as he was saying this, there were fiery speeches in Johannesburg aimed at Hollanders and bureaucrats.

The Volksraad sat in May, and in June a new arrival in Pretoria was Onze Jan Hofmeyr, balding, and blinking through thinly rimmed spectacles. He had been sent by Sir Henry Loch to pave the way for a Swaziland Convention in August. Hofmeyr's Afrikaner Bond was becoming a powerful political machine at the Cape. He sympathized with the aspirations of Rhodes and was at this stage totally fascinated by him, as were all those who were dazzled by power, money and grandiose schemes. Sir Henry Loch was not going to have a great man like Rhodes thwarted by contemptible peasants such as Kruger and his Transvaalers. Another reason why he had sent Hofmeyr was because the new British Resident at Pretoria, Sir Jacobus de Wet, had been taken ill. In sympathy with Rhodes and Loch, Hofmeyr might have been, but they were to be reminded that he was also a great Afrikaner.

'It appeared to me,' Hofmeyr reported to the High Commissioner,

> that not only in the Executive Council and in the Volksraad, but also among the burghers throughout the length and breadth of the South African Republic, there is an intensely strong feeling prevalent with reference to Swaziland, viz. that that territory both historically and geographically, belongs to the Republic, and should be incorporated with it. I feel firmly convinced, that this feeling is so strong, that if no arrangement had been arrived at, and Her Majesty's Govern-

ment had, under article 11 of the London Convention, appointed a Commissioner in Swaziland to maintain order, and had supported such Commissioner by force, many Transvaal burghers would have offered armed opposition to such a course, whatever the attitude of their President and Government, and the results may have been most disastrous for the peace of South Africa.[230]

For the time being joint British and Boer control over Swaziland was to prevail, and the Transvaal was granted a strip of land not more than three miles wide to Kosi Bay, on condition that no treaties were made by the Transvaal with Natives to the north and north-west. The Natal railway extension was not to be opposed, and the Chartered Company was to be assisted as much as possible. Kruger did not have to wonder about Rhodes's role in the Swaziland Convention; the whole thing bore his imprint. The development of Kosi Bay depended on the Transvaal's willingness to enter a customs union. Kruger and his Government found this Convention most unsatisfactory, for they were losing more than they were gaining; and was Kosi Bay really worth anything? The matter would have to be taken up again.

A Boer was basically a trusting person, but once his confidence was shattered it was almost impossible to restore it. This was also true of Kruger, and his suspicions of Rhodes's designs on the Transvaal (the gold appeared endless) only deepened as 1890 drew to a close. Other concerns were a fresh church dispute as a result of attempts at consolidation, Native unruliness in the Zoutpansberg, and a new movement amongst his people to trek to the north. This was the so-called Adendorff Trek which Kruger, according to the Swaziland Convention, forbade in a proclamation in April 1891, as it endangered the interests of the Chartered Company. Kruger's firm stand on this Trek, as well as his attempts to end the church dispute, made many think him autocratic and a meddler. He was also accused of squandering State funds, of giving away all rights and privileges in the guise of concessions and of overloading the civil service with 'loathsome' Hollanders. Kruger's popularity was apparently on the wane.

He visited Natal the same month, passing through Wakkerstroom where he made a speech on the church dispute which largely involved the fate of church properties. As his own church remained aloof from a United Church or Verenigde Kerk, of concern to Dutch Reformed and Hervormdes, he was thought presumptuous in trying to find a solution. But, as he declared, 'As a Christian and Head of State, I feel it my duty to do everything in my power to promote harmony, love and peace in this State.' General Joubert was there too on his own stamping ground, back from a visit to the United States and Europe during which he had pleaded the Transvaal cause at the Swaziland Convention in London. A large number of burghers escorted Kruger and Joubert to Charlestown where they were welcomed by the Governor of Natal. The occasion was the opening of the Natal railway line to that spot on 7 April.

This line was as yet of no interest to Kruger, and he went for diplomatic reasons only. He feared that a Natal link with the Witwatersrand could seriously jeopardize his Delagoa line by way of competition. But he could not very well refuse a friendly invitation to the function, and he was furious when Joubert made a speech in English in which he said that he hoped the line would soon be extended into the Transvaal and that full co-operation between Natal and the Transvaal would come about. He had said so before, knowing how much it annoyed Kruger. The President considered Joubert's sort of love-overture to Natal uncalled-for, precipitate and not in the best interests of the Transvaal.

But the Natalians loved him for it, while Kruger was seen as grumpy and rude, still refusing to speak English and with apparently a different scheme of things in mind. The general feeling and hope in Natal was that Kruger would be beaten, preferably by Joubert, in the next presidential election. The Natalians could see that Joubert had become much more in tune with the younger generation as well as the new population, without having lost the esteem of some of the most important men of his country. Kruger might be a national symbol, but Joubert and his 'Progressives' could only be for the good of all South Africa.

Both men were present in May at the reinterment of Andries Pretorius in what is now called Pretoria's old cemetery. Thoughts went back to so much that had become history. The Volksraad was in session, and back at work Kruger brought up the planned Adendorff Trek for formal discussion. By this time it appeared to be a pan-South African movement, and it could lead to war should this stream of people pour over the Limpopo. In his correspondence, the High Commissioner made it clear that any move into Lobengula's domains would not be tolerated. The Joubert party opposed Kruger's clamp-down on the Trek, maintaining that ownership of the territory was in dispute, that people all over South Africa were involved, that the Chartered Company itself was luring immigrants, and that Kruger was going too far in curtailing freedom of movement. Nellmapius once made the observation that the Boers will not be driven, although they are so easily led.[231]

But Kruger, watching Rhodes and Loch carefully, stood firm on the Adendorff Trek (L. D. Adendorff was only one of various leaders) and the movement began to fizzle out. Mostly Free Staters went, some 112, and were halted at the Limpopo by Bechuanaland police, Rhodes's settlers and a short, bright-eyed man, Dr Leander Starr Jameson, a Rhodes stalwart since the early Kimberley days. Though a medical man, Jameson had been leader of Rhodes's Mashonaland Expedition and was now Administrator. As he used tactful persuasion there was no fight, and some of these trekkers were indeed to settle down in the country to be named Rhodesia. It is surprising that a trek spirit should still be alive decades after the Great Trek. Members of Kruger's family supported it, and so did Joubert and other of the old burghers.

The Second Volksraad functioned in conjunction with the First, not that it seemed more than an advisory body, and brought Ewald Esselen to the political fore in opposition to Kruger. Esselen was one of the many who put his hopes on Joubert for the presidential election of 1893 which was already being planned in 1891. The railway race continued apace, and Kruger's voice was heard in various parts of the Republic. One of his major speeches was at Paardekraal on 16 December 1891 when he addressed some ten thousand persons. It was the tenth aniversary of restored independence as well as the fifty-third of Blood River. Kruger's speeches were beginning to sound more and more like sermons, with endless allusions to God and the Bible, prostrations as it were before the Lord. But he always knew how to hold interest:

> Even when our forefathers left the Cape Colony, you will note God's hand, His Almightiness, His great mercy and divine guidance, a guidance not from man, for all human glory is excluded. Mark the ways of God, and we know ourselves. In the years 1835 and 1836 the Trek from the Cape Colony began towards the North-East to a strange land . . . I was then a boy of ten. My father was one of the first to cross the border and that in 1835, while the Great Trek began in 1836. I am telling you my age, as, my brothers and sisters, all of you present here, I do not know if I will have the opportunity again to address you from here and I do not wish to tell you history as I have it from books, but history of which I

> was an ear- and eye-witness and which I have lived through to this day. In it I will show you God's way, and prove to you that it was God's hand which led us out of the Cape Colony and gave us our freedom . . .

He then went on to tell history as he knew it up to the time of the Annexation.

> Before the country was annexed, people said: 'See how rich it is; gold has been found, but the stupid Boers are not capable of developing it.' And what happened during the Annexation? Then scientific reports from mineralogists were sent in, and from these it appeared that there was gold but it was not payable. You see, thus it was kept hidden by God until our independence was restored, and then at the appointed day the stupid Boers found the gold. The earth was opened and revealed her treasures . . .

Many people were deeply moved by Kruger, but, and this must be repeated, just as many thought him a devout old hypocrite. Kruger gave the Psalms to be sung and concluded: 'Amen. I have spoken.'[232]

It became habitual for Kruger to use the month of March for personal appearances in the eastern and southern parts. Although he was in his sixty-seventh year, he still showed little sign of fatigue. A new generation beheld him with some astonishment: the bulky figure, the booming voice, a face which already seemed beyond time and place—for it was now appearing on coins—the top hat and frock-coat. South Africans were beginning to see him as later generations were to look upon Jan van Riebeeck, founder of their white society, recognizing the person but hardly knowing the man. 'Look at me closely,' Kruger said in one of his speeches, 'and make the effort to understand me.' What he meant was not scrutiny of him as a man but as the embodiment of the Transvaal, of Boerdom, or the word which was being used more and more: Afrikanerdom. The whole concept of Afrikanerdom flowed from the Afrikaner Bond, via Du Toit, Hofmeyr and others: a concept of identity, made by Africa, speaking a language with ancient origins but made in the same way. The extraordinary thing about Paul Kruger is that he already knew, and long before 1892, that he was the personification of Afrikanerdom for as long as it should exist.

Vanity? He was the least vain man ever. But with his historical awareness he knew that he was not only standing in history but making it, like Cromwell, Lincoln, Bismarck (to name some with whom he has been compared)—amazing men who flame out like stars in recorded history and who had no doubt shared a similar concept of destiny. Kruger's significance was also recognized by the Bantu; very recently a great personality among the Xhosas died, surrounded by Krugeriana. This is where it becomes difficult to get Kruger into perspective, to sort the man from the concept when so many factors are involved: a great personality, a superior intellect, destiny, divine selection, purpose, drive. He knew that his critics were often right, that he was woefully lacking in qualities which should be at the command of a maker of history, but then there were compensations, and God had a purpose with him. To understand Paul Kruger one must accept his total personal unselfishness, dedication to land and people, and above all his prostration before the beauty, the wrath, the power, the will and the purpose of God in which he believed utterly.

In his political life it was being said that Kruger was a puppet in the hands of Leyds, that behind every gesture and word of the man casting such a large shadow was Leyds, that it was Leyds who was intoxicated with nation-building within the context of his own nationality. It was the same with Rhodes, his nationalism fed by his dreams of Empire. Leyds, it would appear, also had his dreams, but of Dutch glory which he felt he could fulfil through this ageing man who had somehow landed himself riches beyond the dreams of men. It takes little effort of the imagination to see Leyds in a kind of swoon over past Dutch glories—when his tiny land had been one of the great forces in world economics—and believing that they could be regained through the Witwatersrand. That was why he could not bring himself to leave a Transvaal he loathed. And for the same reason Rhodes could not leave the Transvaal alone.

Kruger was in Johannesburg on 25 March 1892. 'To say that this country is governed by Dr Leyds,' he shouted at Richard Loveday, 'is quite untrue, and it is about time that a law was passed to prohibit the Press from spreading such lies!'[233] The intrigue building up around him took time to be seen in perspective, and then only the British role was taken into account. Nobody took Kruger as seriously as did his Hollander bright boys, and particularly Leyds. It gave them concern that Kruger's 'Hollanderism' was cooling off, that he was beginning to see the South African Republic more in terms of Africa than the Netherlands—with German aid.

Those close to Kruger were surprised and concerned by his sudden attacks of asthma. He was almost too ill to open the Volksraad in May. But, knowing that there were forces abroad to weaken his Government, he pulled himself together. In dealing with dissentients among his own people, he discovered a new trump-card—the threat of resignation. The Volksraad, he roared, could go to hell, and he flung himself from the Raadzaal. The shock was great, for the Volksraad was the Transvaal and the Transvaal was Paul Kruger. The asthma is a key to his emotional disturbance at this time, for his popularity had reached its lowest ebb, and he had to accept the possibility that he could very well fall out in the next election. What then was God's purpose with him?

The presidential campaign of 1892 was the liveliest in the South African Republic's history. The candidates were Kruger, Joubert and, rather surprisingly, Chief Justice John Gilbert Kotzé (1849–1940), a lively and controversial personality in legal affairs, a prolific author and of varied interests. He was still very young when President Burgers imported him from the Cape, small and delicately made (Anthony Trollope called him a 'boy judge'), arriving at the time of the Annexation and then serving under Shepstone. Nobody could have expected that this frail, wide-eyed little man would outlive everybody, even Reitz.

Kotzé's real name was Johannes Gysbert, and he only became Sir John in 1917. His candidacy for the presidency in 1892 caused much talk, for he had not been known for political leanings. His aim was either to split the votes, to strengthen Joubert whom he preferred to Kruger or because he had political ambitions which nobody felt could be taken seriously. Anyway, his candidacy added spice to the campaign, by no means a polite one, and he was aided and abetted by Ewald Esselen who was chairman of Joubert's election committee. It was not so much a matter of principle but a contest of personalities. Johannesburg, where a National Union had been formed, also watched with keen interest, putting hopes on Joubert as the more pliable man.

In the speech-making, which lasted up to December, Kruger again said, as at Boksburg, that he had come to the conclusion that the Uitlanders had to be given certain rights, particularly as to the franchise, full electoral privileges having at the time of the creation of the Second Volksraad been stepped up from five to fourteen years' residence in the State. Having gone so far, Kruger was now prepared to reduce it, so long as the independence of the State ran no risk of being undermined, as Kruger said at Krugersdorp. On his return to Pretoria, he was comforted by the warm way he was welcomed back and touched when 1,500 children sang the Volkslied. In looking at children, Kruger always saw the future, and more and more he included them in whatever he had to say.

The election results were astonishing in their closeness. Kruger gained 7,854 votes as against 7,009 for Joubert. Kotzé did not count with his 81. The Joubert party immediately lodged a protest that voting papers had been tampered with and that it was Joubert who had won. The contest being so close and the accusation so serious, a committee was appointed to hold a scrutiny. Wild rumours were rife, so two recountings were made, the results varying slightly every time. But Kruger remained in the lead and was declared legally elected. Many Joubert supporters were unconvinced and remained so ever after, but he, though he had reservations, showed his sound character in letting the matter drop for the sake of national unity. The results had in any case bolstered his ego no end, and champagne flowed in Visagie Street.

President Kruger held his inaugural speech on 12 May 1893, speaking from the balcony of the new Government Building (which covered an entire block) to a great crowd gathered on Church Square. He rarely made notes for his speeches, at least he never read from any, and spoke in his forceful way as pens scribbled in the background. His discourse invariably only dealt with those subjects he wished to raise. To the newly naturalized citizens he said that they were entitled to all the privileges granted by law. 'But nobody can serve two masters, and I am sure that you will co-operate with us; as long as I am Head of State I will do my utmost to meet your demands.'[234] And to the Uitlanders: 'You are welcome among us and by obeying the laws of the land you will be entitled to all the privileges granted by law.'

Kruger then turned to Joubert and shook him warmly by the hand. Whenever the President was moved he took a man's hand in both of his. He made the same gesture to the diminutive Justice Kotzé. Kruger then turned to the children. So much lay with them: Church and State, Christian education, honour for their own language, love, duty, reverence— 'If you become indifferent to your language, you also become indifferent to your forefathers and indifferent to the Bible . . .' He meant Dutch, but as the Afrikaans language movement was already in swing for full recognition, one can say Dutch-Afrikaans, for the translation of the Bible into Afrikaans was already being made.

Kruger was known for simplicity and lack of affectation, but he had steadily gained in dignity and had developed his own presidential style, groomed, as I have said on page 134, by Jorissen, Bok and Leyds. Even a man like Lord Randolph Churchill who found the

Boers loathsome, described Kruger as extremely gracious and genial. To the new generation, staring at the large man in black with his top hat and Sash of State, it was unthinkable that a President could look any different. It was also difficult to contemplate that a time would come when he would no longer be there.

Even as Kruger was addressing his people and the friends in their midst, and feeling a warm closeness to them, sentiments only a short distance away were very different. 'If I were President Kruger,' Cecil Rhodes once declared, 'I might not have given the Uitlanders the franchise, because that might have ended my own power. But I would have made my new population more comfortable and given them justice.'[235] A great many of them were extremely comfortable by any standards, and as for justice, the Gold Laws were among the fairest in the world; what was wrong there still had to be discovered if not invented. Rhodes was nearer the mark when he said: 'If only one had a Johannesburg, one could unite the whole country to-morrow . . .'[236] And if Rhodes wanted something, it had to be acquired, somehow.

CHAPTER FIFTEEN

The Third Presidency

Shortly after Paul Kruger's inauguration, preparations began in Pretoria for the visit of Sir Henry and Lady Loch, accompanied by a large staff. The 'Englishness' of Pretoria could again be observed in the tremendous display put on to receive His Excellency. The main purpose of his visit was a new Convention of Swaziland, and with all the festivities arranged people wondered how he and Kruger could get down to anything.[237] The Lochs arrived on 3 June 1893, and a provisional Convention was signed on the 9th. It is noteworthy that Kruger had by this time totally dismissed Kosi Bay as of any value as a harbour, and that he was more determined than ever not to enter a customs union until he had established a satisfactory harbour link-up.

In the Volksraad Kruger and the members dealt with a law which was intended to inhibit irresponsibility in the Transvaal newspapers. The outpourings during the presidential campaign had been so distasteful and personal that the need was felt to do something about it, no matter that any attempt to curb the freedom of the Press throughout South Africa was always resented. Further, there were railway matters, like the lines from Charlestown to Johannesburg, and Pretoria to Pietersburg as the Delagoa line came ever closer. Rhodes and his ambitions also came up for discussion in connexion with the turbulence along the Witwatersrand where there were increasing riotous elements who apparently had as their aim Imperial intervention of some kind. These agitations have been compared to a slowly burning fire, continually fanned by meetings, speeches, editorials and the signing of memorials. When a deputation of the self-styled National Union, founded by the attorney Charles Leonard to press for constitutional reform along peaceful lines, called on Kruger to protest against their limited political scope and the import tariffs which crippled the importation of essentials, the President was friendly and thoughtful but non-committal.

Hearings were more easily granted than concessions. It is one of the notable features of Kruger's rule that he always maintained personal contact with his people all over the country, in the same way as he did in Pretoria at his residence, in church and at Church Square. He was also just as accessible to foreigners and those who though part of them could hardly be considered of the *volk*. There was the Jewish community of Johannesburg, for example, who invited him to open their new synagogue and treated him as the grand old man of South Africa. The story is often told that he opened the synagogue in the name of Jesus Christ, a story which caused much laughter through the years, no matter that it was yet another invention. What is important is that a Jew like Hyman Morris could get up and say: 'The liberal attitude Your Honour has always adopted towards our religion is a shining example which deserves to be followed throughout the world.'[238]

One of Kruger's concessions which remained under steady attack was that of dynamite, this being an essential commodity in the mining operations. It was granted to Edouard Lippert, a cousin but no friend of the magnate Alfred Beit, and he made a small fortune out of the concession. As the dynamite was inferior and sold at an extortionate price, this became an increasingly serious matter as the mines developed, for imported explosives could be had at nearly half the price. When it was found that the dynamite *was* imported and still sold at the extortionate price, the concession was cancelled and turned into a Government monopoly which was thought even more obnoxious. Kruger was determined not to allow a free trade in dynamite, because, as Van Oordt points out, that would also allow a free trade in gunpowder, and automatically in fire-arms. When one considered the thousands of Natives within the borders and the unscrupulous white element there and still coming in, this would spell dire danger. Dynamite and independence were, to Kruger and his Volksraad, closely linked.[239]

President Kruger's fame was spreading daily. Years before, the historian Froude had already referred to him as 'this famous President'. But his way of life remained the same. He and Gezina were rarely by themselves at home. Apart from the streams of callers, there were 120 grandchildren, most of them Eloffs, drifting in and out. They had to be well-mannered and quiet during meals, but laughter and high spirits were not frowned upon. Kruger was getting indigestion from his quick way of eating, and perhaps also from his enormous consumption of tobacco; but like all that smoking, his eating habits were difficult to shake off. On formal occasions when it was unseemly to smoke, he would alleviate the craving by eating an orange.[240]

Kruger clearly loved his work and took it very seriously. He could hardly wait to rush off to his office, and that was probably why he ate so quickly. The Government had expressed disapproval at his going to the office on foot. With so many new foreign elements about, it was thought more fitting for him to be conveyed there, with an escort. The arrival and departure of the presidential carriage, later a coach, at and from the Government Building became one of the sights of Pretoria, like the Changing of the Guard elsewhere. On 25 July a rivet in one of the wheels snapped, causing the carriage to tilt and the horses to bolt. The coachman was flung from his seat, but passers-by quickly rushed up and secured the horses. With a smile Kruger expressed his thanks, not in the least perturbed.

He invariably did something surprising. At about the time of the carriage incident the question came up whether to raise the salaries of Generals Joubert and Smit. Kruger at once approved, suggesting that his own salary be cut by £1,000. This still left him £7,000, of which he spent little. Although his days of financial concern had long since passed, he still handled money with care. His private fortune was made by what he put aside and by land deals; since his youth he had always been acquiring land. But in this respect too there are fantasies, such as that he bought up 600,000 acres for a trifling £500. What is true is that one of his most successful transactions was made in 1886, shortly after the Reef discoveries, when he and his son-in-law Frikkie Eloff bought the Geduld-Springs farm for £700. In 1891 Kruger bought Eloff's half for £3,000 and later sold the farm as a whole to the Springs Real Estate Company for £107,700.[241]

At the beginning of 1894 the railway line from Johannesburg to Charlestown was approved. That from the Cape had already reached the Rand. Kruger did not look upon these as *his* lines, though on his last visit to Johannesburg he had travelled by train to Vereeniging on the Vaal River. The line from Delagoa Bay had reached Waterval-Onder, through difficult terrain, and also at the beginning of 1894 the section from Pretoria could be begun. The railway squabbles between syndicates, colonies and republics in South Africa are both complicated and tedious, and are merely referred to here—apart from the Delagoa line which had become an obsession with Kruger. He was no longer apprehensive of the Natal line, this colony not being under the domination of Rhodes.

On a visit to Krugersdorp (the town named after him and originating as from 1887 at Paardekraal) Kruger spoke on such questions as dynamite, Swaziland and the franchise. 'I can't possibly give all Uitlanders the vote just like that,' he said. He was, however, considering the curtailment of the residential period in the case of some responsible persons. No wonder, as since 1890 he had, as Nathan put it, 'effectively banged, bolted and barred the door against new citizens'.[242] He had created full burghers and second-class burghers, the latter having to be over forty, Protestants, owners of land within the Republic and resident for fourteen years. These restrictions were all the more amazing in that the Transvaal was open to immigration and badly needed it. But the influx had become so enormous that Kruger could not think of any other way of avoiding being swamped. At first he did not expect the franchise restrictions to become an issue, for he knew perfectly well that few immigrants were bothered by them and even less were willing to relinquish their British citizenship.

But should it be desired, Kruger was prepared to be accommodating, as he also was in other spheres such as the case of an outspoken Joubert man, Ewald Esselen. The office of State Attorney being vacant, and Esselen recommended, Kruger accepted him, no matter all the unkind and even untrue things Esselen had said about him in the past. One of the most hurting was: 'I wish to ask you if you can believe what Mr Kruger says, namely that he wishes to promote the unity of the two races. All his actions of the past ten years prove to the contrary . . .'[243] Apart from seeking conciliation, Kruger probably gave Esselen the job as a sop to the Joubert Party. It did not stop Esselen from speaking his mind, however, and he even spoke from a National Union platform. It became clear, there being a limit to Kruger's accommodating attitude, that their daily association in their respective offices would not last long.

'Sooner or later,' General Joubert kept saying, 'the Zoutpansberg will go up in flames.' He was referring to the Native unrest which nothing seemed to quell; and indeed the unrest became more and more turbulent throughout 1893 and into 1894, involving first one chief then another. By May things were getting out of hand, and Joubert was ordered to put an end to the insurrections. The State Artillery was at his disposal, well-trained young men in smart uniforms, and men were commandeered to form a strong commando. Nationalities were not taken into account in safe-guarding the State. Boer youths, Germans, Hollanders and Englishmen were among the commandeered. The Englishmen, as British subjects, refused to go. It was said that they saw no reason to fight for 'the damned Boers'. They had the support of British clergy and the National Union, but when they appealed to their Agent in Pretoria, he said that they *had* to do commando service like everybody else. They then called on the British Premier, Lord Rosebery, for his backing.

Kruger knew that this was a political move and also a test case. The National Union had begun to refer to unjust and oppressive laws, and it was the beginning of seeking pretexts for interference. The matter was referred to the Supreme Court, Esselen appearing for the State and Advocate J. W. Leonard for the five men involved. The Court, Chief Justice Kotzé presiding, decided in favour of the State. The men were put under armed escort to the commando, and as a demonstration with a Union Jack took place when this was done the political angle was perfectly plain.[244] Intense interest in the matter was aroused all over the country, the more so when it leaked out that H.M. Government was conducting correspondence with the Transvaal in connexion with it, and that Sir Henry Loch had mobilized Bechuanaland police on the Transvaal border and was hurrying to Pretoria.

Loch's instructions were two-fold : to deal with the commandeering question and, as the time was opportune, again the question of Swaziland. The British elements in Johannesburg and Pretoria were greatly excited, and they were seen streaming through the streets of the seat of Government. Sir Henry Loch was due at Pretoria's new railway station (connexion with the south had outstripped that to the east) on Monday, 25 June. Kruger, Leyds and a member of the Executive went to meet him and found a huge crowd gathered there. A corps of the Pretoria Volunteers struck up 'God Save the Queen' as the train steamed in, and this unleashed a wave of emotion. Kruger and his guests almost had to push their way through to their carriages, the President and His Excellency taking seats together. Exuberant men promptly began to unharness the horses, a man with a huge Union Jack clambered on the coachman's seat, and to the singing of 'God Save the Queen' and 'Rule Britannia', the men set off at a lope with the carriage to the Transvaal Hotel where Sir Henry and staff were to stay.

On reaching this hotel, there were cheers and singing, and the presentation of an Address to Loch. He appeared embarrassed by this tumultuous welcome directed at him alone, and so asked for a cheer for the President. This was given, though rather feebly, and Kruger now sat alone in the carriage, stranded without horses. Some Boers pushed the mob aside and swept the President away. Although outwardly calm, Kruger was furious. This pro-British demonstration was so large and sudden, and so insulting to the host, that many wondered to what extent it was organized from Johannesburg (many Uitlanders were present), and if Sir Henry Loch really was surprised by it all.

A number of Englishmen went straight to Kruger to express their strongest condemnation of what had taken place. The subject was also at once brought up in the Volksraad, for it was an open insult to the State, and immediate steps had to be taken to prevent such demonstrations. Kruger was not angry for long. 'I have not for a moment believed,' he declared, 'that decent Englishmen were involved. But, I am afraid, this is only oil on the fire, and that bitter feelings between the old and new section of the population are aggravated . . .'

If the agitators had expected to intimidate him, they produced only the opposite reaction. Kruger was more resolute than ever to deal firmly with those who insulted the country and treated the laws with contempt. He also now had proof that all his apprehensions were valid. As the High Commissioner had an invitation to Johannesburg where great excitement prevailed, Kruger sent him a note in which he said that it would be a gesture of international friendship should His Excellency *not* go there. What with torchlight processions, deputations and telegrams flying about, Sir Henry complied, though developments could have been interesting, General Joubert and the Artillery being away in the Zoutpansberg.

'When the National Union discovered that the visit to Johannesburg was not to take place,' the Kruger *Memoirs* say, 'they sent some of their members, including Tudhope and Leonard,[245] to Pretoria with an address to Sir Henry Loch. The address contained the most insulting accusations against the Government and Volksraad. But this caused no surprise to those who knew its source. In public, Sir Henry Loch advised the deputation to carry their complaints quietly before the Volksraad. In secret, he asked them how many rifles and how much ammunition they had at Johannesburg, and how long they could hold out against the Government, until he was able to come up to their assistance with English troops from outside.'[246]

In substantiation of this there has survived a letter from one of the magnates, Lionel Phillips, to Julius Wernher in which he says: 'Sir Henry Loch (with whom I had two long private interviews alone) asked me some very pointed questions, such as what arms we had in Johannesburg, whether the population could hold the place for six days until help could arrive, etc., etc., and stated plainly that if there had been 3,000 rifles and ammunition here, he would certainly have come over. He also informed me, in a very significant way, that they had prolonged the Swazie [*sic*] agreement for six months, and said he supposed in that time Johannesburg would be better prepared, as much as if to say, if things are safer then we will actively intervene . . .'[247]

This was written on 1 July 1894, showing how far a capitalist take-over of the Transvaal was already planned. The bulk of mining men had nothing or little to do with these designs, but the magnates and dreamers of empire were involved and able to exert pressure, even on those not British. From the viewpoint of Rhodes, the acquisition of the Transvaal, by now almost completely surrounded by the British sphere of influence, is perfectly understandable as capital and empire went together. He showed no interest in the Orange Free State, for it was accepted that once the South African Republic fell, this State would go with it and would no doubt also reveal mineral riches. Not all magnates, J. B. Robinson for one, felt like this, and there was as yet no general agreement about what sort of government, or flag for that matter, should supplant the Vierkleur.

Having alluded to Lionel Phillips, who was like a wounded dragon-fly in appearance, thoughts turn to his wife Florence, who only a few years later was to make the following reference to Kruger: 'His clumsy features and small cunning eyes, set high in his face, with great puffy rings beneath them, his lank straight locks, worn longer than is usual, the fringe of beard framing his face, even his greasy frock coat and antiquated tall hat have been portrayed times without number . . .' However, she admitted, 'once seen, he is not easily forgotten,' and had to add, 'He has a certain natural dignity of bearing, and I think his character is clearly to be read in his face—strength of character and cunning.' But to her he was a peasant, of manners none and customs beastly. She thought Kruger quite ignorant of conversation, an autocrat, and she noted his habit of throwing short jerky sentences at one, generally allegorical, 'partaking largely of scriptural quotations or misquotations . . .'[248] Elsewhere Lady Phillips makes the amazing statement that Kruger was certainly not a Christian. All this from a woman who, in her own way, was just as passionately South African as he was and who was to become a leading cultural driving-force in the country.[249]

The Swaziland Question dragged on to a kind of settlement ratified in 1895. The second convention dated from 1893 when Kruger met Sir Henry Loch at Colesberg, Loch following this up by his memorable visit to Pretoria with his wife and two daughters. Talks were not conclusive and were again taken up at Volksrust in 1894, the so-called Third Convention, according to which the Republic was allowed to take over Swaziland without incorporating it. But, Kruger having hardly had 'time to breathe', England promptly annexed the eastern region called Sambaanland and Umbigesaland, cutting off the

Transvaal's access to the coast. Kruger found this step inexplicable, unless it was to vex and harass him, for England had no need of this outlet and no right whatever to annex the region.[250] He should, however, have reflected on the reaction to his overtures to Germany.

But all was not vexation for Kruger. A dream of his life was realized in 1895 when the railway line to Delagoa Bay was opened. This rail link was actually completed towards the end of 1894, Kruger being the one to tighten the last bolt, but the official opening only took place in July the following year. Again he thought of President Burgers whose obsession with this line had nearly deranged him and on which he had wasted something like £90,000 at a time of bankruptcy. Now Kruger could get the Volksraad to vote £20,000 for all those who wished to take a joy-ride to Lourenço Marques. It was a gala occasion, the leading officials of all neighbouring territories being present, also Sir Hercules Robinson who had succeeded Sir Henry Loch, and among governors and administrators, Sir Sidney Shippard of Bechuanaland.

Guests were British, Dutch, German, Portuguese, Afrikaans, in a swirl of flags, decorations and bands playing. Happily Kruger took his seat in the packed train which steamed off for the east. At Delagoa Bay lay many vessels, and Kruger was taken aboard a German gunboat and given a telegram of congratulations from the Kaiser. Special medallions could be handed out, and with pride Kruger could at last speak of 'our national railway'. The Portuguese Governor was almost as excited as he was. In a toast Sir Hercules Robinson paid tribute to Kruger, the line being there mainly through *his* determination and perseverance.[251] 'This railway changed the whole internal situation in the Transvaal,' said the *Memoirs*. 'Until that time, the Cape railway had enjoyed a monopoly, so to speak, of the Johannesburg traffic.'[252]

It was inevitable that a tariff war ensued. As Premier of Cape Colony, Rhodes wanted the lion's share. Johannesburg had grown to be the biggest town in South Africa, and traffic to and fro was enormous. The Free State Railway was controlled by the Cape up to Vereeniging, on the Transvaal border, and from there by the Netherlands Company. It was Kruger's desire that the profits on goods and passenger traffic should be divided in equal shares between Cape Colony, Natal and the Transvaal, but Rhodes wanted 50 per cent as the Cape controlled by far the longest stretch. The outcome was that Rhodes lowered the tariff up to Vereeniging, while the Transvaal raised it from there to Johannesburg, a short stretch, to restore the balance.

But the tariff for this was really excessive, though Rhodes had caused it. So goods were off-loaded at Vereeniging and taken by transport wagons to Johannesburg from where wagons again rolled south. This refusal to use the train service forced Kruger to close the fords or drifts in the Vaal used by the wagons, looking upon them as 'import ports'. This 'Closing of the Drifts' became a *cause célèbre*, though it applied only to goods from overseas. Rhodes saw it as contrary to Article 13 of the London Convention and accordingly an opportunity to call for intervention. Kruger received an ultimatum from Joseph Chamberlain, now Secretary of State for Colonies, via Rhodes, demanding that he reopen the drifts. On 1 November, Chamberlain arranged with the Cape Government to send an armed force at joint expense to do so forcibly.[253]

Five days later Kruger blandly withdrew his proclamation and the drifts were open; he was convinced that just about anything could provoke British intervention while Rhodes was on the scene, now aided and abetted by a Joe Chamberlain who had made a political somersault into imperialism. This 'Drifts Crisis' of October–November 1895 was seen even by Cape politicians as unjust, illegal and wholly unwarrantable. In the opinion of J. X. Merriman, the threat of armed intervention was a revelation to Kruger as to the reality of his military position and the point from which he began to plan armament for the Transvaal.[254]

The years 1894 and most of 1895 were among the most placid of Kruger's life. He could even give attention to non-political matters like game preservation. 'If we don't do something,' he was heard to remark, 'our grandchildren won't know what a kudu, an eland or a lion looked like.' For the past ten years he had fought to have part of the eastern Transvaal put aside for a reserve, between the Sabie and Crocodile Rivers, but had met with total indifference in this respect. Game was there to shoot, his people believed, the idea of conservation being a novelty. This was not odd when one considers that there was, I believe, only one game sanctuary in the world at that time, in the United States. But Kruger persevered, proclaimed protection for rhinoceros, eland, giraffe and buffalo and achieved the Pongola Game reserve in 1894. His ultimate achievement was the Kruger National Park, a dream brought to reality after his death by James Stevenson-Hamilton.

Kruger's wisdom, even when people did not understand him, was becoming proverbial. The story was often told of two brothers who had inherited a farm and were at loggerheads about its division. Kruger's advice was that the eldest was to make the division and the other the selection. A story not so well known is of a farmer who went to Pretoria and booked in at one of the town's numerous hotels. Having £100 on him in cash, he gave this to the manager for safe-keeping, those being days when childlike trust was still common in such things. When he asked for his money back, the manager pretended that the transaction had never taken place, there having been no witnesses. The farmer took his dilemma to the President. Kruger reflected a while, then took £100 from his safe and said: 'Take this to the man also, but have witnesses around. Tomorrow, on your own, ask for your money. I'm sure he won't hesitate to give it you. Later bring your witnesses and ask for the second £100.' It worked.

Kruger's sense of humour was often tickled by the names of people, their appearance, their mannerisms and eccentricities. Many people were given nicknames, often apt, like Windhond (Greyhound) to a man very reminiscent of such an animal. Kruger's observation remained as keen as ever. Some Dutch surnames are hilarious to Afrikaner ears, but whereas this was usually covered up politely, on occasion Kruger let out a hearty guffaw, puzzling afterwards how such a surname had come into being. He enjoyed companionship, of both sexes, and found many people endearing. 'As long as officials do their duty,' he observed in his paternal manner, 'one need not be concerned with their religious convictions.' He accepted people the way they were, but more and more people appeared to expect him to be other than he was, and nearly everything he said began to raise eyebrows.

'The power of the Volksraad is supreme in the land and everyone must show obedience to its decisions.' It was by now generally accepted that Kruger *was* the Volksraad. At the beginning of 1895 he addressed the German community as follows:

> During my visit to Europe in 1884 I had the pleasure of meeting the Kaiser of Germany, Wilhelm I. He received me as his equal and with the greatest courtesy and friendliness. I was used to looking upon this Republic as a small child, yet the Kaiser received me as Head of an important, independent State. The present Kaiser was also then at Court, and I have nothing but pleasant memories of the young Prince. I am convinced that he is following in the footsteps of his forefathers and that it is his aim to strengthen the ties between our respective States ...
>
> As for my German subjects, I have found them ever loyal, and willing to obey the laws of the land. I have had many difficulties with the Natives in this Republic, and I must say that, though Her

> Majesty's subjects behave well and are loyal to the State, in times of trouble they turn to Great Britain and declare that they are the subjects of Her Majesty. The Germans, in this State, will not behave in a similar manner. Joyfully and willingly they obey the laws of this land and are not involved in the incitement of Transvaalers against these laws . . .[255]

Apprehension of 'Hollander' influence in the Transvaal had been supplanted by a dread of German dominance. Already Wilhelm II had decorated Kruger with the Order of the Red Eagle, and the strengthening of Boer–German ties was of deep concern to British imperialists.

Later that year, Kruger scanned a petition from the Witwatersrand, requesting a revision of the franchise, signed by 38,500 persons, many of the signatures clearly fictitious as even W. E. Gladstone featured among them. The conspiracy against his young country was being better organized, following the successful appeal to Great Britain over the closing of the drifts, a domestic matter which he had had a perfect right to carry out as he saw fit. As Dr Leyds was off to Germany to seek medical treatment for his throat, Kruger made use of the opportunity to entrust him with an order for guns, rifles and ammunition. To survive, the Transvaal had to be properly armed, but neither Kruger nor Joubert as yet took armament in all seriousness.

Rhodes was not bellicose like Sir Henry Loch. The confederation Rhodes wanted for South Africa was to be achieved without violence. Various means were considered, one of them having been the prolongation of the Swaziland issue. Another was a co-ordination of an Uitlander rising with the intervention of British troops, an idea Rhodes did not care for and which was frowned upon by Lord Ripon at the Colonial Office. A further idea was to invite Kruger to London and gain franchise reform, which would mean a hold on the Transvaal, by tantalizing him with a revision of Article IV of the London Convention. The invitation was sent, but Kruger declined to go. He felt that negotiations could very well take place in South Africa, as they had done at Volksrust.[256]

The Johannesburg Press was becoming more and more insulting to him personally. Kruger was hardly ever seen reading a newspaper, but secretaries did so for him, and a word which was becoming overfamiliar was 'Krugerism'. He was disturbed by the number of capitalists who had previously taken scant interest in politics and who were now letting their voices be heard and giving support to the National

Union. On the other hand, there was comfort in the cordiality of the Labour Union which 'was bold enough to assert that every honest, well-disposed law-abiding working man . . . had no better friend, no more sincere well-wisher than his worthy President, Paul Kruger.'[257] But this Union had little political significance. When Johannesburg invited Kruger to open the first Rand Show in March 1895, he went, and was pleased to find that there were no unpleasant incidents, though there were apparently some agitated persons among the fashionable crowd.

Of great importance to Kruger in July was the appointment of Joseph Chamberlain (born 1836) as Minister of the Colonies in a Conservative cabinet, though he had so long been known for his outspoken liberal views. He had even been anti-imperialist at one stage, and had shown sympathy for the Boers in the War of Independence. But all that was to go by the wayside as South African affairs 'swept him away in a rushing torrent'.[258] He began to devote his life totally to the cause of British Imperialism. It had come as a surprise to Kruger to discover at the time of the Drifts Crisis that Chamberlain was, after all, no friend of theirs and quite ready to use armed force.[259]

It was commonly being said that Johannesburg was in a state of 'ferment'. 'Rhodes,' declared Kruger, 'had long entertained the project of making himself master of the Republic in one way or another; and he devoted his money, his influence and his position as Premier of Cape Colony to this object.'[260] Only later did he have reason to reflect on the visit of Rhodes and Dr Jameson to England at the beginning of 1895 when the Chartered Company managed to extend its territory to the north of Mafeking, hugging the Transvaal's western border. This region was becoming ominously dangerous, a zone that could be used for smuggling arms into Johannesburg, or even as a point from which an invasion could be launched, Rhodes having become the main shareholder in the Simmer and Jack Mine. But that he would really attempt anything along unconstitutional lines, Kruger found difficult to credit.

On his return from his annual tour of the districts, Kruger found that he had to keep a close watch on the rebellious elements in Johannesburg. All the talk of ridding the country of 'Krugerism' naturally meant Kruger himself, and a revolt in Johannesburg *was* possible, though it could only succeed with proper organization and support from the west. He took pains, even accepting humiliations, to stick to every article of the last convention, and showed constant willingness to deal with grievances—and yet there was something building up. 'You must give the tortoise time to put its head out,' he began to say, 'before you can catch hold of it.' He liked the idea of the tortoise for he used it many times, phrased in different ways: in order to cut its head off, in order to know what to do. It was the sort of symbolism he liked, putting things in his own terminology, beasts, soil, stars, terms of the veld from which he had sprung.

President Paul Kruger celebrated his 70th birthday at Boekenhoutfontein, still in the hands of his family. Three head of cattle were given to the Natives there to be slaughtered for a feast. On the Sunday morning, Kruger held a service for them as they sat about him on the grass. The great voice rang out in air he loved: 'Look here, you are black and I am white. I do not know if your young missionary is teaching you right. This whiteness of ours is only a colour, but we all have a soul for which Christ suffered and gave His blood. If the black man has his soul washed white, he will go to heaven. But it may well be that some white men have blacker souls than you and so will go to hell . . .'[261]

CHAPTER SIXTEEN

Kruger, Raiders and Reformers

As President Paul Kruger prepared to say farewell to 1895, there followed such a swift sequence of sensational events that the beginning of 1896 was to be one of the most memorable experiences of his life. It was only after it was all over that people began to fit all the pieces together, and even then many years were to pass in the sifting process because so many of the people involved were still living. What is surprising is how much was already known while Kruger was still alive.[262]

Rhodes was frustrated in his attempts to get the Transvaal into a customs union. Matabeleland and Mashonaland, now called Rhodesia, obstinately refused to reveal riches like those of the Transvaal. His further northern expansion had been blocked by the Germans and the Belgians. His health was deteriorating, and it was quite possible that he could die before he had achieved even half of what he had dreamed to do. The Rhodes-controlled Press mirrored his frustrations. As a protectorate was proclaimed over Tongaland, finally cutting off Kosi Bay, Kruger concentrated solely on Delagoa Bay, which though Portuguese was neutral and much closer than Table Bay, and the Transvaal was strengthened in her purpose to go it alone. Rhodes even offered to *buy* Delagoa Bay, but Portugal, though in need of funds, and under pressure from Berlin, declined. If only Kruger had rejected Chamberlain's ultimatum over the drifts, Rhodes felt, there could have been some action, but the old man was too wily for that. Rhodes held that he had no argument with the Boers but solely with Kruger.[263]

Throughout 1895 Rhodes worked for some kind of revolt in Johannesburg. As time was running out, he dropped his reservations about the use of force, and had the support of Chamberlain, of the leaders of the National Union and his henchmen of whom Jameson, conqueror of Matabeleland, was the most important. Oddly enough they believed the Boers to be a minority in the Transvaal, when there were 150,000 Republican burghers by now as against 75,720 Uitlanders, of whom 41,275 were British—not 100,000 as Rhodes thought.[264]

He was also curiously blind to the lack of unity among this British element when it came to plans for revolt. It was made abundantly clear when they packed the trains leaving Johannesburg that December, ostensibly off for their Christmas holidays when they knew what was in the air. One cannot say that Rhodes underrated the military qualities of the Boer (he was certainly not anti-Boer), but he gave the military angle little thought, beyond considering that *their* end of the year festivities were to his advantage.

Kruger denied that he knew anything beforehand, and this can be questioned. General Joubert was given two tip-offs; one he received from a Scottish carpenter as early as 22 December, on his return to Wakkerstroom from a visit to Durban.[265] He also received a telegram from the Acting State Secretary to say that an Uitlander insurrection was imminent and that he had to return to Pretoria at once. This proves that Kruger must have known something—Wormser also confirms it: '*Kruger wist alles*', knew everything. Dr Jameson had turned up on the western border with troops and had spent months at Pitsani in Bechuanaland preparing to 'rescue' Johannesburg. Other members of the Government did not know or were not expecting anything untoward as they were having Christmas at their farms. Mrs De la Rey has described her utter bewilderment in her unpublished memoirs when she heard that Jameson had invaded the Transvaal.

He started out on 28 December to 'relieve' Johannesburg, acting on an appeal, he maintained, from the citizens to protect their property, wives and children. Kruger heard that the National Union now styled itself the Reform Committee, and that they were distributing arms and ammunition to a corps of volunteers. He was not alarmed, but to avoid a collision he had the police, called ZARPS, confined to barracks, while he waited to see what the 'theatrical revolutionaries' would do. The story that he slept with a loaded rifle at his bedside and that his horse stood ready saddled is quite untrue. He had not mounted a horse for years, though he would have done so if necessary, and even then in anything but panic.

The Executive met on 30 December to deal with the proclamation calling the rebellious elements in Johannesburg to law and order, and it was also to consider concessions which had been on the agenda for some time. As they were conferring, General Joubert, who was thought to be at Wakkerstroom, stalked in with a telegram and waved it about. It was a telegram he had received from the Commissioner of Mines at Ottoshoop in reply to one he had sent from Zeerust. 'This morning,' Joubert read out, 'half past five, 800[266] men of the Chartered Company's troops, armed, and with six Maxims and other guns passed through Malmaniesoog in the direction of Johannesburg.' Jameson's men had cut the telegraph wires, but by the oversight of a drunken aide the line between Zeerust and Pretoria had been left intact. 'What am I to do?' Joubert asked Kruger. 'You are the Commandant-General,' the old man said calmly. 'You should know what to do now.'

He did. A guard was put round the President's residence and telegrams were sent off in all directions. The thoroughness and swiftness of Joubert's mobilization was later described as almost incredible. Men came streaming from Rustenburg, Potchefstroom, Krugersdorp and elsewhere at a moment's notice, particular zeal being shown by Commandant Piet Cronjé who had led the siege of Potchefstroom in the War of Independence. In no time some ten thousand men rode off to Krugersdorp, the terminus of the Netherlands Railway Company, where large quantities of provisions and forage had been stored by conspirators in Johannesburg, and where Jameson was obviously heading.[267] With full faith in Joubert's military abilities, Kruger turned to diplomacy. He had already shown a more conciliatory mood before things started moving, and now appointed a committee in Johannesburg to act with the utmost cordiality. He was also ready to receive deputations of Reformers. Support for Jameson began to crumble and then to collapse.

All South Africa was electrified by those few fast and furious days. Sir Hercules Robinson wired an offer of friendly mediation and was ready to leave for Pretoria at once. His proclamation ordering Jameson out of the Transvaal was believed by many, such as W. P. Schreiner, effective in averting war.[268] Kruger wired back that he would take no steps, beyond halting Jameson and his troops, until the arrival of the High Commissioner. Jameson could no longer comply with all the entreaties to withdraw, as he was nearly at Krugersdorp and his supplies exhausted. His troops and the Boers had their first clash on the hills near the town, and Jameson and his military commander, Sir James Willoughby, were forced to ignominious surrender at Doornkop. Many Boers were of the opinion that a court martial should have been held there and then, Jameson and his officers shot.[269] But Kruger and Joubert took care that no such thing happened, Jameson already having lost seventy in killed and wounded. The Raiders were disarmed and escorted to Pretoria in a friendly way, the scare being over and their stand having been utterly farcical.

But Kruger knew that his burghers in general felt anything but friendly. This was clear even before Jameson was taken prisoner, when a commandant passed through Pretoria with four hundred men. They halted to greet Kruger and told him that when they captured Jameson they intended to march straight on to Johannesburg and to shoot down 'that den with all the rebels in it'. They had been provoked long enough. But Kruger brushed these words aside. 'No, brother,' he said, 'you must not speak like that. Remember there are thousands of innocent and loyal people at Johannesburg, and the others have been for the most part misled. We must not be revengeful; what would be the result of such a step?' But the commandant persisted until Kruger pretended to lose his temper. 'Very well,' he shouted, 'if you will not listen to me, you can depose me from the presidency and govern the country after your own fashion.' When this had the desired effect, Kruger added quietly: 'Then, if you will listen to me, *do* what I say and leave the rest to me.'[270]

In anti-Kruger books it is heatedly stated that he had every intention of having the ringleaders, both of the raiders and also of the conspiracy in Johannesburg, shot. But from the start it was his intention to hand the organizers of the Raid to the British Government for punishment and to give the Reformers fair trial. What his commandants felt was a different matter. The Raid itself was a putrid affair, but its repercussions were tremendous, and particularly when the Kaiser, in a moment of madness, as some thought, sent Kruger a telegram of congratulations on 3 January 1896. Rhodes's political future was ended, the split with the Afrikanerbond being total, and in England there was indignation that their countrymen could have made themselves the laughing-stock of the world. Chamberlain, though deeply implicated with Rhodes, had to repudiate Jameson, while Rhodes, resigning as Premier of the Cape, forgave him for ignoring his last-minute instructions to remain at Pitsani. Rhodes was always loyal to his friends.

The remarkable thing about the Jameson Raid was the calm if not cool way it was handled by Kruger and the insight he showed once he had his facts straight. He had taken note of a manifesto by Charles Leonard with its grievances and demands published in the Johannesburg papers, had declined to allow the German consul to bring up fifty German marines ostensibly to guard the consulate, and was quick to discern the lack of unity among the two deputations that came to see him from the Rand. Moreover, he readily accepted the mediation offered by Sir Hercules Robinson, not knowing that His Excellency had been fully informed all along, and that the collapse of a stand in Johannesburg had sent his plans awry.[271] But if Sir Hercules, aged and ailing in his second term of office, thought he could bully Kruger he was very wrong. When he talked of the removal of grievances and the fate of Jameson, the old man cut him short by saying that that could wait.

'First we have to deal with Johannesburg, and must prevent further bloodshed. Johannesburg must surrender her arms.' Sir Hercules wished to know on which conditions. 'Unconditionally!' roared Kruger. And should the arms be refused, 'I will fetch them!' He had up to twelve thousand burghers and the State Artillery at the ready to attack Johannesburgh. 'I'll give them twenty-four hours to surrender their arms,'[272] he added in a tone of voice which allowed no argument. As for Jameson and his officers, their fate would be decided. According to Van Oordt the burghers, the veldcornets, the commandants—the Transvaal people demanded the final penalty for these freebooters. 'Even the members of the Executive Council were of the same opinion. Only one man said "*No*".' That man was Kruger.

His battle with contrary opinion took place on the afternoon of 6 January at 4 o'clock and lasted for four hours with the commandants, the Executive being present, as well as Orange Free State deputies and his legal team. 'What do the lives of these people matter to us?' Kruger wanted to know. 'The future does. Thousands of Englishmen live in our country, and no matter how just the sentence, how well-deserved the death-penalty, the seven or nine executed will be so many martyrs and will make schism between Burghers and Englishmen unbridgable.' On these lines he argued: hand them over to the British Government, and even if they were not punished, the Transvaal would still gain, for then 'that proud nation will lose its last claim to civilized procedure'.[273] The Transvaal could deal with the Reformers herself.

The aftermath of the Raid revealed Kruger as both crafty and humane, even if it was 'magnanimity by inches'. He had entered a new phase of popularity, was calm, collected and absolutely sure of himself. A cat-and-mouse game, when not at a disadvantage, appealed to the politician in him and also to his sense of humour. Raiders and Reformers who had never bothered to take a long, slow look at Kruger were now, in fear of their lives, inclined to look too carefully and to interpret more than was there. They speculated about his sincerity, his reliability, his hypocrisy and theatricality. These speculations became more and more intense as the plot against the Transvaal was being unravelled, starting with a box of incriminating papers found on the outskirts of Krugersdorp.

Sir Jacobus de Wet, the British Agent in Pretoria, telegraphed to the Reform Committee about the unconditional surrender of Johannesburg. This had no effect and De Wet and Sir Sidney Shippard had to face the crowds in person. On their heads be it that the erroneous impression was given that the life of Dr Jameson depended on their procedure. 'It is hardly necessary to say that they complied before the twenty-four hours had expired,' Kruger related, 'for, with the exception of Colonel Rhodes [Francis William, Cecil's elder brother] and perhaps one or two more, there was not one among the conspirators but would have taken to his heels so soon as the first shot was fired. They had wooed and organized rebellion only in the hope that England would pull the chestnuts out of the fire for them.'[274]

Chamberlain had no option but to express his gratitude to Kruger in the name of the Queen for sparing Jameson and his officers. All that Johannesburg surrendered were 1,814 rifles and three damaged Maxims. The Boers resented this, believing that there were at least ten thousand rifles—until it transpired that the town was not at all as well-armed as had been rumoured. Jameson and his men were handed over to the Governor of Natal to be sent to England for trial. On 9 January Kruger issued a proclamation in which he granted general amnesty, except for the leaders of the Reform conspiracy, a total of sixty-four men, of whom Lionel Phillips, John Hays Hammond (an American), Frank Rhodes and George Farrar were the most important. They were arrested at their homes and clubs on the 9th and imprisoned at Pretoria on a charge of high treason. It was strange to think of these wealthy swashbuckling men languishing in that 'filthy' gaol.

The next day Kruger published another proclamation in which he said that he looked upon only a small number of crafty men as the conspirators. He had already promised the abolition of food duties, lower railway charges and would continue to consider a more liberal franchise. Furthermore, Johannesburg could have her own municipality. 'For months and months,' he said, 'I have considered which changes and improvements would be desirable in the Government of the State; but the atrocious incitement, particularly of the Press, made me hesitate. The same men, who have now publicly acted as leaders, demanded reforms from me in a manner they would not have dared to adopt in their own fatherland . . . I ask you in all seriousness, put your hand to your hearts and answer me this question: "Can and may I, after what has happened, propose to have representation of the people?"' He meant in the running of Johannesburg, and answered the question by saying Yes, for he was prepared to appear before the Volksraad with the motto of 'forgive and forget'.[275]

The hysterical outpourings of some people, like Florence Phillips,[276] are rather difficult to comprehend when one considers what would

Queen Wilhelmina's Accession, 1898: Taking the Oath in the New Church, Amsterdam

President Marthinus Steyn

Dr W. J. Leyds

Lord Alfred Milner, by Malcolm Stewart

Cecil John Rhodes

An 1896 cartoon shows Kruger hunting Rhodes

The Glorious Trio: De Wet, De la Rey and Botha

President Kruger, September 1899

The Last View of Africa. With President Kruger is Manie Bredell

President Kruger at Marseilles: Arrival at the Hotel Noailles

President Kruger's 77th Birthday, 10 Oct. 1902, Utrecht. With him in the front row are, from left to right: General C. R. de Wet: General Louis Botha; W. J. Leyds; General Koos de la Rey

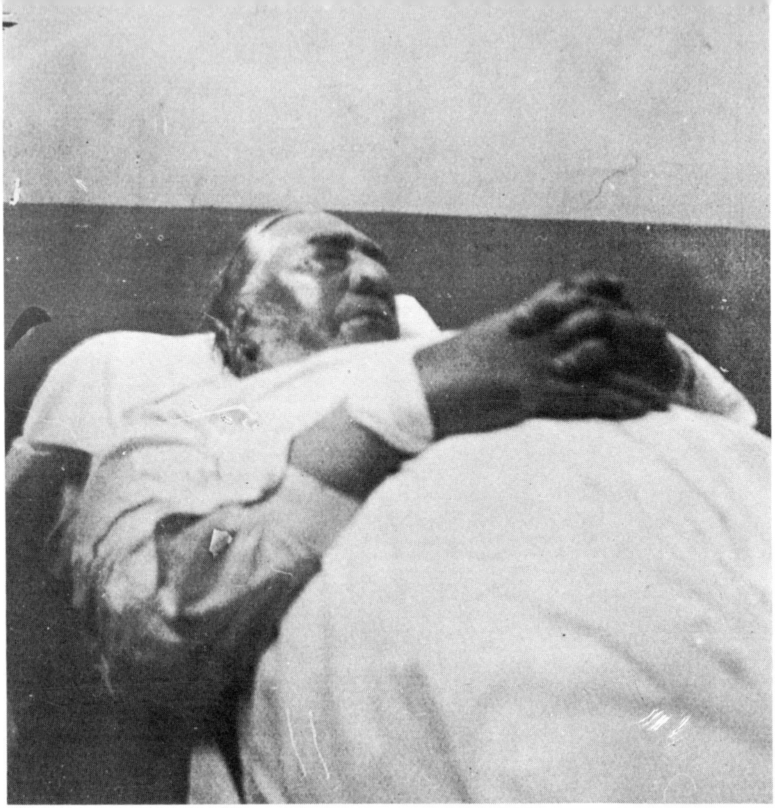

President Kruger in Death

The Monument to President Kruger, Pretoria

have happened had the plot against Kruger come off. 'If filibustering fails,' Lord Salisbury wrote to Chamberlain, 'it is always disreputable.' Words like 'gruesome', 'tyranny', 'injustice' and 'Boer oligarchy' were in common usage, when in fact Kruger showed clemency in the face of strong opposition from a large sector of his people, and also at a time of 'extraordinary outburst of Jingo feeling' in its most repulsive form, as Jan Hofmeyr observed.[277] 'One would have thought,' he went on, 'that the flagrant and indefensible violation of all justice and honour would have been obvious even to the most violent Jingo, especially when we consider that outside of Johannesburg, there had hardly been any sympathy displayed with the Uitlander grievances before the Raid.' The reason for this must largely be sought in the indignation felt throughout the English-speaking world at the Kaiser's telegram to Kruger and its implications.

Rhodes was to tell the Commons Committee of Inquiry into the Raid that he participated in the plot largely because of his fear of German interference in South Africa.[278] Germany already had huge footholds to the west and in East Africa, and had been influential in keeping Delagoa Bay out of British hands. All this was true, and because of the Kaiser, Rhodes and Jameson were the heroes of the hour in England. In South Africa the Afrikaners found Kruger's overtures to Germany as the obvious great power for support perfectly understandable. He was encouraged by Dr Leyds and, as has already been shown, Kruger made no secret of his desire for German backing, diplomatically, politically and economically. That British diplomats resented this is also understandable.[279] And now the Kaiser himself had poked his nose into Boer and British relations.

'I express my sincere congratulations,' he cabled to Kruger, 'that, supported by your people, without appealing for help of friendly powers, you have succeeded by your own energetic action against armed bands which invaded your country as disturbers of the peace, and have thus been enabled to restore peace and safeguard the independence of the country against attacks from outside.' British reaction to this, Virginia Cowles maintained in her biography of the Kaiser, 'tore a breach in Anglo–German relations which never wholly mended'.[280] Apparently the Kaiser put his signature to the telegram with great reluctance, as it had little to do with positive action and would only draw wrath on his own head; but it was thought by his advisers to be positive as a step in the progressive establishment of a Continental bloc against England, particularly with the co-operation of France and Russia.

'My dear William,' Victoria wrote to him, 'As your Grandmother to whom you have always shown so much affection and of whose example you have always spoken with so much respect, I feel I cannot refrain from expressing my deep regret at the telegram you sent President Kruger. It is considered very unfriendly towards this country, which I am sure it is not intended to be, and has, I grieve to say, made a very painful impression here. The action of Dr Jameson was, of course, very wrong and totally unwarranted; but considering the very peculiar position in which the Transvaal stands to Great Britain, I think it would have been far better to say nothing . . .' It would also have been so for Kruger, for his hopes of Germany had only been strengthened. One wonders if he ever considered that if it was not for Britain, Germany could just as well have grabbed the Transvaal.

Kruger and his advisers decided to have a judge from outside to preside at the trial of the Reformers. They decided on the State Attorney of the Orange Free State, Reinhold Gregorowski (1856–1922), a rotund man with sweeping moustaches and gleaming eyes behind pince-nez. He readily accepted the invitation which in the circumstances could only be seen as fabulous. The preparatory examination began on 3 February and lasted for the rest of the month. It was indeed a most dramatic month, for on the 19th, fifty-five tons of dynamite in trucks at Braamfontein, long one of Johannesburg's major stations, exploded, killing 80 people, wounding 700 and leaving 1,500 homeless. It was a scene of ghastly devastation, with corrugated iron strewn for miles around.

Kruger at once hurried to the scene, visited the wounded hospitalized at the Wanderers, and was impressed by the sympathy of the Uitlanders shown all round. They had at once opened a relief fund to which the mining companies and citizens subscribed £70,000 within two days. 'Blessed are the merciful, for they shall obtain mercy,' Kruger murmured. He offered £25,000 from his Government, and the Netherlands Railway Company made a first contribution of £10,000. The Braamfontein dynamite explosion ranks among South Africa's major disasters.[281]

Also in February Kruger was in telegraphic communication with Joseph Chamberlain. Kruger had again been invited to London to confer on Transvaal matters, and was urged to go by his businessman friend Samuel Marks and by Sir James Sivewright, a member of the Cape ministry. Should Kruger come, it would be a coup for Chamberlain, the opportunity of resuming the initiative, though he had no intention of modifying Article IV of the London Convention. As this was the only article which still restricted the Transvaal in her foreign relations, it was the only subject Kruger would have liked to discuss. If it was not on the agenda, not even a special ship as H.M.'s guest would tempt him to go.

Disappointed, Chamberlain sent off another dispatch 'in which he proposed that a sort of Home Rule should be granted to Johannesburg, and he published this dispatch in the London official press before I had received it,' Kruger related. 'When one reflects that it was the very question of Home Rule for Ireland that caused Mr Chamberlain to withdraw from Gladstone's party and barter his Radicalism for his present Jingoism, one must stand astounded at the effrontery of his proposal, especially under the existing circumstances.'[282] But of course Rhodes was in London.

Kruger was not going to have publicity given to views which the British Government thought fit to adopt towards the Transvaal before he even knew what they were. Nor was he going to allow any interference in her internal affairs. What he wanted was a treaty of peace, commerce and amity to replace the London Convention. The retention of Article IV in any kind of new Convention made a trip to England pointless. This contentious article reads :

> The South African Republic will conclude no treaty or engagement with any State or nation other than the Orange Free State, nor with any native tribe to the eastward or westward of the Republic, until the same has been approved by Her Majesty the Queen.
>
> Such approval shall be considered to have been granted if Her Majesty's Government shall not, within six months after receiving a copy of such treaty (which shall be delivered to them immediately upon its completion), have notified that the conclusion of such treaty is in conflict with the interests of Great Britain or of any of Her Majesty's possessions in South Africa.[283]

As Chamberlain saw no way of giving Kruger a hopeful purpose to visit London, the invitation was withdrawn on 25 February.

The Reform Committee members were committed for trial in April. A jury was found unnecessary as Phillips, Farrar, Frank Rhodes and Hammond pleaded guilty to high treason, and the rest to a lesser form of it. Mr Justice Gregorowski (much was made of his melodramatic or diabolic glee) sentenced the four leaders to death, while the remaining sixty were sentenced to two years' imprisonment and a fine of £2,000 each, and thereafter banishment from the State for a further three years. The effusive expressions of horror or jubilation can be dismissed, as few people could possibly have taken these sentences seriously, no matter that they were in accordance with Roman Dutch Law, for almost immediately Kruger was bombarded with appeals for mercy. But one could hardly call the whole trial 'a monstrous farce' as was done by Florence Phillips.[284] 'Kruger is much inclined to clemency,' the jurist James Rose Innes wrote to his wife after calling on the President, 'and I think there is every possibility that the sentence will be commuted to one of banishment.'[285]

As Kruger had kept his head throughout, even to the extent of playing a cat-and-mouse game, there was no reason why he should lose his head now. He wished to give the whole matter careful thought, and in his own time. Like all Boers he had an aversion to capital punishment. Nothing lived on so tenaciously in the Boer mind as the hangings by the British Government of insurgent Boers at Slachtersnek in 1815 when four of the ropes snapped and the men were prepared for hanging all over again. The event, true reasons and facts having been obscured by the mists of time, had become symbolic of dire oppression, British oppression. It had even been given as one of the reasons for the Great Trek. The arrival in Pretoria at this time of part of the Slachtersnek gallows, destined for the National Museum, caused a stir, as it was expected to be put up on a public square and *used*.[286] How little the Boer mind was understood.

When some burghers called on Kruger and insisted that the four leaders be hanged, he said quietly: 'What do you think of Slachtersnek?' They expressed their outrage at this 'foul deed' committed back in the days of the arrogant Lord Charles Somerset. 'And now?' Kruger asked. 'Do you want a second Slachtersnek for the English?' The implications were at once understood. ('Blood shed on a scaffold,' Olive Schreiner once remarked, 'is always fresh.') The President had clearly given the subject much thought, and the matter was dropped. All the more reason for him to be furious when Chamberlain anticipated his Government by sending a cable on 29 April in which he said that he was certain that His Honour would commute the sentences and that he had already said so in Parliament. A curt reply was sent to the High Commissioner that it was already decided that morning to commute the sentences.

The bargaining which commenced was perhaps inevitable with men who were mainly interested in money, and consequently also 'ignoble' as Dr Hans Sauer saw it. The four leaders were finally released on paying a fine of £25,000 each, an enormous sum by ordinary standards but not for men who could well afford it and had made a fortune out of the country they had hoped to seize. I believe that between them they possessed something like forty million pounds. Conditions were that they were not to interfere in Transvaal politics for fifteen years. The others were released on payment of their £2,000 and were not to meddle in politics for three years. Those who could not pay their fines were helped out by the Consolidated Gold Fields Company. When the question of bail was still under consideration, Kruger was asked not to allow his human nature to be influenced by malign factors. He jumped up in a rage and shouted, 'Ja, you always say it is somebody else! First it was Jorissen, then Nellmapius, and then it was Leyds. Well, Jorissen is done for; Nellmapius is dead, and Leyds is in Europe—who is it now?'[287] This anecdote rings true, and shows Kruger's resentment about the supposed hold others had on him, as if it was impossible for him to have a brain and a will of his own.

Kruger's clemency, which does appear to have been unnecessarily protracted, has been ascribed to the influence of the Cockney millionaire, Barney Barnato. He was not in the Transvaal at the time of the Raid but was back for the Reform trial. Barnato, like J. B. Robinson, had long been on a friendly footing with Kruger who always got on well with Jews. Barnato too was outraged by the trial, for he could not see how any civilized Court of Law in the world could have accepted a plea of guilty on such grave charges, and he volubly abused Judge Gregorowski in the uproar that followed the passing of sentence. Dressed in mourning, Barnato called on Kruger and was eventually moved to shout: 'I'm not bluffing, Mr President, I have twenty thousand whites and a hundred thousand blacks on my payroll. If I close down, I will put more white men alone out of work than you have burghers in your State. My concerns spend £50,000 a week which would be lost to you. Already, thanks to the political crisis, the mines have lost £20 million in production. D'ye want to ruin your country for good and all? Do you?'

'No one else could have done what I did,' Barnato said proudly after the sentences were commuted. In London a cartoon was published showing Barnato the conjuror hypnotizing Kruger on stage, with Chamberlain seated in the stalls murmuring: 'How does he do it?'[288] The story fits the Barnato legend, only Kruger was not scared and not easily bluffed, and he had already decided against capital punishment before Barnato, who denied any part in the Raid, had returned to Johannesburg. And when Kruger said: 'Wealth cannot break laws', he meant it. Barnato tried to patch up their friendship by a gift of two marble lions which were placed beside the steps to Kruger's front door, and there they still are. Barnato begged the lions off Leo Weinthal who had had them made for his own house, as he could think of no more suitable gift to Kruger on his 71st birthday. Kruger tolerated these lions in the same way as he now did the young guards who were henceforth posted on his sidewalk, but it was a friendship not to be revived, and it has not been recorded what Kruger thought when an apparently deranged Barnato jumped into the sea on a voyage to England the following year.

The excitements of the early part of 1896 were alarming to Gezina Kruger for additional reasons. For once her precious privacy was invaded by scores of elegantly gowned Uitlander women pleading clemency. Many of these ladies clapped eyes on her for the first time, a plump little woman in black, her face inscrutable, who carried on as usual with such daily tasks as peeling peaches when in season. 'Please Mrs Kruger,' she was begged, 'use your influence on the President on our behalf . . .' Gezina said that she would do all she could. 'I am very sorry for you all, although I know that none of you thought of me that night when we heard that Jameson had crossed the border, and we were afraid the President would have to go out and fight, and when they went and caught his old white horse that he had not ridden for eight years. But all the same I am sorry for you all—'[289]

'If the heads of the Boer Government had not been wise men,' was the comment of Mark Twain after his South African visit, 'they would have hanged Jameson, and thus turned a very commonplace pirate into a holy martyr. But even their wisdom has its limits, and they will hang Mr Rhodes if they ever catch him. That will round him and complete him and make him a saint. He has already been called by all other titles that symbolize human grandeur, and he ought to rise to this one, the grandest of all. It will be a dizzy jump from where he is now, but that is nothing, it will land him in good company and be a pleasant change for him.'[290]

CHAPTER SEVENTEEN

Kruger in the Prelude to War

For some time there had been severe criticism of President Kruger in Cape Colony and also the Orange Free State. One outcome of the Jameson Raid was a tremendous Afrikaner swing towards him. This softened Kruger's heart towards the Cape Afrikaners, and from now on he was more ready to employ them. Kruger's name was a household word throughout the world, and in South Africa his personality aroused more interest than ever before. Streams of Afrikaners visited Pretoria, as well as English-speaking persons and other nationalities. To their pleasure there was still no difficulty in gaining an audience. Among them were many writers, from Olive Schreiner to Frank Harris, Americans and Continentals. On being invited to a recital of Negro spirituals which was said to be very fine, Kruger told the Negro leader of the group: 'Ah, but you haven't heard *me* sing. I sing bass . . .' But he attended and was moved.

A young Hollander, fresh from the Netherlands and of very good family, was introduced to the President who watched his grand air with some amusement. 'Well, what are you doing in the Transvaal?' asked the old man. 'I am looking for employment, Your Honour, preferably in the civil service, and I hope that I can be of help to you.' Kruger blew out a large cloud of smoke. 'Indeed. And what can you do?' The young man seemed to be able to do anything and began to list all his qualifications. When he had at last finished, the President said: 'But don't you need clever people in Holland?' The reply being in the affirmative, Kruger ended the interview by saying: 'Then why didn't you *stay* there?'[291]

Another outcome of the Raid was the revelation of how badly the Republic was armed in case of an emergency, something already suspected at the time of the Drifts crisis. There were burghers who did not possess firearms of any kind. As this was General Joubert's department, he was asked to deal with the matter forthwith. As from January 1896 he ordered thousands of Guedes rifles, Martini-Henrys and eventually Mausers, which the Boers liked best, as well as millions of rounds of ammunition, Creusots, Krupps, Maxim-Nordenfeldts, Maxims, field-guns, siege-guns, howitzers, and so on.[292] An enormous sum of money was involved, and although the Transvaal could afford it, this caused Joubert to hesitate until prodded by his Artillery officers who still felt that they did not have enough.

Up to October 1899 the country was armed to the teeth with the very best and most modern arms made, and would have been even better armed had Joubert shown more zeal and had all orders been delivered in time. Kruger's contention was that their objective was solely to protect the Republic against further filibustering raids, but of course he knew from the Raid that war with Great Britain was not a remote possibility. Rhodes was a hero in England, Chamberlain's complicity in his schemes was revealed, and Jameson was released after only four months in prison. The rate at which the Transvaal was arming herself caused much talk, and even among the disapproving a feeling of outrage that the bulk was bought from Germany and France, and not England.

The general lack of understanding of Kruger the man has been shown in the pressure put on him to show clemency to the Reform leaders. I must add that mayors and town councillors from all over came to Pretoria for a mass deputation—when Kruger had already decided which action to take—on 11 June. The death sentences having been commuted, Kruger was given a rapturous reception as he drove home from the Government Buildings. Men surged forward to unharness the horses in order to draw the carriage themselves, but this Kruger, perhaps from past experience, would not allow. Receiving the mayors that afternoon, the President said:

'I am pleased to see so many deputies from so many towns, but I must assure you that petitions have had no influence on me. In what I have done, I have been guided by the Book. Should people threaten me with war or wish to kill me, I will still act according to the Book, guided by its teaching . . . I look upon the Reformers as naughty boys, deserving punishment, but not as guilty as the man who incited them by shouting "*Sa!*" [The Afrikaans way of setting off a dog.] That man *must* be punished.' Everybody knew that he meant Rhodes, and it was Rhodes who never left his thoughts from now on.[293]

At the Volksraad session of May, attention was given to a stricter enforcement of the Press Law, aimed at the mouthpieces of the Reformers who had persistently preached revolt and had made the most vicious personal attacks on the President. Another law was taken up for the expulsion of undesirable elements, and another for prohibiting their entry. At the same time the greatest caution had to be exercised not to infringe the Convention in any way under the watchful eyes of Joseph Chamberlain. Although Kruger had become the greatest personality in South Africa, and after the Raid a symbol of Afrikanerdom, this by no means silenced his critics. They were as vociferous as ever against the Press Law, the Passport Law and the Aliens Expulsion Act, for these were seen as moves against the Uitlanders. Opposition was not confined to the foreign element, but was growing among a new generation of Afrikaners who wanted Kruger to be a worthy symbol, instead of sliding back to the Middle Ages.

The people who were convinced that he would never unbend and would only become more dictatorial and retrogressive were comforted by the thought that he could not live for ever. And Kruger was ageing in front of their eyes. The bags under his eyes were becoming more pronounced, making his eyes look smaller than they were. Hair and beard were turning silver, and the great shoulders slumped. He was now accompanied by a mounted escort to the Raadzaal, in the corridors of which he was preceded by constables with drawn sabres. In the chamber armed men stood on guard. The old man was still capable of rapid movement, and when roused could pound his walking-stick with notable vigour.

Kruger no longer wore anything but black, the usual frock-coat and top hat. His ways remained the same, rising at dawn, lighting his first pipe and drinking coffee on the stoep with his male callers. About now he had some alterations and improvements made to the house. As always his advice was sought on every imaginable subject, and the stoep gatherings livened up when the Volksraad was in session. Having his breakfast just before eight, the President was in his office on the stroke of nine. Impassively he endured the ceremonies attending his departures and arrivals.

From 9 a.m. until noon Kruger was fully occupied, the Executive sitting almost every day, and he still expected everybody to work as hard as he did. He had luncheon shortly after midday and was back at his office from two until four-thirty. Back home, the afternoon stoep sessions would commence, usually the calling time for foreigners when an interpreter would be present. The session over, the President went indoors when he now received only members of his family and old friends. Supper followed, and shortly after nine Kruger retired to bed. His hearing had begun to deteriorate, and this increasing deafness (varying from day to day) was to be coupled with a most painful affliction of the eyes—ingrowing eyelashes. Those close to him noted his moodiness, from the lightheartedness of a schoolboy to abject despair, moods which changed overnight.

Magdalena Eloff, whom Kruger gave the incongruous (coming

from him) nickname of 'Aurora', related that when Gezina wished to get something out of him, she used to rub his knee, a signal Kruger knew well. At one time she wanted some money needed by a son-in-law, a request he frowned upon. But he went to the safe in his bedroom, jerked out a drawer too far and there was the crash of coins spilling in all directions. Kruger reappeared and called to Magdalena and a maid to pick up the money. Mrs Kruger too, in spite of her enormous girth, began to snatch up gold coins and pop them into her apron pocket. Kruger ignored this but kept a close watch on Magdalena and the maid. Magdalena found the last sovereign under the bed and begged to have it. Kruger refused, so she popped it into her mouth. 'Let the child be,' said Gezina, 'before she swallows it.' The next day the old man fiddled in his pocket and produced something as he looked at Magdalena. He knew that she would expect another gold coin, so it was a peppermint, the expression on her face giving him great amusement.[294]

At his age it was only to be expected that Kruger felt at times that he was outliving all his contemporaries. In March 1896, for example, his beloved crony General Nicolaas Smit died. But others took their place, and one of them was Mr Justice Marthinus Theunis Steyn who succeeded Frank Reitz as State President of the Orange Free State. Although they had met when Steyn was a mere youth, it is unlikely that Kruger had forgotten him as he hardly ever forgot anything. Steyn was sworn in as President that same month. The very next day, 5 March, Steyn asked his Volksraad to give financial aid to the victims of the dynamite disaster at Braamfontein some weeks before, and then went on to propose a meeting with President Kruger at Viljoensdrift.

M. T. Steyn was only thirty-nine. He had started losing his hair in youth, and one was impressed by his broad bare brow, his fine brown eyes and his beard which straggled over his chest. He was descended from well-known, affluent and influential families, had continued his studies in the Netherlands and London, was highly intelligent, cultured and amusing; he was such a delightful man that he was always surrounded by friends whose devotion to him never flagged. He was also blessed in his marriage to Rachel Isabella Fraser, daughter of a Scottish parson who had become absorbed by the Afrikaners, a charming, intelligent and gracious woman.

On his assumption of office, Steyn was somewhat embarrassed by his youth, but he could only hope that the passing of time and the gaining of experience would remedy that. One of his first aims was to win

Kruger's confidence, for he sensed that theirs was to be a close and dramatic relationship. There was nothing anti-British about Steyn, but the annexation of the diamond fields which were part of his country came as a shock in his youth, and gave him a national awareness which only deepened. In the Transvaal War of Independence, while he was in London, he identified himself with Boer aspirations. The Jameson Raid outraged him and gave priority to the relationship between the two republics. The fate of the diamond fields made Steyn reflect with some apprehension on the fate of the goldfields.

Kruger was able to sort out Steyn's background in a matter of minutes, for he knew the clans of Steyn, Wessels and De la Rey well. Kruger was also pleased with Steyn's legal background and obvious intelligence. No matter the great difference in their ages, Kruger never talked down to him and treated Steyn in every way as a Head of State and colleague. 'His heroism,' say the Kruger *Memoirs* of Steyn, 'his resolution and his patriotism are known to all the world; and write what one may, it will always remain an impossible task to give a description of the feelings of attachment, respect and love that fill the hearts of all true Afrikaners for President Steyn. He will certainly be handed down in the memory of his people to the furthest generation as one of the greatest and noblest men that have seen the light of South Africa.'[295] This has proved to be so.

Steyn won Kruger's confidence from the start by being absolutely straightforward with him at Viljoensdrift. 'We did not hide from ourselves the fact that our existence in South Africa was in danger,' Steyn said in his memoirs. 'President Kruger acknowledged that it was essential to do as much as possible not to provoke future confrontations . . . But our main purpose was to be the protection of the interests of our two States along peaceful lines.' Kruger too was always open-hearted with Steyn, 'and even where we differed from each other at times, it was not because of a lack in confidence but in difference of opinion . . . The more I worked with him the higher rose my esteem for his deep insight, power of thought, true patriotism and deep-felt piety. I will thus always look upon it as one of my greatest privileges that it was allowed me to work with him . . .'[296]

The friendship of Steyn gave Kruger strength of heart as Chamberlain's campaign against him intensified and became more and more open. The Transvaal was being bombarded with dispatches mainly concerned with what were considered infringements of the London Convention. The Republic sinned by joining the Geneva Convention, by passing the Press and Immigration Laws, by concluding an extradition treaty with Portugal, and so on. The most amazing step that Chamberlain took was to revive the assumption of British suzerainty, annulled back in 1884. To maintain that suzerainty still existed, struck Kruger as 'nonsensical'. Lord Derby himself had struck out the line 'subject to the suzerainty of Her Majesty, her heirs and successors'. But Chamberlain closed his eyes to this, the claim of suzerainty being a powerful weapon against Kruger.

'I am not going to run away from Africa and I will remain here unofficially and carry out the big idea,' Cecil Rhodes wrote to W. P. Schreiner. Kruger was only temporary, but what he feared was 'a huge English-speaking republic in the Transvaal which will absorb the North and leave the Cape out at the shank end of the Continent'. Rhodes was still bent on his aim of union under the English flag with responsible government.[297] The problem was that even the Uitlanders were rather indifferent as to which flag they lived under, being more interested in making money and having their grievances remedied. Even Jameson had considered replacing Kruger with Lucas Meyer. After the Raid, the drama was one of British Imperialism against Afrikaner Nationalism, the former finding expression in the founding of the South African League. This League had as its aim the Rhodes–Chamberlain determination to have British supremacy with equal political rights for all whites in a united South Africa under the Union Jack.[298]

Anti-Kruger books were beginning to make frequent reference to a vast pan-Afrikaner conspiracy, Boers 'scheming, plotting and planning night and day, back door and front door, how to become the undisputed master of South Africa as a whole.' Chamberlain declared: 'The Dutch in South Africa desire, if possible, to get rid altogether of the connexion with Great Britain, which to them is not a motherland, and to substitute a United States of South Africa which, they hope, would be under Dutch influence.' L. S. Amery talked of the 'mischievous ideal of a purely Dutch South Africa'.[299] This myth begun by Rhodes was gaining wide credence and could justify war, particularly to those blind to the South African structure. Kruger's reply was that if the Republic were then to belong to England, a price would have to be paid which would stagger humanity. War would either mean their practical extinction or getting what they want. The sole question was one of freedom or death. 'If we live to be subdued,' he went on, 'our children would be slaves. If we die for our freedom, then our children can draw the greatest advantage from our example. This we know, that if a self-governing people places itself under the yoke of another, its moral fall is assured.'[300]

The Raid had fixed the attention of the whole world on Paul Kruger, and it was kept there by the continuing repercussions and intrigues. It was also by now more and more apparent that the Witwatersrand was undoubtedly the greatest repository of gold known. Kruger took all the limelight in his matter-of-fact way. He sat for endless photographic studies, and stood patiently as photographers scrambled about with naphtha flares to take shots of him laying foundation stones and taking part in all kinds of functions. He was also becoming used to cartoons in the Press,[301] his personal appearance being the delight of all cartoonists. A variety of coins had his head in profile, and so many medallions were struck, even long after his death, that they have warranted an entire book.

Kruger was generously decorated by the various Powers. For such an unostentatious man it must have been wearisome, but at the request of the Volksraad he wore these jewels or *Ridderordes*: the knightly orders of Portugal, the Netherlands, Belgium and France. The malicious were wont to say that he was decorated like a Christmas tree. (President Steyn who received his share of orders never wore them.) But if Kruger forgot to put them on or could not be bothered, he was rebuked by the Volksraad. In a photograph used by Florence Phillips, one of his decorations hangs from a safety-pin, clearly painted in, as no photographer could have let it pass. The resplendent Sash of State, with its coat of arms, tassels and fringes, must have been uncomfortably wide and long.

The Kruger personage also began to move into the world of sculpture. Through a combination of the President's kindness, the business opportunities of the Transvaal and his own financial acumen, Kruger's crony, Sammy Marks, had become a millionaire. As a token of appreciation he offered Pretoria a statue of the President in bronze. The project was estimated at £10,000 and the commission went to a burly young Dutch sculptor, Anton van Wouw, who had settled in the Transvaal and had become totally identified with the Boer people. Van Wouw's conception was ambitious, a standing Paul Kruger surrounded by four crouching Boers from different periods of their history, larger than life-size, as well as panels in bas-relief—a large monument indeed.

Kruger disliked the whole idea, partly on religious grounds. When he saw the maquette (he never posed for Van Wouw's numerous studies of him)[302] he said that he hoped the young artist did not consider himself God. Kruger did not pose as he said he did not wish to cause comment. Actually Van Wouw was such a meticulous sculptor that he preferred to work from photographs and to study his subject in his ordinary way of life. Mrs Kruger asked that the top of the top hat be left open as a bird-bath, something which convulsed the Reitzes.[303] Kruger never saw his monument erected, and it was to have a chequered history before it found its final position on Church Square in 1954. The crouching Boers are masterpieces—no wonder Lord Kitchener used two of them to decorate his garden in England until they were returned.

As 1896 drew to a close preparations for a conference between Presidents Kruger and Steyn at Bloemfontein were finalized. Their preliminary conference had been at Viljoensdrift. As everybody knew, it mainly concerned closer union between the two republics, something which had been disrupted by the illness and resignation of Steyn's predecessor, Reitz. On 10 March 1897 Kruger and his entourage arrived in Bloemfontein by train (a mode of travel the President found most agreeable), to be met by Steyn and his commission. There was a rapturous crowd and the flags of the two States fluttered everywhere. They drove off to the presidency, a palatial building in comparison with Kruger's modest home.

'Even should President Steyn try to restrain his burghers from closer union, God will bring it about,' Kruger said in a speech. 'But if closer union should have as a consequence the absorption of the one State by the other, then I too will oppose it. You are a free republic as we are. Our burghers are not only our soldiers but the pillars of the State. I stand here as Paul Kruger, but if my people do not wish to co-operate I can do nothing . . .'[304] So much for the great Afrikaner conspiracy to form one vast republic. At a luncheon Kruger remarked: 'You know that we have to stick to the Convention, and Queen Victoria is an irascible (*kwaaie*) woman.' This little joke caused an uproar out of all proportion, the word *kwaai* in Afrikaans does not mean the same as *kwade* in Dutch. The first means irascible, cross or ill-tempered and can be used humorously, while the second means bad. The English papers fumed that Kruger had dared to call Victoria a bad woman, when he had said nothing of the kind, and in any case he was the last person on earth to call a woman names. The reaction of the Jingo Press utterly bewildered him.

The conference was an unqualified success. A Treaty of Trade and Friendship, as negotiated by Reitz, was concluded, and the Treaty of Political Alliance needed revision in the light of the Jameson Raid. This was done, and the Orange Free State was now bound to stand by the Transvaal should her independence be threatened, or *vice versa*, not that the Orange Free State drew much attention. But she wished to have some control over steps taken by the Transvaal which could endanger both States by having a right to oppose them if this was thought necessary. Kruger readily granted this right, clearly wanted by Steyn. A Federal Board, with an equal number of members from both States, drew the tie even closer. In future the rights which a Transvaaler enjoyed in the Free State would be granted to Free Staters in the Transvaal. Burghers of the Orange Free State had in the past shown their willingness to give the Transvaal military co-operation; but it stood to reason that should the Transvaal land in a full-scale war, the willingness of the Orange Free State as a whole would have to be put to the test.

While at Bloemfontein Kruger received news that his Ambassador in Europe, Jonkheer Beelaerts van Blokland, had died. Kruger asked his host what he was to do now and was taken aback when Steyn proposed that Blokland be replaced by Kruger's blue-eyed boy, Dr Leyds. This was adroit, for Steyn knew well enough how Leyds was loathed and thought to be responsible for everything wrong with the Kruger régime. 'This astute and ambitious Hollander,' Leo Weinthal wrote some years later, 'studied the President's character so closely, at the same time hypnotizing the old autocrat so effectively with the idea of his personal importance, that he was practically the President, dictator, and ruler of the Transvaal from 1888 and 1898 . . .'[305] With the removal of Leyds, Steyn felt, the anti-Hollander movement would collapse. Kruger was most reluctant to send Leyds away, but when Steyn offered him one of his best men, Abraham Fischer, and in the general spirit of *bonhomie*, Kruger was open to persuasion.

'We need a first-rate man in Europe,' Steyn told him, 'thoroughly conversant with South African affairs and trusted by the people.' In this respect too Steyn was right: no better man than Leyds as Ambassador and Plenipotentiary Extraordinary to the Courts of Germany, Russia, the Netherlands, Belgium and Portugal could be found in the Transvaal. Moreover, if anybody could follow up German hints of support, that man was Leyds. Abraham Fischer declined to succeed Leyds as State Secretary of the Transvaal, so the office was offered to Frank Reitz, once again in perfect health, who readily accepted. As Reitz would never neglect the interests of his previous State, this appointment suited Steyn even better as he saw in it a means to closer co-operation with the Transvaal.

Also at Bloemfontein Steyn proposed that the two Reformers still in prison, Aubrey Wools Sampson and Walter D. Davis, be released, 'for not only are they seeking cheap notoriety, but are being used by the English Press to whip up further ill-feeling. It would be a significant gesture if they were released on the occasion of Queen Victoria's Diamond Jubilee . . .'[306] Kruger was not happy about this proposal either, the men having refused to pay their fines when they could easily have done so, but he gave in. Steyn asked no more for the time being, but assured of Kruger's eagerness to co-operate, he felt confident that he could influence Kruger to diminish the franchise restrictions and to do away with the Dynamite Monopoly which caused so much vexation. Steyn was democratic to such a degree that at times he was thought lacking in leadership. People still had to find out that he was even more stubborn and tenacious than Kruger.

A new name flashed on to the South African scene in 1897 as successor to Sir Hercules Robinson—Sir Alfred Milner, a self-confessed British (primarily English) Nationalist, Imperialist and Race Patriot.[307] It is doubtful if Kruger had heard of Milner before, but the man was obviously hand-picked by Chamberlain 'with a view of driving matters in South Africa to extremes'. Initially, however, Sir Alfred Milner kept quiet, and Kruger had other things on his mind. His term of office was coming to an end and the machinery for the next presidential election began as usual to work a long time in advance. Instead of giving room to younger men, Kruger and Joubert were to stand again, with a surprise third in Schalk Willem Burger (1852–1918), surprising in that Burger had long been a Joubert supporter. All he could succeed in doing now was to split the votes for Joubert, while Kruger knew that since the Raid his own position was stronger than ever before.

Uitlander agitations continued unabated, but a new crisis was a judicial one which involved Chief Justice Kotzé. A conflict between the Executive and the Judiciary had been building up, made more complex by Kotzé's personal political motivations. It will be recalled that he stood against Kruger in a previous presidential election. 'It was a generally accepted principle,' say the Kruger *Memoirs*, 'that the resolutions of the Volksraad were valid in law, even if they conflicted with the Constitution.' After having accepted and acknowledged this principle for a time, the Supreme Court and particularly Kotzé now refused to do so. 'This decision would have upset the whole country, for a number of rules concerning the goldfields, the franchise and so on depended on resolutions of the Volksraad.' In a rapidly changing country like the Transvaal, 'it was absolutely necessary that, at any given moment, certain interests could be protected and dangers averted from the State by decrees of the Volksraad.'[308]

The Chief Justice of the Cape supported Kruger, and in the mediation that followed De Villiers upheld the decrees of the Volksraad. Kruger promised a revision of the Constitution, for not long before a law had been passed by which judicial functionaries were not allowed to test the laws as to their validity. As Kruger took too long in effecting this revision, in Kotzé's opinion, the Judge considered himself free to test the validity of all the resolutions of the Volksraad by the Constitution. As there was not to be a Volksraad session until May 1898, Kruger had no opportunity as yet to introduce a bill for the revision promised. By claiming drastic powers of judicial review, Kotzé now cast doubts on the validity of most of the laws in force.[309] This was deliberate provocation, and Kruger waited for the results of the presidential election before taking action.

One of the celebrities who called on him in the course of 1897 was the explorer, Henry M. Stanley, at 5.30 a.m. on 24 November. One could dismiss the ten pages of Stanley's *Autobiography*[310] on Kruger had they come from anybody else and had he been introduced by other than Sammy Marks. I will ignore the slanderous things he has to say and pick out what is true to character: 'His features were amiable and human . . . not a bad kind of man . . . a little obstinate, perhaps, but on the whole well-meaning . . . a choleric and passionate old man . . . his right hand went up and down like a sledge-hammer . . . irascibility . . . impatience . . . unbending nature . . . stubborn old fellow . . .' When Stanley gives Kruger an inch of forehead, small and dull eyes, as well as villainy which passes all credibility, one looks with narrowed eyes at this gullible man whose individual rape of Africa on behalf of Leopold of the Belgians is beyond comment.

When Kruger did not get his way with the Volksraad, he threatened to resign. Or when he was about to lose his temper, he would take a drink of water from the mantelpiece and visibly calm down.[311] Once when he proffered the usual resignation, he was startled when a new member jumped up and moved that the resignation be accepted. This was the blue-eyed Louis Botha at his first session as member for Vryheid in 1897. A debate followed, as Botha related, and the President 'was very chary of again threatening to resign'. Louis Botha (1862–1919) was a Joubert man and thought Kruger a great personality but not a good speaker or debater. But the old man knew his own mind and doggedly fought for what he wanted. Though General

Joubert was a much better and quicker speaker, he was invariably worsted by the President.

'In the first speech that Kruger made,' Botha told Lord Buxton,

> on any question before the Volksraad he would take a strong line and emphatically express his opinion as to what he wanted the Volksraad to do, and tried to get his way by storming and 'frightfulness'. If he found that opinion was going against him, he would in his second speech try to persuade them and take up a conciliatory attitude. If, even after that, he could not get what he wanted, he would then quote from the Bible, solemnly declaring that the quotations were all on his side, and usually got his way . . . President Kruger was allowed to speak as often as he liked. Of this privilege he took full advantage, and nearly always wound up the debate as well. This in time became intolerable, and a Bill was introduced to limit the President to one speech in each debate. Kruger fought this proposal to the last stage. He was defeated and then said—'Very well, gentlemen, I won't oppose the Bill any further and you can pass it. But I shall break it as soon as it is passed and you can then punish me.' The Bill was dropped.[312]

Rumour had it that Kruger was about to retire on pension, like M. W. Pretorius who was now living in Pretoria as Acting Historian [*sic*], and requisitions poured in to ask Kruger to stand again, signed by some ten thousand people. It is to be doubted if he for a moment considered retirement, not when he had to have all his wits about him in order to deal with Chamberlain, Rhodes and Milner. In his reply Kruger expressed his gratification that the confidence shown him since 1882 still held sway.

> 'In spite of my feelings of inadequacy at that time, I was not sanguine enough to decline the call to accept the most important office of State President. More than ever am I aware of my shortcomings and tremendous responsibility at this time, for when I first answered your call after our restored independence, so much has happened to impress on us the necessity to stay on guard and gird our loins not to lose the independence granted us by God . . . You know me. You know my weaknesses, but also my heartfelt love for the Fatherland, my continual striving to guard our independence . . .'[313]

He referred to the rinderpest which was ravaging the country and the measures to combat it, protection for Church and School, National Education, international relations, and in particular with the sister republic, neighbouring states and colonies. There was little new in all this. The burning questions of the day were not mentioned, nor any sort of programme indicated. Perhaps it was unnecessary as he had already done all his speaking in the Volksraad. Joubert and Burger, on the other hand, talked about finance, an improved Constitution and Civil Service, State Railways, concessions, and so on. Both of them had Uitlander support, Burger more so than Joubert. The election campaign lasted up to 3 January 1898 when the voting began and continued for a month.

The result was a foregone conclusion but even so caused astonishment, for Paul Kruger, in spite of his age and so much adverse propaganda, entirely stole the show this time. For Schalk Burger there were 3,753 votes, for Joubert 2,001, while Kruger gained 12,853. There was no question of irregularities, and for Joubert it was a humiliation to be beaten by Burger, a man of rather vague personality. This was Kruger's fourth and last presidency. Apart from national drama, his age would have precluded another term of office.

During his election campaign he appeared exhilarated, even jolly, and regaled his audiences with jokes and the crazy anecdotes which appealed to his sense of humour, such as the hunting fantasies already referred to. Never was he in better form, and perhaps because his popularity was at its peak as a result of the Raid and Chamberlain's impertinent and meddling correspondence. Even people who had looked upon Kruger with aversion were indulgent. On 12 May 1898 Pretoria was colourful, the Vierkleur, Union Jack, the flags of the Orange Free State, the Netherlands and, invariably, the United States, fluttered everywhere. Six thousand people thronged Church Square, and there were military divisions and regimental bands.

The band of the mounted police of Johannesburg, followed by 250 armed men (mainly Rustenburgers) preceded the new presidential coach emblazoned with the Republican coat-of-arms and drawn by four magnificent brown stallions. As escort there was the head of the State Artillery, the Police Commissioner, commandants and veldcornets, followed by vehicles bearing worthies and by a section of the smartly uniformed State Artillery. Officers were resplendent in gold braid and plumed helmets, as was Kruger in full dress and sitting impassively in the coach with its mounted silver eagles, coachman and lackeys in green and silver. The cavalcade passed through a triumphal arch at the western entrance of Church Square. Bands struck up and the crowd roared.[314]

President Kruger was received under an awning on the balcony of the Government Buildings by high officials, the presidents of the First and Second Volksraad, representatives of the Orange Free State and foreign countries, the latter in sumptuous ambassadorial array. The ceremony was opened with prayer, and then Kruger began his address, his voice at times audible right across the square, which took him *three hours* to deliver. It was the longest speech he ever made, for in a way it was several speeches in one, directed to the Volksraads, the Executive, the Orange Free State, the diplomatic corps, his burghers, the naturalized foreigners, the new immigrants, the judges, the clergy, the schools and the children. Much of all this he had said before, and as usual he spoke *ex tempore,* but he had made certain that his speech was written down as he did not want it later 'for one reason or another' to be misunderstood.[315]

From two in the afternoon, after that strenuous morning, the Krugers received such a stream of callers, deputations, diplomatic and consular corps, bodies and officials, that they had to be admitted in groups. Gezina received the ladies and kept trays of coffee and cake circulating. The opulence of the Transvaal could be noted in the magnificent gowns of the ladies, the smart conveyances, the elegance of the men, the glitter, polish, even grandeur. But Kruger and his wife were as they had always been, simplicity being the keynote of their lives. On tables lay stacks of congratulatory telegrams from all over—except from the Governments of Cape Colony and Great Britain.[316] There were also many Addresses, including some from the Municipality and Jewish schools of Johannesburg. In the evening Pretoria was illuminated and there was a music festival in Burgers Park.

So Paul Kruger was launched on his new term of office, head of a large country growing ever wealthier, the old ways of the Boer transformed by pomp and ceremony. To Sir Alfred Milner, the old man's triumph was a blow, as this was not what he had expected from the reports of the anti-Kruger forces in the Transvaal. To Milner it was the end to 'reform', but not the end of his plans. Between him, Chamberlain and indirectly Rhodes, a way had to be found to acquire the Transvaal. Should Kruger put a foot wrong, he would know it. And he did so right after the results came out by promptly dismissing Chief Justice Kotzé for defying him in resuming the 'testing right' of laws passed by the Volksraad which went contrary to the Constitution. Kotzé rushed off to Cape Town to appeal to

Milner, and to Victoria as 'Suzerain' of the Transvaal, thereby convincing Kruger that he was no patriot and in league with the Uitlanders.

Milner had to admit that Kruger's dismissal of Kotzé was not a breach of the Convention, but he saw it as 'the end of real justice in the Republic' and that Kruger's step 'threatened all British subjects and interests there'.[317] Indignation increased when Kotzé was replaced by Judge Gregorowski who had presided at the Reform Trial and was thought most sinister, for in connexion with the Testing Rights Law of 1897 ('rushed by Kruger through the Volksraad') Gregorowski had declared 'that in his opinion no honourable man could possibly accept the position of judge while that law remained on the statute book.'[318] And now he blandly accepted the job of Chief Justice in a land where, in Uitlander opinion, the Volksraad (which meant Kruger) could legislate as they pleased.

In his address to the Judiciary in his inaugural speech, Kruger had Kotzé in mind. Here are some excerpts :

> You, by virtue of your office, represent the solidity of the State. It depends on you to confirm confidence in the country, but it also depends on you that confidence in the country should not be shocked . . . The Volksraad is the highest authority in the land, the legislative body, which passes laws and resolutions, and you must administer them to the best of your knowledge and power . . . There is no longer an appeal from the High Court; and if you, honourable judges, in your own judgement, set aside a decree of the Volksraad, then you adopt the right of criticism from the Devil; but if, perhaps, from human weakness, you pronounce a judgement which is not purely in accordance with the law, but is pronounced to the best of your knowledge and conscience, then you are not indictable either before God or man . . .

And then he took up the Kotzé controversy which was now another Uitlander grievance. Kotzé with some of his colleagues 'adopted the right of criticism and became as wanton as a fish in the water that was free to swim about as it pleased. However, he jumped out of the water, that is to say, out of the law, on to dry land. The Volksraad then passed a resolution, with reference to the laws of the land, to the effect that, if a judge refuses to submit to them, I must dismiss him.' As Kotzé refused to acknowledge the law as Kruger understood it, he had to let him go. Kotzé had also refused to help with the revision of the Constitution, so, having won the election, Kruger dismissed him.

'What does he do next?' He says, in a manifesto, that if the people will not help him, he will apply to England . . . He knows that he has taken the oath, not only as regards his office, but that his oath is binding upon him as a burgher of the country, and he knows that a burgher is not allowed to appeal to another Power: if he does, he is guilty. Moreover, he himself has repeatedly declared that the suzerainty no longer exists in our internal government, and yet he flies to that. But I do not take this amiss of him now, for in my eyes he seems to have lost his senses.'[319]

Apart from the exit of Kotzé, there were several important changes in 1898. Dr Leyds, though he was reappointed State Secretary that May, accepted the office of Envoy Extraordinary in Europe where, according to his enemies, he caused so much mischief from his headquarters at Brussels that the onus of the course of events was to a large extent placed on him. Frank Reitz, recently made a judge in the South African Republic, accepted the office of State Secretary. Next to Kruger, Reitz was now the most important member of the Executive, and also a man with a mind of his own, so that there were to be some rows with 'the old man'. Reitz was appointed in June, and if British statesmen at first pinned their hopes on him, as he was such a well-educated, enlightened and courteous man, they still had to find out that Reitz fully shared in Kruger's obsession with their independence, and also that Reitz, in full vigour, was much more aggressive. His son Deneys at seventeen thought Kruger the ugliest man he had ever seen, though of strong, rugged personality, and he says that he often saw Mrs Kruger with pails in her yard, as she kept cows and sold milk to the neighbours.[320]

It was Reitz who introduced Olive Schreiner and her husband to Kruger. The President led them into the parlour, Olive Schreiner being an attractive woman of international fame, and as Kruger laid his pipe down he gave the couple a keen look. This small rotund woman had published a savage indictment of Rhodes and his Chartered Company the year before in her *Trooper Peter Halket of Mashonaland*, a pacifist allegory which had raised eyebrows the world over. It was to be marvelled that Rhodes had refused to have the book suppressed. Kruger did not read fiction, but he knew a lot about Olive Schreiner. Her husband, Cronwright, recorded that Kruger even in old age impressed them with his massive frame, 'his powerful bone, the quick step and the hold his foot took of the ground as he walked, the way it seemed to grip the ground and lift him along, and the look of alertness and energy' which still indicated a man 'as outstanding physically as he was in character and in certain mental qualities'.[321]

According to F. W. Reitz, in his incomplete memoirs published by his son Hjalmar Reitz, he only once had a serious quarrel with the President. This was when the newly-appointed Chief Mining Commissioner, Kleynhans, found that Kruger appointed officials to his department without consulting him. Reitz protested, only to get an angry and rude response. He wondered if he could carry on, but the next day Kruger, who had been advised to eat dates by his personal physician, silently placed some dates before Reitz and gave his knee a gentle squeeze under the table. It was an apology in his own way which Reitz at once accepted.[322]

To have a previous State President of the Orange Free State as State Secretary was quite something, but even more remarkable was the appointment of a thin fair young man as State Attorney—Jan Christiaan Smuts (1870–1950). Both Reitz and Smuts were born Cape Colonials, Smuts even having been before the Raid a Rhodes disciple. Reitz again had family ties with the Schreiners, his sister Fanny having married Bill Schreiner (Olive's brother) who was soon to be Premier of Cape Colony. Jan Smuts was not yet thirty, but he had made such a name for himself as advocate in the eighteen months he had spent in Johannesburg that Kruger readily accepted his recommendation. Those blind to Kruger's perspicacity thought he was losing his mind in appointing such a young man (looking even younger than he was) to such an important office. But Kruger knew what he was doing. Had Smuts been older he could even have been State Secretary.

Kruger looked upon Smuts as a representative of the younger generation of Afrikaners, but perhaps neither of them expected that such a close friendship would result, for Smuts was, after all, a Cambridge graduate with an intellectual range which was to cause astonishment for decades. 'He is one of the cleverest lawyers in South Africa,' Kruger remarked, 'and a man of versatile attainments besides. He is personally a very simple man, and, to meet him, one would not suspect that he possesses so iron a will and so determined a character as he does . . . Smuts will yet play a great part in the future history of South Africa.'[323] Yes, that was what Kruger told the world in 1902. Their friendship has been described as one of the most extraordinary in history, but then they had much in common and their relationship was free of the clashes which so often soured Kruger's other governmental relationships. Kruger's only criticism of Smuts was that he was inclined to crack his whip too loudly.

Kruger also got on well with Smuts's wife, the endearing, brilliant, eccentric Isie (born Krige). When the President first met her, he turned to Smuts and with a twinkle in his eye said: 'What on earth made you marry such an ugly woman?' The young couple were speechless. Then Kruger turned to Isie and said: 'And what on earth made *you* marry such an ugly man?' They all burst out laughing, the Smuts couple grasping Kruger's type of Boer humour. They were actually a very good-looking couple, otherwise Kruger would not have said what he did, and he was much taken with them.[324]

Another story which Smuts himself told was that when after a period he asked the President why he had given such an important office to an inexperienced youth, Kruger replied laughingly: 'Because I had heard that your wife is much cleverer than you are.' It was not an easy job for Smuts, as he found himself surrounded by intrigue, political and official enemies, liquor syndicates, scheming concessionaires and 'powerful evildoers in high places'. Even Kruger's champions had to admit that although the old man was not personally implicated, there was undoubted corruption, professional graft and maladministration, and that he was simply too old and weary to deal with these problems. For years Smuts was to refer to Kruger as 'the greatest of all Afrikaners', but Smuts's son thought that this meant as a colourful character and personality rather than as a statesman.[325]

His Government as from May 1898 was the strongest and in some ways the most remarkable the Transvaal had ever known. Even among his Opposition were men who were to astonish the world. And to deal with Milner, who was beginning to show his hand, Kruger had his man in Smuts, not that he and Smuts together were a match for the British Empire. 'There can be little doubt,' said Iwan-Müller in 1902, 'that Mr Smuts was one of the foremost, if not the foremost, of the abettors of Mr Kruger in his violently anti-English policy. It is an unquestioned fact that he was also on terms of the closest intimacy with Mr Hofmeyr and the wire-pullers of the Afrikaner Bond.' Then he adds sarcastically: 'And it was from the ranks of that confederacy that the future rulers of a United South Africa were to be selected.'[326] Nothing could have astonished him more than that was exactly what was to happen.

Kruger was still much more concerned with Rhodes and Chamberlain than with Milner and the real plot behind the Jameson Raid.

'Do you think,' Kruger said to J. B. Robinson, 'that we are so innocent as not to know that Mr Rhodes held a pistol at the heads of certain men in England, and said to them: "If you do not support me, I will denounce you and your complicity in the Raid."' Rhodes by that time had a reputation for squaring people. Sir Robert Williams once asked Rhodes why he did not try to square Kruger who was apparently attracted by money. 'You are quite wrong!' Rhodes replied heatedly. 'Kruger is a patriot. You cannot square a patriot! How do I know he cannot be squared? Because I have tried!'[327]

Kruger first took serious note of Sir Alfred Milner early in 1898 when the High Commissioner, after keeping quiet while he studied the situation and the Dutch language (knowing German this was not difficult), made a sensational speech at Graaff-Reinet in the Karoo. Never did Milner make an uncalculated move. When he came to South Africa he said that he would wait a year before he showed his hand. And he did just that in his endeavour, as he said, to break the power of Afrikanerdom by driving matters to extremes. His motivation was that he had as his guiding star throughout his career the intense belief in the future of the Empire and the beneficial part it was to play in the great drama of human progress.[328]

In the Transvaal Milner saw two wholly antagonistic systems: 'a medieval race oligarchy, and a modern industrial state, recognizing no difference of status between various white races which could not permanently live side by side in what is after all *one country*. The race oligarchy has got to go, and I see no signs of it removing itself.' Unless it was through war, as he implied at Graaff-Reinet.[329] At this Kruger sat up in astonishment, for he had been concentrating on Rhodes as 'the curse of South Africa', and here now was a potentially even greater curse in this cold, intellectual, calculating man.

One of the many remarkable woman who called on Kruger was the social worker Mary Brown, a member of the distinguished Solomon family of the Cape. On a hot day in the summer of 1898 she and her Scottish husband, Dr John Brown, visited Kruger on their return after a long absence from South Africa. 'We found him sitting on the stoep of his house,' she recalled, '. . . smoking, quietly puffing as he conversed with a military-looking man beside him. This was General Joubert—who left soon after our arrival and introduction. President Kruger was a massive old man, suggestive of great physical strength and also of mental power. He looked at us critically and said a word or two of greeting, and then gave me a seat beside himself and as he did so laid down his pipe. I was told afterwards, by one who knew him well, that this was an act of special courtesy . . .'

Mary Brown was not the sort of person to share the prejudices of the times and was too impressed not to see beyond 'the calumnies so liberally bestowed' on the President. Kruger spoke in Afrikaans to the person who introduced them, but when he turned to Mrs Brown, he spoke *in English* : 'Do you know Rhodes? Do you like him?' She said that she had never seen Rhodes, nor did she wish to see him. Mary noted a curious look in Kruger's 'keen, deep, sad eyes'. 'What has he done?' the old man went on. 'He has taken his Queen's flag and has drawn it through the mud . . .' Mary Brown knew all about the Raid but said nothing. 'If a man sees a beautiful girl,' Kruger continued, 'and he cannot get her, should he shoot her?' She realized that he meant the Transvaal to be the girl. 'No,' said Mary Brown. Kruger then turned to the company at large and spoke about the position of the Transvaal, of the franchise, and of the type of men who were flooding Johannesburg.

'I came away with a feeling,' said Mary Brown, 'of great respect and pity for that old man—a relic of a past order, a type of rough civilization rapidly passing away. One looks back and sees the forms of Paul Kruger, Rhodes and Chamberlain—all intriguers—but I think the hands of the rough old Boer were the cleanest.'[330]

CHAPTER EIGHTEEN

Kruger and Milner

'What have we in this man,' said Olive Schreiner after looking at Sir Alfred Milner, 'who represents English honour and English wisdom in South Africa? To a certain extent we know. We have a man honourable in the relations of personal life, loyal to a friend, and above all charm of gold; wise with the knowledge of books and men; a man who could not violate a promise or strike in the dark. This we know we have, and it is much to know that; *but what have we more*?'[331] She was soon to find out.

Milner's first challenge to South Africans was to make them choose sides, either to show loyalty to the Queen, or to Kruger, 'I don't trust the High Commissioner,' Kruger declared. 'He reminds me of Sir Bartle Frere who took up a similar line and had the war of 1880–1 . . .'[332] But there was to be a lull, for Chamberlain informed Milner that for the present at any rate what was wanted in South Africa was peace. England had difficulties enough with France, Russia and Germany, and was engaged in an important expedition in the Sudan. Momentarily Milner's hands were tied. 'I have reason to believe that H.M. Government,' he said to Conyngham Greene, British Agent in Pretoria, 'are not at all anxious to bring matters to a head. We must keep up our wickets but not attempt to force the game . . .'[333]

Milner felt better when Britain's international position began to improve during the second half of 1898. General Kitchener defeated the Khalifa at Omdurman, the French withdrew from Fashoda, and Germany renounced interest in the Transvaal. Of these developments Kruger knew little or nothing. Most serious was the financial aid being given by Britain and Germany to Portugal on the security of the Portuguese possessions in Africa, including of course Delagoa Bay. Kruger had been diplomatically isolated without knowing it, and the marked improvement in Anglo-German relations meant that Britain could take firmer measures against the Transvaal. Milner was elated by the elimination of Germany as a *political* influence in the Transvaal and the countries surrounding it, though its immediate effect was not of much consequence. What mattered were future contingencies.[334]

Kruger's tightening restrictions against the Uitlanders were seen as 'only reasonable' from an American point of view after the Jameson Raid which had caused a bigger rift between Afrikaner and Briton than Milner (or Chamberlain, so far from the scene) ever grasped.[335] But the three new laws were intensely resented (Aliens' Expulsion Act, Immigration Law and Press Law) as measures of persecution and oppression, no matter that equivalent acts were in force in most countries of the world. As the Immigration Law was interpreted by Chamberlain to be a violation of Article XIV of the Convention,[336] Kruger had it repealed. The Aliens' Act was enforced only once, and with general approval as the person involved was a convicted murderer. As for the freedom of the Press, it was thought wisest to let it ride, the English papers being almost entirely dominated by Rhodes and other capitalists. Through their medium, Milner had ready backing in building up public feeling against Kruger and his administration. The Afrikaners in general read more English than Dutch, and in many cases with mounting indignation.

With the removal of Leyds, 'Hollanderism' appeared to have died out. Had Kruger stepped down, as he should perhaps have done at his age, it might also have been the end of 'Krugerism'. But neither he nor Joubert even considered retirement, and tenaciously the two old men held on, believing that on them depended the destiny of the Transvaal. And, of course, the one was not going to quit while the other stayed on. More than ever Kruger *was* the South African Republic and Joubert *the* Commandant-General; their staffs and colleagues kept a close watch on their every move, just as the Opposition did.

Improvements were taking place all the time. Smuts was streamlining the police and criminal prosecution departments of Johannesburg. The ZARPS (initials for the South African Republican Police) in general, burly young Boers in blue uniforms with white helmets, were looked upon as a foreign and sinister element in their midst by the Uitlanders. The franchise issue, which was more and more becoming the main target of Milner and Chamberlain, was still being considered for revision, no matter that the British had no intention of renouncing their nationality. In the Volksraad Kruger proposed that the period of residence of fourteen years be brought down to nine. As reforms were made, they were simply ignored by the third Uitlander movement, the South African League, led by men who had not been Reformers and were accordingly not politically silenced. They wanted equal political rights in running the country; in fact, putting everything together, what they really wanted was the country as British subjects.

In September, Wilhelmina, who had become Queen of the Netherlands in 1890, was enthroned in full splendour in the New Church of Amsterdam. She had come of age the month before, a beautiful and highly intelligent young woman, very learned for one so young. The drama in South Africa greatly perturbed her, and she wrote to Queen Victoria: 'You will understand, dear Aunt, the feelings of horror which affect me at the idea of war between two nations to one of which I am attached by bonds of friendship, the other by ties of common origin . . .' Victoria consulted Lord Salisbury who advised her to reply in sympathetic terms in the hope for peace. She did so, adding: 'But I cannot abandon my own subjects who have appealed to me for protection. If President Kruger is reasonable there will be no war . . .'[337]

Although Imperialism was back in fashion, Kruger could take heart when Sir Gordon Sprigg was succeeded by William Philip Schreiner as Premier of Cape Colony in October. Schreiner was a wise, moderate man who had the support of Hofmeyr and the Afrikaner Bond. Schreiner was in sympathy with Kruger's problems, but he shared the opinion of men like Steyn and Hofmeyr that concessions had to be made, and particularly in connexion with the franchise. This issue was beginning to torment Kruger as he did not want to be rushed in a matter of such vital importance for the independence of his country. Already just about anything appeared to give Chamberlain and Milner the right to meddle in his internal affairs.

It also appeared as if he was being deliberately provoked by one thing after the other, with much attendant publicity. There was the Bunu Question—the Swazi King who had been forbidden to put subjects to death at will. As he ignored the Republic in this respect, Bunu was summoned to court in Swaziland. Milner at once contended that the S.A.R. had no right to do so, although it was in accordance with the Swaziland Convention. Bunu fled to Zululand and asked for British protection. Machinery was set in motion to make a major issue of the matter, so Bunu was merely fined and allowed to go home. Then there was an outcry when some coloured persons were arrested for being without passes which they had to have according to the Pass Law. The Uitlanders, never having shown concern for coloureds before, held a rowdy meeting at the Amphitheatre in Johannesburg which turned into a nasty brawl.

Much more sensational was the so-called Edgar case. On 18 December two drunken British Uitlanders, Foster and Edgar, came to blows during the night. Edgar gave Foster such a beating that he left him for dead and fled to his room. The police gave chase and, thinking Foster dead, reached Edgar's lodging to arrest him for murder. He had bolted his door and refused to come out. A Boer policeman with the unlikely name of Jones broke down the door. Edgar attacked him with an iron bar, so Jones shot him. A cry at once went up that Jones be arrested on a charge of manslaughter. This was done, but the constable was acquitted as in the view of the jury it was a case of excusable or justifiable homicide. The British element began to demonstrate, for it was an opportunity to protest against the 'intolerable state of affairs' existing in the Transvaal.

Manfred Nathan saw the Edgar case as 'the starting point of the final agitation which led to war'.[338] Chamberlain mispresented it by stating that Johannesburg policemen now broke into people's houses at night without a warrant, and the League saw their chance to appeal directly to the Queen. Milner was away in England with Conyngham Greene, the person standing in for him being Sir William Butler (1838–1910), the noted British soldier, administrator and author. Butler refused to accept the petition from the Acting Agent in Pretoria. It was signed by 21,000 real or imaginary persons, but it was published before presentation and this should not have been done. Then too—as he cabled to Chamberlain—Butler saw the present agitation as a prepared business, aimed to produce political and financial effect in London and to make government at Johannesburg impossible.

Butler's refusal of the petition was most annoying to Milner. In the Cape, Schreiner shared Butler's view that the whole thing was engineered. The Edgar case could clearly not be used to work up a crisis, yet Chamberlain denounced the action of the Kruger Government, as if *they* had acted. Milner, preparing to return to Cape Town, had every intention of seeing the next petition, which was inevitable, through, no matter that the opinion at the Colonial Office was that such petitions should be prevented to avoid friction.[339] Milner was invigorated and ready to take up various matters, one of them being the dynamite monopoly which was due for renewal for another twelve years. Milner now wanted Chamberlain to take it up as an infringement of the Convention.[340]

But it was just as well that Chamberlain decided not to press the dynamite issue just yet, for to Kruger the monopoly and independence went together. On the other hand he relied more and more on the assertion of suzerainty as it nearly gave the old man at Pretoria 'a fit'. Milner explained to Chamberlain that the mere mention of the words 'suzerainty' or 'paramountcy' exercised a curiously maddening effect on the Boers.[341] Kruger was well acquainted with the ill-feeling towards concessionaires. In his inaugural speech of 1898 he had stressed that his Government would do all they could to assist the goldfields, by decreasing the railway tariffs and import duties, by sanctioning the importation of Native mineworkers from Mozambique, and by reducing the price of dynamite. But as for the abolition of the monopoly, he never got round to that.

'The acknowledged and admitted grievances,' the second petition declared,

> of which your Majesty's subjects complain prior to 1895 not only are not redressed, but exist today in an aggravated form. They are still deprived of all political rights, they are denied any voice in the government of the country, the revenue of which is misapplied and devoted to objects which keep alive a continuous and well-founded feeling of irritation, without in any way advancing the general interest of the State. Maladministration and peculation of public monies go hand in hand, without any vigorous measures being adopted to put a stop to the scandal. The education of Uitlander children is made subject to impossible conditions. The police afford no adequate protection to the lives and property of the inhabitants of Johannesburg; they are rather a source of danger to the peace and safety of the Uitlander population.[342]

This petition asking for the intervention of the British Government, signed by 23,000, was seen by Kruger as part of the long-standing plan to force war on him. He had to move with even greater caution, and wondered if it would avail him anything to be yielding and compliant, while the other party relentlessly pushed matters to extremes. Even so, at Rustenburg and Heidelberg at the beginning of 1899, Kruger talked of a reduction of the franchise restrictions to nine years. At Johannesburg he said he hoped it would be even less. It was only later that he could appreciate how much alarm he would have caused Chamberlain and Milner had he forestalled them before they could carry out their grand design. The second Uitlander petition of March 1899, for example, produced a counter-petition, signed by about an equal number of people who were perfectly satisfied with the Kruger administration.

Agent Conyngham Greene gave the Uitlander petition to Milner who passed it on to H.M. Government. When it came to decisive action, Chamberlain hesitated. 'If we ignore altogether the prayer of the petitioners,' he said in a memorandum to the Cabinet, 'it is certain that British influence will be severely shaken. If we send an ultimatum to Kruger, it is possible, and in my opinion probable, that we shall get an offensive reply, and we shall then have to go to war, or to accept a humiliating check . . .'[343] Kruger in any case believed the signatures (given by him as 21,684) to have been collected 'by every kind of fraud', as the names of deceased and absent persons were included.

The franchise having become the spearhead of the Milner–Chamberlain campaign, it was a bitter thing for Kruger to unbend rather than harden on this point. It touched the raw nerve of his national pride, and he wondered how far he would be pushed. Milner wondered how far he could, and though he looked upon Kruger as a mendacious savage, Milner knew that Kruger would reach the limit of what he could give and still retain his country. Milner's dispatches to London stiffened, the most famous being sent on 4 May. 'The case for intervention is overwhelming,' he declared. 'The spectacle of thousands of British subjects kept permanently in the position of helots, constantly chafing under undoubted grievances, and calling vainly to Her Majesty's Government for redress, does steadily undermine the influence and reputation of Great Britain and the respect for the British Government within its own dominions . . .'[344]

Kruger thought Milner a 'sensation-mongering journalist'. Like Schreiner, Merriman, Sauer, Hofmeyr, Steyn and many others, Kruger knew that Milner was dangerous, but how dangerous was only revealed when the Great Boer War turned out to be Milner's war. Because Kruger did not know, he agreed to a proposal to meet Milner face to face to discuss the franchise question. As the appearance of Milner anywhere near the Witwatersrand, seething with agitators, was out of the question, it was decided to have the meeting at a central point like Bloemfontein, with President Steyn as their host.

The proposal for such a meeting had come first from Schreiner on 6 May in order to see grievances and problems thrashed out, then from Chamberlain himself on the 10th. After voluminous correspondence and endless diplomatic manoeuvres, the conference was fixed for 31 May. Both Steyn and Schreiner, at Milner's express wish, were excluded from it, and it was soon clear why. Steyn's role as mediator with Kruger had already lasted some three years, and he was resolute to stick to this role to the end, even while being merely the host.

Kruger arranged to arrive a little ahead of time to confer with Steyn. Kruger was accompanied by two members of the Executive—

Schalk Burger and A. D. W. Wolmarans—by Jan Smuts, a secretary and the physician now in permanent attendance on the President, Dr Heymans. They were met at Viljoenskroon by Landdrost H. F. D. Papenfus and Major Richard Albrecht of the O.F.S. Artillery. The venerable Abraham Fischer, virtually Steyn's second-in-command, prepared to meet the Milner party at Norvalspont. Steyn and his entourage were on the station to meet Kruger. He looked what he was, an old man with all kinds of ailments, the worst being his inflamed eyes. But with his old warmth Kruger grasped Steyn's hand in both his own. The severity of the occasion could be gauged by Steyn's eyes out of which all laughter had died. But then Steyn had since seen Milner in all his calculating rudeness, whereas Kruger still had to take his measure.

As always, Steyn was candid. 'Much will depend on your attitude,' he told the old man as they left the station. 'You *must* make concessions on the franchise issue, Your Honour. Franchise after a residence of fourteen years is in conflict with the first principles of a republican and democratic government. The Free State expects you to concede, and will give you full support should you do so. Should you not give in on this issue, you will lose all sympathy and all your friends.'[345] Kruger, cupping his ear as had now become necessary, reassured his agitated colleague that he had come to have all their troubles with the British Government removed. Already he had, as Steyn knew, proposed a reduction of the period for the franchise. 'I am prepared to do anything,' Kruger said, 'but they must not touch my independence. They must be reasonable in their demands, as I have my people and my Volksraad to reckon with.' Steyn was reassured, but he dreaded, as he had already confided to Schreiner, that impossible demands would be made of the old man of Pretoria.

The fate of the one Republic would be that of the other. To survive Kruger had to concede all reasonable demands made of him until even the Orange Free State could agree to no more. But not a drop of their blood, Steyn said bravely, would be spilt on behalf of dynamite concessionaires. On this point too Kruger reassured him, and they were both prepared for the arrival of His Excellency whom Steyn met at the station with full honours. From the Afrikaner point of view Milner was discourteous from the start. He arrived late to be introduced to Kruger at the Presidency, and he was again late for the official reception when he walked past Kruger to shake the hands of President and Mrs Steyn before he turned to the old man, who had risen.

It is one of the biographer's nightmares that even eye-witnesses can be totally unreliable. Arthur Barlow, who was there as a young reporter, says that Kruger ignored Milner when His Excellency tried to shake his hand, which is not so. Barlow also goes on to describe Kruger as a *small* man, so short that he needed a footstool for his dangling feet when he sat in the Executive,[346] this when Kruger was even larger than a big man like Louis Botha. Barlow adds that at nine o'clock Kruger said : 'I want to go home.' Anyway, Steyn himself and others balance the picture, and one can take it that Milner behaved with impeccable correctness at the reception, apart from coming late, and that exaggeration took place once it transpired that Milner had decided that the Bloemfontein Conference would fail before it had even begun.

For Kruger personally this conference was a humiliation. As a man he had never lacked poise, but what happened now was all too quick and sinister and diabolically clever to be believed. His own stalwarts at times only aggravated the situation, like Reitz with his outright rejection of Chamberlain's claims to suzerainty. The Republic's independence, Reitz declared in Pretoria, did not rest in the Convention of London but on her inherent right as a sovereign State according to international law. Kruger and Milner sat in the Central Railway Bureau and began discussions of what Milner chillingly called Kruger's 'Kaffir bargain', for all he wished to consider was the franchise issue.

'On the one side sat the cultured Englishman,' said Cecil Headlam, editor of the Milner Papers which were only published after the protagonists were dead, 'single-handed, wise and iron-willed, fully aware that failure must mean ignominy or war; inexorably resolved to establish the rights of British citizens settling overseas and the position of Great Britain as the Paramount Power in South Africa . . .' On the other side there was Paul Kruger, 'the burly Voortrekker in his tightly-buttoned frock coat' whom Headlam saw as cunning, equally strong-willed, 'rooted in the ambition of a lifetime to establish his country as the Predominant State in an all-Dutch Republic'. Said Luke : 'Milner's finely-tempered blade could not penetrate his pachydermatous opponent; and Kruger's bludgeon was harmless against this adroit adversary.'[347]

As if it was not galling enough to confer with Her Majesty's representative about his own domestic affairs, Kruger was to find in those five days, through Abraham Fischer as interpreter, that indeed the more he gave, the more was asked. Kruger offered naturalization after two years' residence, and full franchise after five, thus seven instead of fourteen years. Milner demanded full franchise after five years' residence only, an alteration in the oath of naturalization and increased representation of the new burghers in the Volksraad. Kruger was prepared to increase representation and to have an oath similar to that of the Orange Free State.[348] But immediate enfranchisement he was not going to give to the large body of Uitlanders already there for five years. This refusal was what Milner had expected or hoped, as he could use it to 'manoeuvre so that Kruger should appear in the wrong in whatever he did or said'.[349]

Kruger felt that he was making concessions as far as he could possibly go, and he was not going to make them and get nothing in return. One thing he wanted was the acceptance of the principle of arbitration in the case of differences, but this Milner refused to discuss. Everything was concentrated on the franchise issue, and in the opinion of Steyn and many others it was no small thing for Kruger to have come down from fourteen to seven years, for he was not prepared to hand his country over to strangers. 'If His Excellency wishes me to take advice from someone who has nothing to do with the Government of the State, who then governs?' Milner brushed this aside by proposing an advising council, made up of those not burghers of the State but representing the interests of the Uitlanders. 'How can strangers rule my State?' Kruger cried. 'How is it possible!' Milner murmured that his plan did not affect the government of the State. At this point Kruger burst into tears. 'It is our country you want,' he said with heartbreak and utter conviction now. 'It is our country you want.'

Milner then broke off the conference as planned. Chamberlain's cable to prolong it arrived too late, and one can dismiss Milner's statement to him: 'I think I was wrong in breaking the Conference as quickly as I did.' It was due to fatigue, he said; but this was when so much was at stake, and according to modern revelations he knew exactly what he was doing. Milner considered Kruger dangerous, not as a leader of a primitive pastoral people and an enemy of the goldmines, but as the representative of a reactionary creed which must in the course of time be fatal 'to Milner's ideal and the peace of South Africa'.[350]

It was 5 June. Steyn was frantic when Fischer brought him the news that the conference was ended. Steyn rushed off to Milner, but His Excellency refused to discuss anything but the franchise. Steyn then went to Kruger. 'In my opinion,' Steyn told him, 'Milner has only used this conference in order to justify England in case of war.

We must rectify this. Your Honour must still concede wherever possible, as in the case of the Dynamite Monopoly.' But Milner, sensing triumph over the franchise issue, cared little about that any more. Even so, to pacify Steyn, Kruger that same evening sent Milner a message asking for another meeting the next morning. Sir Alfred replied that he considered it unnecessary, as the conference was ended. Kruger withdrew to his room and, according to Dr Heymans, spent the night in tears and prayer.

On the train back to Pretoria he regained his composure, even seemed to cheer up—unless he was a better actor than his intimates knew. He had the backing of the Free State Volksraad, that he knew, and he was going ahead with the concessions he had proposed, hoping that once they were law more sanity would prevail. After all, how could England go to war in order to make her subjects citizens of another State? Home again, the Volksraad was convened and Reitz instructed to deal with the British Agent about the proposed arbitration tribunal; while Kruger on his own initiative introduced a draft law fixing a seven years' residence for obtaining the franchise, its immediate grant to all those who had been in the country for nine years, and only five for those who had already been there for two years. Representation for the goldfields in each Raad was to be increased by four members.

As from 9 June 1899 the drama between Great Britain and the Transvaal increased in intensity from day to day, for no matter what Kruger gave, more was asked. Nevertheless he yielded to pressure, and he gave Hofmeyr, representing the Afrikaner Bond, an attentive hearing. They asked that Kruger should make the seven years' clause of the new Franchise Law retrospective, in other words immediate enfranchisement for all those who had been in the country seven years. Kruger agreed to this, but the Uitlanders wanted five years, and Milner rejected an Arbitration Court. Openly he was now working for war, rather unnerving Chamberlain who felt that it could still be avoided should the Uitlander grievances find redress.

'President, should there be war between you and England,' Kruger was asked, 'have you any chance of winning?' He replied: 'Suppose that you are going along a road, with nothing but a pocket-knife, and you see a lion, would you be so reckless as to attack the beast with it?' 'Certainly not,' said the man. 'Well,' said Kruger, 'but supposing the lion attacked you, would you be such a coward as not to defend yourself with your pocket-knife?' The man said that he would certainly try to do so. 'It's the same,' said Kruger, 'we can only try.' In the opinion of some, to judge by the way the Transvaal was now armed, he was certainly going to have a jolly good try, no matter that General Joubert, Koos de la Rey and others dismissed as madness any idea of fighting the British Empire. Others like Reitz and Smuts began to feel differently, for Kruger had acted on their recommendations and they could now clearly see where it was all heading.

Now and then it appeared as if the crisis was over, only again to be worse overnight. The Cape Ministry could see no justification for British intervention in the internal affairs of the Transvaal as Kruger was giving way. But Milner saw many justifications, and knew how to outrage Kruger. It was proposed that England and the Transvaal should appoint a joint commission to revise the new franchise law—a direct infringement of the London Convention. To permit it would be a humiliating admission of inferiority. Smuts went to see the British Agent who insisted on Milner's demands, so Smuts and Reitz put their heads together. Reitz then came forward with proposals some thought startling—a five years' retroactive franchise, with a quarter of the seats in the Volksraad for the Witwatersrand—in fact more than Milner had asked at Bloemfontein. But there were conditions. The intervention of the British Government was not to be accepted as a precedent, claims to suzerainty were to be dropped, and future disputes were to be settled by arbitration within South Africa.

'Mr Kruger dribbles out reforms like water from a squeezed sponge,' said Chamberlain, 'and he either accompanies his offers with conditions which he knows to be impossible, or he refuses to allow us to make a satisfactory investigation of these reforms . . . The sands are running down in the glass . . .'[351] The Uitlander Council of the South African League maintained that the franchise reforms were still insufficient, that they wanted much more, such as Boer disarmament and the demolition of the forts built at Pretoria and the one in what was becoming the centre of Johannesburg. Furthermore, Chamberlain insisted that the Uitlander members of the Volksraad were to do their speaking in English. By September it was clear that war was inevitable, and yet so many people—among them, apparently, Rhodes—could not credit that it would actually come to that.

From now on books on South Africa and particularly the Transvaal poured from the presses of the world to become a flood by 1900. Van Oordt's huge book on Kruger and his Republic had already been on sale for some time. To counteract all the anti-Kruger propaganda, Smuts wrote *A Century of Wrong* in impeccable Dutch which his wife translated into English. General Joubert, with his literary leanings, wrote a pamphlet in the form of a letter to Queen Victoria, widely translated, in which he pleaded the Boer cause. Jorissen had already published his memoirs, Butler and Martineau their Lives of Colley and Frere, Statham his study of Kruger. English writers were scribbling like mad in deification of Rhodes, in vilifying Kruger and in justifying war. The most provocative piece of writing, however, lay in a drawer in Pretoria.

It was drafted by Reitz and Smuts; according to J. C. Smuts jnr, by his father alone.[352] In this document H.M. Government was asked that all points of mutual difference should be regulated by a friendly course of arbitration, that the British already on the borders of the Republic be withdrawn, that all reinforcements of troops which had arrived in South Africa since 1 June 1899 be withdrawn, and that Her Majesty's troops which were now on the high seas should not land in any port of South Africa. If she did not want to appear the aggressor, this was just the sort of ultimatum Great Britain was waiting for, and President Steyn telegraphed to stall for time.

'I beg you to see the danger of further delay,' Kruger replied. 'Peace, it appears to me, is quite out of the question, and accordingly the whole situation has to be seen from the military viewpoint. From that viewpoint it is our duty to act with the greatest speed . . .' The British Government had made a final offer, a five years' franchise without conditions, and should this be refused, they would 'formulate their own proposals for a final settlement'. Garrisons were being reinforced, troops were on their way to South Africa. Joubert was told to start mobilizing and to post commandos near the strategic points the British were taking just beyond the borders. It was October, the time for the spring rains to provide pasturage for the horses. To have any measure of success the Boers *had* to strike at once, before the military might of the Empire descended on them.

Assailed by telegrams from Kruger, President Steyn still hesitated, until he was absolutely sure that nothing in the world would avert this war. 'The day I say "War",' he said, and meant it, 'it will be war to the very bitter end.' Kruger's birthday was close at hand, a date which had become significant, when he would be seventy-four. Steyn himself had just turned forty-two, and on 9 October he finally established that the British plan for war was complete. Only then did he give Kruger his consent, and the ultimatum was handed to Conyngham Greene that same afternoon. It was a Monday, and as Tuesday broke, Kruger refused all birthday festivities. He was waiting for the British reply and scarcely glanced at the scores of congratulatory telegrams piling up. On the 11th Kruger was in the Executive chamber with Reitz, Smuts, Wolmarans and Piet Grobler, when Greene was announced early in the afternoon. He handed over the British reply in which it was said that the conditions of the South African Republic were such as Her Majesty's Government deemed impossible to discuss. Greene broke the silence that followed to ask for his passport in order to leave Pretoria. Without a word Kruger signed it.

At five o'clock that same afternoon, as the clock struck, the news was out. Kruger's coach was seen leaving the Government Buildings with a mounted police escort with white helmets, rounding the square on his way home. The telegraph building was besieged by reporters, and the news flashed over the world. After two unnaturally quiet and extremely tense days, Pretoria suddenly began to hum with life, and everywhere there was movement. The busiest place was the station where men from sixteen to sixty put their horses into railway trucks and said farewell to their friends and families. Now it was definitely war, and the farewells more emotional.

Some weeks before, Kruger had said: 'If it should be war, England will not let go of us until the Republic is strangled.'[353] He looked every year of his age, the lines in his face having cut deeper in the past months, hair and beard glinting with a silver sheen, the inflamed eyes appearing to sag in their pouches. But his mouth was as determined as ever, and momentarily he seemed to have dropped the melancholy which had enveloped him for months. The die was cast, the agonizing suspense over, there was work to be done. Kruger drew up his sagging shoulders and gripped his knees with his gnarled old hands, ready to face what God now willed for him and his people.

CHAPTER NINETEEN

Kruger and the War

'The Lord will protect us,' Kruger told his Volksraad on 2 October 1899. 'The Lord orders the flight of bullets. The Lord gave us the triumph of the War of Independence and the capture of Jameson. The Lord will also protect you now, even if thousands of bullets fly about you . . . He will guide us. He will decide and show to us that He rules and none other . . . Moses was a man of God, and the Lord spoke with him; but, at a time of great stress and combat, his friends had to stay up his hands, for he was but a weak mortal. Aaron had to support him in the faith. So let us too remember our generals and fighting-generals in our prayers, and unceasingly offer our prayers to God . . .' Prayers certainly his veggeneraals or combat generals agreed, but this was the first major war between whites in southern Africa and much in addition to prayer was needed. To start with, however, the Lord showed benevolence in granting the Boers an amazing series of triumphs.

Although Kruger was already one of the most famous men in the world, his name now became an international household word. He also gained more and more in sympathy as the months went by, and in Europe he was idolized by the anti-British countries. Because of his age and the state of his health, Kruger was kept out of actual combat. Those were not the only reasons, however, as Commandant-General Joubert was also long past the age of military service and yet at the front. Kruger the man stood for too much to risk any danger to him, and at all costs he was not to be captured. He knew this, so he did what he could in exhortations, prayers, speeches, visits to commandos, giving advice, encouragement, and even funds. Already he had given his sons and sons-in-law a thousand pounds each. To the State Treasury he 'lent' £40,000 and gave no further thought to it, as it was unlikely that it would ever be repaid. And, having always enjoyed hard work, he flung himself into the war cause with an energy and zeal which was thought amazing. As correspondence was almost entirely conducted by telegram, and very lengthily at that, reading and replying took much of his time.

The war in South Africa lured men from all over the world to join the Boers. On 8 December Kruger had an interesting caller in the person of Colonel Count Georges de Villebois-Mareuil, who had come to put his vast military experience (in his opinion) to the service of the Boers. He was astounded to be taken straight to the President when he expressed the desire to meet him, and noted the white-helmeted guards and marble lions as he ascended the steps. Kruger was sitting there in his tall hat, big coat, wearing dark glasses, in a depressed state of mind as he had just heard of the murder of some friends and relations by Natives.

'He has a deep voice,' the Count noted in his diary; 'thinks justly and quickly, has the authority which comes of deep thought and indomitable energy . . . We sat around him quite simply, almost familiarly. He spoke with energy and severity . . . briefly, precisely . . . words revealing neither fear nor hope.'[354] Villebois-Mareuil was greatly impressed, and had fortunately not understood when the President growled at someone to tell the Count to stop bowing and scraping. These foreigners interested Kruger, for he still had high hopes of foreign aid, no matter that Leyds had to tell him over and over again that the Powers would *not* intervene. Nearly all of Europe was sympathetic to the Boers, Leyds had found, but of military aid there was no question. As it turned out, the groups of foreign helpers were more of an embarrassment to the Boers, even Villebois-Mareuil himself, by getting shot in the Free State.

Sitting in his office in Pretoria, Kruger had a better idea of the course of the war on all fronts than anybody else, even Joubert, for as Head of State Kruger was nominally head of the Boer army. He was also in daily contact with President Steyn. Kruger followed his usual daily routine, but from now on he went to bed at eight, to rise at eleven, again at two in the morning, and even more often, depending on what was in the air. Telegraph messengers scurried constantly to and fro, day and night, and as time passed Kruger was to be on call at any time to give advice, hints and consolation.[355] As his generals were nearly all politicians instead of trained soldiers, much of the telegraphing was about military advice, even for junior officers.

Apart from the modern armament, it was almost an old-fashioned war to start with, with great courtesy shown on both sides to wounded and prisoners. The Boers put their trust in old and often-tried tactics, such as investment (Kimberley and Ladysmith), in occupying heights and shooting down, in avoiding exposure and in the swift seizure of strategic points. As they were not fighting Natives, laagers were of no use against bullets. The performance of trained British soldiers soon made it clear that there had to be a revision of fighting methods.

Kruger was one of the first to point out that their greatest advantage lay in mobility, in getting the enemy in the flanks and rear, and in cutting their lines of communication and supply.[356]

The Free Staters put up a poor show to start with, but as their dead wood was removed, a crack fighting force emerged, particularly when they were led by the man who was to become their most famous general, Christiaan Rudolf de Wet (1854–1922), the 'flying fox' of the war. Doddering old generals were steadily weeded out and replaced by younger men with initiative, the most remarkable of them being Louis Botha. On the other hand, some of the older stalwarts began to show military abilities which astounded the world, the most notable being Jacobus Herculaas De la Rey (1847–1914), a man of magnificent appearance who had long been seen in the Volksraad and now electrified a battlefield. Before the British forces were markedly reinformed, sensational victories like Colenso, Magersfontein, Stormberg and Spioenkop were possible. Kruger ordered no jubilation over these successes, and when the reverses came, bowed to the will of God, chastisement being part of his philosophy of life.

It seems very probable that Kruger believed or hoped that this war would follow the same course as the first. When one took into account the world-wide interest and indignation aroused now, as well as the amazing stand put up by the Boers, he perhaps expected that there would be negotiations as in the past and some sort of agreement. Perhaps it only now dawned on him how great was the indignation which still prevailed in the British army as a result of Majuba. The rights and wrongs of this war faded in the light of the military prestige of the Empire, not only in South Africa. Political wrangling, imperialist interests, paramountcy and greed aside, this was a war that *had* to be won. And the general opinion—even of Boer sympathizers—was that it *would* be, within three months.

Members of the Kruger clan were fighting to the west, the east and the south. Of Kruger's own immediate family there were four sons, six sons-in-law and thirty-three grandsons in the lines, and of course there were many other relations, some slain, some captured. As the newspapers were read to the old man and his wife, often by Nettie Eloff, great depression prevailed at times. Gezina felt for all the mothers, even of her enemies, but she also showed the spirit of the Boer Woman which was to keep the war going. When members of the family were murdered by Natives, Gezina demanded an immediate punitive expedition. But Kruger refused, as he suspected British incitement. 'It is but a small part of the sorrow each of us will know in this land,' he said resignedly. 'It is only the beginning. We must be strong.'[357] And one thinks of the words of Dr D. F. Malan on the erection of the Kruger Monument on Church Square in 1954: 'The ability to win may mean greatness, but there is that which is even greater. It is the courage, if called to it, to lose.'

The one who had the least heart in the struggle was General Joubert, and the one who kept him going was his wife. She helped him with his organization, gave advice, was present at battles and was known even to take up position beside the gunners and to tell them where to fire.[358] Neither faith, prayer, nor victories could convince Joubert that the Boers could possibly win this war. But he did his duty, listened to his shrewd Hendrina, and began to lean more and more on the shoulder of young Louis Botha who had always supported him in the Volksraad. That Louis was a born soldier was a revelation to him, as it was also to Louis's first promoter, Lucas Meyer. When Joubert had an accident with his horse, he became almost totally reliant on Botha, the hero of both Colenso and Spioenkop. Joubert at first hinted and finally proposed to Kruger that the man to succeed him as supreme commander in the field was Louis Botha. Kruger showed his usual insight by agreeing, Botha provisionally to be Acting-Commandant-General until such time as he could be legally elected. Some of the older warriors were indignant, but the younger generation was delighted.[359]

Kruger was so busily occupied at Pretoria that so far he had not been on the battlefields, but when the British relieved Ladysmith at the end of February 1900, he went post-haste to Natal to exhort his burghers. After nearly four months of triumph over the English, disaster had come. This centred around General Piet Cronjé, Kruger's old stalwart and crony, who was forced to surrender with about four thousand men at Paardeberg by General Lord Roberts. The drama began with the relief of Kimberley (where Rhodes was among the invested) on 15 February, and to the east the occupation of Hlangwane Hill by General Sir Redvers Buller at Ladysmith on the 19th. The climax came when Cronjé, falling back from Kimberley along the Modder River, was trapped at Paardeberg and brought to surrender after days of terrific bombardment. This débâcle caused an almost total collapse of Boer morale and resistance. Streams of men were riding off home, and there seemed to be no way of stopping them.

Much of the first phase of the war was carried through by the sheer force of Kruger's personality. One of his telegrams to the Natal front ran to twelve pages. Much of his military advice was useful, if not astute, for he had after all served in many campaigns, unlike President Steyn who had no military experience whatever and yet was also the head of the Orange Free State army. Kruger's sudden appearance at Glencoe on 1 March did much to quell panic and to stabilize the new stand along the Biggarsberg. Cowardly behaviour evoked much harshness from Kruger. Had he been but five years younger, he would still have taken on ten men at a time. Hardly back in Pretoria, Kruger prepared to leave for the Free State where total collapse prevailed after the biggest 'bag' of the war and as the large British army descended on Bloemfontein. Men who absconded, Kruger held, should be shot, horse and all.

In reminiscences of Kruger in the last phase of his life, one can read between the lines that he had become very difficult to live with, if not insufferable at times. Since 1897 he had been increasingly moody, swinging from abject depression to elation. His speech had become rushed, and once he was talking it was difficult to get a word in anywhere. His storminess was terrifying to many, not to mention the bursts of ill-temper which he no longer made any effort to control. Alone with Gezina he relaxed, treating her with the gentleness and courtesy he had always shown her. She was often unwell if not ill, and movement of any kind had become an effort. As thousands upon thousands of British troops were landing, their obvious objective being Pretoria, Kruger was tormented by the thought of what was to be Gezina's fate.

This was only one of many worries. Although Leyds kept telling him that there was no hope of European intervention of any kind, certainly not from Germany, France or Russia, Kruger still found it difficult to believe. He had taken it for granted that the whole of Afrikanerdom, as in the vast Cape Colony, would rally to their side, no matter that Onze Jan Hofmeyr had warned him that it would not be so. The sympathy of the Cape Afrikaners was there all right, but only small bands joined the Boer forces. The volunteers from all the quarters of the globe, even an Irish Brigade, could be mustered into a single smallish commando. But England had hundreds of thousands of soldiers which she poured into South Africa from day to day.

The war was already quite beyond the pattern of the first one. There had to be peace with honour, but how? General Joubert, in an even more depressed state of mind since his injury, proposed that they sue for peace, at once. Kruger did not agree, not yet anyway, but as he said to Steyn: 'If General Joubert wishes it, it will be difficult to refuse . . .' Steyn was displeased. He had fought against war until it was no longer possible to do so, and as he was committed to the Transvaal, he wanted to see the thing through 'to the bitter end'—the words he used so often. On the other hand, by sending a weighty cable direct to Lord Salisbury and not, as before, through the High Commissioner, the two Governments would prove to their burghers that they continued to work for peace as long as their independence could be maintained. What every Boer had to understand was that this war was not to give Uitlanders the franchise but to retain their independence. As spirits could not be worse, they were bound to improve. Salisbury's reply marked the end of the first phase of the war. His Lordship considered the war as a punishment for Great Britain in having suffered the two republics to exist. Independence was no longer even a talking-point. So now every Boer knew the facts. Kruger was dejected, as he had somehow not expected things to come to this, and for the first time perhaps understood why a normally placid man like Steyn had been in such an agitated state. Now Steyn was invigorated. If the English wanted war, by God they would have it, and no Boer worth his salt would speak to him again of peace.

While they were waiting for the British Premier's reply, Kruger managed to get Steyn's permission to send cables to Germany, France, Russia and the United States of America to ask for help in ending the war. Steyn agreed as H.M. Government would be forced to make a firm statement that she would allow no intervention. Coupled with Salisbury's declaration, the die was cast. For the first time Steyn began to steal Kruger's thunder. The old man could ramble on about the Almighty as much as he pleased, but it was Steyn who was ready to drink the dregs with his people, to be drawn and quartered with them, to give everything for freedom, justice, independence.

Kruger had hardly returned from the Natal front when he went to Bloemfontein by special train in order to confer with Steyn about their overseas correspondence. He was accompanied by Dr Heymans, his grandson Frikkie Eloff who had become his private secretary, and a small escort. It had become a full-time job for the Dutch doctor to look after Kruger's eyes and some minor ailments. Heymans worried over Kruger's excessive smoking and tried to bring him down to one pipe a day. The old man's co-operation was to buy the biggest pipe he could find. As this was no help, a kind of rationing was begun.

From Bloemfontein Kruger travelled to the Free State front in order to inspirit the men under Generals De Wet and De la Rey, planning a trip of about a hundred miles in a Cape cart to the west to a spot called Poplar Grove. On 7 March, Lord Roberts resumed his advance on Bloemfontein, so Kruger was not to reach his destination. But De Wet was quick to rally round and whisked the President away. A flanking movement by General French put them in danger of being cut off, and it was clear that Kruger's presence was known. General De la Rey, a brilliant strategist, held French back, and Kruger got away, 'shells flying all around us', one just behind the cart in which he was sitting. Instead of showing alarm, Kruger was amused and commented on the explosive quality of the Queen's 'pills'. He reached Kroonstad safely, on his direct route to Pretoria.

As Steyn knew that Bloemfontein had no hope to hold out against the huge British army, he moved his Government to Kroonstad, but neither he nor Kruger expected that the Free State capital would be taken on 13 March with hardly a shot being fired.

Fortunately for the Boers, Lord Roberts was so elated at having taken Bloemfontein that he dallied there long enough to give the Boers time to hold a large Krygsraad at Kroonstad and to start, as it were, the war all over again. This was on the 20th, a unique occasion in that both presidents and nearly all the military commanders of both States were present, even the ailing General Joubert. It was on this occasion that Lord Salisbury's blunt reply was read out and sent to the men who, with the consent of De Wet and De la Rey, had disbanded until the 25th. Its effect, as well as a proclamation by Lord Roberts in which he asked the Boers to lay down their arms, infused the burghers with fresh determination—as Steyn had hoped.

The Kroonstad council of war was attended by some fifty leading officers and they took decisions of great military importance. Encumbrances like wagons were to be done away with, they were to be more mobile and they were to resort to a guerrilla form of warfare. 'Trust in God and your Mausers,' even Joubert was moved to say. Disobedient officers were to be dismissed, all commandos were to be mounted and to move in smaller formation. Everywhere communications were to be cut, attacks were not to be awaited but provoked where the terrain was suitable to themselves. As there were to be no wagons, the word laager could be dropped from vocabulary. Henceforth it would be war solely conducted on horseback. The scattered foreign volunteers were to form a commando under De Villebois-Mareuil who was promoted to General and answerable only to General De la Rey.

Using his 'magnificent presidential railway-carriage', as Count

Villebois-Mareuil described it,[360] Kruger returned to Pretoria, whereas President Steyn was in the field with De Wet. Steyn had shown athletic abilities in youth, but the life of a soldier on active service was new to him, as were the days spent on horseback. But he never complained, was always cheerful, ate and did what everybody did. His staff were nearly all English-speaking but as ardently republican as he was. A large measure of General de Wet's success in keeping the President safe during a series of daring actions was due to his superb young scouts, particularly Danie Theron and Gideon Scheepers who were to die so bravely.

Steyn's example had much to do with the new fighting spirit of the Boers. It had to be conceded that it was quite impossible for Kruger to join a commando (he now even needed a valet to dress him), but it detracted from his popularity and there was a new wave of criticism from his own people. They thought him far too ready to make peace. They disapproved of the cables to Salisbury and the Powers, and they resented that it had been thought necessary to send a special deputation to Europe and America. In consisted of A. D. W. Wolmarans of the Transvaal Executive, C. H. Wessels, president of the Free State Volksraad and Abraham Fischer of the Free State Executive. They had already left for Brussels via Lourenço Marques. Kruger was also criticized for seeking the co-operation of the consular representatives in their midst, and above all they disapproved of the proposals that the President should be got out of Pretoria as soon as possible.

These criticisms were indicative of the new spirit, a fighting spirit which made a handful of Boers come to grips with a British army which eventually numbered nearly half a million men, instead of the forty thousand which Milner had thought would be adequate, over a period of nearly three years instead of three months, at a cost of not the estimated £6,000,000 but £205,000,000.[361] This spirit was largely ascribed to the man whom Louis Botha and so many others called 'the soul of the war'—M. T. Steyn. And of course there were 'the glorious trio': Louis Botha himself, the elusive De Wet and the Lion of the West, Koos de la Rey.

Criticism of Kruger is easy, and yet this was in many respects the most heart-breaking period of his life. Hardly back in Pretoria, he was overcome by the news of the death of General Piet Joubert who had put in an appearance at Kroonstad and gone home. 'I have lost someone,' said Kruger at the Pretoria railway station to the mourners taking the coffin to Wakkerstroom for burial, 'who stood beside me since we were both youths, many years ago. I seem at present the only survivor of the many who in the past fought for land and people . . .' He spoke huskily, his eyes swimming in tears.

> Brothers, what shall I tell you in these hours of national loss? Together we fought for freedom, and the present war we have waged for freedom and right. But weeks ago I still saw the deceased in the fighting line, where humbly and modestly he shared the privations of his burghers as a loyal General, a true Christian and an example for everyone to follow . . .
>
> We are living through dark days; setbacks are ours as a result of the wrong in the land. There will be no change until the cause is removed. In our deceased brother we find an example. He enjoyed the confidence of the people and did his duties diligently. Thus—follow his example and the Lord will grant us peace in His time. Why do we have the sympathy of the whole world? I feel in my heart that the war will come to a favourable end. With the help of the Almighty our tiny nation shall continue to exist. When you think of the precious lives already sacrificed, you will rally round the flag and fight to the last for a righteous cause . . .[362]

The death of Joubert added much to the general gloom which still prevailed, but to Kruger personally it gave an increasing feeling of isolation. Old age, deafness, blurring eyes, remoteness—Paul Kruger was being cut adrift but for the steadying hand of God. When the British army again began operations and the devastation of war spread, his old friend Sammy Marks came to plead with Kruger to end it all, that arms be laid down under protest in order to prevent the further loss of life and goods. As Kruger did not dismiss Marks's proposal, Reitz telegraphed to Steyn who at once went to Pretoria. 'We can do no such thing,' he told Kruger. 'You must never forget all those who have gone into rebellion on our behalf. What is to become of them?' It was true that Kruger at times seemed to forget about these rebels, whereas they were never out of Steyn's thoughts.[363]

As the British came closer, Kruger was urged by Reitz and others to have the goldmines blown up. The gold was seen as the reason for all their woe, and the proposal had been made before. General Louis Botha vehemently opposed such a step, against coalmines as well, the mines being necessary for the rehabilitation of the country once the war was over. Kruger declared that Botha talked sense, for he still had hopes of a peaceful settlement. A new swing had come in the war with De Wet's action at Sannaspost on 31 March and at Reddersburg on 5 April. But nothing halted the British army and by May they were making for their supreme prize—Pretoria.

Kruger's advisers told him that he had to quit the 'capital' (actually it was Potchefstroom, Pretoria being the seat of Government), and that it would be best for the Government to move to the eastern Transvaal. He knew he had to go. 'The thought of this departure lay heavy upon my heart,' he said, 'the more so as my wife was so old and weak that I could not think of taking her with me.'[364] Dr Heymans declared that to move her would mean her death. On the other hand, to leave Gezina behind could mean that he would never again see her in this life. Kruger brooded on this and the uncertain future that awaited him. Cowardice was the last thing anybody could attribute to him, but uncertainty and insecurity are not easily endured in old age. Full of worry and foreboding, Kruger began to compose his opening speech in the Volksraad session beginning on 7 May. No matter what happened, he had to speak with confidence.

The 7th came, a sombre but impressive occasion, the last session of its kind, members in black with white ties. Many seats were vacant, laurel wreaths lying on the chairs of the dead, flags draping those of the absent. Military attachés and consuls from France, Russia, Germany, Italy, Belgium, Portugal, the Netherlands and an American Spectator were in their fine feathers, adding colour and glitter without easing the melancholy. Kruger looked really old and worn out. For once, his speech was written out, and it was read by Frank Reitz. It was a joint session of the two Volksraads. Tributes were paid to the individuals and the sister republic; Louis Botha was formally appointed Commandant-General until such time as an election could be held; and reference was made to the various diplomatic moves and the medical aid given by many countries. Reitz having finished, Kruger rose and began to add to his own speech, speaking with deepfelt emotion in a voice that gained in strength as he stated his belief that it was up to God to allow the war to go thus far and no further.

Also present that day was the Irish-American Michael Davitt who was engaged on a passionately pro-Boer book. It was the first time that he heard the President speak—raucously he says, 'like a valedictory address of a minister committing a body to the custody of a grave'. Then the voice became clearer and the words more coherent, 'the address ringing out in a mingled strain of invective and defiance' —a natural orator, rugged in speech. Davitt was also fascinated by the way Kruger used his hands, notes in his left, notes to which he did not refer, his movements those of the finished platform speaker, the massive right hand thudding down on the desk before him as he gave emphasis to what he said.[365]

The British at last reached Johannesburg and prepared to take Pretoria. Should Kruger be captured, the war would certainly be over. Reports came in that Lord Roberts intended to cut the Delagoa Bay railway with a flying column. There was no time to lose and General Louis Botha was ready to protect Kruger's exit. The President's last day in Pretoria was 29 May 1900. His personal effects were packed and a train was brought in readiness for him and other members of the Government, consisting of compartments for sleeping, a dining saloon, bathroom, kitchen and amenities for a telegraphist. Kruger's destination was to be Machadodorp, something that was kept secret.

Relations and friends came to say their goodbyes, among them unexpected Americans. One was a boy called Jimmy Smith bearing an Address in which 29,000 schoolboys from Philadelphia, New York and Boston sent Kruger a message of sympathy in the defence of his country. The Address was in a leather box weighing 47 lbs.[366] The other Americans presented the President with a Vierkleur embroidered in the United States. This presentation, coming when it did, made a profound impression on Kruger and on the people present. Then it was time to leave.

Kruger called his family together in the sitting room and prayed for their well-being, for God's help and guidance. He got up and took his wife's hand. Together they went to their bedroom. Nobody moved or spoke, the only sounds being the snorting of the carriage horses outside. Then the old couple reappeared. Kruger had his arm around Gezina's shoulder. She was muttering: 'It is the will of God, and my prayer is that He will guard over you.' Kruger pressed her against him and then released her and regarded her intently, silently. He swung round and stalked out to a waiting landau. Gezina threw her apron over her face and withdrew.[367]

The rest of the family stood on the stoep and watched as the vehicles rumbled off in the dusk of Church Street. It was dark as the procession left Pretoria behind for the first station on the eastern line where the special train stood ready at Eerste Fabrieken. From there the Kruger party were on their way via Middelburg to Machadodorp. It was one of the ironies of his life that this railway line for which he had fought so long, so bitterly and passionately, now turned out to be his escape route. Kruger's 'flight' it was called, not only by the British but by his own people and resentful Free Staters. But was it *flight*?

Kruger's full intention was to uphold his Government as vigorously as ever, in the same way as President Steyn had hoped to do after the fall of Bloemfontein. 'The only chance with the Boers,' said Milner, 'is to make them thoroughly understand that our quarrel was not with them, but precisely with the Kruger gang—the authors of the War policy, steeped from head to foot in corruption, who, when they had got their country into an awful mess, ran away and left her . . .'[368]

At Machadodorp, President Kruger lived in his saloon-carriage. Those first days of June were amongst the most terrible he had ever experienced, but he was back at work, just as hard as in Pretoria, and his telegraphist had hardly any rest. The British took Pretoria on the 5th, and Roberts's proclamations had to be met with counter-proclamations. Triumphantly Lord Roberts announced to the world that the war was over. Was it? To Kruger in the first days of June, overwhelmed with grief and feeling at death's door, it seemed so. Pretoria was swarming with English troops, everywhere his burghers were surrendering, or leaving their positions, some even going over to the enemy to betray brothers and friends. In an agonized state of mind Kruger appealed to Steyn to come to him. Could arms not be laid down in protest? Kruger wanted to know. How many men were willing to continue the struggle—a handful?

The Boer people would fight on to the end, Steyn telegraphed to Kruger. Steyn was furious. He could not possibly go to Machadodorp, and there would be no laying-down of arms in protest or whatever it was. The surrender of Bloemfontein was not the Free State, and neither was Pretoria the surrender of the Transvaal. The war would be pursued to the bitter end. 'If I and De Wet and De la Rey are not in the least demoralized, why should you be?' Kruger pulled himself together, finding new strength in Steyn. It would have strengthened him even more had he known that Milner considered any negotiation with him as 'absolutely detestable'.[369]

'Flinch not and fall not into disbelief,' Kruger commanded his people in a new voice, 'for the time is at hand for God's people to be tried in the fire.' Telegrams were sent to all officers forbidding men to lay down their arms, for it would avail them nothing. 'We have resolved to fight to the end. Be faithful and fight in the name of the Lord, for they who flee and leave their positions or run away from commando are fleeing straight to St Helena!' This island had become a major centre for Boer prisoners of war, General Cronjé among them. And so the war did indeed begin all over again, and over a vast field.

'You think you have beaten the Dutch, but it is not so,' said Rhodes at Cape Town. Liberated from Kimberley he was addressing a Jingo audience in a rather surprising way. 'The Dutch are not beaten,' he went on. 'What is beaten is Krugerism, a corrupt and evil government, no more Dutch in essence than English. No! The Dutch are as vigorous and unconquered today as they have ever been; the country is still as much theirs as it is yours, and you will have to live and work with them hereafter as in the past . . . Let there be no vaunting words, no vulgar triumph over your Dutch neighbours; make them feel that the bitterness is past.'[370] These words should have become immortal, but as it turned out, for many Milnerism was much worse than Krugerism. And in any case Krugerism was synonymous with Boer Nationalism.

As it was winter and Machadodorp one of the coldest places in the Transvaal, Kruger was advised to move to Waterval-Onder on the Elands River, where a milder climate prevailed under high mountains. A small house[371] was found for him, and after he moved in on 30 June Kruger's depression began to lift, though in a photograph taken of him on the stoep he looks at least a hundred years old. Machadodorp remained the seat of Government, the State Secretary and Executive travelling to and fro every day. Business was still as usual: decrees, requisitions, provisos for furlough, discipline, punishment, reorganization and all the matters that concern a people in a state of war.

One of the persons who was henceforth the closest to Kruger to the end of his days was Guillaume Marie Albert Heymans, the oculist who had come to Pretoria in 1898, a dark man of medium height with a black moustache. After calling him in once, Kruger was so impressed with Dr Heymans that he appointed him his personal physician. To Gezina Kruger Heymans had made the promise that he would bring the President back to the Transvaal, living or dead, a promise she had also exacted from one of his secretaries, Bredell. Proud of serving the most famous man in the world, Heymans collected all kinds of Krugeriana, no doubt with the intention of writing a book, including a remarkable set of photographs which was not published until 1971.

Others within Kruger's inner circle were his grandson Frederik Christoffel Eloff, always called Frikkie, as assistant secretary to Hermanus Christiaan Bredell (1865–1953), usually called Manie. Bredell kept a diary covering this period up to Kruger's end, a fascinating document which was only published in 1972, edited by A. G. Oberholster. Bredell was a qualified attorney and sworn translator (i.e. he had taken the oath of professional honesty) in Dutch and English. He joined the department of the Commissioner of Police in

1895, and began helping the President with secretarial work just before war broke out. He moved into the Kruger home, and became a kind of bodyguard for the President. Apart from Heymans and Bredell (not so much Eloff) there was always hovering in the background Kruger's devoted young Dutch valet, A. Happé.

Further, at this time, there was daily contact with the lively Frank Reitz, the rather morose Schalk Burger and Louis Johannes Jacobsz (Assistant State Attorney, married to one of the Kruger granddaughters). Jan Smuts had joined General De la Rey and was to become a general in his own right. There were many callers, and telegraphic communication was maintained over a vast area. Smuts came to see Kruger at Waterval-Onder, their last personal encounter. At last President Steyn, too, could come on a visit, reaching Kruger safely at the end of August after being escorted some of the way by General De Wet and through the Bushveld by General Lucas Steenekamp.

Steyn found the Transvaal President much changed in appearance, for his hair and beard had gone snow-white, and he was growing a moustache. Though melancholy, Kruger appeared full of courage, but he was certainly fretting over his wife whom he had heard had again been taken ill. Kruger was wearing thickly-lensed glasses which gave him a rather owlish appearance, as well as small gold rings in his ears, believing them to be an aid to his eyesight, no matter what Heymans had to say about superstition. A mere glance was enough to convince Steyn that Kruger could not possibly remain where he was and needed all the care and comforts he could get. Moreover it was most dangerous for him to remain there, the Battle of Dalmanutha, fought by Louis Botha over a front of thirty-five miles against overwhelming odds, having brought the war too close for comfort. Lord Roberts, exasperated that the war was not yet over, was determined to crush Botha and the Kruger Government in the eastern Transvaal and De Wet and the Steyn Government in the north-eastern Free State, the only important concentration of Boer forces in the field in August 1900.[372]

The British forces broke through at Dalmanutha and were marching on Waterval-Boven, linked by a tunnel with Waterval-Onder, hoping for the catch of the war: Kruger *and* Steyn. With four thousand men Botha could not hope to halt fifty thousand with many heavy guns, and he too urged that Kruger should get away at once. The presidential party moved on to Nelspruit on the Delagoa line (the western section was in British hands), halfway between Waterval-Onder and the Portuguese border. Arriving at Nelspruit, they received the latest proclamation by Lord Roberts in which he annexed the South African Republic to the Empire on 1 September. The Orange Free State had been annexed on 24 May.

The final roar of the Lion of Rustenburg resounded on 3 September from his railway carriage. For ten months the small republics had maintained the unequal contest and they would continue to do so, Kruger said. The South African Republic was not conquered. Their forces were still in the field. Their independence was recognized by nearly all the civilized Powers. 'I do hereby proclaim, in the name of the independent people of this Republic, that the annexation is not recognized and is declared null and void. The people of the South African Republic are and remain a free and independent people and refuse to submit to British rule. Given under my hand at Nelspruit', etc.[373] The British began to move up to Nelspruit, and so the final decision was taken that Kruger should travel on to Lourenço Marques and take ship to Europe.

In the week preceding his departure, Kruger along with Steyn and their respective Governments carefully surveyed the military scene and decided that the commandos had to be broken up into even smaller units. Fighting was to be undertaken exclusively on a guerrilla basis and prongs were to be sent into Cape Colony to lessen pressure on the republics. A desperate telegram from Louis Botha, proposing that now was the opportune time for the two Governments to sue for peace, was dismissed by Steyn. There would be no peace negotiations while he was still alive. Kruger needed Steyn's strength, for another proclamation by Lord Roberts (they were endless) came to say that Mrs Kruger and all the leading Boer women of Pretoria, Mrs Louis Botha also, were to be rounded up and sent to the commandos, for lack of coaches probably in open trucks . . .

'Let them come,' Steyn said to the alarmed Kruger. 'We can charter two ships and send all the women to Europe where, I assure you, their arrival would cause an international outcry.' But it was not to come to that. Roberts, though an irritable little man and embittered by the death of his son in Natal, was not a monster. He had even sent a most courteous telegram of condolence on the death of General Joubert. Gezina Kruger was not molested by the British and was cared for by her household staff and her daughter and son-in-law who lived next door. An armed guard put round the presidential home was there for her own protection. Gezina even had refreshments sent out to them, for after all had the Lord not said that one must love one's enemies?[374]

Kruger was now ready to leave his country. Young Deneys Reitz who happened to be there peered through a window of the saloon carriage and saw the President at a table with a large Bible before him, 'a lonely, tired man', too bowed in thought for conversation.[375] Deneys never saw him again. Actually, a definite decision having been taken, Kruger seemed to lose years in age. He also had an important task in hand in raising Boer support in Europe, perhaps even America as well. The commandos operating in the region came to wish the President farewell, listened to his parting words, and the men pressed forward to shake his old paw, perhaps for the last time. From this point Manie Bredell's *Dagboek* gets into stride.

Officially President Kruger had been granted six months' leave in order to promote the Boer cause in Europe. Schalk Burger was appointed Acting President in his absence. Few people could have believed that Kruger would ever be back alive at his age, but then it depended on the will of God. President Steyn said goodbye to his 'old and loyal brother' at Hectorspruit on 11 September, and was escorted back through the Bushveld to General De la Rey, who was becoming a holy terror for the British army in the western Transvaal. Kruger's tears coursed over his wrinkled cheeks as the train crossed the border at Komatipoort. Someone got up and drew the curtains.

'If my departure from Pretoria was a bitter blow to me,' Kruger said, and this sounds like actual dictation, 'my departure under such sorrowful circumstances, from the land to which I had devoted my life was doubly bitter. I saw it swarming with the enemy, who, in his arrogance, was already declaring that the war was over and that only guerrilla bands now infested the country. I had to bid goodbye to the men who had stood beside me for so many years and to leave my country and my people, my grey-haired wife, my children, my friends and the little band of lion-hearted fighters . . . But I had no choice.'[376]

At Lourenço Marques the train did not stop at the station but was shunted into a siding, and as darkness had fallen Kruger could reach the house of the Transvaal Consul General, Gerhard Pott, unobserved. However, since he had crossed the border, Kruger's every move was known to interested parties, among them the British Consul General, Crowe, who put pressure on the Portuguese Governor, Antonio José de Souza Machado, to deal with the situation. Portugal was heavily committed to Great Britain for financial backing, and since the outbreak of war Lourenço Marques was a hotbed of intrigue and espionage. About Kruger the wildest rumours had been in circulation.[377] It was Kruger's intention to stay with Pott until he could embark on the first outgoing steamer, which was the *Herzog* of the German East Africa Line. The next morning, however, Governor Machado called to say that Kruger was to be the guest of the Portuguese Government and was to accompany him right away.

As Kruger knew that the real Governor of Delagoa Bay was the British Consul, he did as he was requested to do. The Portuguese and the Boers had had friendly relations since the days of the pioneer Voortrekker Louis Tregardt and in his own career Kruger had always had friendly dealings with them. The Boers in general, however, looked upon them as unreliable and fickle in their loyalties.[378] Machado was clearly embarrassed by the role imposed on him, but was friendliness itself, hardly leaving Kruger's side, and even being photographed with him. The presidential escort was restricted to quarters, and were only allowed out in the company of A.D.C.s.

Thus it was that Paul Kruger spent his 75th birthday virtually a prisoner. Boers thronging Lourenço Marques were not allowed to see him and had to shout their congratulations up to the windows. As the days and weeks went by Kruger was exasperated by inaction and his captivity (one cannot call it anything else), as he did not know what to do now. He was no longer allowed even to *see* members of his escort, the British Consul having complained about it. The heat was sweltering, and Kruger felt as if he was suffocating. At last hope came. He would be permitted to leave, as long as it was on a neutral ship and his destination Europe. The world knew of President Kruger sitting shut up in Lourenço Marques, and the thought was particularly unbearable to the young Queen of the Netherlands. Carefully she began diplomatic moves to rescue the old man.

Wilhelmina happened to have a man-of-war, the *Gelderland*, in eastern waters, and Britain showed no objection should she take Kruger on board. Wilhelmina, having Victoria's permission, arranged that the ship did her coaling at Delagoa Bay and picked up President Kruger and his party. As has been shown, Queen Wilhelmina had had grave misgivings even before the war began, and the way the war was dragging on deeply distressed her, for many of her countrymen were involved in it and she had a common tie of ancestry with the Boers. But she wanted to be strictly neutral in a Europe which was largely anti-British and to maintain her excellent relations with England. Kruger was not to be taken through British waters but was to land at Marseilles. With marvellous tact and diplomacy Wilhelmina arranged everything.

Kruger was elated when he heard of her act of mercy and that the

Gelderland was coming to fetch him. Blood was thicker than water after all. Perhaps he could even take Gezina with him, but he was at once informed that she was too weak to undertake a journey of any kind. On 12 October Kruger had his slightly belated birthday present in that the *Gelderland* steamed into Delagoa Bay under the command of Baron Sweerts de Landas. A week later, on the 19th, Kruger went on board with Heymans. Bredell, Eloff and Happé. It was a coincidence that a royal salute was fired, in which British and Portuguese ships joined, to mark the betrothal of Queen Wilhelmina which had just been announced. But it might as well have been for President Kruger who from now on was to know all the honours of royalty.

On the afternoon of 20 October 1900 the *Gelderland* sailed out of Delagoa Bay. Kruger made no comment on his treatment by the Portuguese but, as Bredell was to notice, he never again wore his Portuguese decoration. One of the most striking and moving photographs ever taken of President Paul Kruger was on deck, his large bulk, with top-hat, in silhouette as he stood and watched the fading shore of Africa.

CHAPTER TWENTY

Exile and Death

'Wagtail,' Kruger said with astonishment when he saw the little bird sitting on the ship's rail, 'what are you doing so far out? Will you and I ever see our dear fatherland again?' This thought never left his mind. For the first time he was seasick, but this lasted only a day or so, while the rest of his party was prostrate.[379] They all enjoyed the full hospitality of their Dutch hosts who were somewhat overcome by their historic mission and the sensation it was causing throughout the world. At the first opportunity the ship's officers had themselves photographed with the President. The *Gelderland*'s first port of call was Dar-es-Salaam.

In the heat of the tropics Kruger donned a white jacket and white canvas shoes, as well as a white cap when on deck. This array, together with his unfamiliar white moustache and the dark glasses to protect his eyes, was a startling transformation to those accustomed to the Kruger image. On 25 October they arrived at Dar-es-Salaam where they spent three days. There were gun salutes and the German Governor and high-ranking officers came on board to pay their respects. An invitation to a banquet on land was declined in the circumstances, Leyds having advised Kruger to be as unobtrusive as possible until he was safely in Europe. On no account was Wilhelmina to be embarrassed. But there was wild cheering from passing ships as the voyage continued.

If the Governments of the various countries were in a quandary about Kruger, their peoples were nearly all and frantically on his side. Kruger was the symbol of freedom, the prey of the British lion, the head of a small nation of heroes. The legend of Paul Kruger had become universal, his name familiar to every child of all nationalities. The flood of books on him, his people and country continued unabated in many languages. The newspapers and magazines were full of him. In Great Britain, too, but mainly among the intelligentsia, there was much sympathy with Kruger. Lloyd George looked upon the war as an 'outrage which is perpetrated in the name of human freedom' and as 'damnable, even worse perhaps, a senseless war'.[380]

At Suez, Kruger heard of the reception planned for him at Marseilles. Dr Leyds, fully aware of the international scene, again cautioned discretion and advised the President to grant no interviews and to keep quiet until he was in France. This was in a letter brought on board by C. G. S. Sandberg, a former military secretary of General Louis Botha. Kruger readily obliged, and in any case he was drifting into the remoteness of the aged and deaf. He was also to some extent oblivious or unable to grasp the extent of international intrigue which had momentarily formed around him. It also appears as if it did not occur to him that his arrival was a decided embarrassment to the Powers from which he expected help. The evening before his arrival at Marseilles the Dutch officers gave him a banquet on rolling seas, and on the morning of 22 November 1900 the thunder of Dutch and French gun salutes reverberated, and screaming crowds on land swam into Kruger's blurred field of vision.[381]

It was a perfect sunny day. The ship was actually a day late, but the crowd which had dispersed returned, some sixty thousand people, including the members of the Boer deputation from Brussels, Dr Leyds, the Mayor of Marseilles, leaders of societies and all kinds of dignitaries. Leyds had had much to do with the organization of the reception, for should Kruger be accorded full honours, the precedent would be set for receptions elsewhere. Even if Kruger was unlikely to achieve much, his presence had tremendous propaganda value for the Boer cause in Europe. And he let nobody down. Courteously he parted with the officers and crew of the ship, and was then taken to land in a cutter bearing the Vierkleur, a most dignified old man borne through a multitude of sailcraft. Leyds was the first on shore and held out a hand to Kruger who followed suit with surprising nimbleness, mounted a decorated dais and stood bareheaded as an orchestra struck up with the Transvaal national anthem.[382]

A pathos emanated from Paul Kruger which moved the crowds, as when he concluded a speech (interpreted by Prof. A. G. van Hamel) by saying that their independence would only be finally lost when the Boer people, their women and children, were destroyed. Various speeches having been made, the mood changed back to cheering and shouting, and to the strains of orchestral music and in a rain of flowers Kruger and his party were driven off in garlanded carriages to the roars of '*Vive Kruger! Vive les Boers!*' Their destination was the Hotel Noailles; the flags of the Transvaal and France were waving everywhere, and people were cheering from packed balconies.

A reception followed at the hotel, Kruger appearing on the balcony to greet the cheers of thousands of people, a cheering that went on right through the night. He was so exhausted that he was unable to attend the banquet, so Leyds stood in for him after he had given audience to various deputations and dignitaries. The next morning the party left for Paris by train, crowds surging round the stations they passed, yelling, waving flags and tossing flowers. The remarkable thing was the spontaneity of it all, far more so than Leyds had expected, and indeed it was nothing short of a royal progress, with a triumphal entry into Paris at the Gare de Lyon. Preceded by the mounted municipal guard, Kruger passed through cleared streets between rows of constabulary as all of Paris seemed to converge on his route in frenzied excitement. It was quite unbelievable, or 'indescribably colossal' to Bredell.[383]

The President of France, Emile Loubet, had Kruger conveyed by a glittering cuirassier escort to the Elysée Palace and back. The time had now come in Kruger's life for pageantry and all the trappings of a State visit: troops, plumed horses, orchestras and bands, against a background of a yelling mass of humanity. Personally Kruger had never cared for fuss, and he was dazed by it all, but ever at his elbow was Leyds, suave, correct, impeccable. In the ambassadorial salon of President Loubet, Kruger stood in full dignity, neatly dressed in black, wearing his Sash of State and as sole decoration the Legion of Honour, light falling with a silver sheen on his hair and beard. Glamour and dignity there was all right, but was there to be anything else?

To judge by the mass demonstrations in favour of the Boers in so many countries, the wariness if not indifference of their Governments was very puzzling to Kruger. Could he really have believed that any Power would have risked war with England on account of a small backveld State like the Transvaal? But he did, and for the simple reason that he could not believe that God would allow his country to go under when right was on their side. For a man like Kruger to lose his faith was to lose his reason, and what is remarkable is that he kept faith as his gnarled old fist began to beat against a series of locked doors. Life had become rather unreal for him, and he had begun to drift through it as one sometimes does in dreams.

This phase of his life has been recorded in minute detail, but the accounts are mostly of his movements and tell us little about the man. In the English-speaking world he was vilified beyond belief. 'A criminal of the most brutal type,' Hume Nisbet called Kruger in 1900, 'a mad enthusiast who had fashioned his own God and his own Faith, a murderer, a robber, a cheat, a liar . . .'[384] 'Rubbing his oily hands', wrote H. T. Batts, 'playing off people to gain his ends, a tyrant, quite without feelings for others,' and so on.[385] More balanced books were so numerous that even original works appeared in uniform editions in 1900.

There was a mass of literature in many languages, including biographies published in the United States, as well as extensive pro-Kruger outpourings in German, Dutch, French and Russian; but Kruger himself took scant interest in even the fraction he knew about. Similarly, Continental portrayals of him, surrounded by angels, palm and laurel leaves and all kinds of sentimentalities, must have meant little or nothing to a man of his temperament. Then there were all those medallions struck in his honour, the postcards, busts, plates bearing his effigy, mugs in the shape of his head, pipes too—Krugeriana which were to become a passion with many collectors. I believe a beverage called Kruger Bier is still made. Others took a stand between the poles of vilification and deification, and saw him either as 'a sort of sordid Lear' as did Merriman,[386] or simply as a father of woe.

The homage of France in all its warmth was of little practical help to Kruger. Interviews at top level revealed that he would have the full courtesy of France—but no more. The roars of acclaim when he lifted his top hat in his right hand even made it unnecessary for him to say anything. He had the heart of France but not her head.[387] The next door to try was Germany. After a hectic stay in Paris at the Hotel Scribe up to 1 December, the Kruger party departed by train for Cologne. Dr Leyds had asked the Kaiser for an audience but no reply had yet been received. But as the Kaiser had been on friendly terms with Kruger for years it was thought unnecessary to wait. Kruger's departure from France was accompanied by the same pageantry as with his arrival—carillons, gun salutes, deputations and presentations.

They passed through massed railway stations with bands playing and all the rest up to Cologne where the biggest crowd ever had converged. Kruger was only able to reach his hotel by being taken along a circuitous route. He was shaken and annoyed by the mob hysteria unleashed with his arrival at the station. At his hotel there was a telegram from Kaiser Wilhelm to say that the time was not opportune for an audience. His Majesty was on the point of leaving for a hunting trip. In the circumstances Wilhelm considered a visit to Berlin inadvisable. In other words, as Leyds explained to Kruger, they were told to get out of Germany. The old man was deeply shocked, all his dreams of German help shattered. 'The Kaiser has betrayed us,' Kruger said sadly.[388]

But Leyds was not really surprised. Britain had largely ignored the French demonstrations, but a similar sort of thing in Germany would be a different matter. Instead of helping the Boers, and to make up for past indiscretions, the Kaiser in fact sent suggestions to England as to how the Boers could be vanquished by a scorched earth policy, concentration camps, drives, and so on, measures actually adopted by Lord Kitchener who succeeded Lord Roberts. To his critics the Kaiser explained that he was in no position to go to war with England because he did not have a proper fleet, so it was best to befriend her. Leyds did not know all this, but he had hoped that Kruger's actual arrival would clarify the situation. Now it had been clarified, and he called off a German tour.

Their next door would be the Netherlands, a country which, though it was strictly neutral and could be of no help, was more like home. They departed from Cologne on 6 December to further mass demonstrations and travelled via Arnhem and Utrecht to The Hague. The Hollanders went wild with the arrival of President Kruger and their normally placid capital swarmed with excited crowds. The Dutch looked upon Kruger as a personal possession, and from his arrival in drizzle at four in the afternoon in The Hague, demonstrations continued until half past eight when Kruger could take no more and called a halt.

The Queen Mother, Emma, sent messengers to the Hotel des Indes that same evening to invite Kruger to Court the next day in a private capacity. He was thus enabled to thank Queen Wilhelmina personally for her gracious gesture in giving him the *Gelderland*, and to congratulate her on her betrothal. Wilhelmina replied by saying that she hoped the President would be able to attend her wedding and that he would be able to dine with them in the near future. Nothing controversial was touched on, and after an interchange of courtesies, the call was ended. In the afternoon Wilhelmina's Ministers of Finance and External Affairs paid a return call, but all that the old man could deduce was that he was very welcome as long as he remained in a private capacity.

Wilhelmina could not tell Kruger that she had tried to persuade the Kaiser to intercede on his behalf back in March that year. Wilhelm insisted that he could do nothing without an adequate fleet.[389] More the Queen could not do, beyond giving Kruger hospitality and the sympathy of her lovely intelligent eyes. He was disappointed not to have more, but Kruger knew of the Queen's friendship with England, and he would always revere her for getting him out of sweltering Lourenço Marques. So he began to settle down and to feel like his old self, needing no interpreters, and more at ease as mob hysteria died down.

In those crowded weeks Kruger showed varied interests. In Paris he visited the Eiffel Tower, the Hôtel de Ville and an International Exhibition where the Transvaal too had a pavilion. In Cologne he visited the celebrated Cathedral, and shortly after his arrival in the Netherlands he attended a great reception in the Palace of Arts and Science at Amsterdam, as well as a service in the principal church. His entourage at this stage consisted of his two secretaries, Bredell and Eloff, Dr Leyds, members of the Transvaal Deputation, Fischer, Wessels and Wolmarans, and his embassy secretary Cornelis van Boeschoten who was constantly at loggerheads with Bredell. Young Eloff had been joined by his wife. They were fêted in Amsterdam, Leyden and Haarlem, and Kruger was showered with honours. All the kindness, he said, was like balm to his soul.

He needed it, for the British destruction of the two republics had begun as the war moved into its second year. As farmhouses formed depots for guerrilla bands, they were burnt, and so were all food supplies. Flocks of sheep and herds of cattle were wiped out. The women, who played such an important part in keeping the war going, were rounded up with their children (they were homeless anyway) and put into concentration camps all over South Africa. These measures were condemned by the whole civilized world and were repugnant to many British officers, but Lords Roberts and Kitchener could see no other way of breaking the Boer spirit. The concentration camps became the biggest scandal of the war, the inmates dying in thousands. The deaths of their wives and children only increased the ferocity of the Boer fighters, small as their numbers had become, and they continued to have startling successes against overwhelming odds.

It would appear that Kruger put much of what was happening in the ex-republics from his mind, finding it too unbearable to contemplate. He was becoming increasingly out of touch with what was actually happening, and he had physical disorders which distracted his mind. His eyes were now so painful that surgery was needed. Moreover, he had contracted bronchitis. At Utrecht a successful operation on both his eyes was made by Prof. Dr H. Snellen, assisted by Heymans, and his chest began to clear up. Soon he appeared to be in better condition than he had been for months. He missed the wedding of Wilhelmina and her Hohenzollern Prince, but members of his party attended, and Kruger dined privately with the royal couple, the conversation carefully steered away from all political issues.

It became clear to Leyds that Kruger could not go on staying at The Hague. The President's presence, even if 'private', was an embarrassment to the Dutch Government as his appearance anywhere caused emotional demonstrations. Some members of the Dutch Cabinet were openly hostile to Kruger. So, after living at The Hague and having spent a couple of months at Utrecht, the Kruger party moved to Hilversum at the beginning of April 1901 and stayed at the Villa Casa Cara for eight months. After his operation, Kruger improved so markedly that he could again give Press interviews selected by Leyds. Kruger's upper lip was again shaven and, apart from an occasional incongruous white hat, he was more or less his old self. He spent a kind of holiday with Danie Wolmarans at Scheveningen and visited those Dutch towns still clamouring to see him: Rotterdam, Kampen and Dordrecht, where he saw the sights, attended church and was taken through breathtaking gardens and on sailing trips.

All was well with his wife, he had heard, thus it was alarming to receive cables on his return to Hilversum that she had again taken ill, and finally that she was dead. Kruger did not know what had hastened her end. Eight ailing grandchildren were sent to her from the Krugersdorp Concentration Camp after their mother had died, suffering from measles and malnutrition. Within nine days five of these children died, a blow which hastened Gezina's end two weeks later.[390] The British granted her a funeral befitting her station, and many attended her burial in Pretoria.

It was July and Kruger's grief was obvious to his household. A strange silence seemed to envelop him from now on. Wolmarans had the President brought back to Scheveningen to distract his thoughts, and on his return to Hilversum, Kruger 'lived in absolute retirement, interrupted only by the necessary conferences, and devoted myself entirely to the perusal of my Bible.'[391] He was waiting, and so were those who were with him, though they did not dare admit it, for him to die. It was Dr Jameson who had once remarked that Kruger would outlive them all at a time when Jameson could not possibly have imagined that he was still to become Premier of Cape Colony.

Paul Kruger's life spanned such an extraordinary period of South African history that he was often asked to write his memoirs. True, he had a great story to tell but he was no writer and had always found expression in the spoken word. Pieter Grobler, still working for the Transvaal Government at The Hague, and Manie Bredell felt that they had a duty towards posterity, so they got Kruger to reminisce, collected documents and began to compile what was called Kruger's *Memoirs.* Grobler travelled to and fro between The Hague and Hilversum while the book was in progress. Once he was talked into it, Kruger began to enjoy dipping into the past. Although he was in his 76th year, his memory was as remarkable as ever. When sections were read out to him, he corrected inaccuracies—unfortunately not all of them.

The days followed a set routine of rising, eating, reading, smoking, driving and talking. He read the Bible by himself, and Bredell read him the newspapers and then all the cables from his generals in the field, describing their movements, their triumphs and setbacks. Always there were callers, and occasional sorties out into the open air. Bredell and Heymans arranged their outings to suit the President, but Frikkie Eloff was more often absent than present, as apparently he found the atmosphere around the old man stifling. Kruger constantly reprimanded him for extravagance and irresponsibility. His wife wondered how she was to move in the highest social circles without being a lady of fashion. Then too the young Eloffs wanted to make the most of the artistic feast offered by Europe. They were a far cry from the old Krugers, smart, sophisticated, sociable and cultured.

When not attending church on Sundays, Kruger held his own service for the household. He liked to discuss his text afterwards with Heymans and Bredell, even Happé. But Frikkie Eloff was hardly ever there, and Bredell knew that the old man missed him. Warned, Frikkie saw to it that he was present at luncheon, and was startled suddenly to be commanded to say grace. He mumbled rather incoherently, and Kruger let it pass. 'It's all your fault,' Frikkie snapped at Bredell when they were on their own. 'You've got me into trouble!' Then he was gone again. Having coffee at three that afternoon with Bredell, Kruger suddenly turned to him and said: 'I gave him a fright, didn't I?'[392]

Financially Kruger was comfortable but no longer a rich man. He must have known about the rumours that he had taken millions in gold on his 'flight' from Pretoria, and that most of it was buried somewhere in the eastern Transvaal. This was part of anti-Kruger propaganda, the implication being that he fled his country in its hour of need with a large part of the country's financial resources. It was even said that Kruger took the solid gold hands off the church clock, when that church did not have a clock. One cannot dismiss these stories, as people are still digging for the Kruger Millions to this day. General Smuts took pains to explain what the financial arrangements were when the Government left Pretoria,[393] but all this has been in vain, and the legend lives on. Bredell does make mention that part of his duties on leaving Pretoria was to guard the trucks with gold and money,[394] clearly Kruger's personal fortune to maintain himself and entourage.

Kruger's son Tjaart died on 30 September of pneumonia. Better news was that now that the old lady was dead, their daughter, Elsje Francina, and her husband, Frederik Christoffel Eloff and their children (they had eight) were making arrangements to leave for Europe to look after the President. After many intricate arrangements and devious routes, the Eloffs were actually with him on his birthday. It was quite a diversion to have children in the house again. Life now fell into an even more set routine—less so for Manie Bredell who was in love with the one daughter Nettie, an as yet unrequited love, as Nettie had set her heart elsewhere. (They were to be at last married in October 1905.)

Kruger, his male companions and the Eloff family travelled to Utrecht on 11 December and took adjoining villas. Kruger's was called 'Oranjelust', and the name became well known, for he lived there for ten months. Leyds had found this spacious home for him, in a quiet area, with a beautiful garden. Perhaps the work on the *Memoirs* set Kruger's mind wandering and caused some confusion in his thoughts, strange to those used to his clarity of mind. Occasionally he spoke of subjects like the Flesh and the Devil with a Boer forthrightness which made Bredell and Nettie Eloff squirm with embarrassment. The old man's Biblical obsessions were often wearisome. Oddly enough, three of his intimates, Heymans, Van Boeschoten and Happé were Catholics. Religious differences still did not bother Kruger. His grandson Frikkie Eloff had married a Güttman, daughter of a Jewish Rand pioneer.

The year 1901 was ending with the war in South Africa still continuing, unbelievably so and with a ghastliness that could hardly be imagined. Cape rebels, and others who were not rebels, were being hanged, and shot by firing squads. The Republics were a smoking ruin. Kitchener's blockhouses were strung along the railway lines as far as Wellington in the Cape, the country cut up into 'paddocks' in which drives were led to capture the commandos piecemeal. Concentration camps of canvas tents mushroomed over large areas of veld, and there were all those graves of women and children which aroused in an Englishwoman like Emily Hobhouse the ferocity of a tigress.

Europe had become used to Kruger in their midst, and he was still fêted wherever he went, but greater interest than ever was shown in the exploits of Generals De la Rey, De Wet and Louis Botha, and all the others : Beyers, Malan, Viljoen, Smuts, Kemp, Scheepers, Hertzog, Kritzinger, Lemmer and so on, not to forget President Steyn who was still with his men but had contracted a strange malady.

It was proposed to Kruger that he should leave the Netherlands for a milder climate such as the Riviera, but he did not wish to go even if it would ease his rheumatism. There were to be no luxuries for him while his people were suffering. So he spent most of his time indoors, apparently going more deaf and blind as time passed. Bredell noted that his hearing was better on some days than others. The death of Queen Victoria early in 1901 affected Kruger less than that of Rhodes in March 1902. 'May God have mercy on his soul,' Kruger murmured, 'for he clung so much to worldly things . . .' The Last Will and Testament of Cecil John Rhodes interested the old man when it was read out to him from the newspapers, notably that Rhodes had left his beautiful home with its varied history, 'Groote Schuur', as an official residence for the future Premiers of a united South Africa. 'Perhaps I'll be the first,' Kruger said slyly to Bredell.

The opening months of 1902 held much of interest. Young Commandant Gideon Scheepers, taken ill, was forced to surrender, was court-martialled and shot, though he was a Transvaaler and not a Cape rebel. General Viljoen was captured and banished to St Helena. Queen Wilhelmina bravely tried to offer mediation between England and the Boers. General De la Rey, invincible in the western Transvaal, defeated and captured General Lord Methuen. Instead of executing him to avenge Scheepers, De la Rey set him free—to Kruger's approval. As a result of De la Rey's act, the captured General Kritzinger, with even graver charges against him than in the case of Scheepers, was acquitted. And again there were peace moves, for Lord Kitchener had had his fill of South Africa, and the Boers were reduced to rags and starvation. Kruger's remoteness can be seen in that where he had at times wavered, he no longer saw any reason to sue for peace. Had he been but young and strong again, he would have died at the head of the last commando.[395] He was prepared to go to America to further their cause, but was dissuaded as it was bound to be pointless with the new administration there.

President Steyn believed that had they held out just a few months longer, the outcome would have been different. But he was ill, paralysed, and his death thought imminent, so there was no longer his strength of purpose. From Vereeniging where the final peace talks were held, Steyn was taken away to Krugersdorp for intensive medical care. His one consolation was that his signature was not to be found on any peace document. Neither was Kruger's, but he was so far away that the final decision had to be left to the generals. Should they submit, then he resigned himself to the divine purpose of it all. Even so, when the peace proposals were cabled to him, he bowed his head in abject sorrow. 'Our endeavour,' said Lord Rosebery in consoling tones, 'must be to convert those who have been brave foes into brave friends and fellow-citizens and subjects with us in a new and brighter South Africa . . .'[396]

As long as the flags of the Transvaal and Orange Free State fluttered outside his residence, Kruger found it difficult to believe that it was all over. At sunset on 14 June (the Vereeniging Agreement was signed on 31 May) Bredell had the flags removed.[397] So it was the end. 'My grief is beyond expression,' Kruger said in reply to condolences from Germany. And indeed what did he have to say? He could see his burghers returning to their devastated farms, men who had fought so hard and well, having to start all over again, burdened with grief over the loss of loved ones. Kruger too had lost many dear to him, but where was *he* to go? Boekenhoutfontein was still standing, although a pot-shot had been taken at it, but it could no longer be home for him, not when the houses of Generals De la Rey, Louis Botha and thousands of others were heaps of rubble. On many farms even the trees were gone; there was nothing. Then too, having been born under the British flag, was he to die under it?

'I cannot possibly go home,' Kruger told Bredell. The reasons were numerous. It would be impossible for Kruger to sit quietly at a farm and say nothing. There would only be trouble, for he absolutely refused to be a subject of Edward VII. By remaining in exile he could serve his people far better in their cause which, he still believed, would be resolved by God in His own good time. Anyway, he knew that Generals Botha, De la Rey and De Wet were on their way to Europe in order to raise funds for their stricken people, and he had to see them first before a final decision was taken. And President Steyn too, miraculously surviving from day to day, was being brought over for the best medical treatment available. There was so much to discuss and plan, things to look forward to now that the stream of cables had dried up and the days were becoming long and strangely empty. Also expected were F. W. Reitz and Schalk Burger.

They came, the three generals finding themselves international heroes and given a reception even greater than that accorded Kruger, for they were still vigorous, good-looking and seen in a romantic light. Reitz was the first to call on Kruger, as he was about to depart on a lecture tour of the United States, while his son Deneys was emigrating to Madagascar. On 20 August came the Glorious Trio, accompanied by Leyds and members of the Deputation. It was an emotional reunion after nearly three dramatic years into which all of them had crammed enough experience for a lifetime and had discovered unexpected sides to themselves. Rumour had it that there was a flaming row, 'Mr Kruger having fallen foul of General Botha and bitterly upbraiding him for signing away the independence of the Transvaal.' This was so serious that the generals felt obliged to issue a communiqué in which they strongly denied any such thing and attributed it to malice, credulity, or erroneous information. Knowing Kruger as we do by now, it does not seem so unlikely at all that there *was* a scene of sorts.[398]

Of more importance was a united decision that Kruger should remain in exile. Apart from the fact that it was his own wish, it was also political, for the concept of a broken old man languishing in foreign climes could only be of advantage to the reawakening of Afrikanerdom, Kruger 'as a martyr around whom myths could be woven'.[399] An agreement might have been signed and hostilities ended, but for many the war was not over, and for some it is still not over to this day. Kruger's death in exile could only benefit Afrikanerdom, and this was something he realized himself. The Boer mind found satisfaction in being sacrificed for land and people, a kind of 'sacrifice' to which all three generals had leanings, though in different ways, and were indeed to fulfil : De la Rey in violent death, De Wet in imprisonment by his own people, and Botha in being rejected by an exclusive Afrikanerdom in his bid for South African unity—a full decade after Kruger was laid on the altar.

But it was 1902 and he was still very much alive. He could also not be left unattended. The valet Happé was not straining at the leash (I have often wondered what his full name was and what became of him), and constantly amused Kruger with his affected if not refeened Dutch. But Heymans and Bredell had careers before them and did not relish the thought of being chained to a living chunk of history indefinitely. After some soul-searching, and particularly after more satisfactory payment had been worked out, the two men went to Kruger and gave him their assurance that they would not leave him. Kruger was touched and comforted, not that he was free of the selfishness often found with the aged. Bredell says that financially the old man was a hard nut to crack, to use his own words, and that he was not going to throw his life away for peanuts.[400] Then too, both men had promised to bring the old man back to Pretoria, alive or dead.

A remarkable photograph has survived showing Kruger on his 77th birthday at a special church service in Utrecht, sitting massively in the front row between Botha and Leyds, flanked by De Wet and De la Rey. When the main preachers had done, Kruger was assisted to mount the pulpit and then preached a short sermon, 'the words falling with difficulty from his trembling lips'.[401] In the evening there was a private dinner at 'Oranjelust'. The generals then returned to Brussels where the Transvaal Legation had its headquarters and prepared for their visit to Paris. Although theirs was a 'begging mission', it was more of a triumphal progress, even in England when King Edward and Queen Alexandra were pleased to meet them at both Cowes and Buckingham Palace, honours never given Kruger. The King offered the generals knighthoods which they respectfully declined.

Four days after his birthday, Kruger and his household left for Mentone on the French Riviera for the winter, to settle in a luxurious home among palms and orange trees. They lived there until May 1903. His daughter Elsje and her children were still with him, as were his male companions, and there were always those who wished to see him. It would appear that he no longer had much need of companionship, though it was comforting to know that the others were around. For once he had the leisure to pick up family ties, and many letters were dictated to Bredell and then signed by the old man, a correspondence which must have been quite unnerving to the recipients as it was so unusual coming from their father and grandfather. After various scenes with Frikkie, as usual over extravagance, Kruger preferred postal communication to actual contact with this young Eloff. Even in the midst of his immediate family circle, was there any real contact left with the old man?

'How long, Lord,' he murmured, 'how much longer . . .?' Others wondered the same thing, looking at him slumped in chairs, the incongruous white hat with the black band on his head, hands clasped, the lower lip more pendulous than ever, very deaf and nearly blind, full of bronchitis and rheumatism. 'What news is there from South Africa?' were among Queen Victoria's last words. But the war was only an incident in her life, whereas with Kruger the war and its aftermath had become his total obsession. After the tumult of war, a strange silence had fallen over South Africa, a melancholy for which as yet there were no words. As if the country had not been scourged enough, there was the worst drought in years, as well as pests decimating the few surviving cattle.[402]

There is an old saying that one cannot build happiness on unhappiness. Lord Milner (he had since become a Viscount) experienced this in full measure as he governed from Johannesburg, not Pretoria. Never would he have dreamed that the war would have taken so long and demand such devastation 'to bring a people under' as he put it. Although he had a brilliant administrative staff, his famous 'kindergarten', the Milner Administration was a flop. Even the most vociferous of Uitlanders longed for the old order of things. Milner had the Witwatersrand but nobody to work it. In desperation he imported Chinese when the Natives refused to return to the mines. South Africa had problems enough, Kruger and many others remarked, to import another was too much. This Chinese labour force helped to hasten Milner's eclipse. He was to fade out of South Africa after having been instrumental in the large-scale destruction of the major part of the country and in the deaths of 34,116 Boers, 26,000 of whom were women and children. The British dead numbered 22,000, many of whom had died of sicknesses and who throughout had had only the vaguest notion what the war was all about.[403]

The Boer era was no more. From now on one spoke of Afrikaners. Among them there were cross-currents of thought which gradually found expression. Kruger was in on the beginning of it. To put it very simply, the Afrikaners first wanted to salvage what they could and to clear their minds of the fog of war. Only then could relationships with fellow South Africans be reassessed. The English foe was more readily forgiven than the traitors in their midst. The holy terrors of some concentration camps were not British but men of their own flesh and blood. Gallant young fighters had met disaster through the betrayal of their own kin given the misleading name of 'National Scouts'. Even before his exile, Kruger had expressed his revulsion of this element. Rumour had it that they were paraded along Church Street where Mrs Kruger could see them.

But what was to be done with them? General Louis Botha had long before the termination of the war come to a concept of South Africanism for the white races, irrespective of descent or creed. As time passed he went further: heroes, enemies and traitors, all were to be taken into a common fold for the good of South Africa as a whole. Hence sprang his policy of 'conciliation', which was supported more and more warmly by General Smuts, and viewed favourably by General De la Rey. President Steyn too set as an ideal the fusion of the white races, but first of all he wished to see the Afrikaner find his feet. James Barry Munnik Hertzog, a Free State judge who had become a general and of growing political importance, went further: Botha's conciliation was only possible once the Afrikaner was restored to his full dignity, and even then only if he retained whatever was his own, in the same way as the Englishman retained his—a twin stream of cultures, not one. 'To each his own', was Hertzog's cry, loyalty to all South Africa, not the British Empire, was to come first.

The arrival of President Steyn in Europe, stricken with a malady which had induced almost total paralysis and double vision, also aroused great emotional response from the peoples of Europe. Though a physical wreck, his mind was unimpaired, and he showed it in his determination neither to forgive nor to forget. This did not mean that he was anti-British (I have mentioned that almost his entire staff in the war was English-speaking), but the rapists of South Africa had to be called to account, the graves of women and children had to speak, his people had to find themselves in unity as Afrikaners. Steyn once watched a puddle of blood formed by the slain of opposing sides and had seen it as a vision of the future of South Africa. But this was only possible once men clasped hands as equals and not as victors and vanquished. Much of Steyn's thinking was passed on to Hertzog, and from Hertzog to De Wet. To them Botha's wooing of the British in the post-war period was offensive. It was like garlanding a rapist with flowers.

After Steyn's arrival in Europe, Kruger travelled from Hilversum to see him on 6 August 1902, their first meeting since Komatipoort in September 1900. Kruger was shocked to see the once robust young man hardly capable of a feeble flutter of the hands, and sat at his sickbed rather like, as I have said elsewhere, a tableau of a man and his fate.[404] On rejoining Mrs Steyn, who had shown tremendous courage and had overcome endless obstacles in bringing her husband to Europe, Kruger said to her: 'My child, you must look after him very well. South Africa still needs him so badly. Should he be made to walk again, I'll jump for joy—I'll jump so high . . .' And he indicated one of his leaps in youth. After intensive medical care and endless patience, Steyn indeed began to improve, and in the course of 1903 and the beginning of 1904 was to see Kruger often when at Cannes as they were then within easy travelling distance of each other.

In the summer of 1903 Kruger was back at Hilversum, at the Villa

Djemnah, returning to Mentone in October. With the approach of the summer of 1904 he moved to Clarens in Switzerland. The Eloffs as usual moved into an adjoining villa. The beauty of lakes and mountains was by this time hardly visible to Kruger. His last home was the Villa Dubochet No. 17, a simple but solid structure, run by an efficient Swiss housekeeper. She, Madame Blancpain, recalled: 'The President could no longer move freely. On arrival he went straight to his room on the ground floor and rarely ventured into other parts of the house. From his room a door led out on to a spacious balcony with a view over the lake and French Alps. There, on the balcony, he spent his days in meditation. Dr Heymans and a male nurse carried him in his chair from his room to the balcony and back, and helped him to the bathroom.' Kruger's favourite chair was a distinctive one, its back adorned with carved Boer symbols; it has since been replaced by a replica.[405]

To the end, national and church matters held his interest, as well as labour, education and political evolution. He was never without spiritual comforters, as various ministers of his church saw to his needs. With closed eyes and breathing heavily, Kruger appeared to lose consciousness at such a service. But at the gentle touch of Heymans, the old man murmured: 'Let the minister continue. It is sweet and blissful for me to be close to the Lord.'[406] The dictation of letters was ending, the effort having become too much. But always there was something, like sending a message to the Russian people on their entry into war with Japan. The Russians had almost to a man supported the Boer cause. According to Leyds, the staunchest friend the Boers ever had was the Tsar.

The subject of Kruger's return to South Africa had again come up. Its political significance had taken on a different meaning. Louis Botha and Jan Smuts conferred with Lord Milner on Kruger's possible return, but Milner, although not appearing to oppose the idea, said that it was for the Colonial Office in London to decide.[407] Botha and Smuts now realized that Kruger's death in exile would be detrimental to their policy of conciliation, but they agreed that Kruger could not possibly be expected to take the Oath of Allegiance to the British Crown. The English Press referred to ex-President Kruger and ex-President Steyn, something their own people never did. Kruger no longer gave any thought to going home, and as time passed and he became increasingly feeble, the matter was not raised again.

With both Presidents in Europe, the Afrikaner people had begun to concentrate on General Louis Botha as their leader. Here was a man in the heroic mould, one of them, of dash and daring, intelligent, warm-hearted, possibly as great a statesman as he was a soldier. With the intellectual resources of Jan Smuts behind him, he would certainly fix Milner. Then too Botha had a plan and a policy. The younger generation adored Louis Botha. The word is not too strong; they did not like or love him, they adored him, for Botha was one of those who always aroused strong emotions. Such emotion was felt as the massive man with his striking blue eyes faced a congress of the people on 23 May 1904. Botha stood there as the personification of the political rebirth of the Afrikaner people. Thoughts turned to Paul Kruger, so far away, and it was decided to send him a message of greetings of salutation from the people, *het volk*—in fact the name Botha had taken for his political party: Het Volk.

The reply came in a dying voice from the old man of Pretoria:

> I thank all of you who have come together to confer about past and future and yet remembered your old State President, showing that you have not forgotten the past. He who wishes to create a future must not lose track of the past. Thus; Seek all that is to be found good and fair in the past, shape your ideal accordingly and try to realize that ideal for the future. It is true: much that has been built is now destroyed, damaged, levelled. But with unity of purpose and unity of strength that which has been pulled down can be built again. It is gratifying to me to find you ruled by unity and concord. Never forget the grave warning in the words: 'divide and rule', and never let it be applied to the Afrikaner people. Then our nationality and our language will flower. How much of it I will be vouchsafed to see, rests in the hand of God. Born under the English flag, I do not *wish* to die under it.

And then came the final cadence:

> I have learnt to resign myself to the bitter thought of closing my eyes in foreign climes as an exile, almost totally alone, far from relations and friends whom I'll *probably* never see again, far from the soil of Africa which I'll probably never tread again, far from the land to which I gave my life in order to cut a path for civilization and where I saw my own nation grow. But the bitterness will soften, as long as I may retain the conviction that the work begun will be continued. The hope that the end result of such work will be good shall sustain me. Thus be it. From the depth of my heart I greet you and the entire nation.

The sentiment was wholeheartedly that of Kruger, the words and composition was that of Leyds, the translation is my own. The old man read and approved the letter, signed for the last time, and knew that he had released a political testament which would endure.

On 9 July, Paul Kruger contracted pneumonia. At five minutes past three on the morning of 14 July 1904, the President, to the last eagerly awaiting his Lord, departed this life. He died in the Voortrekker way, no fuss, no bother, his Bible resting open on a table. Dr Heymans took a last photograph, hands clasped on chest on the white coverlet, the face heavily featured and still resolute, a monument of power and will, even in death.

Sources and Notes

References are to books listed in the Select Bibliography

1 By De Villiers, Engelenburg, Preller, Uys, Mossop, Hoge, Jeffreys, Schmidt, Krüger and many others.

2 According to Nathan, 1703.

3 Mossop, p. 249; Krüger, p. 4.

4 L. L. Tomlinson: *Geskiedkundige Swellendam,* Cape Town, Nasionale Pers, 1943.

5 The main scholars involved in this dispute were Prof. C. J. Uys, C. Graham Botha, J. v. G. Bekker and Prof. D. W. Krüger. The President himself added to the confusion by saying or being made to say in his so-called *Memoirs* that he was born at the farm Vaalbank in the district of Colesberg. Uys believed that he was born at the farm Zoutpansdrift to the west of the town Hofmeyr, originally called Maraisburg, founded in 1874. There has also been controversy about the spelling of the surname as Kruger or Krüger, but one can take Prof. Spies's version as correct.

6 For a reproduction see Krüger, vol. 1.

7 Smithers, p. 21. This is an entertaining autobiography, unflattering to Kruger, in which she makes free use of the Bredell-Grobler *Memoirs.*

8 One of them was Mary Solomon, better known as Mrs John Brown, the distinguished social worker and dedicated friend of Olive Schreiner, a South African version of a combination of Mary and Beatrice Webb.

9 *Memoirs,* p. 4.

10 Potgieter & Theunissen, p. 23.

11 As related in Mrs Rompel-Koopman's entertaining slim volume on Mrs General Joubert: *Wat Meurouw Generaal Joubert Verfelt,* Cape Town, H.A.U.M., 1916.

12 *Memoirs,* p. 7.

13 Potgieter & Theunissen, p. 34.

14 *Ibid.,* ch. vii; Theal, vol. vi, p. 292.

15 *The Life of Olive Schreiner,* p. 307. She had contact with just about every important person in South African history after the time of Sir George Grey. She was also one of the stream of

people who passed round Kruger's bier when he lay in State in the Suzanna Hall, in dim electric light, towards the end of 1904, and experienced a thrill of national and historical awareness, as implied in her husband's mutilated compilation of her *Letters.*

16 I have dealt with these battles in some detail in my book *The Voortrekkers,* this study being a sequel.

17 Van Oordt, p. 30.

18 Krüger, pp. 15–17; Engelenburg & Preller, pp. 41–2.

19 *Memoirs,* pp. 19–21. A valid reason why this book cannot be dismissed is that after its publication the old man enjoyed having it read to him and would go off on a spree of reveries which the compilers could only have wished they had had in more detail when they were working on it.

20 Descriptions of Kruger as a young man are all from hearsay. The people who knew him then were not writers, and once he became famous, deductions were made—usually exaggerated. Kruger himself, as I reveal, enjoyed straining the credulity of his audience and more often than not gave a sudden fantastic slant to a story told in all seriousness, more exhilarating to himself than those who could not possibly grasp the satisfaction of such inventiveness.

21 *Memoirs,* pp. 13–14.

22 Nathan, p. 24.

23 Kotzé, vol. i, p. 491.

24 *Memoirs,* p. 19.

25 *Ibid.,* pp. 34–7.

26 Jeppe, pp. 86–7.

27 The details are given in my book *The Voortrekkers.*

28 Facts and figures in the early part of Van Oordt's study are not as reliable as they become later on.

29 Nathan, p. 38.

30 Sir Harry Smith, *Autobiography,* London, Murray, 1903.

31 Krüger, vol. i, p. 36.

32 Preller : *Pretorius,* p. 385.

33 Cf. Smith's *Autobiography,* Preller's *Pretorius,* Malan's *Die Opkoms van 'n Republiek,* Bloemfontein, Nasionale Pers, 1929, and Barnard's *'n Lewensbeskrywing van Majoor Henry Douglas Warden,* Archives Year Book, 1948.

34 Van Oordt, p. 799.

35 Krüger, vol. i, p. 29.

36 Seaver : *David Livingstone,* p. 161.

37 My own deduction is that the Boers did cause mischief there, but the Bakwena also had a hand in it when they broke in to get hold of arms—not Livingstone's 'arsenal' but the property of his hunter friends. The way the books were destroyed does not appear to implicate the Boers, for to even the most backward a book was a Bible.
38 Jan Oordt, p. 69.
39 Seaver, p. 158.
40 Livingstone, *Family Letters,* p. 188.
41 Van Oordt, p. 70.
42 Some writers confuse the campaigns against Setsheli, Montshiwa and Makapan.
43 *Memoirs,* pp. 46–7.
44 Meintjes : *The Voortrekkers,* p. 261.
45 Van Oordt, p. 77.
46 Given as 1853 in the *Memoirs,* p. 46.
47 pp. 82–3.
48 For a repudiation of slavery among the Boers see the *Biographical Memoirs* of the jurist Sir John Kotzé, vol. i, pp. 266 ff. For the opposite see Scoble and Abercrombie, or any anti-Boer book for that matter.
49 Allen : *Kruger's Pretoria.*
50 Van der Walt, Wiid & Geyer, vol. i, p. 348.
51 Van Oordt, p. 90.
52 *Ibid.,* p. 91.
53 *Memoirs,* p. 64.
54 For a more detailed account of this sort of protest see my biography of General De la Rey which also features the Rebellion of 1914.
55 Actually many people wanted Kruger as Commandant-General, but he was determined to pacify Schoeman.
56 *Memoirs,* p. 55.
57 *Ibid.,* pp. 68–70.
58 Cf. Peter Becker : *Hill of Destiny—The Life and Times of Moshesh,* London, Longmans, 1969.
59 Theal, vol. vii, p. 489.
60 Jeppe, pp. 159–70.
61 It was more than that, for the Cape Governor, Sir George Grey, had set his heart on federating the Orange Free State with Cape Colony, British Kaffraria and Natal. This is dealt with in some detail in my study *Sandile.*

62 Theal, vol. viii, p. 443.
63 *Memoirs,* p. 86.
64 Krüger, vol. i, p. 69.
65 *S.A. Biographical Dictionary.*
66 This account of the Civil War is based on Van Oordt; Theal; Krüger; the *Memoirs*; Nathan; Van der Walt; Wiid & Geyer, and others.
67 Krüger, vol. i, p. 76.
68 *Memoirs,* p. 108.
69 Theal, vol. viii, p. 476.
70 Van Oordt, p. 132.
71 Sir John Kotzé comments that the abandonment was not unavoidable, but the blame was not Kruger's. It lay with all those Boers who had not loyally responded to his call to turn out in force, vol. i, p. 255.
72 S. P. Engelbrecht, *Burgers,* pp. 130–1.
73 *Memoirs,* p. 120.
74 Krüger, vol. i, p. 98.
75 *Memoirs,* pp. 122–3.
76 The restoration of the complex was undertaken by the Simon van der Stel Foundation, completed and opened as a museum by Premier B. J. Vorster in 1973.
77 Van der Walt, Wiid & Geyer, vol. i, p. 387.
78 *Ibid.*
79 Van Oordt, p. 151.
80 The Pedi were not independent as the British at first gave out, but subjects of the Republic; and even if they were not, Sir John Kotzé held, punitive steps against them were quite justified, vol. i, p. 292.
81 *Memoirs,* p. 125.
82 Von Oordt, p. 160.
83 Given by Engelbrecht, *Burgers,* p. 206.
84 There is some confusion here between fact and fiction, for Burgers could not possibly have levied a new tax without the consent of the Volksraad, at the session of which Kruger had to be present. This is the kind of thing that happens in ghost-written 'memoirs'.
85 19.8.1876.
86 *Memoirs,* p. 130.
87 Freely adapted from Kruger's letter as given by Engelbrecht, *Burgers,* pp. 244–5.

88 Kotzé, vol. i, p. 307.
89 Engelbrecht, *Burgers,* p. 257.
90 Frere's reaction to the Annexation was: 'Good heavens! What will they say in England?' This is from Martineau's biography and perhaps deliberately misleading. Sir John Kotzé says Frere knew perfectly well what was going on, vol. i, p. 598.
91 *Transvaalsche Herinneringen,* pp. 21–2.
92 Jeppe, *n.* pp. 29–30.
93 Kotzé, vol. i, p. 340.
94 Nathan, p. 119.
95 Kotzé, vol. i, p. 414.
96 In the *Memoirs* it is stated that the party embarked at Port Elizabeth, perhaps a confusion with M. T. Steyn, who did.
97 *Memoirs,* p. 144; Van Oordt, p. 185.
98 According to Steyn whose memoirs were incorporated almost *in toto* by N. J. van der Merwe, his son-in-law and biographer of 1921.
99 Cf. Sir Percy FitzPatrick in his *South African Memories* on General De la Rey at Durban.
100 Cf. Krüger, vol. i, p. 129.
101 *Transvaalsche Herinneringen.*
102 *S.A. Biographical Dictionary.*
103 Krüger, vol. i, p. 144.
104 *Ibid.*
105 Van Oordt, p. 194.
106 She was a forceful personality, more of a soldier than her husband. They were rarely separated, and she accompanied him on all his military campaigns.
107 Van Oordt, p. 208.
108 The main sources on Joubert are by Mouton, Wormser and myself.
109 Van Oordt, p. 210.
110 Lehmann, p. 54.
111 *Ibid.,* pp. 54–5.
112 *Memoirs,* p. 151.
113 The remarkable Mrs Joubert's reminiscences were written down by Mrs L. Rompel-Koopman in 1915 and published in book-form.
114 Martineau, vol. ii, pp. 238–9.
115 Much has been written on this war in Dutch and English as from the 1880s, and later in Afrikaans; the most modern accounts

being by Ransford and Lehmann, the latter's sound study unfortunately marred by his mis-spelling of Afrikaans names.

116 Van Oordt, p. 247.

117 Lehmann, p. 60.

118. Van Oordt, pp. 253–4.

119 Krüger, vol. i, p. 176.

120 Published in full by Van Oordt, pp. 270–3.

121 *Memoirs,* p. 163. More than twenty years later the idea still amused him and he repeated it several times to his secretary, Manie Bredell, who was making notes and writing a diary.

122 *Memoirs,* p. 165.

123 Martineau, vol. ii, p. 386.

124 Van Oordt, p. 297.

125 *Ibid.,* p. 303.

126 *Ibid.*

127 De la Rey Papers, State Archives, Pretoria.

128 Krüger, vol. i, p. 207.

129 Lehmann, p. 101.

130 Van Oordt, p. 315.

131 Mouton.

132 Statistics of casualties throughout this war are surprisingly inconsistent on both sides.

133 Given by Lehmann, p. 121.

134 Van Oordt, p. 321.

135 *Die Boerevrou-boek,* p. 159.

136 It was published in full at the time in the *Staats-Courant,* excerpts quoted elsewhere as by Krüger, vol. i, pp. 220–1.

137 Van Oordt, p. 327.

138 Krüger, vol. i, p. 229.

139 I have such a platter, 18″ × 23″.

140 Lehmann, p. 272.

141 But he gave it in full in his memoirs, quoted by Van Oordt, pp. 336–44.

142 T. B. Barlow, pp. 225–6.

143 Arthur G. Barlow, p. 9.

144 Van Oordt.

145 *Ibid.,* p. 347.

146 Krüger, vol. i, p. 246.

147 Nathan, p. 178.

148 An Afrikaner, from Graaff-Reinet, 1839–87. The inhabitants of Pretoria were largely on the side of the British for economic reasons.

149 From my family papers.
150 Dr O. Geyser: 'Sir Theophilus Shepstone', *Die Huisgenoot,* 24.5.68.
151 Holmes, pp. 94–5.
152 *Memoirs,* pp. 185–6.
153 Van Oordt, p. 354.
154 Davey, p. 304.
155 Jeppe, pp. 111–12.
156 Van Oordt, p. 360.
157 In the latest book on the Historical Monuments of South Africa it is said that the move only took place in 1883.
158 Allen, p. 15.
159 Du Plessis & Eloff, p. 25.
160 *Die Boerevrou-boek,* pp. 159–60.
161 Krüger, vol. i, p. 253.
162 Pp. 112–13.
163 Van Oordt, p. 366.
164 There is a booklet in Afrikaans by Prof. D. W. Krüger on the celebration of Dingaan's Day from 1838 to 1910.
165 Hofmeyr, pp. 217–18.
166 Cf. Alan Paton's *Hofmeyr;* Millin; Fisher; Davenport, etc.
167 It is quoted in full by Van Oordt, pp. 374–6.
168 *Memoirs,* p. 190.
169 Van Oordt.
170 *Memoirs,* p. 385.
171 For a detailed analysis of Kruger the Statesman, often giving the reverse of the popular conception of him, see F. P. Smit *in toto.*
172 Van Hoek, pp. 35–7.
173 Hofmeyr, p. 596.
174 Iwan-Müller, p. 454.
175 For the text see J. S. du Plessis: *Paul Kruger aan die Woord.*
176 Marais, p. 6.
177 *Memoirs,* p. 196.
178 Krüger, vol. ii, pp. 12–17.
179 Van Oordt, p. 403.
180 *Ibid.,* p. 405.
181 Cf. Van Jaarsveld: *Lewende Verlede.*
182 According to Krüger. Van Ooordt, Nathan and others give different dates of departure.
183 Faure, p. 107.
184 Longford, pp. 439–40.

185 Lewsen, vol. i, p. 121.
186 *Memoirs,* p. 199.
187 Krüger, vol. ii, pp. 27–8.
188 Faure, p. 110.
189 Cf. Lewsen, vol. i, p. 143.
190 A detailed description of this tour will take much too long. It has been dealt with by Du Toit, Faure, Van Oordt, Nathan, Krüger and others.
191 Van Oordt, p. 422.
192 There is indeed no proof that Kruger ever met Victoria, but it is odd that Reitz also told similar anecdotes. She was in Scotland when they conferred with Derby, and the possibility cannot be ruled out that Kruger met her when they went there. Much was made of their meeting in a banned (in the U.K. and S.A.) film in German, Nazi propaganda, and I believe in another film, never completed, in which Gwen ffrançon-Davies played Victoria. In the Nazi era Kruger was blatantly used for propaganda purposes, cf. Van Jaarsveld on the Kruger figure in the Second World War in *Lewende Verlede,* ch. xviii.
193 FitzPatrick : *The Transvaal from Within,* pp. 57–8, a book by a delightful man but notable, as has been said, for its 'colourful inaccuracies'. Apart from writing his classic *Jock of the Bushveld,* Sir Percy was no mean photographer and took one of Kruger in action which has the quality of a Rembrandt. His most recent biography also refers to him as 'the first South African', whereas in my opinion this notable personage was General Louis Botha, no matter who says what.
194 Van Oordt, p. 422.
195 W. J. Leyds, *Onze Eerste Jaren in Zuid-Afrika.*
196 Van den Heever : *Hertzog,* pp. 48–50.
197 Engelbrecht : *Burgers,* p. 406; Van Jaarsveld : *Van Van Riebeeck tot Verwoerd,* p. 197.
198 *Transvaal Argus.*
199 Millin : *Rhodes,* pp. 50–1.
200 *The Decline of the West,* vol. i.
201 Cf. Mouton.
202 Lockhart & Woodhouse : *Rhodes,* p. 100.
203 Van Oordt, p. 436.
204 Krüger, vol. ii, p. 71.
205 Lockhart & Woodhouse, p. 102.
206 Van Oordt.

207 Much space is devoted to Kruger and the western border in MacKenzie's *Austral Africa* published in 1887.
208 Lockhart & Woodhouse, p. 103.
209 A substantial bibliography can be given dealing with this subject alone, virtually every book featuring Rhodes.
210 G. A. Leyds: *A History of Johannesburg*, p. 13. Harrison, who should have been a millionaire, disappeared on his way to Barberton, possibly devoured by a lion.
211 Nathan, p. 236.
212 *Memoirs*, p. 206.
213 *Ibid.*, pp. 207–8.
214 Lewsen: *Merriman Correspondence*, vol. i, pp. 234–5.
215 *Ibid.*, pp. 244–5.
216 Meintjes, *De la Rey: Lion of the West*, pp. 56–7.
217 Van Oordt, p. 482.
218 Cf. Marais, p. 10.
219 *Memoirs*, p. 216.
220 *Ibid.*, editorial note, p. 217.
221 *A Banking Centenary—Barclays Bank*, private edition, 1938.
222 Van Oordt, p. 498; Nathan, p. 264.
223 *Memoirs*, p. 222.
224 Allen, p. 40.
225 An example of the amazing stories spun around Kruger can be found in Tromp van Diggelen's autobiography *Worthwhile Journey*, told in all seriousness as fact. He says that it was his father, Col. S. H. van Diggelen, who 'rescued' Kruger from the Wanderers and that they made their get-away on horseback, the President jumping the wall round the Von Brandis house!
226 Van Oordt, p. 511.
227 *Memoirs*, p. 225.
228 Michell, p. 153.
229 For a full account of the Swaziland Question see Garson.
230 Hofmeyr, pp. 402–3.
231 (To Merriman), Lewsen, vol. i, p. 300.
232 The full speech is given by Van Oordt, pp. 552–9.
233 Cf. Van Oordt, p. 564.
234 *Ibid.*, p. 575.
235 Lockhart & Woodhouse, p. 289.
236 Millin, p. 245.
237 Cf. Walker: *Schreiner*.
238 Krüger, vol. ii, p. 139.

239 Cf. FitzPatrick : *Transvaal from Within,* pp. 72 ff.
240 Nathan, pp. 302–3.
241 Krüger, vol. i, p. 79.
242 Nathan, p. 269.
243 Cf. Van Oordt, p. 587.
244 *Ibid.,* p. 590.
245 John Tudhope. The Leonards were Advocate J. W. and his younger brother Charles.
246 *Memoirs,* p. 249.
247 Cf. Nathan, p. 259.
248 Mrs Lionel Phillips, pp. 19–20.
249 Dr Thelma Gutsche's *No Ordinary Woman* (Cape Town, Timmins, 1966) does full justice to her.
250 *Memoirs,* p. 252.
251 Krüger, vol. ii, p. 141. Cf. John R. Day: *Railways of Southern Africa,* ch. 2.
252 *Memoirs,* p. 253.
253 Michell, p. 271.
254 Lewsen, vol. iii, p. 163–4.
255 Van Oordt, p. 609. Scoble & Abercrombie give the full speech in a different translation.
256 Garson, pp. 370 ff.
257 Scholtz, vol. i, p. 283.
258 Wilde, p. xii.
259 Michell, p. 271.
260 *Memoirs,* p. 257.
261 Smithers, p. 281.
262 The standard work on the subject is that by Dr Jean van der Poel.
263 Lockhart & Woodhouse, p. 303.
264 Van der Walt, Wiid & Geyer, vol. i, p. 501.
265 Wormser, p. 97.
266 Actually 508 according to Preller, *Lobengula,* p. 277.
267 Lewsen, vol. ii, p. 197.
268 Walker, p. 72.
269 One of them was Louis Botha, and many years later Jameson said that he quite agreed with him.
270 *Memoirs,* pp. 270–1.
271 Cf. Marais, pp. 94–5.
272 Van Oordt, p. 717.
273 Given by Van Oordt, p. 718, from Jorissen.

274 *Memoirs,* p. 272.
275 *Memoirs,* p. 273–4; Van Oordt, pp. 724–5; Krüger ii, p. 167.
276 Mrs Lionel Phillips, p. 105.
277 Hofmeyr, p. 502.
278 Van der Poel, pp. 157–8.
279 Cf. Marais, p. 48.
280 Cowles, p. 143.
281 *Memoirs,* pp. 274–5; Nathan, p. 372; G. A. Leyds, pp. 175 & 243.
282 *Memoirs,* p. 276.
283 Given in full as Appendix B to FitzPatrick's *Transvaal From Within.*
284 Mrs Lionel Phillips, p. 142.
285 Wright (ed.), *Innes Correspondence,* p. 173.
286 Pakenham, p. 110.
287 Cf. FitzPatrick, p. 108.
288 Jackson, p. 211; Lewinsohn, p. 246.
289 Mrs Lionel Phillips, p. 170.
290 Mark Twain, *Following the Equator,* vol. ii, pp. 383–4.
291 From Van Oordt's short biography of Kruger *Van Schaapwachter tot President—Het leven van Paul Kruger,* in simplified Dutch under his favourite pseudonym, D'Arbez.
292 Cf. Breytenbach. This historian has devoted the major part of his life to a history of the Boer War in Afrikaans.
293 Van Oordt, p. 758.
294 Du Plessis & Eloff, pp. 29–30.
295 *Memoirs,* p. 291.
296 From Steyn's memoirs published by Van der Merwe, extracts of which I translated and published in my *Life of Steyn.*
297 Lockhart & Woodhouse, pp. 141–2; Walker, pp. 81–2.
298 Cf. Le May.
299 Cf. Bell.
300 Cf. Le May.
301 Kruger was a patron of an Art Memento honouring the memory of the political satirist and painter W. H. Schröder who made many cartoons of him through the years. Schröder, who died in 1892, also painted a large portrait in oil of Kruger for the First Chamber of the Raadzaal.
302 According to Van Wouw himself.
303 Deneys Reitz, p. 20.
304 Van Oordt, p. 789.
305 *Men of the Times,* pp. 605–6.

306 Cf. Meintjes: *Steyn,* p. 66.
307 Cf. Marais, p. 172.
308 *Memoirs,* pp. 287–9.
309 Cf. Hancock, *The Sanguine Years,* pp. 69–70.
310 Stanley, pp. 489–99.
311 Hjalmar Reitz published some of his father's memoirs which included Kruger anecdotes in his humorous book *The Conversion of a South African Nationalist.*
312 Buxton, pp. 230–1.
313 Van Oordt, pp. 792–4.
314 Krüger, vol. ii, pp. 192–3; Van Oordt, pp. 842–4.
315 It is given in full in an Appendix to the *Memoirs,* pp. 383 ff.
316 Van Oordt, p. 868. One can take it that he was there and had a good look.
317 Wilde, p. 75.
318 Nathan, p. 409.
319 *Memoirs,* pp. 399–408.
320 Deneys Reitz, p. 20.
321 In his *Life of Olive Schreiner* [Cronwright-Schreiner], pp. 307–8.
322 Hjalmar Reitz, p. 210.
323 *Memoirs,* p. 299.
324 Hancock, pp. 68–9.
325 J. C. Smuts, pp. 39–41.
326 Iwan-Müller, p. 609.
327 Hutchinson & Martelli, p. 99.
328 Iwan-Müller.
329 Le May, p. 14.
330 James & Hills, pp. 96–8.
331 Luke, pp. 140–1.
332 Cf. Marais, p. 207.
333 *Ibid.,* p. 208. Cf. Headlam.
334 Headlam, vol. i, p. 299; Le May, pp. 15–16; Krüger, vol. ii, p. 224.
335 Cf. Middleton, pp. 201 ff.
336 According to this article all persons, except Natives, had liberty of entrance, travel and residence.
337 *Letters,* 3rd series, vol. iii, pp. 394–7; Lewsen, vol. iii, p. 200; *The Graphic,* 17.9.1898.
338 Nathan, p. 422.
339 Marais, p. 243.
340 Le May, p. 17.

341 Wilde, p. 74.
342 Scholtz, vol. ii, pp. 184–5.
343 Garvin, vol. iii, p. 393.
344 Le May, p. 18.
345 Meintjes : *Steyn,* pp. 83 ff.
346 Arthur Barlow, p. 57.
347 Luke, p. 156.
348 *Memoirs,* pp. 308–9.
349 Le May, p. 20.
350 Cf. Wrench, pp. 203 & 359.
351 *Memoirs,* p. 321.
352 Smuts, p. 46.
353 Krüger, vol. ii, p. 239.
354 Villebois-Mareuil, p. 34.
355 *Memoirs,* p. 347.
356 Krüger, vol. ii, p. 242.
357 *Ibid.,* pp. 243–4.
358 Amery.
359 Meintjes : *Botha.*
360 Villebois-Mareuil, p. 327.
361 M. A. Gronum, pp. 5–6.
362 Wormser, pp. 110–11.
363 Meintjes : *Steyn,* p. 123.
364 *Memoirs,* p. 351.
365 Davitt, p. 425.
366 *Vreemde Sending, Panorama,* Oct. 1968.
367 Du Plessis & Eloff, pp. 38–9.
368 Headlam, vol. ii, p. 289.
369 *Ibid.,* vol. ii.
370 Plomer, p. 150.
371 Proclaimed a National Monument in 1962, bearing the name of 'Krugerhof', and almost unchanged to this day.
372 Meintjes : *Botha,* p. 68.
373 *Memoirs,* p. 357.
374 Du Plessis & Eloff, p. 43.
375 Deneys Reitz, p. 113.
376 *Memoirs,* p. 359.
377 Krüger, vol. ii, p. 262.
378 Cf. Weeber.
379 Oberholster (ed.), p. 11.
380 Jones, p. 27.

381 This last chapter is based mainly on Bredell (ed. Oberholster), Beyers, Krüger, Du Plessis & Eloff and numerous magazine articles. *The Graphic* of 1.12.1900 gives full pictorial coverage to Kruger's arrival.
382 Cf. *The Graphic,* above.
383 Oberholster (ed.), p. 14.
384 *For Right and England.*
385 *Pretoria from Within.*
386 Lewsen, vol. iii, p. 299.
387 Krüger, vol. ii, p. 272.
388 Beyers, pp. 33–6.
389 Cowles, p. 179.
390 Related by a grand-daughter, Mrs E. F. Van Broekhuizen in Malherbe (ed.), *Die Boerevrou-boek,* p. 161.
391 *Memoirs,* pp. 271–2.
392 Oberholster (ed.).
393 Cf. Hancock & Van der Poel (eds).
394 Oberholster (ed.), p. 8.
395 Nathan, p. 471.
396 Omond, p. 36.
397 Oberholster (ed.), p. 83.
398 Omond, pp. 111–14.
399 Le May, p. 213.
400 Oberholster (ed.), pp. 63–4.
401 Omond, p. 207.
402 Hancock & Van der Poel (eds), vol. ii, p. 89.
403 M. A. Gronum, pp. 6–7.
404 Meintjes: *Steyn,* pp. 192 ff.
405 *Die Huisgenoot,* 14.10.1966.
406 Krüger, vol. ii, p. 297.
407 Hancock & Van der Poel (eds), vol. ii, pp. 123–4.

Select Bibliography

ALLEN, VIVIEN *Kruger's Pretoria,* Cape Town, Balkema, 1971.

AMERY, L. S. *The Times History of the War in South Africa* (7 vols.), London, Low, Marston, 1900–9.

BARLOW, ARTHUR G. *Almost in Confidence,* Cape Town, Juta, 1952.

BARLOW, T. B. *The Life and Times of President Brand,* Cape Town, Juta, 1972.

BARNARD, C. J. *Louis Botha op die Natalse Front,* Cape Town, Balkema, 1970.

BASSON, M. A. *Die Britse Invloed in die Transvaalse Onderwys,* Archives Year Book, 1956.

BELL, FRED W. *The South African Conspiracy,* London, Heinemann, 1900.

BEYERS, C. *Laaste Lewensjare en Heengaan van President Kruger,* Archives Year Book, 4th series, part I.

BREYTENBACH, J. H. *Die Tweede Vryheidsoorlog* (3 vols.), Pretoria, 1969–74.

BUTLER, W. F. *The Life of Sir George Pomeroy Colley,* London, Murray, 1899.

BUTLER, W. F. *An Autobiography,* London, 1911.

BUXTON, EARL *General Botha,* London, Murray, 1924.

CARTER, T. F. *A Narrative of the Boer War,* Cape Town, Juta, 1896.

COOK, EDWARD T. *Rights and Wrongs of the Transvaal War,* London, Arnold, 1901.

CRONWRIGHT-SCHREINER, S. C. *The Life of Olive Schreiner,* London, Allen & Unwin, 1924.

COWLES, VIRGINIA *The Kaiser,* London, Collins, 1963.

DAVENPORT, T. R. H. *The Afrikaner Bond,* Cape Town, O.U.P., 1966.

DAVEY, ARTHUR M. *The Siege of Pretoria, 1880–1881,* Archives Year Book, 1956.

DAVITT, MICHAEL *The Boer Fight for Freedom,* New York, Funk & Wagnalls, 1902.

DE VILLEBOIS-MAREUIL *War Notes,* London, Methuen, 1902.

DE WET, C. R. *Three Years' War,* London, Constable, 1903.

DOYLE, A. CONAN *The Great Boer War,* London, Bell, 1902.

DU PLESSIS, GEZINA & ELOFF, MAGDALENA *Die President en Ek,* Cape Town, Tafelberg, 1971.

DU PLESSIS, J. S. *Paul Kruger aan die Woord,* Bloemfontein, n.d.

ENGELBRECHT, S. P. *Paul Kruger se Amptelike Briewe,* Pretoria, 1925.
ENGELBRECHT, S. P. *Thomas François Burgers,* Cape Town, H.A.U.M., 1933.
ENGELENBURG, F. V. *General Louis Botha,* Pretoria, Van Schaik, 1929.
ENGELENBURG, F. V. & PRELLER, G. S. *Paul Kruger's Afkomst en Familie,* Pretoria, 1924.
FAURE, D. P. *My Life and Times,* Cape Town, 1907.
FISHER, JOHN *The Afrikaners,* London, Cassell, 1969.
FITZPATRICK, J. PERCY *The Transvaal from Within,* London, Heinemann, 1899.
FITZPATRICK, J. PERCY *South African Memories,* London, Cassell, 1932.
GARDNER, BRIAN *The African Dream,* London, Cassell, 1970.
GARSON, N. G. *The Swaziland Question and a Road to the Sea,* Archives Year Book, 1957.
GARVIN, J. L. *The Life of Joseph Chamberlain* (3 vols.), London, Macmillan, 1932–4.
GIE, S. F. N. *Geskiedenis van Suid-Afrika* (vol. 2), Stellenbosch, Pro-Ecclesia, 1939.
GRIERSON, EDWARD *The Imperial Dream,* London, Collins, 1972.
GRONUM, M. A. *Die Engelse Oorlog,* Cape Town, Tafelberg, 1972.
HANCOCK, W. K. *Smuts—The Sanguine Years,* C.U.P., 1962.
HANCOCK, W. K. & VAN DER POEL, JEAN (eds.) *The Smuts Papers* (4 vols.), C.U.P., 1966.
HEADLAM, CECIL (ed.) *The Milner Papers* (2 vols.), London, Cassell, 1931–3.
HENSMAN, HOWARD *Cecil Rhodes,* Edinburgh, Blackwood, 1901.
HOFMEYR, J. H. *The Life of Jan Hendrik Hofmeyr,* Cape Town, De Villiers, 1913.
HOLMES, PRESCOTT *Paul Kruger,* Philadelphia, Altemus, 1900.
HUTCHINSON, ROBERT & MARTELLI, GEORGE *Robert's People—The Life of Sir Robert Williams,* London, Chatto & Windus, 1971.
IWAN-MÜLLER, G. B. *Lord Milner and South Africa,* London, Heinemann, 1902.
JACKSON, STANLEY *The Great Barnato,* London, Heinemann, 1970.
JAMES, ANGELA & HILLS, NINA *Mrs John Brown,* London, Murray, 1937.
JEPPE, CARL *The Kaleidoscopic Transvaal,* Cape Town, 1906.
JONES, JAMES *Lloyd George,* Harvard, 1951.
JORISSEN, E. J. P. *Transvaalsche Herinerringen,* Pretoria, 1897.
KOTZÉ, J. G. *Biographical Memoirs and Reminiscences,* vol. i, Cape Town, Miller, n.d.

KRÜGER, D. W. *Paul Kruger* (2 vols.), Johannesburg, Dagbreek, 1961 & 1968.

KRUGER, RAYNE *Good-bye Dolly Gray,* London, Cassell, 1964.

KRUGER, S. J. P. *Memoirs,* compiled by Grobler and Bredell, London, Unwin, 1902.

LEHMANN, JOSEPH H. *The First Boer War,* London, Cape, 1972.

LE MAY, G. H. L. *British Supremacy in South Africa,* Oxford, 1965.

LEWINSOHN, RICHARD *Barney Barnato,* London, Routledge, 1937.

LEWSEN, PHYLLIS (ed.), *Selections from the Correspondence of J. X. Merriman* (3 vols.), Cape Town, V.R.S., 1960, 1963, 1966.

LEYDS, G. A. *A History of Johannesburg,* Cape Town, Nasionale Boekhandel, 1964.

LEYDS, W. J. *Onze Eerste Jaren in Zuid-Afrika,* The Hague, 1939.

LOCKHART, J. G. & WOODHOUSE, C. M. *Rhodes,* London, Hodder & Stoughton, 1963.

LONGFORD, ELIZABETH *Victoria R I,* London, Weidenfeld & Nicolson, 1964.

LUKE, W. B. *Lord Milner,* London, Partridge, 1901.

MACKENZIE, JOHN *Austral Africa—Losing it or Ruling it* (2 vols.), London, 1887.

MAGNUS, PHILIP Gladstone, New York, Dutton, 1954.

MALHERBE, K. (ed.), *Die Boerevrou-Boek,* Pretoria, Van Schaik, 1950.

MARAIS, J. S. *The Fall of Kruger's Republic,* O.U.P., 1961.

MARRIS, N. MURRELL *Joseph Chamberlain,* London, Hutchinson, 1900.

MARTINEAU, J. *Life and Correspondence of Sir Bartle Frere* (2 vols.), London, 1895.

MEINTJES, JOHANNES *De la Rey—Lion of the West,* Johannesburg, Keartland, 1966.

MEINTJES, JOHANNES *President Steyn,* Cape Town, Nasionale Boekhandel, 1969.

MEINTJES, JOHANNES *General Louis Botha,* London, Cassell, 1970.

MEINTJES, JOHANNES *The Commandant-General: Piet Joubert,* Cape Town, Tafelberg, 1971.

MEINTJES, JOHANNES *Sandile—The Fall of the Xhosa Nation,* Cape Town, Bulpin, 1971.

MEINTJES, JOHANNES *The Voortrekkers,* London, Cassell, 1973.

Men of the Times, 1906.

MICHELL, LEWIS *Cecil John Rhodes,* London, Arnold, 1902.

MIDDLETON, LAMAR *The Rape of Africa,* London, Hale, 1936.

MILLIN, SARAH GERTRUDE *Rhodes,* London, Chatto & Windus, 1933.

MORRIS, JAMES *Pax Britannica—The Climax of an Empire,* London, Faber, 1968.
MOSSOP, E. E. *Lives of the Earlier Krugers,* Archives Year Book, 1947.
MOUTON, J. A. *Genl. Piet Joubert in die Transvaalse Geskiedenis,* Archives Year Book, 1957.
NATHAN, MANFRED *Paul Kruger,* Durban, Knox, 1944.
OBERHOLSTER, A. G. (ed.), *Dagboek van H. C. Bredell,* R.G.N., 1972.
OBERHOLSTER, J. J. *Die Historiese Monumente van Suid-Afrika,* Stellenbosch, Rembrandt, 1972.
OMOND, G. W. T. *The Boers in Europe,* London, Black, 1903.
PAKENHAM, ELIZABETH *Jameson's Raid,* London, Weidenfeld & Nicolson, 1960.
PHILLIPS, MRS LIONEL *Some South African Recollections,* London, Longmans, Green, 1900.
PIENAAR, P. DE V. (ed.), *Die Kultuurgeskiedenis van die Afrikaner,* Cape Town, Nasionale Boekhandel, 1968.
PLOMER, WILLIAM *Cecil Rhodes,* London, Nelson, 1938.
POTGIETER, CARL & THEUNISSEN, N. H. *Kommandant-Generaal Hendrik Potgieter,* Johannesburg, A.P.B., 1938.
PRELLER, GUSTAV S. *Andries Pretorius,* Johannesburg, A.P.B., 1940.
PRELLER, GUSTAV S. *Lobengula,* Johannesburg, A.P.B., 1963.
RANSFORD, OLIVER *The Battle of Majuba Hill,* London, Murray, 1967.
REITZ, DENEYS, *Commando,* London, Faber, 1935.
REITZ, HJALMAR *The Conversion of a South African Nationalist,* Cape Town, Unie-Volkspers, 1946.
ROBERTS, BRIAN *Churchills in Africa,* London, Hamilton, 1970.
ROSENTHAL, ERIC *General de Wet,* Cape Town, Simondium, 1968.
SCHOLTZ, G. D. *Die Oorsake van die Tweede Vryheidsoorlog* (2 vols.), Johannesburg, Voortrekkerpers, 1948.
Schroder Art Memento, Pretoria, 1897.
SCOBLE, JOHN & ABERCROMBIE, H. R. *The Rise and Fall of Krugerism,* London, Heinemann, 1900.
SEAVER, GEORGE *David Livingstone,* London, Lutterworth, 1957.
SMIT, F. P. *Die Staatsopvattinge van President Kruger,* Pretoria, Van Schaik, 1951.
SMITHERS, ELSA *March Hare,* O.U.P., 1939.
SMUTS, J. C. *Jan Christian Smuts,* London, Cassell, 1952.
STANLEY, HENRY M. *Autobiography,* London, Low, Marston, 1909.
STATHAM, F. R. *Paul Kruger and his Times,* London, 1898.
Suid-Afrikaanse Biografiese Woordeboek, vol. i, 1968; ii, 1972.

THEAL, GEORGE MCCALL *History of South Africa,* vols. 10 & 11, Cape Town, Struik, 1964.

UYS, C. J. *Paul Kruger van die Wieg tot die Graf,* Cape Town, 1955.

VAN DEN HEEVER, C. M. *Generaal J. B. M. Hertzog,* Johannesburg, A.P.B., 1946.

VAN DER MERWE, N. J. *Marthinus Theunis Steyn* (2 vols.), Cape Town, Nasionale Pers, 1921.

VAN DER POEL, JEAN *The Jameson Raid,* Cape Town, O.U.P., 1951.

VAN DER WALT, WIID & GEYER *Geskiedenis van Suid-Afrika* (2 vols.), Cape Town, Nasionale Boekhandel, 1951.

VAN HOEK, KEES *Gesprekke met Dr Leyds,* Pretoria, Van Schaik, 1939.

VAN JAARSVELD, F. A. *The Awakening of Afrikaner Nationalism,* Cape Town, Human & Rousseau, 1961.

VAN JAARSVELD, F. A. *Lewende Verlede,* Johannesburg, A.P.B., 1961.

VAN JAARSVELD, F. A. *The Afrikaner's Interpretation of South African History,* Cape Town, Simondium, 1964.

VAN JAARSVELD, F. A. *Van Van Riebeeck tot Verwoerd,* Johannesburg, Voortrekkerpers, 1971.

VAN OORDT, J. F. *Paul Kruger en de Opkomst van de Zuid-Afrikaansche Republiek,* Amsterdam, Dusseau, 1898.

VILLEBOIS-MAREUIL, G. DE *War Notes,* London, Methuen, 1902.

WALKER, ERIC A. *W. P. Schreiner,* O.U.P., 1937.

WEEBER, E. J. *Op die Natalse Front* & *Op die Transvaalse Front,* Cape Town, Nasionale Pers, 1942.

WILDE, RICHARD H. *Joseph Chamberlain and the South African Republic,* Archives Year Book, 1956.

WORMSER, J. A. *Het Leven van Petrus Jacobus Joubert,* Cape Town, H.A.U.M., 1916.

WRENCH, JOHN EVELYN *Alfred Milner,* London, Eyre & Spottiswoode, 1958.

WRIGHT, HARRISON M. (ed.), *Sir James Rose Innes Selected Correspondence,* Cape Town, V.R.S., 1972.

Index